PassKey EA Review

Part 1: Individual Taxation

IRS Enrolled Agent Exam
Study Guide
2017-2018 Edition

Richard Gramkow, EA
Christy Pinheiro, EA, ABA®
Kolleen Wells, EA
Joel Busch, CPA, JD

PassKey
Learning Systems

Editor: Joel Busch, CPA, JD

This study guide is designed for test-takers who will take their exams in the 2017-2018 EA Exam testing window (May 1, 2017, to February 28, 2018).

PassKey EA Review, Part 1: Individual Taxation, IRS Enrolled Agent Exam Study Guide 2017-2018 Edition

ISBN: 978-0-9986118-0-8

First Printing. 2017.
PassKey EA Review® is a U.S. Registered Trademark

www.PassKeyPublications.com
Online study: www.passkeylearningsystems.com

Table of Contents

4

Recent Praise for the PassKey EA Review Series

(Real customers, real names, public testimonials)

PassKey was the only study aid that I used
Stephen J Woodard, CFP, CLU, ChFC
The guides were an invaluable resource. They were concise and covered the subject matter succinctly with spot-on end of chapter questions that were very similar to what I encountered on the exams.

I passed all three parts.
Robbie Cantoron
I passed all three parts of the EA exam using this book, which is why I'll give it five stars... There are many tax laws I've learned about by studying this book that I haven't encountered yet preparing returns, so I did end up learning a lot. The trick is to focus, (after reading the material), on the multiple choice questions at the end of each chapter and their solutions: this is how you'll apply and practice what you've learned and really learn the details.

This review is the best on the market.
Yaw Asiante-Asamoah
I passed on all three parts on one attempt. The questions in the Review and Workbook are similar to the real exams. I got a big raise and my bonus went up at my seasonal job. It's worth the money, trust me.

This book helped me pass.
Kenichi Mochizukion
I used the PassKey workbook after studying PassKey textbook. The example questions cover all the topics and require good understanding to answer, so it was very helpful to reveal my weak areas prior to the exam.

Wonderful!
Ana Lavallee
PassKey was all I needed to pass the three tests to become an EA in just three months. The books are easy to read and understand. Thank you!

Outstanding!
Derrell L. Chastain
Outstanding! Helped me pass the EA exam...I used all three books!

Highly recommend these materials
Tosha H. Knelangeon

Using only this book and the workbook, I passed all three EA exams on my first try. I highly recommend these materials. As long as you put in the time to read and study all the information provided, you should be well-prepared.

Very useful, I passed 1st and 2nd exams by reading only PassKey!
Shixiong Feng

Very useful, I passed the 1st and 2nd exams by only reading the PassKey EA Review. If you are willing to spend some time to read the whole book thoroughly, then this book is the only thing you need to pass the EA exams.

Worked like a charm!
Brian Lang (New York, New York)

I passed on my first try.

Excellent explanations!
Janet Briggs

The best thing about these books is that each answer has a comprehensive explanation about why the answer is correct. I passed all three EA exams on the first attempt.

I passed!
Ismail Osman

The book is excellent to pass the EA exam. I passed Part 1 on my first attempt. These are great study resources. I love PassKey!

Amazing!
Sopio Svanishvilion

PassKey helped me pass all three parts of the Enrolled Agent exam. They are a "must have" if you want to pass your EA exams.

Almost like the real EA exam!
Charlotte Ennusah

The questions in the book are almost like the questions on the real exams. I recommend this book for everyone who wants to spend less time getting their EA license.

Essential Figures for Tax Year 2016

Part One: Individuals

Here is a quick summary of some of the important tax figures for the current enrolled agent exam cycle (May 1, 2017, to February 28, 2018):

Income Tax Return Filing Deadline: April 18, 2017

Note: The normal filing deadline for individual taxpayers is April 15. The deadline is extended because the Emancipation Day, a holiday in Washington, D.C., will be observed on Monday, April 17, pushing the nation's filing deadline to April 18.

Personal Exemption Amount: $4,050

2016 Personal Exemption Phaseout Thresholds:
- Single: $259,400 -$381,900.
- Head of Household: $285,350 -$407,850
- Married Filing Jointly or Qualifying Widow(er): $311,300 - $433,800.
- Married Filing Separately: $155,650 - $216,900

2016 Standard Deduction Amounts:
- Single or married filing separately: $6,300
- Married filing jointly or Qualifying widower: $12,600
- Head of household: $9,300
- The additional standard deduction for people who have reached age 65 (or who are blind) is:
  - $1,250 for married taxpayers or
  - $1,550 for unmarried taxpayers.

Gross Income Filing Thresholds for U.S. Citizens and U.S. Residents:
- Single: $10,350 (65 or older $11,900)
- Married Filing Jointly: $20,700,
  - 65 or older (one spouse) $21,950;
  - 65 or older (both spouses): $23,200
- Head of Household: $13,350 (65 or older $14,900)
- Married Filing Separately (any age): $4,050
- Qualifying Widow(er) with dependent child: $16,650 (65 or older $17,900)
- Any taxpayer with self-employment income of $400 or more in any taxable year must file a return.

2016 Mileage Rates:
- Business: 54¢ per mile
- Charitable purposes: 14¢ per mile
- Medical and moving: 19¢ per mile

2016 Retirement Contribution Limits:
- Roth and traditional IRAs: $5,500, (catch-up contribution of $1,000 for taxpayers age 50 or older).
- 401(k), 403(b): $18,000, (catch-up contribution of $6,000 for taxpayers age 50 or older).
- Maximum contribution for defined contribution plans is $53,000.
- SIMPLE 401k or SIMPLE IRA contributions limit: $12,500 (catch-up contribution of $3,000 for taxpayers age 50 or older)

2016 Social Security Taxable Wage Base: $118,500
FUTA Wage Base: The FUTA tax rate is 6% on the first $7000 paid to each employee.
Medicare Taxable Wage Base: No limit

2016 Health Savings Accounts (HSAs) Annual Contribution Limits:
- HSA for self-only coverage: $3,350
- HSA for family coverage: $6,750

2016 Estate and Gift Tax Exclusion Amount: $5.45 million per individual
Annual Exclusion for Gifts: $14,000
Non-Citizen Marital Threshold for Gift Tax: $148,000
Top rate on qualified dividends and long-term gains for individuals: 20%

2016 Education Credits and Deductions:
- American Opportunity Credit: $2,500 per student (up to 40% refundable)
- Lifetime Learning Credit: $2,000 per return
- Coverdell Education Savings Account (amount per beneficiary): $2,000
- Tuition and fees deduction: $4,000 (this deduction is set to expire in 2017)
- Student loan interest deduction: $2,500

2016 Maximum Earned Income Tax Credit (EITC):
- $6,269 with three or more qualifying children
- $5,572 with two qualifying children
- $3,373 with one qualifying child
- $506 with no qualifying children

Investment income must be $3,400 or less for the year in order to qualify for the EITC.

2016 Earned Income Tax Credit (EITC) Phaseout Ranges:
To be eligible for the EITC, the taxpayer must have earned income less than:
- $14,880 ($20,430 if MFJ) with no qualifying child
- $39,296 ($44,846 if MFJ) with one qualifying child
- $44,648 ($50,198 if MFJ) with two qualifying children
- $47,955 ($53,505 if MFJ) with three or more qualifying children

2016 Foreign Earned Income and Housing Exclusions:
- Maximum foreign earned income exclusion: $101,300
- Base housing amount: $16,208

2016 Maximum Credit Amounts:
- Adoption Credit: $13,460 per child
- Child Tax Credit: $1,000 per child (unchanged from the previous year)
- Credit for Child and Dependent Care Expenses: $3,000 (one child); $6,000 (two or more)
- Retirement Savings Contributions Credit (Saver's Credit): up to $2,000 ($4,000 if married filing jointly)

Withholding Threshold for "Nanny Tax" or Household Employees: $2,000

"Kiddie Tax" Unearned Income Threshold: All unearned income over $2,100 is taxed at the parents' tax rate.

2016 AMT Exemption Amount
- $53,900 for Single or HOH
- $83,800 for Married Filing Jointly or Qualifying Widow(er)
- $41,900 for Married Filing Separately

Section 179 Deduction
- The $500,000 deduction limit and $2 million reduction threshold were made permanent and also indexed for inflation (there is a $2,010,000 reduction threshold for 2016).
- The special allowance for depreciable software was made permanent in 2016
- Section 179 is now allowed for certain air conditioning and heating units
- The Section 179 election can be revoked (but once revoked, it becomes irrevocable)
- The $250,000 cap attributable to Qualified Leasehold Improvement Property has been removed for 2016, allowing a full $500K deduction for qualifying property.

Bonus Depreciation: 50% Bonus depreciation has been extended. The PATH ACT also introduced a gradual reduction from 50% in 2015-2017, to 40% in 2018, and to 30% in 2019, followed by a complete phase-out of the deduction in 2019.

2016 Affordable Care Act (Obamacare) Penalty: 2.5% of household AGI or a maximum of $2,085 ($695 per adult, $347.50 per child) for those who do not purchase qualifying health insurance and do not qualify for an exclusion. However, on Jan. 20, 2017, an executive order signed by newly-elected President Trump directed federal agencies to exercise authority and discretion available to them to reduce potential burden to taxpayers. Consistent with that, the IRS has decided to make changes that would continue to allow electronic and paper returns to be accepted for processing in instances where a taxpayer doesn't indicate their health coverage status. At the time of this book's printing, the IRS would accept a taxpayer's return even if they do not respond to the Health Coverage question. However, legislative provisions of the ACA law were still in force at the beginning of 2017, and taxpayers remain required to follow the law and pay what they may owe.

New Tax Laws Affecting Individuals in 2016

Accelerated Filing Dates for Certain Information Returns: the PATH Act changed the government copy due date for Forms W-2, Form W-3, and Form 1099-MISC to January 31. This new deadline applies to paper filers as well as e-filed forms. This change only affects Forms 1099 that report nonemployee compensation. The filing deadline for other forms in the 1099 series remains unchanged.

Tax Credit Timing: The PATH Act requires that the IRS cannot send out certain refunds (specifically the EITC and the Additional Child Tax Credit) until February 15, 2017. This affects all 2016 tax returns claiming these refundable credits.

Permanent Tax Law Extensions
- **Educator expense deduction** (the Teacher Credit): The $250 deduction for certain expenses of elementary and secondary school teachers was made permanent and is now also indexed for inflation
- **Sales tax deduction:** The deduction of state and local general sales taxes was made permanent.
- Certain tax-free distributions from IRAs for charitable purposes.
- Beneficial rules for contributions of capital gain real property (real estate) made for conservation purposes are now permanent.

Temporary Extensions (Extended through 2016, set to expire in 2017)
- Energy Credits
- Qualified Principal Residence Debt exclusion
- Mortgage insurance premiums deduction
- Tuition and fees deduction

Section 179 Deduction in 2016
- $500,000 limit and $2 million reduction threshold were made permanent and also indexed for inflation ($2,010,000 reduction threshold for 2016, indexed for inflation)
- Special allowance for depreciable software made permanent
- Section 179 is now allowed for certain air conditioning and heating units
- The election can be revoked (but once revoked, it becomes irrevocable)

Tax Exemptions for American Medalists: Olympic and Paralympic athletes may now exclude the value of their medals and prize money.

Credit disallowance: There are new 2 and 10-year bans for disregarding the Child Tax Credit and American Opportunity Credit rules. In 2016, if a taxpayer claims these credits and is later determined to be ineligible for them, a ban may be imposed on the taxpayer from claiming these credits on future returns.

Truncated SSNs on Form W-2: Effective in tax year 2016, the PATH Act extends IRS authority to require truncated Social Security Numbers on Form W-2.

New FBAR filing deadline: FBARs (FinCen Form 114) will now be due on April 15, with a with a maximum 6-month extension to October 15. Previously, a taxpayer could not request an extension to file the FBAR, and the FBAR was due June 30.

Increase in Failure to File Penalty: The Trade Facilitation and Enforcement Act of 2015 increases the penalty for failing to file a tax return in 2016. The higher penalty applies to individual returns filed in 2017, for the 2016 tax season. The increased failure-file penalty is the lesser of $205 (up from $135) or 100% of the amount of tax owed.

Electronic Filing PIN No Longer Valid: The Electronic Filing PIN, an IRS-generated PIN used to verify a taxpayer's signature on a self-prepared, e-filed tax return, is no longer available. To validate a signature on an electronic return, the taxpayer must now use their prior-year adjusted gross income (AGI) or their prior-year self-select PIN. There were no changes to Practitioner PIN Method.

Form 1098-T Required: A taxpayer must have received a Form 1098-T from an eligible educational institution in order to claim the Tuition and Fees Deduction, American Opportunity Credit, or the Lifetime Learning Credit.

21st Century Cures Act: Signed by President Obama in December 2016, this health bill grants small businesses regulatory relief for employers who wish to offer insurance reimbursements to their employees. Employer reimbursements under this type of Health Reimbursement Arrangement may not exceed $4,950 for the employee (or $10,000 for family coverage).

Sharing Economy: In August 2016, the IRS launched a new online resource center that offers taxpayer guidance called the Sharing Economy Tax Center.

Definition of Marriage: The IRS issued final regulations in September 2016 regarding the definition of marriage after the landmark case of *Obergefell v. Hodges*. These regulations state that a marriage of two individuals is recognized for federal tax purposes if the marriage is recognized by the state, possession or territory of the United States in which the marriage is entered into, regardless of where the couple is living. This clarifies the law to include common law marriage as well as marriages performed in a foreign country.

Waiver of the 60-day time limit on IRA rollovers: Starting in August, 2016, Rev. Proc. 2016-47 allows eligible taxpayers can now qualify for a waiver of the 60-day rollover limit and avoid possible early distribution taxes. Taxpayers will submit the self-certification to their plan administrator or an IRA trustee (NOT to the IRS). In the past, taxpayers who failed to meet the rollover time limit could only obtain a waiver by requesting a private letter ruling from the IRS.

New ITIN Rules: All ITINs issued before 2013 will now expire, unless renewed. Application procedures have also changed. There are now three ways to apply for an ITIN. A taxpayer may use Form W-7, or apply in person with an IRS-authorized Certified Acceptance Agent or make an appointment at a designed IRS Taxpayer Assistance Center.

- Older ITINs will expire if not renewed (any ITIN issued before 2013)
- Newer ITINs will expire if not used for three years or more, unless they are renewed
- Form W-7 has been revised as of September 2016
- The IRS will no longer accept passports of dependents as stand-alone documents that lack a date of entry into the United States.

New IRS Acceptance Agent 2016 Program Changes

- The ITIN Acceptance Agent Certification process changes in 2016
- ITIN Acceptance Agent Applications are now accepted year round
- The IRS is actively recruiting IRS acceptance agents

Form 1098 Changes: The IRS Form 1098, Mortgage Interest Statement, now must include the beginning mortgage balance and the property address (not just the mailing address of the mortgage-holder).

Defending Public Safety Employees' Retirement Act: This new law expands the exemption from the 10% early withdrawal penalty tax on early distributions to qualified public safety employees from defined contribution governmental plans. This law is effective for distributions made in 2016.

Introduction

Congratulations on taking the first step toward becoming an enrolled agent, a widely respected professional tax designation. The Internal Revenue Service licenses enrolled agents, known as EAs after candidates pass a competency exam testing their knowledge of federal tax law. As an enrolled agent, you will have the same representation rights as a CPA, with the ability to represent taxpayers in IRS audits and appeals—an EA's rights are unlimited before all levels and offices of the IRS.

The PassKey study guide series is designed to help you study for the EA exam, which is formally called the *IRS Special Enrollment Examination* or *"SEE."*

EA Exam Basics

The EA exam consists of three parts, which candidates may schedule separately and take in any order they wish. The computerized exam covers all aspects of federal tax law, with Part 1 testing the taxation of individuals; Part 2 testing the taxation of businesses; and Part 3 testing representation, practice, and procedures.

Each part of the EA exam features 100 multiple choice questions, with no written answers required. The exam may include some experimental questions that are not scored. You will not know which of the questions count toward your score and which do not.

> **Computerized EA Exam Format**
> Part 1: Individual Taxation-100 questions
> Part 2: Business Taxation-100 questions
> Part 3: Representation, Practice, and Procedures-100 questions

You will have 3.5 hours to complete each part of the exam. The actual seat time is four hours, which allows time for a pre-exam tutorial and a post-exam survey. An on-screen timer counts down the amount of time you have to finish.

The testing company Prometric exclusively administers the EA exam at thousands of testing centers across the United States and in certain other countries. You can find valuable information and register online at *www.prometric.com/SEE.*

Testing Center Procedures

The testing center is designed to be a secure environment. The following are procedures you will need to follow on test day:

1. Check in about a half-hour before your appointment time, and bring a current government-issued ID with a photo and signature. If you do not have a valid ID, you will be turned away and will have to pay for a new exam appointment. Refunds will not be issued by Prometric if you forget to bring proper ID with you.

2. The EA exam is a closed-book test, so you are not allowed to bring any notes or reference materials into the testing room. The center supplies sound-blocking headphones if you want to use them.
3. No food, water, or other beverages are allowed in the testing room.
4. You will be given scratch paper and a pencil to use, which will be collected after the exam.
5. You will be able to use an onscreen calculator during the exam, or Prometric will provide you with a handheld calculator. You cannot bring your own calculator into the examination room.
6. Before entering the testing room, you will be scanned with a metal detector wand.
7. You will need to sign in and out every time you leave the testing room. Bathroom breaks are permitted, but the test timer will continue to count down.
8. You are not allowed to talk or communicate with other test-takers in the exam room. Prometric continuously monitors the testing via video, physical walk-throughs, and an observation window.

> **Important Note:** Violation of any of these procedures may result in the disqualification of your exam. In cases of cheating, the IRS says candidates are subject to consequences that include civil and criminal penalties.

Exam-takers who require special accommodations under the Americans with Disabilities Act (ADA) must contact Prometric at 888-226-9406 to obtain an accommodation request form. The test is administered in English; a language barrier is not considered a disability.

Exam Content

Each May, using questions based on the prior calendar year's tax law, the IRS introduces multiple new versions of each part of the EA exam. If you fail a particular part of the exam and need to retake it, do not expect to see the identical questions the next time.

Prometric's website includes broad content outlines for each exam part. When you study, make sure you are familiar with the items listed, which are covered in detail in your PassKey guides. The IRS no longer releases test questions and answers from prior exams, although questions from older exams (pre-2005) are still available on the IRS website for review. Be aware that tax law changes every year, so be familiar with recent updates and do not rely too heavily on these earlier questions and answers.

Your PassKey study guides present an overview of all the major areas of federal taxation that enrolled agents typically encounter in their practices and are likely to appear on the exam. Although our guides are designed to be comprehensive, we suggest you also review IRS publications and try to learn as much as you can about tax law in general, so you are well-equipped to take the exam.

In addition to this study guide, we highly recommend that all exam candidates read:

- **Publication 17,** *Your Federal Income Tax* (for Part 1 of the exam), and
- **Circular 230,** *Regulations Governing the Practice of Attorneys, Certified Public Accountants, Enrolled Agents, Enrolled Actuaries, and Appraisers before the Internal Revenue Service* (for Part 3 of the exam).

You may download these publications for free from the IRS website.

Note: Some exam candidates take *Part 3: Representation, Practice, and Procedures* first rather than taking the tests in order, since the material in Part 3 is considered less complex. However, test-takers should know that several questions pertaining to taxation of *Individuals* (Part 1) and *Businesses* (Part 2) are often included on the Part 3 exam.

Exam Strategy

Each multiple choice question has four answer choices. There are several different question formats, and examples of each format are featured in your PassKey study guides.

Format One-Direct Question
Which of the following entities are required to file Form 709, *United States Gift Tax Return*? A. An individual B. An estate or trust C. A corporation D. All of the above
Format Two-Incomplete Sentence
Supplemental wages do not include payments for: A. Accumulated sick leave B. Nondeductible moving expenses C. Vacation pay D. Travel reimbursements paid at the federal government's per diem rate
Format Three-All of the Following Except
There are five tests which must be met for you to claim an exemption for a dependent. Which of the following is not a requirement? A. Citizen or Resident Test B. Member of Household or Relationship Test C. Disability Test D. Joint Return Test

There may also be a limited number of questions that have four choices, with three incorrect statements or facts and only one with a correct statement or fact, which you would select as the right answer.

During the exam, you should read each question thoroughly to understand exactly what is being asked. Be particularly careful when the question uses language such as "not" or "except."

If you are unsure of an answer, you may mark it for review and return to it later. Try to eliminate clearly wrong answers from the four possible choices to narrow your odds of selecting the right answer. But be sure to answer every question, even if you have to guess because all answers left incomplete will be marked as incorrect. Each question is weighted equally.

With 3.5 hours allotted for each part of the exam, you have slightly more than two minutes per question. Try to answer the questions you are sure about quickly, so you can devote more time to those that include calculations or that you are unsure about. Remember the clock does not stop for bathroom breaks, so allocate your time wisely.

To familiarize yourself with the computerized testing format, you may take a tutorial on the Prometric website. However, the tutorial only illustrates what the test screens look like; it does not allow you to revisit questions you have left open or marked for review, as you can do during the actual exam.

Scoring Methods

The EA exam is not graded on a curve, and the IRS does not reveal either a percentage of correct answers needed to pass or a predetermined pass rate. Each question on the exam is worth one point. The IRS determines scaled scores by calculating the number of questions answered correctly from the total number of questions in the exam and converting to a scale that ranges from 40 to 130. The IRS has set the scaled passing score at 105, which corresponds to the minimum level of knowledge deemed acceptable for EAs.

After you finish your exam and submit your answers, you will exit the testing room, and a Prometric staff member will print results showing whether you passed or failed. Test results are automatically shared with the IRS, so you do not need to submit them yourself. Test scores are confidential and will be revealed only to you and the IRS.

If you pass, your printed results will show a passing designation but not your actual score. The printout also will not indicate which specific questions you answered correctly or incorrectly.

If you fail, you will receive a scaled score, so you will be able to see how close you are to the minimum score of 105.

You will also receive the following diagnostic information to help you know which subject areas to concentrate on when studying to retake the exam:

- *Level 1: Area of weakness where additional study is necessary. It is important for you to focus on this domain as you prepare to take the test again. You may want to consider taking a course or participating actively in a study group on this topic.*
- *Level 2: Might need additional study.*
- *Level 3: Clearly demonstrated an understanding of the subject area.*

These diagnostic indicators correspond to various sections of each part of the exam.

If necessary, you may take each part of the exam up to four times during the testing window between May 1 and February 28. You will need to re-register with Prometric and pay fees each new time you take an exam part.

You may carry over passing scores for individual parts of the exam up to two years from the date you took them.

Pass Rates

The yearly pass rates for the SEE vary by exam. In the prior year testing period, the highest pass rate was for Part 3, with a nearly 90% success rate. Just over 80% of test-takers passed Part 1.

The pass rate for Part 2 was much lower, averaging about 60%. Prometric notes that it can be misleading to compare pass rates for the various exams because the same individuals do not take each one. The number of candidates who take Part 1 is nearly double the number of candidates taking either Part 2 or Part 3.

Applying for Enrollment

Once you have passed all three parts of the EA exam, you can apply to become an enrolled agent. The process includes an IRS review of your tax compliance history. Failure to timely file or pay personal income taxes can be grounds for denial of enrollment. The IRS's Return Preparer Office will review the circumstances of each case and make determinations on an individual basis. You may not practice as an EA until the IRS approves your application and issues you an enrollment card, a process that takes up to 60 days or more.

Successfully passing the EA exam can launch you into a fulfilling and lucrative new career. The exam requires intense preparation and diligence, but with the help of PassKey's comprehensive *EA Review*, you will have the tools you need to learn how to become an enrolled agent.

We wish you much success.

Ten Steps for the IRS EA Exam

STEP 1: Learn

Learn more about the enrolled agent designation and explore the career opportunities that await you after passing your EA exam. In addition to preparing income tax returns for clients, EAs can represent individuals and businesses before the IRS, just as attorneys and CPAs do. A college degree or professional tax background is not required to take the EA exam. Many people who use the PassKey study guides have had no prior experience preparing tax returns, but go on to rewarding new professional careers.

STEP 2: Gather Information

Gather more information before you launch into your studies. The IRS publishes basic information about becoming an EA on its website (*www.irs.gov/Tax-Professionals/Enrolled-Agents*). You will also find valuable information about the exam itself on the Prometric testing website at www.prometric.com/see. Be sure to download the *Candidate Information Bulletin*, which takes you step-by-step through the registration and testing process.

STEP 3: Obtain a PTIN

PTIN stands for *Preparer Tax Identification Number*. Before you can register for your EA exam, you must obtain a PTIN from the IRS. The PTIN sign-up system can be found at www.irs.gov/ptin. You will need to create an account, provide personal information, and pay a required fee. Since tax return information is used to authenticate your identity, you should use a previous year's individual tax return if you're applying for a PTIN and you filed your tax return in the past eight weeks. It takes about 15 minutes to sign up online and receive your PTIN. Candidates who choose to use the paper Form W-12, *IRS Paid Preparer Tax Identification Number (PTIN) Application and Renewal*, will have to wait about four to six weeks to have their PTINs processed. Foreign-based candidates without a Social Security number are also required to have a PTIN in order to register to take the exam; they will need to submit additional paperwork with their Form W-12.

STEP 4: Register with Prometric

Once you have your PTIN, you may register for your exam on the Prometric website by creating an account to set up your user ID and password. You must also complete Form 2587, *Application for Special Enrollment Examination*.

STEP 5: Schedule Your Test

After creating an account, you can complete the registration process by clicking on "Scheduling". Your exam appointment must be scheduled within one year from the date of registration. You can choose a test site, time, and date that are convenient for you. Prometric has test centers in most major metropolitan areas of the United States, as well as in many other countries.

You may schedule as little as two days in advance—space permitting—through the website or by calling 800-306-3926 Monday through Friday. Be aware that the website and the phone line show different inventories of available times and dates, so you may want to check both for your preferred testing dates.

The testing fee is nonrefundable. Once you've scheduled, you'll receive a confirmation number. Keep it for your records because you'll need it to reschedule, cancel, or change your appointment.

STEP 6: Adopt a Study Plan

Focus on one exam part at a time, and adopt a study plan that covers each unit of your PassKey guides. You'll need to develop your own individualized study program. The period of time you'll need to prepare for each exam is truly unique to you, based on how much prior tax preparation experience you have and your current level of tax knowledge; how well you understand and retain the information you read; and how much time you have to study for each test. For those without prior tax experience, a good rule of thumb is to study at least 60 hours for each of the three exam sections. *Part 2: Businesses* may require additional study preparation, as evidenced by the lower pass rates. One thing is true for all candidates: for each of the tests, start studying well in advance of your scheduled exam date.

STEP 7: Get Plenty of Rest and Good Nutrition

Get plenty of rest, exercise, and good nutrition prior to the EA exam. You'll want to be at your best on exam day.

STEP 8: Test Day

Be sure to arrive early at the test site. Prometric advises arriving at least 30 minutes before your scheduled exam time. If you miss your appointment and are not allowed to take the test, you'll forfeit your fee and have to pay for a new appointment. Remember to bring a government-issued ID with your name, photo, and signature. Your first and last name must exactly match the first and last name you used to register for the exam.

STEP 9: During the Exam

This is when your hard work finally pays off. Focus and don't worry if you don't know the answer to every question, but make sure you use your time well. Give your best answer to every question. All questions left blank will be marked as wrong.

STEP 10: Congratulations. You Passed!

After celebrating your success, you need to apply for your EA designation. The quickest way is by filling out Form 23, *Application for Enrollment to Practice before the Internal Revenue Service*, on the IRS website. You may also pay online. Once your application is approved, you'll be issued an enrollment card, and you'll be official—a brand new enrolled agent!

Unit 1: Tax Returns for Individuals

More Reading:
Publication 17, *Your Federal Income Tax*
Publication 501, *Exemptions, Standard Deduction, and Filing Information*
Publication 971, *Innocent Spouse Relief*
Publication 519, *U.S. Tax Guide for Aliens*
Publication 552, *Recordkeeping for Individuals*
Publication 54, *Tax Guide for U.S. Citizens and Resident Aliens Abroad*

Overview of EA Exam Part 1: Individuals

For Part 1 of the enrolled agent exam, you will be expected to know a broad range of information about preparing tax returns for individual taxpayers. This information includes the basics of filing status, requirements, and due dates; taxable and nontaxable income; deductions, credits, and adjustments to income; determining the basis of property; figuring capital gains and losses; rental income; retirement income; estate and gift taxes, and much more. We begin with the preliminary work tax return preparers are expected to do in order to prepare accurate tax returns.

Use of Prior Year Returns

When enrolled agents and other tax professionals prepare tax returns for clients, they are expected to perform due diligence in collecting, verifying, and gathering taxpayer data. A preparer is also expected to review prior year tax returns for compliance, accuracy, and completeness. A preparer is required by law to notify a taxpayer of an error or omission on a prior year tax return and the consequences of not correcting the error or omission. However, a preparer is not required to correct the error. The use of prior year returns can help prevent major mathematical errors and alert a preparer to issues specific to a particular client.

In reviewing prior year tax returns, a preparer needs to determine whether there are items that affect the current year's return, including the following:

- Carryovers
- Net operating losses
- Credit for prior year minimum tax (Form 8801)
- Depreciation

Taxpayer Biographical Information

The following information is required to prepare an accurate tax return:

- Legal name
- Date of birth
- Marital status
- Residency status and/or citizenship
- Dependents
- Taxpayer identification number

The IRS requires each individual listed on a federal income tax return to have a valid taxpayer identification number (TIN). That includes the taxpayer, his or her spouse (if married), and any dependents. The types of TINs are:

- Social Security number (SSN)
- Individual taxpayer identification number (ITIN)
- Adoption taxpayer identification number (ATIN)

> **Note:** A taxpayer's personal information is considered highly sensitive and confidential. A preparer who wrongfully discloses taxpayer information could face civil and criminal charges.

A taxpayer who cannot obtain an SSN must apply for an ITIN if he files a U.S. tax return or is listed on a tax return as a spouse or dependent.

ITIN Applications and Renewals

Taxpayers who are ineligible for a Social Security Number must request an ITIN. These taxpayers must file Form W-7, *Application for IRS Individual Taxpayer Identification Number*, and supply documentation that establishes their foreign status and true identity. For example, an ITIN would be required when a soldier marries a foreign spouse and wishes to file jointly. In order to file a joint return, the couple would need to request an ITIN for the foreign spouse.

Starting in 2017, there are now three ways to apply for an ITIN.

- Using Form W-7, or
- Using an IRS-authorized Certified Acceptance Agent or
- In person at a designed IRS Taxpayer Assistance Center.

Also starting in 2017, all ITINs issued before 2013 will now expire unless they are renewed. New ITIN procedures include:

- Enhanced documentation for new Individual Taxpayer Identification Numbers (ITINs)
- Older ITINs will expire if not renewed
- Newer ITINs will expire if not used within three years
- Form W-7 has been revised (as of September 2016)
- The IRS will no longer accept passports of dependents as stand-alone documents that lack a date of entry into the United States.

New ITIN Application Procedures: When a taxpayer applies for an ITIN, his Form W-7 must include original documentation such as passports and birth certificates, or certified copies of these documents from the issuing agency. Notarized copies are no longer accepted.

> **Example:** Laurie is a U.S. citizen with a Social Security number. Laurie lives and works in Mexico. Later in the year, she marries Roman, a citizen of Mexico, who has a daughter from a prior marriage. Laurie decides to file jointly with Roman in 2016 and claim her stepdaughter as a dependent. In order to do so, they must request ITINs for Roman and his daughter.

Note: The issuance of an ITIN does not affect an individual's immigration status or give the taxpayer the right to work in the United States. A taxpayer with an ITIN is not eligible to receive Social Security benefits or the Earned Income Tax Credit. ITINs are for federal tax reporting only, and are not intended to serve any other purpose.

Adoption Taxpayer Identification Number (ATIN)

ATINs are specifically designed for adopted children who are not yet eligible for a Social Security Number. For an adopted child who does not yet have an SSN, a taxpayer may request an ATIN if:

- The child is placed in the taxpayer's home for legal adoption.
- The adoption is a domestic adoption, or the adoption is a legal foreign adoption and the child has a permanent resident alien card or certificate of citizenship.
- The taxpayer cannot obtain the child's existing SSN even though he has made a reasonable attempt to obtain it from the birth parents, the placement agency, and other persons.
- The taxpayer cannot obtain an SSN for other reasons, such as the adoption not yet being final.

An ATIN cannot be used to obtain the Earned Income Tax Credit.

Special Rule for a Deceased Child

If a child is born and dies within the same tax year and is not granted an SSN, the taxpayer may still claim that child as a dependent.

Example: Alice gave birth to a son on October 1, 2016. The baby had health problems and died three days later. He was issued a death certificate and a birth certificate, but not an SSN. Alice can claim her son as a qualifying child in 2016. Alice must paper-file her return in order to claim her deceased son as a dependent. Her son will be considered a "qualifying child" for tax purposes, even though the child only lived a short time.

The tax return must be filed on paper with a copy of the birth certificate or a hospital medical record attached. The birth certificate must show that the child was born alive, as a stillborn infant does not qualify. The taxpayer would enter "DIED" in the space for the dependent's Social Security number on the tax return.

Recordkeeping Requirements for Individuals

Whether a paid tax return preparer is involved or not, a taxpayer is responsible for keeping copies of tax returns and maintaining other records for as long as they may be needed for the administration of any provision of the Internal Revenue Code.

Generally, a taxpayer should keep copies of tax returns and supporting documentation for at least three years from the date the returns were filed or the date they were due, whichever is later.

The IRS does not require taxpayers to keep records in any particular way, but says individuals need good records for the following purposes:

Identify sources of income: Taxpayers receive money or property from a variety of sources. Individuals need this information to separate business from nonbusiness income and taxable from nontaxable income.

Keep track of expenses: Tracking expenses as they occur helps taxpayers identify expenses that can be used to claim deductions.

Keep track of the basis of property: Taxpayers need to retain records showing the original cost or other basis of property they own and any improvements made to them.

Support items reported on tax returns: If the IRS has questions about items on a return, a taxpayer should have records to substantiate those items. In an IRS audit, the burden of proof is on the taxpayer to prove their expenses in order to deduct them.

Prepare tax returns: Good records help taxpayers and their preparers file accurate returns more quickly.

> **Note:** Even if a tax professional prepares and signs an individual's tax return, the taxpayer is ultimately responsible for the accuracy of its contents.

The IRS allows taxpayers to maintain records in any way that will help determine the correct tax. Electronic records are acceptable, as long as a taxpayer can reproduce the records in a legible and readable format. Basic records that all taxpayers should keep include items related to:

- **Income:** Forms W-2, Forms 1099, bank statements, brokerage statements, Schedules K-1.
- **Expenses:** Sales slips, invoices, receipts, canceled checks or other proof of payment, written communications from qualified charities, Forms 1098 to support mortgage interest and real estate taxes paid.
- **Home purchase and sale:** Closing statements, HUD statements, purchase and sales invoices, proof of payment, insurance records, receipts for improvement costs.
- **Investments:** Brokerage statements, mutual fund statements, Forms 1099, Forms 2439.

Basic Tax Forms for Individuals

Form 1040EZ: Form 1040EZ is the simplest tax return form. The one-page form is designed for single and joint filers with no dependents or large deductions. It shows the taxpayer's filing status, income, adjusted gross income, standard deduction, taxable income, tax, Earned Income Tax Credit, amount owed or refund, and signature. A taxpayer may use Form 1040EZ only if:

- Taxable income is below $100,000, and interest income is $1,500 or less.
- The only income is from wages, salaries, tips, unemployment compensation, Alaska Permanent Fund dividends, taxable scholarships and fellowship grants, and taxable interest.
- Their filing status is single or married filing jointly.
- The taxpayer is under age 65 and not blind.
- The taxpayer is not claiming any dependents.
- The taxpayer claims no adjustments to income and no credits other than the Earned Income Tax Credit.

Form 1040A: Form 1040A is a two-page form. Taxable income must be less than $100,000, and there can be no self-employment income. A taxpayer may not itemize deductions when using Form 1040A and is limited to certain adjustments to income and credits.

Form 1040: Form 1040, also called the "long form", is designed to report all types of income, deductions, and credits. Taxpayers who cannot use Form 1040EZ or Form 1040A must use Form 1040. Common reasons a taxpayer must use Form 1040 include:

- Taxable income exceeds $100,000.
- He wants to itemize his deductions.
- He is reporting self-employment income.
- He is reporting income from the sale of property (such as the sale of stock or rental property).

Form 1040NR: Form 1040NR is used by nonresident aliens to report their U.S. source income. The IRS defines an alien as any individual who is not a U.S. citizen or U.S. national. A nonresident alien is an alien who has not passed the green card test or the substantial presence test. Form 1040NR is used by investors overseas, as well as nonresident taxpayers who earn money while in the U.S. The 1040NR is not used by U.S. citizens or U.S. residents.

Example: Cisco is a worldwide boxing champion and a legal citizen and resident of Panama. Cisco receives a non-immigrant visa to fight in a boxing match in the U.S., where he earns $500,000 for the fight. He only remains in the U.S. for six days. After his boxing appearance, he returns to Panama. Cisco is not eligible for an SSN and must request an ITIN to report his U.S. income. Without the ITIN, he would be subject to automatic backup withholding on his U.S. earnings. Cisco's accountant correctly reports his income and tax on Form 1040NR. Cisco does not have to report his worldwide income on his Form 1040NR, only the income he earned in the United States.

Form 1040X, *Amended U.S. Individual Income Tax Return***:** This form is used to correct a previously filed Form 1040, 1040A, or 1040NR. It is also used to change amounts previously adjusted by the IRS, make a claim for a carryback due to a loss or unused credit, correct a liability for the additional Medicare Tax, or make certain elections after the prescribed deadline.

Amended returns cannot be filed electronically.

Federal Income Tax Rates

An individual's federal taxable income is taxed at progressive rates in the United States. The more taxable income a taxpayer has, the higher the percentage of that income he pays in taxes. The IRS groups individuals by ranges of their taxable income level, or *brackets*, and applies increasing tax rates at each successive level.

For tax year 2016, there are seven tax brackets for individuals: 10%, 15%, 25%, 28%, 33%, 35%, and 39.6%. Each year, the IRS adjusts the income ranges for inflation and issues tax tables that show how much tax is owed for specific amounts of taxable income, depending upon a taxpayer's filing status.

For example, in 2016 a single taxpayer with $9,275 of taxable income would be in the 10% tax bracket. If he had $50,000 of taxable income, he would be in the 25% tax bracket, while a taxpayer with more than $500,000 of taxable income would be in the highest tax bracket of 39.6%.

2016 Federal Tax Rates				
Rate	Single Filers	MFJ or Qualifying Widower	Head of Household	MFS
10%	$0 to $9,275	$0 to $18,550	$0 to $13,250	$0 to $9,275
15%	$9,275 to $37,650	$18,550 to $75,300	$13,250 to $50,400	$9,276 to $37,650
25%	$37,650 to $91,150	$75,300 to $151,900	$50,400 to $130,150	$37,651 to $75,950
28%	$91,150 to $190,150	$151,900 to $231,450	$130,150 to $210,800	$75,951 to $115,725
33%	$190,150 to $413,350	$231,450 to $413,350	$210,800 to $413,350	$115,726 to $206,675
35%	$413,350 to $415,050	$413,350 to $466,950	$413,350 to $441,000	$206,676 to $233,475
39.60%	$415,050+	$466,950+	$441,000+	$233,476+

However, this does not mean that a taxpayer in the highest income range owes tax at 39.6% on all of their taxable income. The applicable tax rate for each successive bracket applies only to the additional amounts of taxable income that fall within that bracket.

Example: Cora is single and had $39,000 of taxable income for 2016. For the first $9,275 she is taxed at a 10% rate. For the next segment of her taxable income, from $9,275 to $37,650, she is taxed at a 15% rate. Only for the remaining $1,350, from $37,650 to $39,000, she is taxed at 25%, which is referred to as her marginal tax rate.

In addition to the regular tax in the United States, there is a parallel tax called the alternative minimum tax (AMT). A taxpayer must pay either the regular tax or the AMT, depending on whichever amounts to the greater tax. The AMT is covered in detail later.

Tax Return Due Dates and Extensions

The regular due date for individual tax returns is April 15; if April 15 falls on a Saturday, Sunday, or legal holiday, the due date is delayed until the next business day. For the 2016 tax year, a federal holiday in Washington D.C. pushes the normal filing deadline to April 18, 2017.

If a taxpayer cannot file his tax return by the due date, he may request an extension by filing Form 4868, *Application for Automatic Extension of Time to File*, which may be filed electronically. An extension grants a taxpayer an additional six months to file his individual tax return.

For the 2016 tax year, extended individual tax returns are due by October 16, 2017 (the normal extended due date is October 15).

Note: Although an extension gives a taxpayer extra time to *file* his return, it does not extend the time to *pay* any tax due. A taxpayer will owe interest on any amount that is not paid by the regular filing deadline, plus a late payment penalty if he has not paid at least 100% of the prior year's tax or 90% of the current year tax. Taxpayers are expected to estimate and pay the amount of tax due by the filing deadline.

The IRS will accept a postmark as proof of a timely-filed return. For example, if a tax return is postmarked on April 15 but does not arrive at an IRS service center until April 23, the IRS will accept the tax return as having been filed on time. In cases where a tax return is filed close to the deadline, it is advisable for a taxpayer to pay for proof of mailing or certified mail. This is also called the "mailbox rule".

E-filed tax returns are given an "electronic postmark" to indicate the day they are transmitted.

Filing Deadline Exceptions

Federal Disaster Areas: Taxpayers in federally-declared disaster areas are often granted extensions to file and pay their income taxes and to make estimated tax payments. The IRS may also abate interest and any late filing or late payment penalties that apply to taxpayers in these disaster areas.

This tax relief generally includes individuals and businesses located in a disaster area, those whose tax records are located in a disaster area, and relief workers.

June 15 Deadlines: Three groups of taxpayers are granted an automatic two-month extension to file and pay any tax due:

- Nonresident aliens who have income that is not subject to U.S. withholding.
- U.S. citizens or legal U.S. residents who are living outside the United States or Puerto Rico and their main place of business is outside the U.S. or Puerto Rico.
- Taxpayers on active military service duty outside the U.S.

A citizen or resident alien living abroad must attach a statement to his tax return explaining which situation qualifies him for the special two-month extension. Even if he is allowed an extension, the taxpayer will have to pay interest on any tax not paid by the regular tax deadline of April 15.

Taxpayers Out of the Country: A taxpayer who is out of the country can request an additional discretionary two-month extension of time to file his tax return, beyond the regular six-month extension of October 15. For calendar-year taxpayers, the "additional" extension date would be December 15.

To request this extension, a taxpayer must send the IRS a letter explaining the reason why he needs the additional two-month period of time to file. There is no specific form for this additional extension.[1] Unless the request is denied, the taxpayer will not receive a response from the IRS.

Special Rules for Combat Zones: The deadline for filing a tax return or a claim for refund, and the deadline for payment of tax owed, are automatically extended for any service member, Red Cross personnel, accredited correspondent, or contracted civilian serving in a combat zone. These taxpayers have their tax deadlines suspended from the day they started serving in the combat zone until 180 days after they leave the combat zone. These deadline extensions also apply to the spouses of armed services members serving in combat zones.

---

[1] See IRS Publication 54, *Tax Guide for U.S. Citizens and Resident Aliens Abroad*, for more information about extended deadlines. Publication 54 discusses four extensions: an automatic 2-month extension, an automatic 6-month extension, an additional extension for taxpayers out of the country, and an extension of time to meet certain tests.

Example: Dimitri is a U.S. Marine who has served in a combat zone since March 1, so he is entitled to extra time to file and pay his taxes. The 46 days between the date he entered the combat zone and the April 15 filing deadline are added to the normal extension period of 180 days, so he has a 226-day extension period after he leaves the combat zone. IRS deadlines for assessment and collection are also suspended during any period that a US servicemember is in a combat zone.

Penalties and Interest

The IRS can assess a penalty on individual taxpayers who fail to file, fail to pay, or both. The failure-to-file penalty is generally greater than the failure-to-pay penalty. If someone is unable to pay all the taxes he owes, he is better off filing on time and paying as much as he can, as the IRS will consider payment options with individual taxpayers.

Failure-to-File Penalty: The penalty for filing late is usually 5% of the unpaid taxes for each month or part of a month that a return is late. The penalty is based on the tax that is not paid by the due date, without regard to extensions. The penalty will not exceed 25% of a taxpayer's unpaid taxes.

If both the failure-to-file penalty and the failure-to-pay penalty apply in any month, the 5% failure-to-file penalty is reduced by the failure-to-pay penalty.

Note: The Trade Facilitation and Enforcement Act of 2015 increases the penalty for failing to file a tax return in 2016. The higher penalty applies to individual returns filed in 2017. The increased failure-file penalty is the lesser of $205 (up from $135) or 100% of the amount of tax owed.

If a taxpayer is owed a tax refund, he will not be assessed a failure-to-file penalty.

Failure-to-Pay Penalty: If a taxpayer does not pay his taxes by the due date, he could be subject to a failure-to-pay penalty of ½ of 1% (0.5%) of unpaid taxes for each month or part of a month after the due date that the taxes are not paid. This penalty can be as much as 25% of a taxpayer's unpaid taxes. The failure-to-pay penalty rate increases to a full 1% per month for any tax that remains unpaid the day after a demand for immediate payment is issued, or ten days after notice of intent to levy certain assets is issued.

Interest on the Amount Due: In addition to filing penalties, the taxpayer will also be charged interest on the amount due. Generally, interest accrues on any unpaid tax from the due date of the return until the date of payment in full. The interest rate is determined quarterly and is the federal short-term rate plus 3 percent. Interest compounds daily.

Relief from Joint Tax Liability

In certain cases, a spouse can be relieved of the tax, interest, and penalties on a joint return. When spouses file a joint return, they are both legally responsible for the entire tax liability. However, a taxpayer can file a claim for spousal relief under three different grounds:

- Innocent Spouse Relief
- Separation of Liability Relief
- Equitable Relief

Innocent Spouse Relief: This is when a joint return has understated tax liability due to erroneous items attributable to a taxpayer's spouse or former spouse. Erroneous items include income received by a spouse that is omitted from the return. Deductions, credits, and property basis are also erroneous items if they are incorrectly reported on the joint return.

To be considered an innocent spouse, the taxpayer must establish that he or she did not know (or have reason to know) that there was an understated tax liability at the time of signing the joint return. The taxpayer must request relief within two years after the date on which the IRS begins collection activity.

Separation of Liability Relief: The above restrictions also apply to separation of liability relief. In this case, however, the taxpayer must no longer be married to, or must be legally separated from, his or her spouse, or must be widowed or have lived apart for at least 12 months from the spouse with whom the joint return was filed.

The understated tax, plus interest and penalties, would be allocated to the taxpayer based on the amount for which he or she is responsible.

Equitable Relief: If a taxpayer does not qualify for the first two types of relief, he or she may be eligible for equitable relief. The IRS will review the facts and circumstances of the taxpayer's case and determine whether it would be unfair to hold the taxpayer liable for the understated tax.

Unlike the other two forms of relief, equitable relief may also be granted for an underpaid tax, meaning it was properly reported on a tax return but not paid. Further, in some cases, the spouse requesting relief may have known about the understated or underpaid tax, but did not challenge the treatment for fear of his or her spouse's retaliation.

The taxpayer has up to ten years to request equitable relief under certain circumstances. Form 8857, *Request for Innocent Spouse Relief*, is used to request all three types of relief.

Example: Nataly is a victim of domestic violence who now lives apart from her husband. When she signed her joint return, she knew her husband was underreporting income from his business but was afraid of what would happen if she refused to sign. After the IRS discovered the understated tax, Nataly filed for equitable relief and was able to document her history of spousal abuse using affidavits from family members and other proof. The IRS granted her request for relief of her portion of the understated tax, penalties, and interest.

Injured Spouse Claims

An "injured spouse" claim has a similar-sounding name but is completely different than "innocent spouse" relief. To be considered an injured spouse, a taxpayer must meet the following criteria:

- Have filed a joint return
- Have paid federal income tax or claimed a refundable tax credit
- All or part of the taxpayer's refund was, or is expected to be, applied to his or her spouse's past financial obligations
- Not be responsible for the debt

A spouse who believes that he is entitled to a portion of the refund on a joint return can file Form 8379, *Injured Spouse Allocation.*

> **Example:** Ron filed a joint return with his wife, Valerie, who had delinquent student loans. Valerie incurred the student loan debt before she was married. Ron files Form 8379 to request his portion of their tax refund as an injured spouse. The IRS will retain Valerie's portion of the couple's tax refund to offset her debt, but will allow Ron to obtain his portion of the refund.

Refunds Claims and Amended Returns

In order to claim a refund, a taxpayer must generally file an amended tax return (Form 1040X) within three years from the date the return was originally due or two years from the date the tax was paid, whichever is later. [2] If a claim is not filed within the applicable period, a taxpayer generally will not be entitled to a refund.

However, if the taxpayer files an extension and filed his original return prior to the October 15 extension deadline, the three-year period begins on the date that the taxpayer originally filed his return. Amended returns (Form 1040X) cannot be filed electronically. They must be filed on paper. If a taxpayer is entitled to a refund, he cannot request a direct deposit on Form 1040X.

> **Example:** Don has not filed a tax return for a long time, and now he wants to file several years of delinquent tax returns: 2011 through 2016. Don files the returns and realizes that he was entitled to refunds for each year. If he files all the back tax returns by April 18, 2017, he will receive refunds for his 2013-2016 tax returns. His refunds for 2011 and 2012, however, have expired. He will not receive a refund for those years.

> **Example:** Oleg made estimated tax payments of $1,000 and requested an extension to file his 2013 income tax return. He filed his 2013 return timely, before the extended due date of October 15, 2014. When he filed his return on September 7, 2014, he paid an additional $200 tax due. Oleg later finds an error on the return. Three years after the extended due date, he files an amended return on September 7, 2017, and claims a refund of $700.

> **Example:** Goldie prepared her own 2013 tax return and filed it after the deadline, on July 12, 2014. She did not request an extension, so the return was delinquent when she filed it. She later discovered that she had forgotten to claim the Earned Income Tax Credit. Approximately three years later, she files an amended return on July 10, 2017. Goldie's refund claim is denied because she filed her original return past the due date *without* a valid extension. Therefore, her amended return was not filed timely.

Extended Statute for Claiming Refunds

In some cases, a request for a tax refund will be honored past the normal deadline. These special cases involve:

- A bad debt from a worthless security (up to seven years prior)
- A payment or accrual of foreign tax

---

[2] If the taxpayer had an extension to file (for example, until October 15), but the taxpayer filed earlier and the IRS received it July 1, the return is considered filed on July 1 (Form 1040X instructions).

- A net operating loss carryback
- A carryback of certain tax credits
- Exceptions for military personnel
- Taxpayers in federally-declared disaster areas
- Taxpayers who have been affected by a terroristic or military action

Time periods for claiming a refund are also extended when a taxpayer is "financially disabled". This usually requires that the taxpayer be mentally or physically disabled to the point that he is unable to manage his financial affairs.

> **Example:** Roger has been helping his elderly mother, Mabel, file her tax returns for the last several years. Over time, she has become forgetful of things. In 2016, Roger discovers a large file in his mother's home filled with old brokerage statements. Several of the brokerage statements show losses from worthless securities, dating back many years. Mabel had been putting the statements away because she believed that they were unimportant. Mabel's Form 1099-B from 2010 shows a significant loss from worthless stock (over $10,000 in losses that were never reported). Even though the brokerage statement is six years old, Mabel is still allowed to amend her 2010 tax return in order to claim the stock losses. That is because the IRS allows up to seven years to amend a tax return for losses from worthless securities. Mabel can file a Form 1040X in order to claim the losses and still receive a refund under this extended statute.

Statute of Limitations for IRS Assessment and Collection

The IRS is generally required to assess tax or audit a taxpayer's return within three years after the return is filed or, if filed early, the due date of the return. If a taxpayer files his tax return late, the IRS has three years from the later of:

- The due date of the return, or
- The date the return was actually filed.
- If a taxpayer never files a return, there is no deadline for assessment of tax.
- If the taxpayer files a fraudulent tax return, there is no deadline for IRS assessment or collection.

The statute of limitations for IRS collection is ten years from the date tax is assessed, as long as there is no evidence of fraud. The ten-year period begins to run on the date of the tax assessment, not on the date of filing. So, for example, if the taxpayer owes when they file their tax return, the IRS will send a bill. The bill is the assessment.

The IRS assigns a collection statute expiration date, or "CSED", to every delinquent taxpayer account. Once the CSED expires, the IRS loses its right to seize assets or make payment demands. Certain events can extend the amount of time the IRS has to collect.

The IRS has six years to assess tax on a return if a "substantial understatement" is identified, meaning that gross income was understated by more than 25%.[3]

---

[3] IRC Sect. 6501(e)(1)(A)(i).

Example: Karolyn filed her 2013 tax return on February 27, 2014. The three-year statute period for audit began April 15, 2014, and ends on April 15, 2017. After that date, the IRS must be able to prove fraud or a substantial understatement of gross income to audit the tax return.

Example: Harold has always filed his tax returns in a timely manner. Five years ago, Harold was self-employed and did not understand how to manage his money or pay estimated taxes. He had a large tax bill from that year. Harold still filed his tax return on time and correctly reported the amount due, with the intention of making payments. The IRS issued its assessment and sent Harold a bill for $24,000 (the amount that Harold owes, plus penalties and interest). Harold requested an installment agreement and began making monthly payments towards his tax debt. Shortly thereafter, Harold had a terrible car accident and became completely disabled. He no longer has the means to work or pay the bill. The IRS has five years left to collect on the debt, and after that, the statute for collection expires. Although the interest and penalties will continue to accrue, if Harold does not have any assets or any means to pay the bill, he will likely be deemed "uncollectible".

Estimated Taxes

The federal income tax is a "pay-as-you-go" tax, meaning a taxpayer must pay taxes as he earns or receives income throughout the year.

If a taxpayer earns income that is not subject to withholding, such as self-employment income, rents, and alimony, or if his taxes withheld are insufficient to cover his tax liability, he may be required to make quarterly estimated tax payments. Estimated tax is used to pay income tax as well as self-employment tax and alternative minimum tax.

Safe Harbor Rule: Taxpayers can avoid making estimated tax payments by ensuring they have enough tax withheld from their income. A taxpayer must generally make estimated tax payments if:

- He expects to owe at least $1,000 in tax (after subtracting withholding and tax credits)
- He expects the total amount of withholding and tax credits to be less than the smaller of:
  - 100% of the tax liability on his prior year return
  - 90% of the tax liability on his current year return

Example: Gerald earned $95,000 in 2016 and paid $8,200 in tax. Although he expects his income to increase in 2017, he will not be assessed a penalty for underpayment of estimated taxes, provided he pays at least $8,200 in estimated tax during the year (100% of the tax liability on his prior year return).

A taxpayer will not face an underpayment penalty if the total tax liability on his return (minus the amounts of tax credits or paid through withholding) is under $1,000.

Example: Dominique has a full-time job as a secretary. She also earns money part-time as a self-employed manicurist. In 2016, she did not make estimated payments. However, Dominique made sure to increase her withholding at her regular job in order to cover any amounts that she would have to pay on her self-employment earnings. When she files her tax return, she discovers that she still owes $750. Although she is responsible for paying the tax that is owed, she will not owe an underpayment penalty because the total tax liability is less than $1,000.

A U.S. citizen or U.S. resident is not required to make estimated tax payments if he had zero tax liability in the prior year.

> **Example**: Cassius, age 25 and single, earned $2,700 before he was laid off in 2015, and received $1,500 in unemployment compensation afterward. He did not have to pay income tax because his gross income was less than the filing requirement. In 2016, Cassius began working as a self-employed plumber but made no estimated tax payments during the year. Even though he owed $3,000 in tax at the end of the year, Cassius does not owe the underpayment penalty for 2016 because he had zero tax liability in the prior year.

If a taxpayer wishes to change his withholding amounts from his wages, he must use Form W-4, *Employee's Withholding Allowance Certificate*, and submit the form to his employer.

Safe Harbor Rule for Higher-Income Taxpayers: If the taxpayer's 2016 adjusted gross income was more than $150,000 ($75,000 if MFS), the taxpayer must pay the *smaller of* 90% of their expected tax for 2017 or 110% of the tax shown on their 2016 return to avoid an estimated tax penalty.

Estimated Tax Due Dates for Individuals

The year is divided into four payment periods for estimated taxes, each with a specific payment due date. If the due date falls on a Saturday, Sunday, or legal holiday, the due date is the next business day. A taxpayer must complete Form 1040-ES, *Estimated Tax for Individuals*, to pay his estimated tax.

If a payment is mailed, the date of the U.S. postmark is considered the date of payment.

> **First Payment Due: April 15**
> **Second Payment Due: June 15**
> **Third Payment Due: September 15**
> **Fourth Payment Due: January 15 (of the following year)**

Estimated Taxes for Farmers and Fishermen

Special rules apply to the payment of estimated tax by qualified farmers and fishermen. If at least two-thirds of the taxpayer's gross income in the current year comes from (or in the prior year came from) farming or fishing activities, the following rules apply:

- The taxpayer does not have to pay estimated tax if he files his return and pays all tax owed by the first day of the third month after the end of his tax year (usually March 1).
- The taxpayer does not have to pay estimated tax if his current year income tax withholding is at least two-thirds (.6667) of the total tax liability on his current tax return or 100% of the total tax liability on his prior year return.
- If the taxpayer must pay estimated tax, he is required to make only one estimated tax payment (called the "required annual payment") by the fifteenth day after the end of his tax year (usually January 15).

For this special tax treatment, qualified farming income includes gross farming income on Schedule F, gross farming rental income, gains from the sale of livestock, and crop shares for the use of a farmer's land. This rule also applies to qualified fishermen.

Note: This special estimated tax rule also applies to a person's share of gross income from partnerships and S corporations where the majority of its income is derived from farming or fishing. This safe harbor for estimated payments does not apply to C Corporations, however, regardless of the type of business activity.

Example: Jay is a self-employed owner of a commercial fishing vessel. All of his income is from commercial fishing, so he is not required to pay quarterly estimated taxes. Jay's records are incomplete, so he asks his tax accountant to file an extension on his behalf. Since Jay will be unable to file his tax return by March 1, 2017, his accountant notifies Jay that he is required to make a single payment of estimated taxes by January 15, 2017.

Example: Karla earns 100% of her income from growing organic strawberries. She is a qualified farmer and reports her business income on Schedule F. She is not required to pay quarterly estimated taxes. Karla filed her tax return on February 20, 2017, and enclosed a check for her entire balance due of $4,900. Since she filed before the March 1, 2017, deadline, she will not be subject to any penalty.

Note: If a qualified farmer (or fisherman) files their 2016 Form 1040 by March 1, 2017, and pays all the tax they owe at that time, they do not need to make <u>any</u> estimated tax payments in the previous year. This rule does not apply to any other business activity—it only applies to farmers and fishermen.

Backup Withholding

There are times an entity is required to withhold certain amounts from a payment and remit the amounts to the IRS. For example, the IRS requires backup withholding if a taxpayer's name and Social Security number on Form W-9, *Request for Taxpayer Identification Number and Certification*, does not match its records.

Example: Wesley owns a number of investments through Top Finances Corporation. In 2016, the IRS notifies Top Finances that Wesley's Social Security number is incorrect. Top Finances notifies Wesley by mail that the company needs his correct Social Security number, or it will have to start backup withholding on his investment income. Wesley ignores the notice and never bothers to update his SSN. Top Finances must begin backup withholding on Wesley's investment income.

The IRS will sometimes require backup withholding if a taxpayer has a delinquent tax debt, or if he fails to report all his interest, dividends, and other income. Payments subject to backup withholding may include wages, interest, dividends, rents, royalties, and payments to independent contractors for services.

Note: The backup withholding rate for 2016 is 28% for all U.S. citizens and legal U.S. residents.

Under backup withholding rules, a business or bank must withhold taxes from a payment if:
- The individual did not provide the payor with a valid taxpayer identification number.
- The IRS notified the payer that the TIN or SSN is incorrect.

- The IRS notified the payor to start withholding on interest and dividends because the payee failed to report income in prior years.
- The payee failed to certify that he was not subject to backup withholding for underreporting of interest and dividends.

Unit 1: Study Questions

(Test yourself first, then check the correct answers at the end of this quiz.)

1. Which of the following is not a requirement for a spouse to be eligible for innocent spouse relief?

A. When the taxpayer signed the return, he or she did not know, and had no reason to know, that there was an understatement of tax.
B. The taxpayer must have filed as either MFJ or MFS.
C. The return had an understatement of tax directly related to the spouse's erroneous items.
D. The facts and circumstances show that it would be unfair for the IRS to hold the taxpayer liable for the understatement.

2. Catherine files an extension request (Form 4868), which allows her an additional six months to file her tax return. When she finally prepares her return, she realizes that she owes a substantial amount of tax. She pays the tax when she files the return, which she does before the extended due date. Which penalties, if any, will Catherine be likely to owe?

A. She will owe interest on the amount owed and a late payment penalty.
B. She will owe interest on the amount owed and a late filing penalty.
C. She will owe interest on the amount owed, a late payment penalty, and a late filing penalty.
D. She will not owe any penalties because she filed before the extended due date and paid the taxes owed with the return.

3. Isla files as single and has no refundable credits. She is not self-employed. Based on the figures below, is she required to pay estimated tax in the current year?

AGI for prior tax year	$73,700
Total tax on prior year return	9,224
Anticipated AGI for current year	82,800
Total current year estimated tax liability	11,270
Tax expected to be withheld in current year	$10,250

A. Yes, she is required to make estimated tax payments.
B. No, she is not required to make estimated tax payments.
C. She is not required to make estimated tax payments because she does not have self-employment income.
D. None of the above is correct.

4. Generally, how long should taxpayers keep the supporting documentation for their tax returns?

A. Four years from the date the return was filed, or the return was due, whichever is later.
B. Three years from the date the return was filed, or the return was due, whichever is later.
C. Two years from the date the return was filed, or the return was due, whichever is later.
D. Ten years from the date the return was filed, or the return was due, whichever is later.

5. Ricky files his 2016 tax return on February 15, 2017. He has a balance due of $800 on the return. How long can he wait to pay the amount owed and not incur a penalty?

A. He will owe a late payment penalty unless he pays his tax liability when he files his return.
B. He has until the due date of the return (not including extensions) to pay the amount owed and not pay a penalty.
C. He has until the due date of the return (including extensions) to pay the amount owed and not pay a penalty.
D. He does not have to pay the amount due by a certain date because it is less than the safe harbor amount of $1,000.

6. Which of the following taxpayers is required to have an individual taxpayer identification number (ITIN)?

A. A nonresident alien with a Social Security number which moves outside the U.S.
B. A nonresident alien who must file a return and is not eligible for a valid Social Security number.
C. Anyone who does not have a Social Security number.
D. All nonresident and resident aliens.

7. Clark's 2013 tax return was due April 15, 2014. He filed it on March 2, 2014. Later, Clark discovered that he is eligible for an education credit that will result in a refund. He neglected to take this credit on his 2013 return. What is the latest date that Clark can amend his 2013 tax return in order to receive a refund?

A. April 15, 2016
B. April 18, 2017
C. March 2, 2017
D. March 2, 2016

8. The current backup withholding rate for U.S. taxpayers is:

A. 0%
B. 13.5%
C. 25%
D. 28%

9. Cynthia is divorced, files as head of household, and has two dependents. Cynthia is a citizen of Canada and a legal U.S. Resident (green card holder). She earned $43,000 in 2016 and plans to itemize her deductions. Which tax form should Cynthia use?

A. Form 1040.
B. Form 1040A.
C. Form 1040EZ.
D. Form 1040NR.

10. All of the statements about estimated tax payments are correct except:

A. An individual whose only income is from self-employment will generally have to pay estimated payments.
B. If insufficient tax is paid through withholding, estimated payments may be necessary.
C. Estimated tax payments are required when the amount of taxes withheld is greater than the overall tax liability.
D. Estimated tax is used to pay not only income tax, but self-employment tax and alternative minimum tax as well.

11. Which of the following is not an acceptable reason for extending the statute of limitations for claiming a refund past the normal deadline?

A. A bad debt from a worthless security.
B. Living in a federally-declared disaster area.
C. Exceptions for military personnel.
D. Living outside the country for three years.

12. If a taxpayer files his tax return more than 60 days after the due date or extended due date, what is the minimum penalty he will face?

A. A minimum of 25% of his unpaid taxes.
B. A minimum of 5% of his unpaid taxes.
C. The smaller of $205 or 100% of the unpaid tax.
D. The greater of $135 or 100% of the unpaid tax.

13. Which of the following documents will be accepted as valid means of identification for a taxpayer applying for an ITIN?

A. Notarized copies of birth certificates and passports.
B. Original birth certificates and passports.
C. Certified copies of birth certificates and passports.
D. Both B and C.

14. Dottie is a U.S. resident who paid estimated tax in 2015 totaling $2,500. In 2016, she closed her business as a self-employed florist and is now unemployed. Dottie expects to have zero tax liability in 2016. Which of the following statements is correct?

A. She is still required to make estimated tax payments in 2016.
B. She is not required to make estimated tax payments in 2016.
C. She must pay a minimum of $2,500 in estimated tax payments in 2016, or she will be subject to a failure-to-pay penalty.
D. She must make a minimum of $2,250 (90% × $2,500) in estimated tax payments in 2016, or she will be subject to an underpayment penalty.

15. What is the statute of limitations for an IRS assessment on a tax return from which more than 25% of the taxpayer's gross income was omitted?

A. There is no statute of limitations on a return in which gross income was omitted.
B. Three years from the date the return was filed, or the return was due, whichever is later.
C. Six years from the date the return was filed.
D. Ten years from the date the return was filed.

16. Rochelle is a United States citizen who lives in England. She owes $5,000 of tax for 2016. Which of the following statements is correct regarding her filing and payment requirements?

A. She must file and pay her taxes by April 18, 2017.
B. She is allowed an automatic two-month extension to file her tax return, but she must pay her taxes by April 18, 2017.
C. She is allowed an automatic two-month extension to file and pay her taxes, but she must attach a statement to her return explaining why she qualifies for the extension.
D. If she files by June 15, 2017, she will not owe any additional interest on her tax liability.

17. Sally and Albert file a joint return. Their tax refund will be applied toward Albert's unpaid child support obligations from an earlier relationship. To request her portion of their refund, Sally should file:

A. As an innocent spouse.
B. As a damaged spouse.
C. As an injured spouse.
D. For equitable relief.

18. Forrest is single and earned $200,000 as a self-employed software consultant during the current year. Under the estimated tax safe harbor rules for high-income taxpayers, he can avoid an underpayment penalty if he pays _____ of his prior year tax liability:

A. $1,000
B. 90%
C. 100%
D. 110%

19. Leah is a self-employed architect and must make estimated tax payments. What is the due date for her *third* estimated tax payment for the tax year 2016?

A. October 15, 2016
B. August 15, 2016
C. September 15, 2016
D. January 15, 2017

Unit 1: Quiz Answers

1. The answer is B. Innocent spouse relief is available only for a spouse who has filed *jointly* and is therefore legally liable for the understatement of tax. Therefore, a taxpayer who filed MFS wouldn't qualify. To qualify for innocent spouse relief, the taxpayer must meet all of the following conditions:

- The taxpayer filed a joint return that has an understatement of tax directly related to the spouse's erroneous items.
- The taxpayer establishes that, at the time of signing the joint return, he or she did not know, and had no reason to know, that there was an understatement of tax.
- Taking into account all the facts and circumstances, it would be unfair for the IRS to hold the taxpayer liable for the understatement.

In order to apply for innocent spouse relief, a taxpayer must submit Form 8857, *Request for Innocent Spouse Relief*, and sign it under penalty of perjury.

2. The answer is A. Even though she files Form 4868, Catherine may owe interest and a late payment penalty on the amount owed if she does not pay the tax due by the regular due date. However, she will not be assessed a late filing penalty (failure-to-file) because she filed her tax return before the extended due date.

3. The answer is B. Isla does not need to pay estimated tax because she expects her income tax withholding in the current year ($10,250) to be greater than both, 90% of the tax to be shown on her current year return ($11,270 × 90% = $10,143) and 100% of her prior year tax liability ($9,224). Therefore, Isla qualifies for the safe harbor rule and is not required to make estimated tax payments. A taxpayer is not required to pay estimated tax if:

- The taxpayer had no tax liability in the prior year,
- The taxpayer was a U.S. citizen or resident alien, and
- The prior tax year covered a 12-month period.

A taxpayer also does not have to pay estimated tax if she pays enough through withholding so that the tax due on the return is less than $1,000. In most cases, a taxpayer must pay estimated tax if she expects withholding (plus any refundable credits) to be less than the smaller of:

- 90% of the tax to be shown on the current year tax return, or
- 100% of the tax shown on the prior year tax return.

4. The answer is B. Taxpayers should keep the supporting documentation for their tax returns for at least three years from the date the return was filed or three years from the date the return was due, whichever is later. This includes applicable worksheets, receipts, and other forms.

5. The answer is B. Ricky has until the original due date of the return (not including extensions) to pay the amount owed and not incur a penalty. Taxpayers should submit their payment of taxes due on or before April 15 (or the next business day if April 15 falls on a Saturday, a Sunday, or a legal holiday). For the 2016 tax year, taxpayers have until April 18, 2017, to pay the amount he owes.

6. The answer is B. If a taxpayer must file a U.S. tax return or is listed on a tax return as a spouse or dependent and is not eligible for a Social Security number, he must apply for an ITIN.

7. The answer is B. If Clark has his amended return postmarked on or before April 18, 2017, it will be within the three-year limit, and the return will be accepted. If the amended return is postmarked after that date, it will fall outside the three-year statute of limitations, and he will not receive the refund. In order to claim a refund, the amended return must be filed the later of three years from the date the return was due or two years from the date the tax was paid.

8. The answer is D. The current backup withholding rate is 28%. The IRS may require backup withholding if a taxpayer has a delinquent tax debt; if he fails to report all his interest, dividends, and other income; or if his Social Security number does not match records provided to the IRS.

9. The answer is A. Since Cynthia plans to itemize her deductions, she must file Form 1040. She cannot use a Form 1040A or a Form 1040EZ. Form 1040NR is only for nonresident taxpayers. With few exceptions, green card holders are taxed as US Citizens and do not file Form 1040NR. Nonresidents cannot file as Head of Household or take any dependency exemptions.

10. The answer is C. If a taxpayer's withholding exceeds his tax liability, no estimated payments would be required. The taxpayer would receive a refund of the overpaid tax when he files his tax return.

11. The answer is D. Living outside the country is not a valid reason to extend the statute of limitations for claiming a refund. In some cases, a request for a tax refund will be honored past the normal three-year deadline. Exceptions exist for military personnel, individuals who are financially disabled, taxpayers who live in federally-declared disaster areas, and taxpayers who have bad debts from worthless securities.

12. The answer is C. The minimum penalty is $205 or 100% of the unpaid tax (whichever is less) for a taxpayer who files his return more than 60 days late. This is an increase from the previous year. The higher penalty applies to individual returns filed in 2017, (for the 2016 tax season). The increased failure-file penalty is now the lesser of $205 (up from $135) or 100% of the amount of tax owed.

13. The answer is D. Only original documents of birth certificates and passports are accepted, or documents that have been certified by the original issuing agency. Notarized documents are no longer accepted.

14. The answer is B. A taxpayer is not required to pay estimated tax if she expects to have zero tax liability for the current tax year.

15. The answer is C. If a taxpayer omitted more than 25% of his gross income on his return, the IRS has up to six years to assess a deficiency.

16. The answer is C. A U.S. citizen or resident alien living outside the United States has an automatic two-month extension to file and pay her taxes. The same is true for members of the military who are serving outside the U.S. Rochelle must attach a statement to her tax return explaining why she qualifies for the extension. She will still owe interest on the tax that was due on April 18, 2017, if she does not pay the amount due by that date.

17. The answer is C. Sally should file a claim as an injured spouse to request her portion of their tax refund. She would do so by filing Form 8379, *Injured Spouse Allocation*. If the request is granted, the IRS will retain her husband's portion of their tax refund to offset his unpaid child support but will allow Sally to obtain her portion of the refund. In contrast, innocent spouse relief is when tax has been incorrectly reported on a joint return, and one spouse is relieved of the obligation to pay the other spouse's portion of the tax liability.

18. The answer is D. To avoid an underpayment penalty, Forrest must pay the smaller of:
- 110% of his prior year tax liability or
- 90% of his expected tax for the current year.

This estimated tax safe harbor rule applies to higher-income taxpayers with adjusted gross income of more than $150,000 ($75,000 if filing a married filing separately return).

19. The answer is C. The third quarter payment for individual estimated tax is due September 15. For estimated tax payments, a year is divided into four quarterly payment periods. Each period has a due date. The payments are due as follows:

Periods	Due Date
Jan. 1-March 31	April 15
April 1-May 31	June 15
June 1-Aug. 31	September 15
Sept. 1-Dec. 31	January 15 (following year)

Unit 2: Taxpayer Filing Status and Residency

> **For additional information read:**
> Publication 17, *Your Federal Income Tax*
> Publication 501, *Exemptions, Standard Deduction, and Filing Information*
> Publication 54, *Tax Guide for U.S. Citizens and Resident Aliens Abroad*
> Publication 519, *U.S. Tax Guide for Aliens*

The IRS uses a taxpayer's filing status to determine filing requirements, standard deductions, eligibility for certain credits, and the amounts of tax owed. There are five filing statuses, with rules governing each, including special rules for annulled marriages and widow(er)s with dependent children.

In general, a taxpayer's filing status depends first on whether he or she is married or unmarried as of the last day of the year. For federal tax purposes, a marriage was traditionally defined as a legal union between a man and a woman as husband and wife.

For tax years 2013 and beyond, a marriage between same-sex spouses is also recognized as a legal union, as long as the marriage was performed in a domestic or foreign jurisdiction that recognizes the validity of same-sex marriage.[4]

Then, on June 26, 2015, in the landmark case *Obergefell vs. Hodges*, the U.S. Supreme Court held in a 5 to 4 decision that the Fourteenth Amendment requires a state to license a marriage between two people of the same sex, and to recognize a marriage between two people of the same sex when their marriage was lawfully licensed and performed out-of-state, or in another country.

This new ruling made the law uniform for legally married same-sex couples in all 50 states and the District of Columbia. However, individuals who have entered into a registered domestic partnership, civil union, or other similar relationship that is not considered a marriage under state law are not considered married for federal tax purposes.

> **Study Alert:** Expect to be tested on the concept of same-sex marriage on the EA Exam. Remember that registered domestic partners or those in civil unions are NOT considered "married" for federal tax purposes, and you may see a question on the exam regarding this current tax law issue.

Single

A taxpayer is single for the entire tax year if, on the last day of the tax year, he or she was:

- Unmarried
- Legally separated or divorced, or
- Widowed (and not remarried during the year). However, special rules apply to widowed taxpayers. We will cover those rules later.

---

[4] Revenue Ruling 2013-17 was issued in response to the Supreme Court case, *Windsor vs. United States*, in which the court ruled that the Defense of Marriage Act (DOMA) was unconstitutional under the equal protection clause and held that federal law must recognize a same-sex marriage that was valid under applicable state law. Under that ruling, the state where the marriage ceremony was performed determined whether it was recognized as legal under federal law.

> **Example:** Kenneth and Jennifer legally divorced on December 31, 2016. They do not have any dependents. They cannot file either as married filing jointly or married filing separately for 2016. Instead, each must file as "single" for 2016.

Married Filing Jointly (MFJ)

The married filing jointly status typically provides more tax benefits than filing a separate return. On a joint return, spouses report all of their combined income, allowable expenses, exemptions, and deductions. Spouses can file a joint return even if only one spouse had income. Both spouses must agree to sign the return, and both are responsible for any tax owed, even if all the income was earned by only one spouse. A subsequent divorce usually does not relieve either spouse of the liability associated with the original joint return (see exceptions related to innocent spouse relief, covered earlier).

Taxpayers can file jointly if they are married as of December 31 and:

- Live together as husband and wife or as a legally married same-sex couple
- Live together in a common law marriage recognized in the state where they now reside or in the state where the common law marriage began
- Live apart but are not legally separated or divorced[5]
- Are separated under an interlocutory (not final) divorce decree

In addition, a widowed taxpayer may use the married filing jointly status and file jointly with his deceased spouse if his spouse died during the year and he or she has not remarried as of the end of the year.

A U.S. resident or U.S. citizen who is married to a nonresident alien can elect to file a joint return as long as both spouses agree to be taxed on their worldwide income.

> **Note:** Federal law does not allow Registered Domestic Partners to file a joint return. This rule also applies to civil unions.[6] The IRS *does* recognize common-law marriages. Currently, the only states that recognize common law marriage are Alabama, Colorado, the District of Columbia, Iowa, Kansas, Montana, Rhode Island, South Carolina, Texas and Utah.

Married Filing Separately (MFS)

The MFS status is for taxpayers who are married and either:

- Choose to file separate returns, or
- Do not agree to file a joint return.

If one spouse chooses to file MFS, the other is forced to do the same, since a joint return must be signed by both spouses.

---

[5] State law governs whether a taxpayer is married or legally separated under a divorce or separate maintenance decree. In certain states, a legally separated couple may agree to file jointly or as married filing separately, or they may be required to do so until a divorce becomes final.
[6] See Revenue Ruling 2013-17.

> **Example:** Jerry and Danielle have always filed jointly in the past. However, Danielle has chosen to separate her finances from her husband this year, even though they are living together. Jerry wants to file jointly with Danielle, but she has refused. Danielle files her tax return using married filing separately as her filing status; therefore, Jerry is forced to file MFS as well.

The MFS filing status means the two spouses report their own income, exemptions, credits, and deductions on separate returns, even if one spouse had no income. This filing status may benefit a taxpayer who wants to be responsible only for his own tax, or if it results in less tax than filing a joint return.

Typically, however, a married couple will pay more tax on a combined basis when filing separately than they would by filing jointly.

Specific features of the MFS filing status include the following:

- The tax rates are generally higher at the same levels of taxable income than those applicable to MFJ.
- The exemption amount for the alternative minimum tax is half that allowed on a joint return.
- Various credits, including the Earned Income Tax Credit, the Premium Tax Credit, and those for child care, education, adoption, and retirement savings, are either not allowed or are much more limited than on a joint return.
- The capital loss deduction is limited to $1,500, half that allowed on a joint return.
- The standard deduction is half the amount allowed on a joint return and cannot be claimed if the taxpayer's spouse itemizes deductions.

> **Example:** Dinesh and Maya keep their finances separate and choose to file MFS. Dinesh plans to itemize his casualty losses, so Maya is forced to either itemize her deductions or claim a standard deduction of zero.

One common reason a taxpayer may choose the MFS filing status is to avoid an offset of his refund against his current spouse's outstanding prior debt.

This might include delinquent child support or student loans, or a tax liability a spouse incurred before the marriage.

> **Example:** Tom and Judith were married in 2016. Tom owes delinquent taxes from a prior year. Judith chooses to file separately from Tom, so her refund will not be offset by his overdue tax debt. If they were to file jointly, their entire refund might be retained in order to pay the debt.

Amending Filing Status from MFS

There are rules for when married taxpayers are allowed to change their filing status for a given year's return.

Taxpayers generally cannot change from a joint return to a separate return *after the due date* of the return. For example, if a married couple filed their joint 2016 tax return on March 13, 2017, and subsequently decided they wanted to file separately instead, they would have only until April 18, 2017, to file amended returns using the MFS filing status (the due date of the original return).

An exception allows a personal representative for a deceased taxpayer to change from a joint return elected by the surviving spouse to a separate return for the decedent, for up to a year after the filing deadline.

> **Example:** Kurt and Susan have always filed jointly. Susan dies suddenly in 2016, and her last will names Harriet, her daughter from a previous marriage, as the executor of her estate. Kurt files a joint return with Susan for tax year 2016, but Harriet, as the executor, decides that it would be better for Susan's estate if her tax return were filed MFS. Harriet files an amended return claiming MFS status for Susan, and signs the return as the executor.

To change from separate returns to a joint return, taxpayers must file an amended return using Form 1040X and may do so at any time within three years from the due date of the separate returns (not including extensions).

Same-Sex Spouses

Same-sex spouses who are legally married must file as either married filing jointly or married filing separately. They do not have the choice to file as single. However, be aware that civil unions and registered domestic partnerships are not legally considered "marriages" for IRS purposes.

Registered domestic partners (or partners in a civil union) may not file a federal return using a married filing separately or jointly filing status. Therefore, these taxpayers are not married for federal tax purposes.

> **Example:** Curtis and Antonio are registered domestic partners in the state of California. They consult Marilynn, an EA, who prepares their tax returns. Curtis and Antonio wish to file jointly. However, registered domestic partners are not married under state law. Therefore, they must file as Single for Federal tax purposes.

Head of Household (HOH)

A taxpayer who qualifies to file as head of household will usually have a lower tax rate than the rates for single or MFS, and will receive a higher standard deduction.

The head of household status is available to taxpayers who meet all three of the following requirements:

- The taxpayer must be single, divorced, legally separated, or "considered unmarried" on the last day of the year.
- The taxpayer must have paid more than half the cost of keeping up a home for the year.
- The taxpayer must have had a qualifying person living in his home for more than half the year. There are exceptions for temporary absences, such as school, or for a qualifying parent, who does not have to live with the taxpayer. This would include hospitalization and stays in a nursing home.

"Considered Unmarried" for HOH Status

There are some instances where a taxpayer can be considered unmarried (for tax purposes only). To be "considered unmarried" on the last day of the tax year, a taxpayer must meet all of the following conditions:

- File a separate return from the other spouse.
- Pay more than half the cost of keeping up a home for the tax year.
- Not live with his spouse in the home during the last six months of the tax year.
- Maintain the home as the main residence of a qualifying child, stepchild, or foster child for more than half the year.
- Be able to claim an exemption for the child (although there is an exception for divorced parents, explained later).

For the purpose of determining this filing status, valid household expenses used to calculate whether a taxpayer is paying more than half the cost of maintaining a home include:

- Rent, mortgage interest, property taxes
- Home insurance, repairs, utilities
- Food eaten in the home

Valid expenses do not include clothing, education, medical treatment, vacations, life insurance, or transportation. Welfare payments are not considered amounts that the taxpayer provides to maintain a home.

For purposes of the head of household status, a "qualifying person" is defined as:

- A qualifying child,
- A married child who can be claimed as a dependent, or
- A dependent parent.

The qualifying person for HOH filing status must generally be related to the taxpayer either by blood, adoption, or marriage. However, a foster child also qualifies if the child was legally placed in the home by a government agency.

A taxpayer's qualifying person may include the taxpayer's child or stepchild, sibling or stepsibling, or a descendant of any of these. For example, a niece or nephew, stepbrother or stepsister, or grandchild may all be eligible as qualifying persons for the HOH filing status.[7]

> **Example:** Lewis's unmarried daughter, Araceli, lived with him all year. Araceli turned 18 at the end of the year. She does not have a job, did not provide any of her own support, and cannot be claimed as a dependent by anyone else. As a result, Araceli is Lewis's qualifying child. Lewis may use the HOH filing status.

An unrelated individual may still be considered a "qualifying relative" for a dependency exemption, but will not be a qualifying person for the HOH filing status.[8]

---

[7] A taxpayer cannot file as head of household if the taxpayer's only dependent is his or her Registered Domestic Partner.
[8] The rules for qualifying children and relatives will be covered in detail in the next unit, *Personal and Dependency Exemptions.*

Special Rules for HOH Status

Divorced or Noncustodial Parents: A taxpayer can file as HOH and not claim the qualifying child as their dependent. This happens most often with divorced parents. This is because the head of household filing status applies to the taxpayer who maintains the main home of a qualifying child.

However, a custodial parent may choose to release the dependency exemption to a noncustodial parent. In this scenario, the custodial parent would claim head of household filing status, while the noncustodial parent would claim the dependency exemption.

> **Example:** George and Elizabeth have been divorced for five years. They have a 12-year-old daughter named Rebecca who lives with her mother during the week and only sees her father on weekends. Therefore, Elizabeth is considered the custodial parent. They agree, however, to allow George to claim the dependency exemption for Rebecca on his tax return. In 2016, George correctly files as single and claims Rebecca as his dependent. Elizabeth may still file as HOH if she otherwise qualifies, but she will not claim the dependency exemption for Rebecca.

The "considered unmarried" rules apply in determining who can claim a child for dependency and HOH purposes. A couple, even if not formally separated or divorced, must live apart for *more than half the year* in order for either spouse to claim HOH status.

> **Example:** Luke and Pauline separated in February 2016 and lived apart for the rest of the year. They do not have a written separation agreement and are not yet divorced. Their six-year-old daughter, Kennedy, lived with Luke all year, and he paid more than half the cost of keeping up the home. Luke files a separate tax return and claims Kennedy as a dependent because he is the custodial parent. Luke can also claim head of household status for 2016. Although Luke is still legally married, he can file as HOH because he meets all the requirements to be "considered unmarried".

> **Example:** Janine and Richard separated on July 10, 2016, but were not yet divorced at the end of the year. They have one minor child, Madeline, age eight. Even though Janine lived with Madeline and supported her for the remainder of the year, Janine does not qualify for HOH filing status because she and Richard did not live apart for the last six months of the year.

Death or Birth during the Year: A taxpayer may still file as head of household if the qualifying child is born or dies during the year. The taxpayer must have provided more than half of the cost of keeping up a home that was the child's main home while he was alive.

> **Example:** Velma gives birth to a son in September 2016 who dies within two months of his birth. She can claim him on her tax return as a qualifying child even though he only lived a short while.

Dependent Parents: If a taxpayer's qualifying person is a dependent parent, the taxpayer can file as HOH even if the parent does not live with the taxpayer.

The taxpayer must pay more than half the cost of keeping up a home that was the parent's main home for the entire year. This rule also applies to a parent in a rest home. A qualifying "parent" may be a stepparent, in-law, or grandparent who is related to the taxpayer by blood, marriage, or adoption.

> **Example:** Sharon is 54 years old and single. She pays the monthly bill for Shasta Pines Retirement Homes, where her 78-year-old mother lives. Sharon's mother has lived at Shasta Pines for two years and has no income. Since Sharon pays more than half of the cost of her mother's living expenses, Sharon qualifies for head of household filing status.

> **Example:** Tina is single and fully financially supports her mother, Rue, who lives in her own apartment. Rue dies suddenly on May 2, 2016. Tina can claim her mother as a dependent and file as HOH for 2016, even though Rue was not alive for the whole year.

Nonresident Alien Spouses: A taxpayer, who is married to a nonresident alien spouse, may elect to file as HOH by "disregarding" the nonresident alien spouse. This is a unique rule that only applies to taxpayers who are married to nonresidents.

This is true even if both spouses lived together throughout the year. The taxpayer must not elect to treat the spouse as a resident and he must have a qualifying child (or other qualifying dependent, such as a parent) to qualify for the HOH status.

> **Example:** Two years ago, Tim, a U.S. citizen, met and married Mina, a nonresident alien who is a citizen and resident of Greenland. The couple lived together in Greenland while Tim was on sabbatical from his university teaching position. They have a son who was born in 2016. Mina does not wish to file jointly with Tim and does not wish to make the election to be treated as a U.S. resident. Tim can file as head of household, even though he and Mina lived together all year because Mina is a nonresident alien.

Annulments

Annulment is a legal procedure for declaring a marriage null and void. If a taxpayer obtains a court decree of annulment that holds no valid marriage ever existed, the couple is considered unmarried even if they filed joint returns for earlier years.

Unlike divorce, an annulment is retroactive. Taxpayers who have annulled their marriage must file amended returns (Form 1040X) claiming single (or head of household status, if applicable) for all the tax years affected by the annulment that are not closed by the statute of limitations.

> **Example:** Sara and Robert were granted an annulment on October 31, 2016. They were married for two years. Robert has sole custody of one son from a prior relationship. For 2016, Sara must file as single and must amend the prior two years' tax returns to single as well. Robert must also amend his joint returns. If he otherwise qualifies, Robert can amend his returns to head of household filing status.

Qualifying Widow(er) With a Dependent Child

Qualifying widow(er) with a dependent child is the least common filing status. A qualifying widow(er) receives the same standard deduction as married taxpayers who file jointly. In the year of the spouse's death, a taxpayer can generally file a joint return.

However, if a surviving spouse remarries before the end of the year, the married filing separately status must be used for the decedent's final return.

Example: Marian and her husband, Lou, have an infant son. Lou dies suddenly of a heart attack on February 1, 2016. Marian remarries on December 10, 2016. Since she remarried in the same year her former husband died, she no longer qualifies for the joint return filing status with her deceased husband. However, Marian does qualify to file jointly with her new spouse. Therefore, Lou's filing status for his final tax return in 2016 must be MFS.

For each of the two years following the year of the spouse's death, the surviving spouse can use the qualifying widow(er) filing status if he has a qualifying dependent and does not remarry. After two years, the taxpayer's filing status converts to single or HOH, depending upon which status applies.

For example, if a taxpayer's spouse died in 2015 and he did not remarry, the taxpayer could use the qualifying widow(er) filing status for 2016 and 2017 if he has a qualifying dependent.

Example: Barbara's husband died on July 3, 2015. She has one dependent child who is ten years old. Barbara does not remarry. Therefore, Barbara's filing status for 2015 is MFJ (the last year her husband was alive). In 2016 and 2017, she can file as a "qualifying widow with a dependent child", which is a more favorable filing status than single or HOH. In 2018, she would file as HOH, assuming she remains single and does not remarry.

To be eligible for the qualifying widow(er) filing status, the taxpayer normally must:

- Not have remarried before the end of the year.
- Have been eligible to file a joint return for the year the spouse died; it does not matter if a joint return was actually filed.
- Have a qualifying child for the year. A qualifying child can be a child or stepchild, but does not include a foster child for the purposes of this filing status.
- Have furnished over half the cost of keeping up the qualifying child's home for the entire year.

Note: A taxpayer's marital status on the last day of the year (December 31) determines their marital status for the entire year, for tax purposes.

Determining Residency for Tax Purposes

In order to file an accurate tax return, a taxpayer must determine whether he is considered a *resident* or a *nonresident*. There are multiple types of tax residency.

For IRS purposes, an "alien" is an individual who is not a U.S. citizen. Aliens are further classified as nonresident aliens and resident aliens. Residency status is important because these taxpayers are taxed in different ways:

- **Resident aliens** are generally taxed on their worldwide income, the same as U.S. citizens.
- **Nonresident aliens** are taxed only on their income from sources within the United States and on certain income connected with the conduct of a trade or business in the U.S.
- **Dual status aliens** are both nonresident and resident aliens during the same tax year, with different rules applying for the part of the year a taxpayer is a U.S. resident and the part of the year he is a nonresident.

Residency for IRS purposes is not the same as legal immigration status. An individual may be considered a U.S. resident for tax purposes based upon the time he spends in the United States, regardless of immigration status.

A nonresident alien could be someone who lives outside the U.S. and simply invests in U.S. property or stocks and is therefore required to file a tax return to correctly report his earnings.

> **Example:** Chloe Jones is a folk singer and a popular recording artist in her home country of Australia. Chloe comes to the U.S. on tour, playing a variety of different venues during the month of April. Afterwards she returns to her home country. Chloe is not a U.S. resident for tax purposes. However, she is required to report her U.S. source income. Chloe's accountant files a Form 1040NR to report the income that she earned while she was touring in the U.S. She will only report and be taxed on her U.S. source income.

Tax Residency Tests

If a taxpayer is an alien, he is considered a nonresident alien for tax purposes unless he meets at least one of two tests: the *green card* test or the *substantial presence* test.

Green Card Test

An alien taxpayer is automatically considered a U.S. resident if he is a "lawful permanent resident[9]" of the United States at any time during the tax year. A taxpayer generally has this status if he is a lawful immigrant and has been issued an alien registration card, also known as a "green card".

An alien who has been present in the U.S. any time during a calendar year as a lawful permanent resident may opt to be treated as a resident alien for the entire calendar year.

Substantial Presence Test

An alien taxpayer without a green card is considered a U.S. resident for tax purposes only if he meets the substantial presence test for the calendar year. To meet this test, he must be physically present in the United States for at least:

- 31 days during the current tax year (2016), and
- 183 days during the three-year period that includes the current year (2016) and the two years immediately preceding the current year.

For purposes of the 183-day requirement, all the days present in the current year (2016) are counted, along with:

- 1/3 of the days present in the previous year (i.e., 2015), and
- 1/6 of the days present in the second year before the current year (i.e., 2014).

---

[9] Image provided by Department of Homeland Security, U.S. Citizenship and Immigration Services Verification Division.

Note: If an individual meets the requirements of the substantial presence test, he is considered for federal tax purposes a resident alien of the United States, even though he may be an undocumented immigrant.

Numerous exceptions are considered when counting days for the substantial presence test. Days in the United States are not counted if the alien taxpayer:

- Regularly commutes to work in the U.S. from a residence in Canada or Mexico, generally more than 75% of the workdays during the applicable working period (this is deemed a "closer connection to home country").
- Is present in the U.S. as a crew member of a foreign vessel.
- Is unable to leave because of a medical condition that arose while in the United States.
- Is a professional athlete in the U.S. to compete in a charitable sports event. These athletes exclude only the days in which they actually competed in the sports event, but do not exclude days used for practice, travel, or promotional events.
- Is an exempt individual. Exempt individuals include aliens who are:
  - Foreign government-related individuals in the U.S. temporarily, (such as foreign diplomats).
  - Teachers on temporary visas.
  - Visiting Scholars or researchers. Scholars are exempt for two years.
  - Students on temporary visas who do not intend to reside permanently in the U.S. Students are exempt from the substantial presence test for five years.

If the taxpayer does not meet either the green card test or the substantial presence test, he is considered a nonresident alien for tax purposes and is subject to U.S. income tax only on his U.S. source income.

Study Tip: You should memorize details of the substantial presence test for the EA exam, including the 183-day requirement and exceptions to the rule.

Example: Juliana is a Brazilian citizen who was physically present in the United States for 15 days in each of the years 2014, 2015, and 2016. She is not a green card holder. Juliana earned $32,000 in 2016 as a Portuguese translator for the U.S. government. Since the total days she was present in the U.S. for the three-year period do not meet the substantial presence test, Juliana is not considered a resident for tax purposes for 2016 and her earnings are taxed as a nonresident. Juliana is required to file Form 1040NR, *U.S. Nonresident Alien Income Tax Return*.

Example: Chow is a Chinese citizen and a renowned scientist. Chow was invited to the US to teach an advanced course at Yale University. Even though Chow is physically present in the United States for the entire tax year, he is not considered a resident for tax purposes, because he is a visiting scholar. Chow is required to file Form 1040NR, *U.S. Nonresident Alien Income Tax Return* to report his U.S. earnings.

Tax Residency through Marriage: A nonresident alien who does not meet the substantial presence test and does not have a green card may still elect to be treated as a resident for tax purposes if he is married to a U.S. citizen or resident. This election can be made only if:

- At the end of the year, one spouse is a nonresident alien, and the other is a U.S. citizen or resident, and
- Both spouses agree to file a joint return and to treat the nonresident alien as a resident alien for the entire tax year.

> **Example:** Lola and Bruno are married, and both are nonresident aliens at the beginning of the year. In February, Bruno becomes a legal U.S. resident alien and obtains a green card and a Social Security number. Lola and Bruno may both choose to be treated as resident aliens for tax purposes by attaching a statement to their joint return. Lola is not eligible for a Social Security number, so she must apply for an ITIN. Lola and Bruno must file a joint return for the year they make the election, but they can file either joint or separate returns for later years.

> **Example:** Mei, a citizen of South Korea, is in the U.S. as a graduate student on an F-1 visa status. She has resided continuously in the U.S. since arriving on August 15, 2011. She was in the U.S. all of 2016. Because international students are exempt from the substantial presence test for five years, Mei became a resident alien for federal income tax purposes in 2016. Mei is married to Quon, who lives in South Korea and is a nonresident alien. Mei and Quon can both elect to be treated as U.S. residents for tax purposes on a jointly filed return.

Students: Most international students and scholars fall under the status of nonresident aliens. An international student is anyone who is temporarily in the U.S. on an F, J, M, or Q visa. Immediate family members of a student, including spouses and unmarried children under age 21 who reside with the student, are also considered students for tax purposes.

Any part of a calendar year in which the student is present in the U.S. counts as a full year.

> **Example:** Nayan first came to the U.S. in 2010 from India as an F-1 student at a university. She studied in the U.S. until the end of 2011 and then returned home. She re-entered the U.S. as a J-1 student in 2016 in order to attend graduate school. For federal income tax purposes, Nayan is a nonresident alien because she has been in the U.S. for less than five years as a student.

Dual Status Aliens: A taxpayer is considered a dual-status alien when he has been both a resident alien and a nonresident alien in the same tax year. The most common dual-status tax years are the years of arrival and departure.

A taxpayer's status on the last day of the year determines whether he is a resident alien or a nonresident alien for the tax year.

For the part of each year, the taxpayer is a nonresident alien, he is taxed only on his U.S. source income. For the part of each year, the taxpayer is a resident alien, he is taxed on his worldwide income. This applies even if the income was earned earlier in the year while the taxpayer was a nonresident alien, but was received after he became a resident for tax purposes.

Example: Abbas legally became a U.S. resident for tax purposes on January 1, 2016. On January 15, 2016, he received $2,000 of income for contract work he did the previous year. Even though the income was earned while he was a nonresident alien, it was received after he became a resident. This income is reported and taxed on Form 1040, not on Form 1040NR.

Tax Treaties

The United States has income tax treaties with a number of foreign countries. Under these treaties, residents of foreign countries may be taxed at reduced rates, or be exempt from U.S. income taxes on certain items of income they receive from U.S. source income. These reduced rates and exemptions vary among countries and specific items of income.

Treaty provisions generally are reciprocal. Therefore, a U.S. citizen or resident who receives income from a treaty country and who is subject to taxes imposed by foreign countries may be entitled to certain credits, deductions, exemptions, and reductions in the rate of taxes of those foreign countries.

Income received by a nonresident alien that is effectively connected with a trade or business in the United States is, after allowable deductions, taxed at the rates that apply to U.S. citizens and residents. Withholding would be made at the highest applicable rate.

Note: For nonresident aliens, income or gains from U.S. sources is generally subject to backup **withholding at 30%**, unless a lower treaty rate applies. The backup withholding rate for U.S. citizens and U.S. residents is a flat 28% rate.

2016 Filing Requirements

Not every person is required to file a tax return. A taxpayer is required to file a tax return if his 2016 gross income exceeds the combined total of the standard deduction and personal exemption amounts. The IRS defines gross income as <u>all income</u> a taxpayer received in the form of money, goods, property, and services that are not exempt from tax. Sometimes, a taxpayer is required to file a tax return even though none of his income is taxable.

Note: **"Earned income"** includes all the taxable income a taxpayer receives from working, such as wages, salaries, tips, and other employee compensation. Earned income also includes self-employment earnings that a taxpayer earns by owning a business or farm. Most other types of income are considered **unearned income**, including interest income, dividends, capital gains, retirement income, inheritances, and prizes.

The 2016 filing requirement thresholds, expressed as levels of gross income, are as follows:

Gross Income Filing Thresholds for U.S. Citizens and U.S. Residents:
- Single: $10,350 (65 or older $11,900)
- Married Filing Jointly: $20,700,
    - 65 or older (one spouse) $21,950;
    - 65 or older (both spouses): $23,200

- Head of Household: $13,350 (65 or older $14,900)
- Married Filing Separately (any age): $4,050
- Qualifying Widow(er) with dependent child: $16,650 (65 or older $17,900)
- Any taxpayer with self-employment income of $400 or more in any taxable year must file a return.
- A taxpayer who earned $108.28 or more as a church employee. For the purposes of this rule, a "church employee" is an employee of a church or religious organization that has a certificate in effect electing an exemption from employer social security and Medicare taxes. [10]

> **Example**: Adrienne and Marvin are married and plan to file jointly. Adrienne is 63 and had gross income of $12,225 for the year. Marvin is 66 and had gross income of $7,500 for the year. Since their combined gross income was $19,725, they are not required to file a tax return. The filing requirement threshold for joint filers when one spouse is 65 or older is $21,950 in 2016.

> **Example**: Rita is 66, married, and had $9,500 of wage income in 2016. Her husband, Roger, also 66, had $8,700 in wage income. They have no dependents. Normally, Roger and Rita would not have a filing requirement because their gross income is under the filing threshold for joint filers age 65 and over. However, Rita wants to file separately from her husband. She is therefore required to file a tax return because the filing threshold for MFS taxpayers of any age is $4,050 in 2016. Roger must also file a tax return because his filing status is MFS by default. Roger cannot choose to file jointly with his wife unless she agrees, since both spouses are required to sign a joint return.

> **Example**: Laurel is 36, single, and had gross income of $17,500 last year. She does not have any children. She is required to file a tax return since her income was more than $10,350 in 2016. She will use the single filing status.

Filing Requirements for Self-Employed Taxpayers

There are different requirements for taxpayers who are self-employed. Generally, a taxpayer is required to file a tax return if he has net self-employment earnings of $400 or more.

> **Note:** Do not confuse the filing threshold amount for self-employed taxpayers with the filing requirement for information returns (most notably, Form 1099-MISC, *Miscellaneous Income*). Form 1099-MISC is used to report a number of different types of payments, but it is most commonly used to report payments to an independent contractor who is paid at least $600 during the year.

Dependent Filing Requirements

All dependent children who earn more than $6,300 of earned income in 2016 must file an income tax return. The threshold is much lower for unearned income (investment income). When unearned income exceeds $1,050 in 2016, a tax return must be filed for the dependent. A dependent's standard deduction is calculated differently. In 2016, it normally equals the larger of:

---

[10] For the purposes of this rule, a "church employee" does not include a minister, a member of a religious order, or a Christian Science practitioner.

- $1,050 (of unearned income, such as interest or dividends) or
- Their earned income plus $350, with a maximum standard deduction of $6,300.

Example: Cesar is a 16-year-old high school student who is claimed as a dependent on his parents' tax return. He worked as a pizza delivery boy ten hours a week and earned $3,200 of wages in 2016. He also had $1,100 of interest income from a certificate of deposit that his grandmother gave him last Christmas. Cesar is required to file a tax return because his unearned income exceeds $1,050. If Cesar did not have any interest income, he would not be required to file a return. The investment income is what triggers his filing requirement.

Example: Annette is 17 and is claimed as a dependent on her mother's tax return. Working at an ice cream parlor during the school year, Annette earned a total of $6,600 in wages in 2016. She had no other income. Annette must file a tax return because her total earned income is more than $6,300. Her mother can still claim her as a dependent.

Example: Marc is 20, single, and a full-time college student. Marc's parents claim him on their joint tax return. He received $200 of interest income and earned $4,750 of wages from a part-time job. Marc's total income of $4,950 is below the gross income filing threshold for dependents. His investment income is also below the filing requirement. Marc is not required to file a tax return in 2016.

Even if a taxpayer is not legally required to file a tax return, he should do so if he is eligible to receive a refund. A taxpayer should file a tax return if he:

- Had income tax withheld from his pay,
- Made estimated tax payments or had prior year overpayments,
- Qualifies for the Earned Income Tax Credit, or
- Qualifies for any other refundable tax credits.

Example: Holly is single, has a young son, and qualifies for HOH filing status. In 2016, she earns $11,000 of wages and $700 of self-employment income from cleaning houses. Although Holly makes less than the filing threshold for the HOH filing status, she must file a tax return because her earnings from self-employment exceed $400. Even if Holly did not have self-employment earnings, she should still file a tax return, because she likely qualifies for the Earned Income Tax Credit. The EITC is a refundable credit which could give Holly a refund.

Additional Filing Requirements

Sometimes a taxpayer is required to file a tax return even if the gross income threshold is not met, such as in the previous example of self-employment earnings of $400 or more. Other examples include the following:

- Church employees who are exempt from employers' Social Security and Medicare taxes and have wages above $108.28.
- If the taxpayer owes Social Security tax or Medicare tax on tips not reported to his employer.
- If the taxpayer must pay the alternative minimum tax.
- If the taxpayer owes additional tax in connection with a qualified plan, an IRA, a health savings account, or other tax-favored health plan.

- If the taxpayer received a Medicare Advantage MSA, Archer MSA, or health savings account distribution.
- If the taxpayer owes household employment taxes for a household worker, such as a nanny.
- If the taxpayer must recapture an education credit, investment credit, or other credit.
- If the taxpayer received advance payments of the Premium Tax Credit for himself, his spouse, or a dependent who enrolled in coverage through the Health Insurance Marketplace.

Unit 2: Study Questions

(Test yourself first, then check the correct answers at the end of this quiz.)

1. Seven years ago, Vladimir and Pablo were legally joined in a civil union in the state of Vermont. They now live in California. What is the correct statement about their filing status for 2016?

A. Vladimir and Pablo must file jointly.
B. A civil union of same-sex spouses in Vermont is not recognized in California, so they must file joint federal returns and separate state returns.
C. Vladimir and Pablo have the choice to file as single, married filing jointly, or married filing separately.
D. Civil unions are not recognized as legal marriages for IRS purposes. Vladimir and Pablo must file as single for federal tax purposes.

2. Dana's husband died on January 14, 2016. She has one dependent son who is eight years old. She did not remarry. What is the most beneficial filing status for Dana to use for 2016?

A. Married filing jointly.
B. Single.
C. Qualifying widow(er).
D. Head of household.

3. Madison and Todd are not married and do not live together, but they have a two-year-old daughter named Amanda. Madison and her daughter lived together all year while Todd lived alone in his own apartment. Madison earned $13,000 working as a clothing store clerk. Todd earned $48,000 managing a hardware store. He paid over half the cost of Madison's apartment for rent and utilities, where his daughter Amanda lives. He also gave Madison child support and extra money for groceries. Todd does not support any other family member. Which of the following statements is correct?

A. Todd can file as head of household.
B. Madison can file as head of household.
C. Todd and Madison can file jointly.
D. Neither can claim head of household filing status.

4. Helen, age 65, and Norman, age 72, were married in 2016. They have no dependents. Helen had gross income of $2,000, and Norman had gross income of $28,000 for the year. Norman wants to file jointly, but Helen wants to file separately. Which of the following statements is correct?

A. Norman is required to file a tax return using the MFS status. Helen is not required to file a return.
B. Norman may still file jointly with Helen and sign on her behalf, as long as he notifies her in writing.
C. Norman and Helen are both required to file tax returns, and they must both file MFS.
D. Norman and Helen may both file as single.

5. Annie's husband, Enzo, has neither a green card nor a visa. He was physically present in the United States for 150 days in each of the years 2014, 2015, and 2016. Is Enzo a resident alien under the substantial presence test?

A. Yes, he is a resident alien for tax purposes.
B. No, he is a nonresident alien for tax purposes.
C. Enzo is a nonresident alien for tax purposes, but he may elect to file as a resident with his spouse.
D. None of the above is correct.

6. Trinity, age 22, is single and a full-time college student who is claimed as a dependent on her father's tax return. In 2016, Trinity earned $7,350 of wages from her part-time job as an administrative assistant. She had no other income. Is she required to file a tax return?

A. Yes.
B. No.
C. Trinity is only required to file a tax return if she is a full-time student.
D. Trinity should file a return because she will receive a refund, but she is not required to file.

7. Clarence takes care of his ten-year-old grandson. How long must his grandson live in Clarence's home in order for Clarence to qualify for head of household status?

A. At least three months.
B. More than half the year.
C. The entire year.
D. More than 12 months.

8. Zora is a citizen of Russia who is granted a green card while abroad and comes to the U.S. to work as an engineer. Zora arrives in the U.S. on November 1, 2016. She earns a total of $26,000 of U.S. wages in November and December. Which of the following statements is correct?

A. She is not required to file a U.S. tax return.
B. She is required to file a U.S. tax return, and she must file using Form 1040NR.
C. She is required to file a U.S. tax return, and she must file her return using Form 1040, 1040A or 1040EZ.
D. She is not required to file a U.S. tax return in 2016, but she will be required to file a return in 2017.

9. When may a taxpayer amend a joint tax return from "married filing jointly" to "married filing separately" after the original filing deadline?

A. Never.
B. Only within the statute of limitations for filing amended returns.
C. Only when a marriage has been annulled.
D. An estate's personal representative may amend a joint return elected by the surviving spouse to a separate return for the decedent.

10. Kathy's marriage was annulled on February 25, 2016. She was married to her husband in 2014 and filed jointly with him in 2014 and 2015. She has not yet filed her 2016 tax return. Kathy has no dependents. Which of the following statements is correct?

A. She must file amended returns, claiming single filing status for all open years affected by the annulment. She will file single for the current tax year.
B. She is not required to file amended returns. She can file jointly with her husband in 2016 because she was still married for part of the year.
C. She is not required to file amended returns. She must file as married filing separately on her 2016 return.
D. She is not required to file amended returns. She must file as single on her 2016 return.

11. A U.S. resident or citizen who is married to a nonresident alien can file a joint return as long as both spouses:

A. Sign the return and agree to be taxed on their worldwide income.
B. Are living overseas.
C. Have valid Social Security numbers.
D. Are physically present in the United States.

12. Huang is a student temporarily in the U.S. on an F-1 Visa. You are his tax preparer and you are trying to determine residency for tax purposes. Huang was present in the U.S. all year. How long is he exempt from the substantial presence test?

A. One year.
B. Three years.
C. Five years.
D. There is no exemption to the substantial presence test.

13. Which of the following statements is correct regarding the head of household filing status?

A. The taxpayer must be unmarried in order to qualify for head of household filing status.
B. The taxpayer's spouse must live in the home during the tax year.
C. The taxpayer's dependent parent does not have to live with the taxpayer in order to qualify for head of household filing status.
D. The taxpayer must have paid roughly half of the cost of keeping up the house for the entire year.

14. The married filing separately (MFS) status is for taxpayers who:

A. Are legally divorced on the last day of the year.
B. Are married and choose to file separate returns.
C. Are unmarried, but engaged to be married.
D. Are unmarried, but have a dependent child.

15. Victor is 39 years old and has lived apart from his wife, Eleanor, since February 1, 2016. Their divorce was not yet final at the end of 2016, and they were not legally separated under a separate maintenance decree. They have two minor children. Since they split up, one child has lived with Victor and the other with Eleanor. Victor provides all of the support for the minor child living with him. Eleanor refuses to file jointly with Victor in 2016. The most beneficial filing status that Victor qualifies for is:

A. Married filing separately.
B. Single.
C. Head of household.
D. Married filing jointly.

16. Lisa and Stuart were married. Stuart died in 2015. Lisa has not remarried, and she has one dependent child. Which filing status should Lisa use for her 2016 tax return?

A. Single.
B. Married filing jointly.
C. Head of household.
D. Qualifying widow with a dependent child.

17. Mary and Troy are married and lived together all year. Mary earned $7,000 in 2016, and Troy earned $42,000. Mary wants to file a joint return, but Troy refuses to file with Mary and instead files a separate return on his own. Which of the following statements is correct?

A. Mary can file a joint amended tax return and e-file it if Troy refuses to provide a signature.
B. Mary and Troy must both file separate returns.
C. Mary can file as single because Troy refuses to sign a joint return.
D. Mary does not have a filing requirement because her income is below the filing threshold.

18. Which dependent relative may qualify a taxpayer for head of household filing status?

A. An adult stepdaughter who lives in her own apartment who is supported by the taxpayer.
B. A cousin who lives with the taxpayer all year.
C. A parent who lives in his own home and not with the taxpayer.
D. An adopted child who lived with the taxpayer for five months of the tax year.

19. All of the following individuals are required to file an income tax return except:

A. A taxpayer who owes household employment tax for a nanny.
B. A church employee who is exempt from payroll taxes and who earned $106 of wages in 2016.
C. A 54-year-old qualifying widower who earned $18,000 in 2016.
D. A single taxpayer who earned $6,500 in 2016 and who owes excise tax on withdrawals from a health savings account.

20. Kylie is an 18-year-old senior in her last year of high school. She worked as a grocery store bagger on weekends and earned $1,400 in wages during 2016. She also received $2,300 for a winning scratch-off lottery ticket. Her parents claim her as a dependent on their tax return. Does Kylie have to file her own return?

A. Yes, because of the amount of her unearned income.
B. Yes, because of the combined amount of her unearned and earned income.
C. No, because her earned income is below the threshold for a dependent.
D. No, because it is illegal for a high school student to play the lottery.

21. Ezequiel and Angela are married, but they choose to file separate returns for 2016 because the IRS is investigating Ezequiel for a previous tax issue. Ezequiel and Angela file their MFS returns on time. A few months after filing their separate returns, the investigation is over, and Ezequiel's previous tax issue has been resolved. He then wishes to file amended returns and file jointly with his wife in order to claim the Earned Income Tax Credit. Which of the following statements is correct?

A. Ezequiel is prohibited from changing his filing status in order to claim this credit.
B. Ezequiel and Angela can amend their MFS tax returns to MFJ in order to claim the credit.
C. Ezequiel and Angela can amend their MFS tax returns to MFJ, but they cannot claim the credit.
D. Angela cannot file jointly with Ezequiel after she has already filed a separate tax return.

22. Louisa legally separated from her husband during 2016. They have a 9-year-old son. Which of the following would prevent Louisa from filing as head of household?

A. Louisa has maintained a separate residence from her husband since March 1, 2016.
B. Her son's principal home is with Louisa.
C. Louisa's parents assisted her with 40% of the household costs.
D. Her son lived with Louisa from July 3, 2016, to December 31, 2016.

23. Carol and Raul were married four years ago and had no children. They split up in 2015 but did not file for divorce. Although they lived apart during all of 2016, they are neither divorced nor legally separated. Which of the following filing statuses can they use?

A. Single or married filing separately.
B. Married filing jointly or married filing separately.
C. Married filing separately or head of household.
D. Single or qualifying widow(er).

24. Alexandra's younger brother, Sebastian, is 18 and lived with friends in January and February of 2016. From March through July of 2016, he lived with his sister Alexandra. On August 1, Sebastian moved back in with his friends and stayed with them the rest of the year. However, since Sebastian did not have a job, Alexandra gave him money every month and provided the majority of his financial support for the remainder of the year. Alexandra has no other dependents. Which of the following statements is correct?

A. Alexandra can file as head of household.
B. Alexandra can file jointly with Sebastian.
C. Alexandra cannot file as head of household.
D. Sebastian can file as head of household.

25. Taxpayers are considered to be married for the entire year if:

A. One spouse dies during the year and the surviving spouse does not remarry.
B. The spouses are legally separated under a separate maintenance decree.
C. The spouses are divorced on December 31 of the tax year.
D. The spouses had their marriage annulled on December 31 of the tax year.

26. Janet and Harry are married and file jointly. During 2016, Janet turned 67, and Harry turned 66. Janet's gross income was $19,000, and Harry's gross income from self-employment was $620. Harry had no other income. Based on this information, which of the following statements is correct?

A. Janet and Harry are not required to file tax returns.
B. Janet and Harry are required to file tax returns.
C. Only Janet is required to file a tax return.
D. Only Harry is required to file a tax return.

27. Which of the following dependency relationships would not qualify a taxpayer to claim qualifying widow(er) as their filing status after the death of a spouse?

A. A biological child
B. A foster child
C. An adopted child
D. A step-child

Unit 2: Answers

1. The answer is D. Same-sex marriage is now legal in all 50 states and the District of Columbia. However, for federal tax purposes, civil unions are not treated as legal marriages. Civil unions offer same-sex couples some of the same benefits of marriage under state law, but they are not recognized as "marriages" for federal tax purposes. The IRS recognizes a marriage of same-sex spouses that was validly entered into in a domestic or foreign jurisdiction whose laws recognize same-sex marriage. Therefore, Vladimir and Pablo must file as single.

2. The answer is A. If a taxpayer's spouse died during the year, the taxpayer is considered married for the whole year and can file as MFJ. Therefore, Dana should file a joint return for 2016.

3. The answer is D. Todd provided over half the cost of maintaining a home for Madison and Amanda, but he cannot file as head of household since Amanda did not live with him for more than half the year. Madison cannot file as HOH either because she did not provide more than one-half the cost of keeping up the home for her daughter. However, either Todd or Madison may still claim Amanda as a dependent.

4. The answer is A. Since Norman and Helen are married, they can file either jointly or separately. If Helen does not agree to file jointly with Norman, Norman must file MFS. The filing requirement threshold for married filing separately is $4,000. Norman is required to file a return because his gross income exceeded this threshold. Helen is not required to file a tax return because her gross income in 2016 was $2,000, below the MFS filing requirement threshold.

5. The answer is A. Enzo meets the substantial presence test and is considered a resident alien for tax purposes. He is considered to have been present in the United States for a total of 225 days. The full 150 days are counted for 2016; 50 days for 2015 (1/3 of 150); and 25 days for 2014 (1/6 of 150).

6. The answer is A. A single dependent whose earned income was more than $6,300 in 2016 must file a return.

7. The answer is B. A relative must have lived with the taxpayer more than half the year (over six months) and be the taxpayer's dependent. A taxpayer's dependent parent is an exception and does not have to live with the taxpayer.

8. The answer is C. Zora is required to file a U.S. tax return in 2016, and she must file using Form 1040, Form 1040A, or Form 1040EZ. Zora is a green card holder, and therefore she is treated as a U.S. resident for tax purposes, regardless of how much time she has been present in the United States. As a resident alien, Zora will be taxed on income from worldwide sources, including any income she earned while she was in Russia.

9. The answer is D. An executor for a deceased taxpayer can amend a joint return to an MFS return up to one year after the filing deadline. This is the only exception to a rule that generally prevents a taxpayer from amending his married filing jointly return to a married filing separately return past the filing deadline.

10. The answer is A. Kathy must file amended tax returns. She cannot file jointly with her former husband in 2016. If a couple obtains a court decree of annulment, the taxpayer must file amended returns (Form 1040X) claiming single or head of household status for all tax years affected by the annulment that are not closed by the statute of limitations for filing an amended tax return.

11. The answer is A. A U.S. resident or citizen who is married to a nonresident alien can elect to file a joint return as long as both spouses sign the return and agree to be taxed on their worldwide income. A Social Security number is not required, because a nonresident spouse that is ineligible for an SSN may request an ITIN.

12. The answer is C. In determining residency status for tax purposes, students temporarily in the U.S. on an F, J, M, or Q visa are exempt from the substantial presence test for five years. In addition, an individual who is in either of the following categories is temporarily exempt from counting days toward the substantial presence test:
- Teacher or trainee: This includes any non-immigrant temporarily present in the U.S. on a J or Q visa who is not a student. The definition includes physicians, au pairs, short-term scholars, summer camp workers, and cultural exchange visitors temporarily present in the U.S.
- Closer connection to home country: This includes individuals who have a tax home in a foreign country and have a closer connection to that country than they do the U.S.

13. The answer is C. A dependent parent does not have to live with a taxpayer in order for the taxpayer to elect the head of household filing status. This special rule applies to parents who are related to the taxpayer by blood, marriage, or adoption if the taxpayer pays more than half of the qualifying parent's household costs. Answer "A" is incorrect because a married person can still qualify for head of household if they are "considered unmarried" for tax purposes. A married person can be "considered unmarried" in certain circumstances if they live apart from their spouse and can file as head of household.

14. The answer is B. The married filing separately (MFS) status is for taxpayers who are married and either:
- Choose to file separate returns, or
- Do not agree to file a joint return.

15. The answer is C. Victor qualifies for head of household filing status because he can be "considered unmarried" for tax purposes. His child lived with him for more than six months, he did not live with his spouse the last half of the year, and he paid more than half the cost of keeping up a home for the year for a qualifying child. Couples who are living apart but not yet divorced or legally separated are allowed to file jointly, but both spouses must agree to do so. Therefore, since Eleanor refuses to file jointly with Victor, the most beneficial filing status is head of household.

16. The answer is D. In 2016, Lisa is eligible for "qualifying widow(er) with dependent child" filing status. Lisa and Stuart qualified to file MFJ in 2015, the year he died, with Lisa signing the tax return as a surviving spouse. The year of death is the last year for which a taxpayer can file MFJ. For each of the two years following the year of the spouse's death, the surviving spouse can use the qualifying widow status, if she has a qualifying dependent and does not remarry.

17. The answer is B. Married couples must agree to file jointly. If one spouse does not agree to file jointly, they are individually subject to the MFS filing threshold. In this case, both spouses are required to file tax returns because both are above the applicable earnings threshold for MFS.

18. The answer is C. A parent is the only dependent relative who does not have to live with the taxpayer in order for the taxpayer to claim head of household status. In order to file for head of household, the "qualifying person" must be one of the following: a birth child, adopted child, grandchild, stepchild, foster child, brother, sister, half-brother, half-sister, stepbrother, stepsister, or a descendant of any of those. A cousin does not qualify because they do not meet the relationship test. The adopted child in answer "D" does not qualify because the child lived with the taxpayer for less than ½ the year.

19. The answer is B. Church employees who are exempt from Social Security and Medicare taxes and have wages of $108.28 or more for the year are required to file a tax return. In answer B, the church employee's wages were below that threshold. In all of the other answers, the taxpayer would be required to file a return.

20. The answer is A. Kylie has to file a tax return because of the amount of her unearned income: the $2,300 lottery prize. A dependent with unearned income of more than $1,050 in 2016 is required to file a tax return. Her earned income—$1,400—was not high enough to trigger a filing requirement, but the lottery winnings (unearned income) do trigger a filing requirement. Answer "D" is incorrect because most U.S. states allow 18-year olds to play the state lottery.

21. The answer is B. Ezequiel and Angela are allowed to amend their separate returns to a joint return in order to claim the credit. If a taxpayer files a separate return, he may elect to amend the filing status to married filing jointly at any time within three years from the due date of the original return (not including any extensions). However, the same does not hold true in reverse. Once a taxpayer files a joint return, he cannot choose to file a separate return for that year after the due date of the return (with a rare exception for deceased taxpayers).

22. The answer is D. For Louisa to file as head of household, her home must have been the main home of her qualifying child for more than half the tax year (over six months). Since her son started living with her in July, he would not have been in the household sufficient time to qualify her for this filing status.

23. The answer is B. As long as they are married and are neither divorced nor legally separated, Carol and Raul can file a joint return or file separately. They cannot file as single.

24. The answer is C. Alexandra cannot claim head of household status because Sebastian lived with her for only five months, which is less than half the year.

25. The answer is A. Taxpayers are considered married for the entire year if:
- They were married on the last day of the tax year, or
- One spouse died during the year, and the surviving spouse has not remarried as of the end of the year.

26. The answer is B. Janet and Harry must both file tax returns. Normally, Janet and Harry would not be required to file because their combined gross income was less than the filing requirement in 2016, and they are both over 65 (this threshold applies if both spouses are 65 or over and they are filing jointly). However, because Harry's self-employment income exceeds $400, he is required to file. Further, if Janet did not wish to file a joint return with Harry, she would nevertheless be required to file separately because her income exceeds the applicable threshold of $4,050 for MFS filers. Whether they choose to file jointly or separately, both are required to file tax returns for 2016.

27. The answer is B. To be eligible for the qualifying widow(er) filing status, the taxpayer normally must have a dependent child. For the purposes of this filing status, a qualifying child can be a child, adopted child, or stepchild, but does not include a foster child. Adopted children are always treated as biological children for tax law purposes.

Unit 3: Personal and Dependency Exemptions

> **For additional information read:**
> Publication 501, *Exemptions, Standard Deduction, and Filing Information*
> Publication 504, *Divorced or Separated Individuals*
> Publication 519, *US Tax Guide for Aliens*

Exemptions are like tax deductions, as they reduce taxable income. Exemption amounts are indexed for inflation and are generally updated every year. For tax year 2016, the exemption amount is $4,050 per person. Taxpayers may qualify to claim two kinds of exemptions:

- **Personal exemptions,** which taxpayers claim for themselves.
- **Dependency exemptions,** which taxpayers claim for their dependents.

Only one exemption is allowed per person.

Married Couples: On a joint tax return, a married couple is allowed two personal exemptions, one for each spouse. Also, on a joint return, one spouse is never considered the dependent of the other spouse.

Example: Jenny married Rick in April of 2016. Jenny and Rick can claim two personal exemptions on their jointly filed return. Because they are married, they cannot claim each other as a dependent.

Example: Cyrus and Mandy are married with three young children. They file jointly. In this scenario, they would be able to claim five exemptions: two personal exemptions (one each for Cyrus and Mandy) and three dependency exemptions (one exemption for each of their three children). This would be a total of $20,250 in exemptions that they could claim on their tax return ($4,050 per person X 5= $20,250).

If a married couple files separate returns, each spouse can claim a personal exemption for himself or herself. However, if a spouse files a separate return, the taxpayer can claim an exemption for his spouse only if that spouse had no gross income, is not filing a return, and could not be claimed as the dependent of another taxpayer.

A taxpayer who is divorced at the end of the tax year cannot claim an exemption for a former spouse. If a taxpayer's spouse dies during the year and the surviving spouse does not remarry before the end of the year, he can claim an exemption for the deceased spouse on a jointly filed return.

Example: Barrett's wife died in 2016. He did not remarry. Barrett can claim personal exemptions for himself and his deceased wife on their jointly filed return for 2016. Therefore, his tax return would have two exemptions ($4,050 X 2), and Barrett would sign the return as a surviving spouse.

A taxpayer can claim one dependency exemption for each qualified dependent. Examples of dependents include a child, stepchild, brother, sister, or parent.

Example: Hao and Binh are married and have four dependent children. On their jointly filed return, they can claim a total of six exemptions: four dependency exemptions for their children and two personal exemptions for themselves.

Personal Exemption Phaseout

Personal and dependency exemptions are phased out or eliminated for taxpayers with adjusted gross income above specified thresholds. For an individual subject to this limitation, the total exemption amount that can be claimed is reduced by 2% for each $2,500 increment by which his AGI exceeds the applicable threshold. In 2016, the phase-out will occur over the following income ranges:

Filing Status	Phaseout Begins	Phaseout Ends[11]
Single	$259,400	$381,900
Head of Household	$285,350	$407,850
MFJ or Qualifying Widow(er)	$311,300	$433,800
MFS	$155,650	$216,900

Note: In 2016, exemptions are fully phased out once AGI reaches $381,900 for single filers. For joint filers, the phaseout occurs when AGI reaches $433,800. When taxpayers reach these thresholds, they cannot claim any exemptions—they are completely phased out. These phaseout thresholds are adjusted for inflation each year.

Tests for Dependency

In order to determine if a taxpayer can claim a dependency exemption for another person, there are three main tests:

- Dependent taxpayer
- Joint return
- Citizenship or residency

Test #1. Dependent Taxpayer Test

If a taxpayer can claim another person as a dependent, even if the taxpayer does not do so, the dependent cannot take a personal exemption on his own tax return or claim another person as a dependent, even if he has a qualifying child or qualifying relative.

Thus, there is only one personal exemption that applies to a person who qualifies as a dependent, whether he files his own return or is listed as a dependent on someone else's return.

Example: Eva is a 17-year-old single mother who has an infant son. Eva lives with her parents and has a part-time job, but she does not make enough money to support herself or her infant son. Eva is claimed as a dependent by her parents, so she cannot claim an exemption for herself, and she is prohibited from claiming her infant son as a dependent on her own tax return.

Sometimes an individual meets the rules to be a qualifying dependent of more than one person. Regardless, only one person can claim an individual as a dependent on his tax return.

---

[11] Rev. Proc. 2015-53

> **Example:** Dan and Linda are unmarried and live together with their daughter, Savannah. Savannah is a qualifying child for both Dan and Linda, but only one of them can claim her as a dependent on their tax return.

Test #2. Joint Return Test

If a married individual files a joint return, he normally cannot be claimed as a dependent by another taxpayer.

> **Example:** Ellen is 18 years old and had no income in 2016. She got married on December 1, 2016, to Rex, who is 22 years old. Ellen's new husband earned $26,700 during 2016, and they file jointly, claiming two personal exemptions on their tax return. Ellen's father supported her throughout the year and even paid for their wedding. However, her father cannot claim Ellen as his dependent because she is filing jointly with her new husband.

There is one narrow exemption to this test. The joint return test *does not apply* if the joint return is filed by the dependent only to claim a refund and neither spouse would have a tax liability, even if they filed separate returns.

> **Example:** Greg and Taylor are both 19 years old and married. They live with Taylor's mother, Michelle. In 2016, Greg earned $2,800 from a part-time job. That was the only income that either Greg or his wife earned all year. Neither Greg nor Taylor is required to file a tax return, but they file a joint return to obtain a refund of the taxes that were withheld from Greg's wages. As the exception to the joint return test applies, Michelle can claim exemptions for both Greg and Taylor on her tax return, as long as Greg and Taylor did not claim the exemptions for themselves and all the other tests for dependency are met.

Test #3. Citizenship or Residency Test

The dependent must be a citizen or resident of the United States, or a citizen or resident of Canada or Mexico (with an exception for foreign-born adopted children).

> **Example:** Maurice is a Canadian Citizen and a legal U.S. Resident (green card holder). He provides all of the financial support for his two children, ages 6 and 12, who are also Canadian citizens. His children live in Canada with Maurice's sister. Maurice can still claim his children as dependents, even though they are not U.S. Citizens or U.S. residents. This is because of the special exception that allows for residents and citizens of Canada and Mexico to be claimed as dependents.

Dependency Relationships

A taxpayer cannot claim a person as a dependent unless that person is either his **qualifying child** or his **qualifying relative**. There are very specific tests to identify the difference between the two.

> **Note:** Both "qualifying children" and "qualifying relatives" must meet all of the general dependency requirements already specified: the dependent taxpayer, joint return, and citizenship or residency tests.

Tests for a Qualifying Child

The tests for a "qualifying child" are more stringent than the tests for a "qualifying relative". Having a qualifying child entitles a taxpayer to claim a dependency exemption as well as numerous tax credits, including the Earned Income Tax Credit and the Child Tax Credit. Having a qualifying relative, on the other hand, does not qualify a taxpayer for these credits.

There are five tests for a qualifying child:

- Relationship
- Age
- Residency
- Support
- Tie-breaker (for a qualifying child of more than one person)

Test #1. Relationship Test

The qualifying child must be related to the taxpayer by blood, marriage, or legal adoption. Qualifying children include:

- A child, stepchild, or adopted child
- A sibling or stepsibling
- A descendant of one of the above (such as a grandchild, niece, or nephew)
- An eligible foster child

Test #2. Age Test

In order to be a qualifying child, the dependent must be:

- Under the age of 19 at the end of the tax year, or
- Under the age of 24 at the end of the tax year and a full-time student, or
- Permanently and totally disabled at any time during the year, regardless of age.

A child is considered a full-time student if he attends a qualified educational institution full-time for at least five months during the year.

Note: For the purposes of the age test, in order to qualify as a student, the taxpayer's child must be enrolled in the number of hours or courses the school considers full-time during some part of at least five months of the year.

A child who is claimed as a dependent must be younger than the taxpayer who is claiming him, except in the case of dependents who are disabled. For taxpayers filing jointly, the child must be younger than one spouse listed on the return but does not have to be younger than both spouses.

Example: Owen and Sydney are 22 years old, married, and file jointly. Sydney's 23-year-old step-brother, Parker, is a full-time student and lives with Owen and Sydney, who provide all of his support. Parker is not disabled. Owen and Sydney are both younger than Parker. Therefore, Parker is not their qualifying child, even though he is a full-time student.

> **Example:** Lucius, age 34, and Paige, age 20, are married and file jointly. Paige's 21-year-old brother, Jason, is a full-time student, is single, and lives with Lucius and Paige. They provide all of Jason's support. In this case, Lucius and Paige can claim Jason as a qualifying child on their joint tax return because he is a full-time student and is younger than Lucius.

> **Example:** Andrew is 45 years old and totally disabled. Karen, his 37-year-old sister, provides all of Andrew's support and cares for him in her home, where he lives with her full-time. Despite Andrew's age, he is considered a qualifying child and a dependent for tax purposes because he is completely disabled. Karen can claim Andrew as her qualifying child, and she can also file as head of household.

Test #3. Residency Test

A qualifying child must live with the taxpayer for more than half the tax year (over six months). Exceptions apply for children of divorced parents, kidnapped children, children who were born or died during the year,[12] and temporary absences, (such as for summer camp or a missionary trip).

A temporary absence includes illness, college, vacation, military service, and incarceration in a juvenile facility. It must be reasonable to assume that the child will return to the home after the temporary absence.

> **Example:** Scott is unmarried and lives with his 10-year-old son, Elijah. Scott provides all of Elijah's support. In 2016, Elijah became very ill and was hospitalized for seven months. Elijah is still considered Scott's qualifying child because the hospitalization counts as a temporary absence from home. Scott can claim Elijah as his qualifying child, and he can also file as head of household.

> **Example:** Marty's nine-year-old granddaughter, Quinn, lives with him for five months of the year, with her mother for three months, and with her aunt for four months. Quinn is not Marty's qualifying child because the residency test is not met. However, she may be Marty's qualifying relative if other tests are met.

Test #4. Support Test

A qualifying child cannot provide more than one-half of his own support. A full-time student does not take scholarships (whether taxable or nontaxable) into account when calculating the support test.

> **Note:** The definition of **support** includes only income actually used for living expenses. For example, if a child earns income that is saved to a bank account rather than spent on the child's living expenses, the amounts are not included in the support test.

> **Example:** Douglas and Andrea file jointly. They have a daughter named Isabella, age 26. She earned $4,000 in wages before she was laid off in March and moved back in with her parents. Douglas and Andrea provided the majority of Isabella's support for the rest of the year. Isabella got a new job in December and moved out. She is not a qualifying child for federal tax purposes. Isabella meets the support test, as well as the residency test. However, she does not meet the age test.

---

[12] A taxpayer cannot claim an exemption for a stillborn child. The child must be born alive, even if he lived only for a short time.

Example: Kevin has a 19-year-old daughter named Tiffany. Kevin provided $5,000 toward his daughter's support for the year. Tiffany also has a part-time job and provided $13,000 of her own support. Therefore, Tiffany provided over half of her own support for the year. Tiffany does not pass the support test, and consequently, she is not Kevin's qualifying child. Tiffany can file a tax return as single and claim her own exemption.

Example: Penelope, age 12, had a small role in a television series. She earned $30,000 as a child actor, but her parents put the money in a trust fund for her. She lived at home with her parents all year. Penelope meets the support test since her earnings were not used for her own support. She meets the tests for a qualifying child, so she can be claimed as a dependent by her parents.

Payments received from a child placement agency for the support of a foster child are considered support provided by the agency, rather than support provided by the child.

Example: Gina is a foster parent who provided $3,500 toward her 10-year-old foster son's support for the year. The state of Nevada provided $6,000, which was considered support provided by the state, not by the child. Gina's foster child did not provide more than half of his own support for the year. Therefore, Gina can claim her foster son as a qualifying child.

Test #5. Tie-Breaker Test

Only one person can claim a qualifying child, even if the child qualifies for more than one person. If more than one taxpayer could claim the same child under the normal dependency exemption rules, the tie-breaker rules apply, meaning the child is treated as a qualifying child in the following sequence:

- By the child's parents, if they file a joint return
- If only one of the taxpayers is the child's parent, by that parent
- By the parent with whom the child lived the longest during the year
- By the parent with the highest AGI, if the child lived with each parent for the same length of time during the tax year
- By the taxpayer with the highest AGI, if neither of the child's parents can claim the child as a qualifying child
- By a taxpayer with a higher AGI than either of the child's parents who can also claim the child as a qualifying child, but does not

Example: Sophia is single and has a three-year-old son named Preston. They live with Sophia's father, Theodore (the child's grandfather). Sophia claims Preston as her qualifying child, which means the child may not be the qualifying child of Theodore, the grandfather.

Example: Penny and her sister, Rosa, live together. Their seven-year-old niece, Brianna, lived with her aunts all year while Brianna's mother was incarcerated. Penny's AGI is $12,600. Rosa's AGI is $19,000. Brianna is a qualifying child of both Penny and Rosa because she meets the relationship, age, residency, and joint return tests for both aunts. However, Rosa has the primary right to claim Brianna as her qualifying child because her AGI is higher than Penny's.

Note: The tie breaker test only applies when two people <u>attempt</u> to claim the same child. In cases where the parents are in agreement, there is no tie-breaker test.

Qualifying Relative

A person who is not a qualifying child may still qualify as a dependent under the rules for qualifying relatives. Even an individual who is not a family member can be a qualifying relative. Unlike a qualifying child, a qualifying relative can be any age. To be claimed as a qualifying relative, the dependent must meet the following four tests:

- Not a qualifying child
- Member of household or relationship
- Gross income
- Support

Test #1. Not a Qualifying Child Test

If a child is already a qualifying child for any taxpayer, he cannot also be a qualifying relative of another taxpayer.

Test #2. Member of Household or Relationship Test

A dependent who is not related to the taxpayer normally must have lived with the taxpayer the entire tax year in order to meet the member of household or relationship test. However, a family member who is related to the taxpayer in any of the following ways does not have to live with the taxpayer to meet this test:

- A child, stepchild, foster child, or descendant of any of them (for example, a grandchild)
- A sibling, stepsibling, or half sibling
- A parent, grandparent, stepparent, or other direct ancestor (but not a foster parent)
- A niece or nephew, son-in-law, daughter-in-law, father-in-law, mother-in-law, brother-in-law, or sister-in-law

Example: Ernie's 12-year-old nephew, Josh, lived with him for three months in 2016. For the rest of the year, Josh lived with his mother, Melody, in another state. Melody is Ernie's 32-year-old sister. Even though Josh and Melody lived in another state, Ernie still provided all of their financial support. Josh is not Ernie's qualifying child because he did not live with Ernie for more than half the year and therefore does not meet the residency test. However, Josh does meet the requirements to be Ernie's qualifying relative.

Note: For the relationship test, "family members" do not include *cousins*, who are treated as unrelated persons. A cousin must live with the taxpayer for the entire year and also meet the gross income test in order to qualify as a dependent, and even then, a cousin cannot be a qualifying child—only a qualifying relative.

Any relationship that is established by marriage does not end as a result of death or divorce. For example, if a taxpayer supports his mother-in-law, he can continue to claim her as a dependent even if he and his ex-spouse are divorced or if he becomes widowed.

> **Example**: Mia and Caleb have always financially supported Mia's elderly mother, Gertrude, and claimed her as their dependent on their jointly filed returns. In 2014, Mia died and Caleb becomes a widower. Caleb remarries in 2016, but he continues to support his late wife's mother. Caleb can still claim Gertrude on his tax returns, even though he has remarried.

> **Example:** Thomas lived all year with his girlfriend, Ava, and her two children in his home. Their cohabitation does not violate local laws. Ava does not work and is not required to file a 2016 tax return. Ava and her two children are not related to Thomas as family members, but they may be qualifying relatives if they meet all the other tests.

Test #3. Gross Income Test

A qualifying relative cannot earn more than the personal exemption amount, which is $4,050 in 2016. Please note that there is no "gross income test" for a qualifying child—only for a qualifying relative.

Test #4. Support Test

In order to claim an individual as a qualifying relative, the taxpayer must provide more than half of the dependent's total support during the year. Support includes amounts from Social Security and welfare payments, even if that support is non-taxable. Support does not include amounts received from nontaxable scholarships.

Support can include the fair market value of lodging.

> **Example:** Harry's mother, Penny, received $2,400 in social security benefits and $300 in interest during 2016. Penny paid $2,000 for food and lodging and $400 for recreation. She put the $300 in interest in a savings account. Even though Harry's mother received a total of $2,700 ($2,400 + $300), she spent only $2,400 ($2,000 + $400) for her own support. If Harry spends more than $2,400 for her support and no other support was received, he would have provided more than half of his mother's support, and would be able to claim her as a qualifying relative.

Rules for Divorced and Separated Parents

Generally, to claim a child as a dependent, the child must live with the taxpayer for more than half the year. However, special rules apply if the dependent is supported by parents who are divorced or separated, or who live apart.

In most cases, the child is the qualifying child of the custodial parent. However, a custodial parent may allow the noncustodial parent to claim the dependency exemption. The noncustodial parent must attach Form 8332, *Release/Revocation of Release of Claim to Exemption for Child by Custodial Parent*, to his tax return to claim the dependency exemption.

A child may be treated as the qualifying child of the noncustodial parent if all the following conditions apply:

- The parents are divorced or legally separated, or if they lived apart at all times during the last six months of the year.

- The child received over half of his support for the year from the parents (multiple support agreement rules do not apply in this case).
- The child is in the custody of one (or both) parents.
- The custodial parent signs a written declaration (Form 8332 or a similar statement) that he will not claim the child as a dependent for the year and the noncustodial parent attaches this declaration to his return.

This rule is an exception to the normal residency test for a qualifying child. It does not apply to determination of head of household filing status or to eligibility for the Earned Income Tax Credit. These benefits can be claimed only by the custodial parent, even if the noncustodial parent claims the dependency exemption. If a divorce decree does not specify which parent is the custodial parent or which parent receives the dependency exemption, the exemption goes to the parent who has physical custody for the majority of the year.

Example: Gary and Frieda are divorced and have one child. Frieda is the custodial parent, but she agrees to release the dependency exemption to Gary by signing Form 8332. Gary files as single and claims his son as his dependent. Frieda may still file as head of household, even though she does not claim the dependency exemption for her son because she maintained the home where he lived for most of the year.

Example: Alexis and Nathan are divorced. They have one child named Dylan. In 2016, Dylan lived with Alexis for 300 nights and with Nathan for 65 nights. Therefore, for federal tax purposes, Alexis is the custodial parent and has the right to claim Dylan as her qualifying child. However, Alexis may choose to release the exemption to Nathan by signing Form 8332.

If the child lived with each parent for an equal number of nights during the year, the custodial parent is deemed to be the parent with the higher adjusted gross income.

The custodial parent can revoke a release of exemption for a child using Part III of Form 8332. A copy of the revocation must be attached to the tax return for each year the child is claimed after the revocation.

Multiple Support Agreements

A *multiple support agreement* is when two or more people jointly provide for a person's support. This happens commonly when adult children are taking care of their parents. In order for the dependency exemption to apply under a multiple support agreement, family members together must pay more than half of the person's total support, but no one member individually may pay more than half.

In addition, the taxpayer who claims the dependent must provide more than 10% of the person's support. Only one family member can claim the dependency exemption in a single year. Different qualifying family members can claim the dependency exemption in other years.

Example: Benjamin, Matthew, and Pamela are siblings who support their disabled mother, Abigail. Abigail is 83 and lives with Benjamin. In 2016, Abigail receives 20% of her financial support from Social Security, 40% from Matthew, 30% from Benjamin, and 10% from Pamela. Under the IRS rules for multiple support agreements, either Matthew or Benjamin can take the exemption for their mother if the other signs a statement agreeing not to do so. Pamela cannot claim the dependency exemption because she does not provide more than 10% of the support for her mother.

Example: Graciela and Pilar are sisters who help financially support their 64-year-old father, Alonso. Each pays approximately 20% of his care in a residential facility for elderly people. The remaining 60% is paid for by a wealthy friend who is not related to Alonso. Because more than half of Alonso's support is provided by someone unrelated who cannot claim an exemption for him, no one can claim the dependency exemption.

Rules for Alien Exemptions

A resident alien can claim the same exemptions as U.S. citizens. A nonresident alien, whether single or married, can claim only one personal exemption for himself, as long as he cannot be claimed as a dependent on any other U.S. tax return. He generally cannot claim any dependency exemptions.

Nonresident aliens who are married generally cannot file jointly and instead must file MFS, unless one of the spouses is a U.S. citizen or resident alien at the end of the year.

Example: Leandro and Alina are Swiss citizens who are living temporarily in the United States as nonresident aliens. Leandro is working as a visiting scholar at Harvard on a J-1 visa. Alina does not work. They have three children who live with them. Leandro must file separately. Nonresident aliens cannot file jointly with their spouses. Leandro can claim an exemption only for himself on his Form 1040-NR. He cannot claim any dependency exemptions for his children.

Exceptions to these rules include the following:
- Residents of Canada and Mexico can claim additional exemptions for a spouse and dependents if:
    - The spouse had no gross income,
    - The spouse was not the dependent of another U.S. taxpayer, and
    - The dependents otherwise qualify as dependents.
- There are special tax treaty rules for certain residents of South Korea and India, in which additional exemptions for spouses and dependents may be claimed.

Unit 3: Study Questions

(Test yourself first, then check the correct answers at the end of this quiz.)

1. Tony and Isabelle provide the sole support of all the following individuals (all are U.S. citizens, but none live with them, file a tax return, or have any taxable income):

- Jennie, Tony's grandmother
- Julie, Isabelle's stepmother
- Jonathan, father of Tony's first wife
- Timothy, Isabelle's cousin

How many exemptions may Tony and Isabelle claim on their joint return?

A. Three.
B. Four.
C. Five.
D. Six.

2. Dina has three children: Luther, Tim, and Mary. Each child contributes toward her support. Luther and Tim each provide 45%, and Mary provides 10%. Which of Dina's children would be eligible to claim a dependency exemption for her in 2016 under a multiple support agreement?

A. Luther or Tim.
B. Both Luther and Tim may claim an exemption for Dina.
C. Luther, Tim, or Mary.
D. None of the three are eligible to claim the dependency exemption because no one child provided more than half of his or her mother's support.

3. All of the following statements are correct about the rules of exemptions except:

A. One spouse is never considered the dependent of the other spouse.
B. A divorced spouse cannot claim an exemption for his former spouse.
C. A taxpayer may take any personal exemption he is entitled to, regardless of adjusted gross income.
D. Exemption amounts are updated for inflation and are generally adjusted annually.

4. Giovanni and Lucia are married and classified as nonresident aliens for U.S. tax purposes. How many exemptions would they qualify for when they file their U.S. tax return(s)?

A. None.
B. One each on returns filed separately.
C. One each on a joint return.
D. It depends how many dependents they have.

5. Alyssa is 19 years old and a full-time student who is claimed as a dependent on her parents' tax return. Over the summer, she worked in a clothing boutique and earned $7,000. Alyssa wants to file a tax return to report her wage income and receive a refund. How many exemptions may she claim on her tax return?

A. Zero.
B. One.
C. Two.
D. Three.

6. Roy is a client who tells you that his wife died in February 2016. Based on this information, Roy can claim:

A. Only the personal exemption for himself.
B. Only the personal exemption for his wife.
C. Personal exemptions for both himself and his wife.
D. A personal exemption for himself and a partial exemption for his wife, prorated based on the number of months she lived during the year.

7. John provides the sole support for his mother. To claim her as a dependent on his Form 1040, John's mother must be a resident or citizen of which of the following countries?

A. The United States.
B. Mexico.
C. Canada.
D. Any of the above.

8. Amber lives with Chad, her 16-year-old son. She provided $5,100 toward his support for the year. Chad also has a part-time job and provided $12,900 toward his own support. Can Amber claim her son as a dependent?

A. Yes, she can claim her son as a qualifying child, because he is a minor.
B. Yes, she can claim Chad as a qualifying relative.
C. No, Chad provided more than half of his own support for the year. Therefore, he is neither Amber's qualifying child nor her qualifying relative.
D. None of the above.

9. Dani and Ted divorced years ago. They have six-year-old twins who live with Dani. Her AGI is $41,000, and Ted's AGI is $48,000. Although Dani is the custodial parent, their divorce decree states that Ted can claim the children on his tax return. However, Dani refuses to sign Form 8332. Which of the following statements is correct?

A. Ted can claim one child as a dependent.
B. Ted and Dani can each claim the children as dependents on their respective tax returns.
C. Since Dani is the custodial parent and refuses to sign Form 8332, Ted cannot claim either child.
D. Neither Dani nor Ted can claim the children as dependents.

10. Joseph, 52, is a single father who lives with an adopted son named Wyatt who has Down syndrome. Wyatt is 32 years old and permanently disabled. Wyatt had $800 of interest income and $5,000 of wages from a part-time job in 2016. Joseph provided $25,000 toward Wyatt's support. Which of the following statements is correct?

A. Joseph can file as head of household, with Wyatt as his qualifying child.
B. Joseph does not qualify for head of household, but he could still claim Wyatt as his qualifying relative because Wyatt does not meet the age test for a qualifying child.
C. Joseph can file as head of household, with Wyatt as his qualifying relative.
D. Joseph must file as single, and he cannot claim Wyatt because of the amount of Wyatt's income.

11. Personal and dependency exemptions are phased out:

A. For higher income taxpayers.
B. For all taxpayers who itemize deductions.
C. For all taxpayers with AGI over $100,000.
D. For all nonresident aliens.

12. Cheryl is 46 and unmarried. Her nephew, Bradley, lived with her all year and turned 18 years old on December 28, 2016. Bradley did not provide more than half of his own support. He had $4,200 of income from wages and $1,000 of investment income. Which of the following statements is correct?

A. Bradley is Cheryl's qualifying child.
B. Bradley is not a qualifying child; however, Cheryl can claim him as a qualifying relative.
C. Bradley is not a qualifying child or qualifying relative because he had income that exceeded the personal exemption amount.
D. Cheryl can claim Bradley only if he is a full-time student since he is no longer a minor child.

13. Terrence is single and 18 years old. He works a part-time job at night and goes to school full-time. His total income for 2016 was $10,500. Terrence lives with his parents, who provided the majority of his support. His parents are claiming him as a dependent on their tax return. Which of the following statements is correct?

A. Terrence is not required to file his own return.
B. Terrence's parents cannot claim him as a dependent because he earned more than the standard deduction amount for 2016.
C. Terrence is required to file his own return, and he can also take an exemption for himself.
D. His parents can claim Terrence as their qualifying child. He is required to file a tax return, but he cannot claim a personal exemption for himself.

14. Haley is 22 and a full-time college student. During the year, she lived at home with her parents for four months and lived in the college dorms for the remainder of the year. She worked part-time and earned $6,000, but that income did not amount to half of her total support. Can Haley's parents still claim her as a dependent?

A. No, because Haley earned more than the personal exemption amount.
B. No, because Haley did not live with her parents for more than half the year, and she does not meet the age test.
C. Yes, her parents can claim her as a qualifying child.
D. Yes, her parents can claim her as a dependent, but only as a qualifying relative.

15. Ursula and her son live together. Dave is 34 years old, not disabled, and has a part-time job. Ursula provides more than half of Dave's support. Ursula can claim Dave as a qualifying relative, as long as he does not earn _____ or more in 2016.

A. $1,050
B. $3,500
C. $4,950
D. $4,050

16. Ingrid and Bill file for divorce. Ingrid has one son from a prior marriage named Greg, age 15. After the divorce is final, Ingrid develops a drug problem and disappears. In 2016, Greg lives for nine months with his former stepfather, Bill, who provides all of Greg's support. Which of the following statements is correct?

A. Bill can claim Greg as his qualifying child.
B. Bill can claim Greg as his dependent but not as a qualifying child because the divorce dissolved any legal relationship between them.
C. Bill cannot claim Greg as his dependent because they are not related persons.
D. Only Ingrid can claim Greg as her dependent.

17. Sean's wife, Jackie, died in 2016. Sean did not remarry during the year, and he has one dependent child who is 16 years old. Based on this information, how many exemptions can Sean claim on his 2016 tax return?

A. Only the personal exemption for himself.
B. Only the personal exemption for himself and the dependency exemption for his son.
C. Exemptions for himself, his son, and his deceased wife.
D. A personal exemption for himself and a partial exemption for his deceased wife.

Unit 3: Answers

1. The answer is C. They may take three dependency exemptions on their tax return, and two personal exemptions for themselves (3+2 =5 total exemptions). Tony and Isabelle may take dependency exemptions for all the dependents listed, except for Timothy, since he is Isabelle's cousin. Timothy would have to live with Tony and Isabelle all year for them to claim him as their dependent. Parents (or grandparents, in-laws, stepparents, etc.) do not have to live with a taxpayer to qualify as dependents. Tony can claim Jonathan, because Jonathan was once his father-in-law, and relationships that are established by marriage do not end with death or divorce.

2. The answer is A. Only Luther, or Tim is eligible to claim the exemption under a multiple support agreement in 2016. Answer B is incorrect because only a single taxpayer can claim the exemption in a tax year. Mary is not eligible because she does not provide more than 10% of her mother's support.

3. The answer is C. At certain higher income levels, exemptions are phased out completely. The thresholds for phase-outs are determined by a taxpayer's filing status and AGI.

4. The answer is B. As nonresident aliens, each would qualify for only one personal exemption, and they would be required to file separate tax returns. They would not be able to claim exemptions for their dependents.

5. The answer is A. Since Alyssa is claimed as a dependent on her parents' tax return, she cannot claim an exemption for herself. Therefore, her total number of exemptions is zero. Regardless, she can still file a tax return in order to claim a refund.

6. The answer is C. In 2016, Roy can claim a personal exemption for his deceased wife and a personal exemption for himself. A taxpayer whose spouse dies during the year can file jointly (MFJ) in the year of death.

7. The answer is D. A dependent must be a citizen or resident alien of the United States, Canada, or Mexico.

8. The answer is C. Chad provided more than half of his own support for the year, so he is not Amber's qualifying child or her qualifying relative. To meet the support test, the child cannot have provided more than half of his own support for the year.

9. The answer is C. Without Form 8332, *Release/Revocation of Release of Claim to Exemption for Child by Custodial Parent,* signed and attached to the return, the IRS will not recognize the dependency exemption claimed by a noncustodial parent, regardless of what the divorce decree states. If a divorce decree does not specify which parent is the custodial parent or which parent receives the dependency exemption, the exemption automatically goes to the parent who has physical custody for the majority of the year.

10. The answer is A. Even though Wyatt is over the normal age threshold for a qualifying child; he is considered a qualifying child for purposes of the dependency exemption and head of household filing status. This is because Wyatt is permanently disabled and Joseph provides his financial support and care. The normal age thresholds for "qualifying children" do not apply in the case of permanently disabled individuals.

11. The answer is A. Personal and dependency exemptions are phased out or eliminated for taxpayers with adjusted gross income above specified thresholds. For taxpayers subject to this limitation, the total exemption amount that can be claimed is reduced by 2% for each $2,500 increment by which AGI exceeds the applicable threshold. For married couples filing jointly, exemptions are fully phased out once their AGI reaches $433,800; for a single filer, exemptions are fully phased out when AGI reaches $381,900.

12. The answer is A. Bradley is Cheryl's qualifying child because he meets the age test, support test, and relationship test. Also, because Bradley is single, he is a qualifying person for Cheryl to claim head of household filing status. Bradley is not required to be a full-time student because any child under the age of 19 at the end of the tax year will be treated as a qualifying child if all the other tests are met. Bradley is only 18 years old and therefore passes the age test.

13. The answer is D. His parents can claim him as their qualifying child because Terrence is under the age of 19 and does not provide more than half of his own support. He is required to file a tax return, but he cannot claim an exemption for himself. The gross income test only applies to a qualifying relative, not to a qualifying child.

14. The answer is C. Haley meets all the qualifying child tests: the relationship test; the age test (because she is under 24 and a full-time student); the residency test (because the time spent at college is a legitimate temporary absence); and the support test (because she did not provide over half of her own support). Therefore, her parents can claim her as a dependent.

15. The answer is D. Dave cannot be a qualifying child because he does not meet the age test, but he can be claimed as a qualifying relative. The 2016 limit for gross income for qualifying relatives is $4,050. Therefore, if Dave earns less than during the year, his mother can claim him as a dependent on her tax return.

16. The answer is A. A qualifying child must be related to the taxpayer by blood, marriage, or legal adoption. A step relationship formed by a legal marriage is not dissolved by divorce or death. Since Greg did not live with his mother, but did live with his stepfather, Bill, for more than half the year, Bill is considered the custodial parent for tax purposes, and he can claim his stepson as a qualifying child.

17. The answer is C. Sean can claim three exemptions on his tax return. Because they were married at the time of Jackie's death, Sean may file a joint return in the year of her death and claim a personal exemption for his deceased wife, along with a personal exemption for himself. He can also claim a dependency exemption for his son.

Unit 4: Taxable and Nontaxable Income

For additional information read:
Publication 525, *Taxable and Nontaxable Income*
Publication 15-B, *Employer's Tax Guide to Fringe Benefits*
Publication 3, *Armed Forces' Tax Guide*

The Internal Revenue Code (IRC) describes types of income that are taxable and nontaxable. Over the course of the next few units, we will cover the most common types of both. In this unit, we focus on various forms of employee compensation, but we start with a look at broader concepts regarding the taxability of income.

Federal tax law sets forth that all income is taxable unless it is specifically excluded. "exclusion" is not the same as a deduction, and it is important to understand the distinction because many deductions are phased out as a taxpayer's gross income increases. Excluded income, on the other hand, retains its character without regard to the amount of the taxpayer's gross income.

Most types of excluded income do not have to be reported on a tax return.

Example: Monte is a popular recording artist who made more than $600,000 of taxable income last year. Because of his high income, many deductions are phased out for Monte. However, in 2016, Monte is involved in an auto accident and sustains major injuries. Monte sues the other driver and receives an insurance settlement of $95,000. The settlement is excluded from his gross income because compensation for physical injuries is not taxable to the recipient, regardless of his taxable income level.

Calculating Taxable Income

For a taxpayer to figure out how much tax he owes, he first needs to determine his **gross income**.

Definition: Gross income is all income a taxpayer receives in the form of money, goods, property, and services that are not exempt from tax. In addition to wages, salaries, commissions, tips, and self-employment income, gross income includes other forms of compensation, such as interest, dividends, capital gains, taxable fringe benefits, and stock options.

Next, the taxpayer calculates his **adjusted gross income (AGI)** by subtracting from gross income certain specific deductions or adjustments. These deductions include IRA contributions, certain expenses for self-employed individuals, alimony payments, and moving expenses. The amount of a taxpayer's AGI is important because it helps determine eligibility for certain deductions and credits.

Finally, the taxpayer calculates his **taxable income** by subtracting additional deductions (standard or itemized) and exemptions from AGI.

Earned Income vs. Unearned Income

Earned income such as wages, salaries, tips, professional fees, or self-employment income is received for services performed. *Unearned income* includes interest, dividends, retirement income, alimony, and disability benefits. Earned income is generally subject to Social Security and Medicare taxes (also called FICA taxes). Investment income and other unearned income are generally not subject to FICA taxes.

The amount of taxable income is used to determine the taxpayer's gross income tax liability before applicable credits. The table below is a simplified example of how to calculate income tax.

How to Calculate Taxable Income and Tax Liability
Start with gross income
Subtract adjustments to income ("above the line" deductions)
= Adjusted gross income (AGI)
Subtract greater of itemized deductions or standard deduction
Subtract personal and dependency exemptions
= Taxable income
× Tax rate
= Gross tax liability
Subtract credits
= Net tax liability or refund receivable (based on amount of pre-paid tax, if any)

Constructive Receipt of Income

The doctrine of constructive receipt requires that cash-basis taxpayers be taxed on income when it becomes available and is not subject to substantial limitations or restrictions, regardless of whether it is actually in their physical possession. Income received by an agent for a taxpayer is constructively received in the year the agent receives it.

Example: Jerrald is a landlord who owns several rental properties. On December 30, 2016, a customer delivers to Jerrald's payment lock-box a $500 check for repairing a plumbing leak. Jerrald does not collect the customer deposits in the lock-box on the 30th and leaves town later that day to celebrate New Year's Eve. Jerrald does not take physical possession of the check until January 5, 2017, the same day he deposits the check in his bank account. He is considered to have constructive receipt in 2016 and must include the $500 of gross income on his 2016 tax return because the check was available to Jerrald at that time without any substantial limitations or restrictions.

Note: Most individuals are cash-basis taxpayers who report income when it is actually or constructively received during the tax year. This concept of constructive receipt would not apply to accrual-basis taxpayers who recognize income when it is earned rather than when it is received. We will cover accrual basis taxpayers in Book 2.

Funds must be available without substantial limitations under the constructive receipt rules. If there are significant restrictions on the income, or if the income is not accessible to the taxpayer, it is not considered to have been constructively received.

Income is also not considered to have been constructively received if a taxpayer declines it, as in the case of a prize or an award.

> **Example:** Kathryn won front-row concert tickets valued at $1,200 from a local radio station. Kathryn would be required to pay taxes based on the fair market value of the tickets. However, on the day of the concert, the radio station does not receive the tickets in time from the promoter, and Kathryn is not able to attend the concert. Since she never received the proceeds, the prize is not taxable to her because she never had constructive receipt of it.

> **Definition:** The IRS defines **fair market value** (FMV) in this way: The price at which a property would change hands between a buyer and a seller when both have reasonable knowledge of all the necessary facts and neither is being forced to buy or sell. If parties with adverse interests place a value on property in an arm's-length transaction, that is strong evidence of FMV. If there is a stated price for services, this price is treated as the FMV unless there is evidence to the contrary.

Claim of Right Doctrine

Under the claim of right doctrine, income received without restriction (over which the taxpayer has complete control) must be reported in the year received, even if there is a possibility it may have to be repaid in a later year.

If there is a dispute and income is later repaid, the repayment is deductible in the year repaid. As a result, the taxpayer is not required to amend his reported gross income for the earlier year.

> **Example:** In 2016, Courtney sells a painting in her art gallery for $25,000. She properly includes $25,000 in her gross income and pays taxes on the income for the 2016 tax year. On March 2, 2017, the customer discovers the painting is a forgery and returns it for a full refund of $25,000. Since Courtney pays back the $25,000 in 2017, she is entitled to deduct the amount from her gross income in 2017. She does not have to amend her 2016 tax return.

Worker Classification

For federal tax purposes, the IRS classifies workers in two broad categories: employees or independent contractors. These workers are taxed in different ways, and it is critical for businesses to identify the correct classification for each individual to whom it makes payments for services. In general, a business must withhold and remit income taxes, Social Security and Medicare taxes, and pay unemployment tax on salaries and wages paid to an employee. A business generally does not have to withhold or pay taxes on payments to independent contractors.

Self-Employed Taxpayers

Self-employment income is earned by taxpayers who work for themselves. A taxpayer who has self-employment income of $400 or more in a year must file a tax return and report the earnings to the IRS.

Taxpayers who are independent contractors usually receive Forms 1099-MISC from their business clients showing the income they were paid. The amounts from the Forms 1099-MISC, along with any other business income payments, are reported by most self-employed individuals on Schedule C, *Profit or Loss from Business*, of Form 1040.

Self-employed farmers or fishermen report their earnings on Schedule F, *Profit or Loss from Farming*, of Form 1040. Self-employment income also includes:

- Income of ministers, priests, and rabbis for the performance of services such as baptisms and marriages.
- The distributive share of trade or business income allocated by a partnership to its general partners or by a limited liability company to its members. The income is reported on IRS Schedule K-1 (Form 1065).

A taxpayer does not have to conduct regular full-time business activities in order to be considered self-employed. A taxpayer may have a side business in addition to a regular job, and this is also considered self-employment.

Example: James earned $45,000 as a full-time employee for Regal Roofing. He also advertises general handyman services online. During the year, James did several handyman side-jobs on the weekends for clients. James received payments of $9,000 from several different individuals for his handyman work. He did not receive Forms 1099-MISC for the $9,000 (because they were individuals who are not required to issue Forms 1099-MISC), but he must report these payments as self-employment income on Schedule C.

Example: Jennie runs a popular taco truck with her brother, Colin. They both split profits and losses equally, and they work together as a partnership. They correctly file Form 1065, *U.S. Return of Partnership Income*, to report the gross income from the taco stand. Jennie and Colin both receive a Schedule K-1 from the partnership every year. Jennie and Colin must each report their distributive share of income from the taco stand on their respective Forms 1040, Schedule E (Part 2). The income is considered self-employment income and is subject to self-employment tax.

FICA Tax (Payroll Taxes)

The Federal Insurance Contributions Act (FICA) tax includes two separate taxes: one is Social Security tax and the other is Medicare tax. The current rate for Social Security is 6.2% for the employer and 6.2% for the employee, or 12.4% total. The current rate for Medicare is 1.45% for the employer and 1.45% for the employee, or 2.9% total.

The combined FICA tax rate for 2016 is 15.3% and applies up to $118,500 of a taxpayer's combined earned income, including wages, tips, and net earnings from self-employment. If the taxpayer's combined earned income exceeds $118,500, a rate of 2.9%, representing only the Medicare portion, applies to any excess earnings over $118,500. There is no cap on earnings subject to the 2.9% Medicare tax.

An additional Medicare surtax of 0.9% is applied to wages and self-employment income above certain thresholds.[13]

---

[13] The Additional Medicare Tax applies to wages, railroad retirement (RRTA) compensation, and self-employment income over certain thresholds.

Note: The 7.65% tax rate is the combined rate for Social Security and Medicare. The Social Security portion (also called "OASDI") is 6.2% on earnings up to the applicable taxable maximum amount ($118,500 in 2016). *Remember:* the Medicare portion is 1.45% on *all* earned income. There is no yearly maximum for Medicare tax.

Self-Employment Tax

Self-employment tax (SE tax) is imposed on self-employed individuals in a manner similar to the Social Security and Medicare taxes that apply to wage earners. Self-employed individuals are responsible for paying the entire amount of Social Security and Medicare taxes applicable to their net earnings from self-employment.

If a taxpayer has wages in addition to self-employment earnings, the Social Security tax on the wages is paid first.

Example: Haywood is a self-employed graphic designer. After deducting all his expenses, he reports $120,000 in net self-employment income on Schedule C. Haywood will pay $14,694 (12.4% X $118,500 [the maximum threshold]) for the social security part of the self-employment tax in 2016. This is the maximum Social Security tax he will pay for 2016, even if he has other sources of income. He also owes 2.9% Medicare tax on the gross amount (2.9% X $120,000 = $3,480). Haywood's total self-employment tax for 2016 is $18,174 ($3,480 Medicare tax + $14,694 Social Security tax).

There are two adjustments related to the self-employment tax that reduce overall taxes for a taxpayer with self-employment income.

- First, the taxpayer's net earnings from self-employment are reduced by 7.65%. Just as the employer's share of Social Security tax is not considered wages to the employee, this reduction removes a corresponding amount from the net earnings before the SE tax is calculated.
- Second, the taxpayer can deduct the employer-equivalent portion of his self-employment tax in determining his adjusted gross income.

Self-employment tax is calculated on IRS Schedule SE.

More Than One Business: If a taxpayer owns more than one business, he must net the profit or loss from each business to determine the total earnings subject to SE tax. However, married taxpayers cannot combine their income or loss from self-employment to determine their individual earnings subject to SE tax.

Example: Tanner is a sole proprietor who owns a barbershop. He has $19,000 of net income in 2016. His wife, Erin, has a candle-making business, which has overall losses of ($12,000) in 2016. Tanner must pay self-employment tax on $19,000, regardless of how he and Erin choose to file. That is because married couples cannot offset each other's income from self-employment, even if they file jointly, for self-employment tax purposes. The income of each business is allocated to each individual.

Example: Darren is a single taxpayer who is a sole proprietor with two small businesses, a computer repair shop and a car wash business that he runs only during the summer months. The computer business has net income of $50,000 in 2016, while the car wash has a net loss of $23,000 in 2016. Darren only has to pay self-employment tax on $27,000 ($50,000 - $23,000) of income because he may net the income and losses from both his businesses.

Employee Compensation

Wages, salaries, bonuses, tips, and commissions are compensation received by employees for services performed. This compensation is taxable income to the employee and a deductible expense for the employer. Employers are required by January 31 to issue Forms W-2, which show the amounts of wages paid to employees for the previous year.

Employers are required by law to withhold Social Security and Medicare taxes from an employee's wages. If the employer fails to withhold these taxes, the employee is required to file Form 8919, *Uncollected Social Security and Medicare Tax on Wages.*

Note: If a taxpayer has more than one employer and his total compensation is over the $118,500 Social Security base limit for 2016, too much Social Security tax may have been withheld. In this case, a taxpayer can claim the excess as a credit against his income tax. If he files Form 1040, he would enter the excess amount on line 71.

Advance Wages: If an employee receives advance wages, commissions, or other earnings, he must recognize the income in the year it is constructively received, regardless of whether he has earned the income. If the employee is later required to pay back a portion of the earnings, the amount would be deducted from his taxable wages at that time.

Example: Maddox requests a modest salary advance of $1,200 on December 18, 2016, so he can take a two-week vacation. His employer gives him the check on December 20, 2016. Maddox must recognize the income on his 2016 tax return, even though he will not actually "earn" the money until 2017 when he returns from his vacation.

Supplemental Wages

Supplemental wages are compensation paid to an employee in addition to his regular pay. These amounts are listed on the employee's Form W-2 and are taxable just like regular wages, even if the pay is not actually for work performed. Vacation pay and sick pay are examples of supplemental wages that are taxable just like any other wage income, even though the employee has not technically "worked" for the income. Supplemental wages may also include:

- Bonuses, commissions, prizes
- Severance pay, back pay, and holiday pay
- Payment for nondeductible moving expenses

Garnished Wages

An employee may have his wages garnished for various reasons, such as when he owes child support, back taxes due, or other debts. Regardless of the amounts garnished from the employee's paycheck, the full amount of his gross wages must be included in his taxable wages at year-end.

Example: Holden's employer garnishes part of his salary for back child support. Since the amount would have normally been included in Holden's paycheck, he must recognize the income as if he had received it himself.

Property in Lieu of Wages

An employee who receives property for services performed must generally recognize the fair market value of the property when it is received as taxable income. However, if an employee receives stock or other property that is restricted, the property is not included in income until it is available to the employee without restriction.

Example: Barry's company gives him 500 shares of stock, valued at $5,000. He cannot sell or otherwise use the shares for five years. If Barry quits his job, he forfeits the shares. He does not have to recognize the stock as income in the year he receives it because the stock is subject to substantial restrictions. Barry will report it as taxable income when the restrictions lapse and he gains complete control over the stock.

Tip Income

Tips received by food servers, baggage handlers, hairdressers, and others for performing services are taxable income. An individual who receives $20 or more per month in tips must report the tip income to his employer. An employee who receives less than $20 per month in tips while working one job does not have to report the tip income to his employer. Tips of less than $20 per month are exempt from Social Security and Medicare taxes, but are still subject to federal income tax.

Example: Lydia works two jobs, as an administrative assistant during the week and as a bartender on the weekends. She reports her tip income from the bartending job of $3,000 to her employer. Her Forms W-2 show wage income of $21,000 (admin) and $8,250 (bartender). Lydia must report $29,250, the total amount earned at both jobs, on her Form 1040. Since she reported the tip income to her employer, her bartending tips are already included on her Form W-2 for that job.

An employee who does not report all of his tips to his employer generally must report the tips and related Social Security and Medicare taxes on his Form 1040. Form 4137, *Social Security and Medicare Tax on Unreported Tip Income,* is used to compute the additional tax.

Noncash tips (for example, concert tickets or other items) do not have to be reported to the employer, but they must be reported and included in the taxpayer's income at their fair market value.

Taxpayers who are self-employed and receive tips must include their tip income in gross receipts on Schedule C.

Taxable Fringe Benefits for Employees

Employers often offer fringe benefits to employees; common fringe benefits include health insurance, retirement plans, and parking passes.

Although most employee fringe benefits are nontaxable, some benefits must be reported on the employee's Form W-2 and included in his taxable income. Examples of taxable fringe benefits include:

- Off-site athletic facilities and health club memberships
- The value of employer-provided life insurance over $50,000
- Any cash benefit or benefits in the form of a credit card or gift card
- Season tickets to sporting events, although single tickets can be excluded in certain cases
- Transportation benefits, if the value of a benefit for any month is more than a specified nontaxable limit[14]
- Employer-provided vehicles, if they are used for personal purposes

---

Example: Tanning Town Inc. owns a tropical resort that its employees may use free of charge. Becker visits the resort with his family for two weeks. The fair market value of the stay is $5,000. Even though Becker paid nothing for the trip, the $5,000 FMV of the vacation must be included in his taxable wages.

Example: Great American Bank pays for country club memberships for all its top executives. Membership costs $8,000 a year per person. Bank executives use the club to entertain prospective clients and investors. Even though the club membership is used for business purposes, this type of fringe benefit is taxable compensation to the employees. Great American Bank must include the full amount of the club membership ($8,000) in an employee's wages.

Nontaxable Fringe Benefits for Employees

Most fringe benefits are not taxable and may be excluded from an employee's income. For example, the value of accident or health plan coverage provided by an employer is not included in an employee's income. The following are explanations of some common types of nontaxable employee fringe benefits.

Retirement Plans

Employer contributions on behalf of their employees' qualified retirement plans are not taxable to the employees when they are made. However, when an employee receives distributions from a retirement plan, the amounts received are taxable income.

Retirement plans may also allow employees to contribute part of their pretax compensation to the plan. This type of contribution is called an elective deferral and is excluded from taxable compensation for income tax purposes, but is subject to Social Security and Medicare taxes.[15]

---

[14] The non-taxable benefit for both mass transit and parking for 2016 was $255 per month. Any expense over that amount is included in the employee's taxable income as wages.

[15] The tax provisions of retirement plans are covered in detail later.

Cafeteria Plans

A cafeteria plan provides employees an opportunity to receive certain benefits on a pretax basis. Participants in a cafeteria plan must be permitted to choose from at least one taxable benefit (such as cash) and one qualified (nontaxable) benefit. Qualified benefits include:

- Accident, dental, vision, and medical benefits (but not Archer medical savings accounts or long-term care insurance).
- Health care flexible spending accounts (FSA, as opposed to a health savings account that a taxpayer may establish and fund on his own. An employee who is covered by an FSA generally cannot make contributions to an HSA).
- Adoption assistance.
- Dependent care assistance.

Employee contributions are usually deducted based upon salary reduction agreements.

Salary reduction contributions are not considered actually or constructively received by the employee and therefore are not considered to be taxable wages. Thus, they are generally not subject to income tax withholding, or to FICA (Social Security and Medicare taxes) or FUTA (unemployment tax). An employer may choose to make benefits available to employees, their spouses, and dependents.

Flexible Spending Arrangement (FSA): An FSA is a form of cafeteria plan benefit that reimburses employees for expenses incurred for certain qualified benefits, such as health benefits. The benefits are subject to annual maximum limits and have traditionally been subject to an annual "use-or-lose" rule, with a short (two-and-a-half-months) grace period after year-end to use any remaining balance.

In 2016, employee salary reduction contributions to a health care FSA are capped at $2,550.

> **Note:** Both employer and employee may contribute to an employee's health FSA, but contributions from all sources combined must not exceed the annual limit ($2,550 in 2016).

If a taxpayer over-contributes to their health care FSA, the taxpayer must pay income tax, plus a 6% excise tax, on any excess contributions and related earnings for each tax year the excess contributions remain in the account. In order to avoid the excise tax on excess contributions, the taxpayer must remove the year's excess contributions and related investment earnings before the last day to file federal income taxes for the pertinent tax year, generally April 15.

> **Example:** Huey has a health care FSA at his current job. In 2016, he contributes the maximum of $2,550 to his account. In November, he switches jobs and mistakenly contributes to the HSA that his new employer offers him. At the end of 2016, Huey has contributed a total of $4,500 to both accounts. He has an excess contribution for 2016. If Huey does not withdraw the excess contribution by the filing deadline (April 18, 2017), he will be subject to a 6% excise tax, as well as income tax, on the excess contribution and any related investment earnings. These penalties will continue year after year, until the excess contribution is corrected.

Up to $500 of unused FSA money per account may be carried over to the following year. An employer must choose between either the grace period or the carryover option.

Adoption Assistance in a "Cafeteria Plan": An employee can exclude amounts paid or reimbursed by an employer under a qualified adoption assistance program ($13,460 for 2016).

Dependent Care Assistance: An employee can exclude up to $5,000 in 2016 ($2,500 if MFS) of benefits received under a qualified dependent care assistance program each year. Amounts paid directly to the taxpayer or to a daycare provider qualify for exclusion.

Highly Compensated Employees (HCEs)

A cafeteria plan cannot have rules that favor eligibility for highly compensated employees to participate, contribute, or benefit from a cafeteria plan. If a benefit plan favors HCEs, the value of their benefits become taxable. This is to discourage companies from offering excellent tax-free benefits to their top executives while ignoring the needs of lower-paid employees. For purposes of a cafeteria plan, an HCE is any of the following:

- An officer;
- A shareholder who owns more than 5% of the voting power or value of all classes of the employer's stock;
- An employee who is highly compensated based on the facts and circumstances; or
- A spouse or dependent of a person described above.

Employer-provided benefits also cannot favor "key employees".

In 2016, a key employee is defined as:

- An officer[16] having annual pay exceeding $170,000.
- An employee who for 2016 is either one of the following:
  - A more than 5% owner of the business.
  - A 1% owner of the business whose annual pay exceeds $150,000.

> **Example:** Fengrew Inc. is a C corporation with 300 employees, 25 of whom are considered highly compensated employees. Fengrew's cafeteria plan and its benefits are available to all full-time employees; therefore, the discrimination rules do not apply, and the employees' benefits are not taxable.

A plan is considered to have favored HCEs if more than 25% of all the benefits are given to HCEs.

Other Types of Employee Fringe Benefits

Educational Assistance: An employer can offer employees educational assistance for the cost of tuition, fees, books, supplies, and equipment. The payments may be for either undergraduate or graduate-level courses, and do not have to be work-related.

In 2016, $5,250 in educational assistance may be excluded per year per employee. If an employer pays more than $5,250, the excess is generally taxed as wages to the employee.[17]

---

[16] For larger companies, the maximum number of officers that are counted towards this particular testing is 50 (or if there are fewer than 50, the greater of: three officers, or 10-percent of the total number of officers).

The cost of courses involving sports, games, or hobbies is not covered, unless they are related to the business or are required as part of a degree program. The cost of lodging, meals, and transportation is also not included.

Tuition Reduction: An educational organization can exclude the value of a qualified undergraduate tuition reduction to an employee, his spouse, or a dependent child. A tuition reduction is "qualified" only if the taxpayer receives it from, and uses it at, an eligible educational institution. Graduate education only qualifies if it is for the education of a graduate student who performs teaching or research activities for the educational organization.

> **Example:** Deborah is a graduate teaching assistant at Northern Arizona University. As part of her employment agreement with the college, Deborah is offered a 50% tuition waiver, reducing the cost of her own graduate tuition at the school. The normal graduate tuition cost is $14,000 per year. Because of the tuition waiver, Deborah only pays $7,000. The tuition reduction is not taxable to Deborah.

Meals and Lodging: An employer may exclude the value of meals and lodging provided to employees if they are provided:

- On the employer's business premises, and
- For the employer's convenience.

For lodging, there is an additional rule: it must be required as a condition of employment. Lodging can be provided for the taxpayer, his spouse, and the taxpayer's dependents and still not be taxable.

> **Example:** Dominick is a project supervisor for Franklin Construction. He is provided free hotel lodging at remote job sites, where he is required to stay on-site for months while timber is cleared and the grounds are prepared for construction projects. The value of the lodging and meals is excluded from his income because it is primarily for his employer's convenience.

The exclusion from taxation does not apply if the employee can choose to receive additional pay instead of lodging. Meals may be provided to employees for the convenience of the employer on the employer's business premises for a number of reasons, such as when:

- Police officers and firefighters need to be on call for emergencies during the meal period
- The nature of the business requires short meal periods
- Eating facilities are not available in areas near the workplace
- Meals are furnished immediately after working hours because the employee's duties prevented him from obtaining a meal during working hours

> **Example:** Paramedic Transport Inc., regularly provides meals to employees during working hours so that paramedics are available for emergency calls during the meal. The employees are not allowed to take regular lunches because of the nature of their employment. The value of the free meals is therefore excludable from the employees' wages, and the employer is allowed to deduct the cost of the meals as a business expense.

---

[17] There is an exception for job-related education. If the education is directly job related, amounts in excess of the $5,250 limit may qualify for exclusion as a working condition fringe benefit.

Meals furnished to restaurant employees before, during, or after work hours are also considered furnished for the employer's convenience and are not taxable to the employee.

Transportation: Employers may provide transportation benefits to their employees up to certain amounts without having to include the benefits in the employees' taxable income. Qualified transportation benefits include transit passes, paid parking, and a ride in a commuter highway vehicle between the employee's home and workplace. In 2016, employees may exclude from taxable income:

- $255 per month in combined commuter highway vehicle transportation and transit passes, and
- $255 per month in parking benefits.

An employer can also reimburse an employee up to $20 per month for reasonable expenses incurred when using a bicycle to commute to work.

Example: Joe is employed by a lumber company. He drives an employer-provided pickup truck, hauling equipment on job sites and delivering lumber to customers. He also gets to take the truck home in the evenings. In 2016, Joe drives the truck 20,000 miles, of which 4,000, or 20%, are personal miles (4,000/20,000 = 20%). The truck has an annual lease value of $4,100. Personal use is therefore valued at $820 and is included in Joe's wages.
Example: Clementine was offered a lucrative new job in New York City as a computer programmer. As part of her employment contract, she negotiates a parking space for her car. Her new employer agrees to pay the cost of the space at the garage across the street from her work. Monthly parking is quite expensive in New York City, and the monthly parking fee at the garage is $550. Since this amount exceeds the allowable limit for parking fringe benefits, a portion of the parking costs will be taxable to Clementine as wages. In 2016, the allowable transportation benefit for parking is $255. Therefore, an additional $295 ($550-$255) would be taxable to Clementine each month. This amount would be deductible by the employer as regular wages and subject to employment taxes for both the employer and the employee.
Note: The use of a company car for commuting purposes or other personal use is a taxable benefit. Therefore, the value of the vehicle's use for either of these purposes is considered taxable wages to the employee.

Cell Phones: The value of the business use of an employer-provided cell phone may be excluded from an employee's income to the extent that, if the employee paid for its use, the payment would be deductible. There must be substantial "noncompensatory" reasons for the use of a phone that relate to the employer's business.

Legitimate reasons include the employer's need to contact the employee in the event of work-related emergencies and the employee's need to be available to speak with clients when away from the office. If a cell phone is provided simply to promote goodwill, to boost an employee's morale, or to attract a prospective employee, the value of the cell phone must be added to the employee's wages.

No-Additional-Cost Services: Nontaxable fringe benefits also include services provided to employees that do not impose any substantial additional cost to the employer because the employer already offers those services in the ordinary course of doing business. Employees do not need to include these no-additional-cost services in their income.

Typically, no-additional-cost services are excess capacity services, such as unused airline seat tickets for airline employees or open hotel rooms for hotel employees.

> **Example:** Bella is a flight attendant with Jet Way Airlines. She is allowed to fly for free on stand-by flights when there is an extra seat. This fringe benefit is allowed at no additional cost to the employer and is therefore nontaxable to the employee.

If an employee is provided with the free or low-cost use of a health club on the employer's premises, the value is not included in the employee's compensation. The gym must be used primarily by employees, their spouses, and their dependent children. However, if the employer pays for a fitness program or use of a facility at an off-site location, the value of the program is included in the employee's compensation.

Group-term Life Insurance Coverage: Up to $50,000 of life insurance coverage may be provided as a nontaxable benefit to an employee. The cost of insurance coverage on policies that exceed $50,000 is a taxable benefit.

Moving Expense Reimbursements: Reimbursements of moving expenses, if paid under an accountable plan for expenses that would otherwise have been deductible by the employee, generally are not taxable to the employee.

> **Definition:** An "accountable" plan is an employee reimbursement allowance arrangement or a method for reimbursing employees for business expenses that complies with IRS regulations.

Employee Achievement Awards: Employers may generally exclude from an employee's taxable wages the value of awards given for length of service or safety achievement. The tax-free amount is limited to the following:

- $400 for awards that are not qualified plan awards. A qualified plan award is one that does not discriminate in favor of highly compensated employees.
- $1,600 for all awards, whether or not they are qualified plan awards.

The exclusion for employee awards does not apply to awards of cash, gift cards, or items such as vacations or tickets to sporting events.

Employee Discounts: Employers may exclude the value of employee discounts from wages up to the following limits:

- For services, a 20% discount of the price charged to nonemployee customers.
- For merchandise, the company's gross profit percentage multiplied by the price nonemployee customers pay.

De Minimis (Minimal) Benefits: This is a property or service an employer provides that has so little value that accounting for it would be impractical. Examples of de minimis benefits include the following:

- Occasional personal use of a company copying machine
- Holiday gifts with a low fair market value
- Beverages such as coffee or soft drinks for employees

Cash and gift cards are not excludable as de minimis benefits unless they are for occasional meal money or transportation fare.

Reimbursement of Employee Business Expenses

When a business reimburses its employees for certain business expenses, such as meals and travel, reimbursements are not taxable income if employees meet all of the following requirements of an accountable plan:

- Have incurred the expenses while performing services as employees
- Adequately account for travel, meal, entertainment, and lodging
- Provide evidence of their employee business expenses, such as receipts or other records
- Return any excess reimbursement within a reasonable period of time

Under an accountable plan, a business may advance money to employees; the cash advance must be reasonably calculated to equal the anticipated expenses, and it must be advanced within a reasonable period of time. If any expenses reimbursed under this arrangement are not substantiated, they are considered taxable income for the employee.

> **Example:** Viviane runs a tax preparation business. She advances $250 to her employee, Mel, so that he can become a notary. Mel spends $90 on a notary course and then another $100 to take the notary exam. Mel returns the unused funds ($60), as well as copies of his receipts to Viviane. The expenses are qualified expenses under an accountable plan, so the amounts paid are not taxable income for Mel, and still deductible as business expenses by Viviane.

Qualifying expenses for travel are excludable from an employee's income if they are incurred for temporary travel on business away from the area of the employee's tax home. Travel expenses paid in connection with an indefinite work assignment cannot be excluded from income. Any work assignment in excess of one year is considered "indefinite." Travel expense reimbursements include:

- Costs of travel to and from the business destination (such as flights and mileage reimbursements)
- Transportation costs while at the business destination (such as taxi fares and shuttles)
- Lodging, meals, and incidental expenses
- Cleaning, laundry, and other miscellaneous expenses

> **Example:** Woody works for a travel agency in Detroit. He flies to Seattle to conduct business for an entire week. His employer pays the cost of transportation to and from Seattle, as well as lodging and meals while there. The reimbursements for substantiated travel expenses are excluded from Woody's income.

Taxation of Clergy Members

There are special rules regarding the taxation of clergy members, defined as individuals who are ordained, commissioned, or licensed by a religious body or church denomination. A clergy member's salary is reported on Form W-2 and is taxable. Offerings and fees received for performing marriages, baptisms, and funerals must also be reported as self-employment income on Schedule C.

Housing Allowance: A clergy member who receives a housing allowance may exclude the allowance from gross income to the extent it is used to pay the expenses of providing a home. The exclusion for housing is limited to the lesser of:

- Fair market rental value (including utilities), or
- The actual cost to provide the home.

The housing allowance cannot exceed reasonable pay and must be used for housing in the year it is received. Salary, other fees, and housing allowances must be included in income for purposes of determining self-employment tax. Even if a minister is considered an employee, churches cannot withhold Social Security and Medicare taxes from his wages. They are treated as self-employed for purposes of these taxes.

Example: William is an ordained minister who receives $32,000 of salary in 2016. He receives an additional $4,000 for performing marriages and baptisms. His housing allowance is $500 per month, for a total of $6,000 per year, and is excluded from his gross income. William must report the $32,000 as salary and the $4,000 as self-employment income. The $6,000 housing allowance is subject to self-employment tax, but not to income tax.

Example: Abby is a full-time ordained minister. Her church allows her to use a cottage that has a rental value of $5,000. She is paid a salary of $12,000, and her church does not withhold Social Security or Medicare taxes. Her income for self-employment tax purposes is $17,000.

A clergy member may apply for an exemption from self-employment tax if he is conscientiously opposed to public insurance because of his religious principles. If the exemption is granted, the clergy member will not pay Social Security or Medicare taxes on his earnings, and he will not receive credit toward those benefits in retirement.

If a clergy member is a member of a religious order that has taken a vow of poverty, he is exempt from paying SE tax on his earnings for qualified services. The earnings are tax-free because they are considered the income of the religious order, rather than of the individual clergy member.

Combat Pay and Veterans' Benefits

Wages earned by military personnel are generally taxable. However, there are a number of special rules for military personnel regarding taxable income.

Combat zone wages (combat pay) are not taxable income. Hazardous duty pay is also excludable for certain military personnel. Enlisted personnel who serve in a combat zone for any part of a month may exclude their pay from tax. For officers, pay is excluded up to a certain amount, depending on the branch of service.

Example: Lee is a Navy pilot who served in a combat zone from January 1, 2016, to November 3, 2016. He is only required to report his income for December 2016, because all of the other income is excluded from taxation as combat zone pay. Even though Lee only served three days in November in a combat zone, his income for the entire month of November is excluded.

Similarly, veterans' benefits paid by the Department of Veterans Affairs to a veteran or his family are not taxable if they are for education (the G.I. Bill), training, disability compensation, work therapy, dependent care assistance, or other benefits or pension payments given to the veteran because of disability.

Disability Payments

Disability retirement benefits are taxable as wages if a taxpayer retired on disability before reaching the minimum retirement age. Once the taxpayer reaches retirement age, the payments are no longer taxable as wages. They are then taxable as pension income.

As a general rule, long term disability payments from an insurance policy are excluded from income if the *taxpayer* pays the premiums for the policy. If an *employer* pays the premiums, the employee must report the payments as taxable income. If both an employee and his employer have paid premiums for a disability policy, only the employer's portion of the disability payments would be reported as taxable income.

Disability Insurance Premiums	Taxability of Benefits
Employer pays 100%	100% taxable
Employer pays a portion and employee pays balance with post-tax dollars	Yes, the taxable percentage is based on the premiums paid by the employer
Employer pays portion and employee pays balance with pre-tax dollars	100% taxable
Employee pays 100% with post-tax dollars	Not taxable
Employee pays 100% with pre-tax dollars	100% taxable

Example: Hortense becomes disabled in 2016 and begins to receive a long-term disability benefit of $4,200 a month. The original insurance policy was paid for by both her employer and herself. Before Hortense became disabled, her employer paid 80% of the disability insurance premiums. Hortense paid the remaining premium amount (20%) with post-tax dollars. In this case, because the employer paid 80% of the policy premiums, then 80% of the benefits received would be taxable to Hortense. This means that $3,360 ($4,200 x 80%) would be taxable. The remaining benefits $840 (20% X $4,200) would not be taxable since Hortense paid that portion of the insurance premium with her own post-tax dollars.

Note: Do not confuse sick pay with disability pay. Sick leave is always taxable as wages, just like vacation pay and holiday pay.

Worker's compensation paid to a taxpayer under a worker's compensation act or other statute is always exempt from tax. Veteran's disability benefits (also called *VA Disability Compensation*) are exempt from taxation if the veteran was terminated through separation or discharged under honorable conditions.

Life Insurance Payments and Payouts

Life insurance payouts generally are not taxable to a beneficiary if the payment was the result of the death of the insured. This is true even if the proceeds were paid under an accident or health insurance policy. However, interest income received as a result of life insurance proceeds is usually taxable. Further, if a taxpayer surrenders a life insurance policy for cash, he must generally include in income any proceeds that are more than the cost of the policy.[18]

Sometimes, a taxpayer will choose to receive life insurance proceeds in installments rather than as a lump sum. In this case, part of the installment generally includes interest income. If a taxpayer receives life insurance proceeds in installments (also called a life insurance annuity), he can exclude part of each installment from his income. To determine the excluded part, the amount held by the insurance company (generally the total lump sum payable at the death of the insured person) is divided by the number of installments to be paid. The taxpayer would include any amount over this excluded portion as taxable interest income.

> **Example:** Libby's brother died in 2016, and she is the sole beneficiary of his life insurance. The face amount of the policy is $75,000. Rather than take a lump sum payment, Libby chooses to receive 120 monthly installments of $1,000 each. The excluded part of each installment is $625 ($75,000 ÷ 120), or $7,500 for an entire year. The rest of each payment, $375 a month (or $4,500 for an entire year), is taxable interest income to Libby.

---

[18] There are limited exceptions when the policy holder is deemed to be terminally or chronically ill.

Unit 4: Study Questions

(Test yourself first, then check the correct answers at the end of this quiz.)

1. Debby broke her leg in a car accident in 2016 and was unable to work for three months. She received an accident settlement of $13,000 from her insurance company. During this time, she also received $7,500 of sick pay from her employer. In addition, she received $5,000 from the accident policy she had purchased herself. How much of this income is taxable to Debby?

A. $5,000
B. $7,500
C. $12,500
D. $18,000

2. Income was constructively received in 2016 in each of the following situations *except*:

A. Wages were deposited in the taxpayer's bank account on December 26, 2016, but were not withdrawn by the taxpayer until January 8, 2017.
B. A taxpayer was informed his check for services rendered was available on December 15, 2016. The taxpayer did not pick up the check until January 30, 2017.
C. A taxpayer received a check by mail on December 31, 2016, but did not deposit the check until January 5, 2017.
D. A taxpayer's home was sold on December 28, 2016. The payment was not received by the taxpayer until January 2, 2017, when the escrow company released the funds.

3. Lavina received the following income and fringe benefits in 2016:

Wages	$30,000
End-of-the-year bonus	2,000
Parking pass per month	90
Employer contributions to her 401(k) plan	900
FMV of free use of a gym on the employer's premises	500

How much income must Lavina report on her 2016 tax return?

A. $30,000
B. $32,000
C. $32,500
D. $34,480

4. Which of the following tip income is exempt from federal income tax?

A. Tips of less than $20 per month.
B. Noncash tips.
C. Tips not reported to the employer.
D. All tips are taxable.

5. Bartholomew is a naval officer who was injured while serving in a combat zone. He was later awarded Veterans Affairs (VA) disability benefits. How are these payments reported on Bartholomew's tax return?

A. 100% of the disability benefits may be excluded from income.
B. Up to 50% of the disability benefits may be excluded from income.
C. 100% of the disability benefits may be excluded from income for enlisted personnel, but not for officers.
D. The disability benefits are taxable.

6. Which of the following fringe benefits is taxable (or partially taxable) to the employee?

A. Health insurance covered 100% by the employer.
B. An employer-provided company car that is used for commuting.
C. Group-term life insurance coverage of $50,000.
D. Employer contributions to an employee's 401(k) plan.

7. What is adjusted gross income?

A. The sum of all sources of taxable income that the taxpayer receives during the year.
B. The amount of earned income a taxpayer receives during the year.
C. Another term for taxable income.
D. Gross income minus certain allowable deductions or adjustments, calculated before exemptions and the standard deduction or itemized deductions are taken.

8. Self-employment income does not include:

A. Income of ministers, priests, and rabbis for the performance of services such as baptisms and marriages.
B. The share of partnership ordinary income allocated to general partners on Schedule K-1.
C. Wages earned by a temporary employee.
D. Payments to independent contractors.

9. Foster owns a restaurant. He furnishes his daytime waitress, Alida, two meals during each workday. Foster encourages (but does not require) Alida to have her breakfast on the business premises before starting work so she can help him answer phones. She is required to have her lunch on the premises. How should Foster treat this fringe benefit to Alida?

A. None of Alida's meals at the restaurant are taxable.
B. All of Alida's meals at the restaurant are taxable.
C. Alida's lunch is not taxable, but her breakfast is.
D. Alida's meals are taxed at a flat rate of 15%.

10. Orrin is an ordained minister in the Evangelical Church of Chicago. He owns his home, and his monthly house payment is $900. His monthly utilities total $150. The fair rental value in his neighborhood is $1,000. Orrin receives a housing allowance from his church in the amount of $950 per month. What amount of his housing allowance would he include in his gross income?

A. $0
B. $100 per month
C. $150 per month
D. $950 per month

11. Which of the following types of fringe benefits are deductible by an employer but not taxable to the employee?

A. De minimis fringe benefit.
B. Use of an employer's apartment, vacation home, or boat.
C. Membership in a country club or athletic facility.
D. A gift card.

12. Salvador is an enlisted soldier in the U.S. Army who served in a combat zone from January 30, 2016, to September 2, 2016. He returned to the United States and received his regular duty pay for the remainder of the year. How many months of his income are taxable in 2016?

A. Zero. All the income is tax-free.
B. Three months are subject to tax.
C. Four months are subject to tax.
D. Twelve months are subject to tax.

13. Which of the following fringe benefits provided by the employer will result in taxable income to the employee?

A. A cell phone used by a salesperson to talk to clients while on the road.
B. Reimbursements paid by the employers for qualified business travel expenses.
C. Use of a company van for daily commuting.
D. Occasional personal use of an office copy machine.

14. Marco is employed as an accountant by a large firm. When he travels for his audit work, he submits his travel receipts for reimbursement by his firm, which has an accountable plan for its employees. Which of the following statements is correct about accountable plans?

A. The reimbursed amounts are not taxable to Marco.
B. Marco may still deduct his travel expenses on his tax return.
C. His employer cannot deduct the travel expenses, even though Marco was reimbursed in full.
D. Reimbursed expenses are taxable to the employee, and the employer can also deduct the expenses as they would any other current expense.

15. Faye was the beneficiary on her mother's life insurance policy. Her mother died on December 12, 2016. Faye received the following payments on January 31, 2017:

- $160,000 death benefit from her mother's life insurance policy
- $175 of interest income on the life insurance proceeds

What is the proper treatment of these payments?

A. The insurance benefit and interest income are both taxable in 2016, since that is the year that the policy holder died.
B. The insurance benefit and interest income are both taxable to Faye in 2017.
C. Only the $175 of interest income is taxable in 2017. The life insurance proceeds are not taxable.
D. None of these payments are taxable to Faye. Instead, they are taxable to her mother's estate.

16. Of the following, only _____ is not taxable income:

A. A holiday bonus.
B. Overtime pay.
C. Vacation pay.
D. A travel reimbursement.

17. Brendan is a flight attendant who earned wages of $30,000 in 2016. The airline provided free transportation on standby from his home in Little Rock to the airline's hub in Charlotte. The fair market value of the commuting flights was $5,000. Brendan also received advances under an accountable plan of $10,000 for overnight travel, but only spent $6,000. He returned the excess ($4,000) to his employer. Brendan was injured on the job and received worker's compensation of $4,000. What amount must he include in gross income?

A. $30,000
B. $34,000
C. $35,000
D. $37,000

18. Orval and Rae are married and both are self-employed. Orval owns a business that has a $9,750 net profit in 2016. His wife, Rae, has an overall business loss of ($11,100) for 2016. They both file Schedules C to report their self-employment income. Which of the following statements is correct?

A. On their joint return, they will not have to pay self-employment tax, because the losses from Rae's business will offset Orval's income.
B. They can file MFS and offset each other's self-employment tax.
C. Orval must pay self-employment tax on $9,750, regardless of his wife's income or losses.
D. If they choose to file separate returns, they may split the profits and losses equally between their two businesses.

19. Elaine is a cash-basis taxpayer and sells cosmetics on commission. On December 25, 2016, Elaine receives $10,000 of income from commissions, plus an advance of $1,000 for future commissions in 2017. She also receives $200 of expense reimbursements from her employer after turning in her receipts as part of an accountable plan. How much income should Elaine report on her 2016 tax return?

A. $0
B. $11,000
C. $11,200
D. $10,200

Unit 4: Answers

1. The answer is B. Only Debby's sick pay is taxable as wages. Sick pay from an employer is taxable as wages and is therefore included in Debby's gross income. Settlements for personal injuries from an accident are not taxable. If a taxpayer pays the full cost of an accident insurance plan, the benefits for personal injury or illness are not included in income. If the employer pays the cost of an accident insurance plan, the amounts are taxable to the employee.

2. The answer is D. A taxpayer does not need physical possession of income in order to have constructive receipt. However, income is not considered constructively received if the taxpayer cannot access the funds because of restrictions. Since the taxpayer's control of the receipt of the funds in the escrow account was substantially limited until the transaction had closed, the taxpayer did not constructively receive the income until the following year.

3. The answer is B. Only the wages and the bonus are taxable ($30,000 + $2,000). The parking pass is a nontaxable transportation benefit, and the employer contributions are not taxable until Lavina withdraws the money from her retirement account. Lavina does not have to report the use of the gym, because it is on the employer's premises and therefore not taxable.

4. The answer is D. All tip income is subject to federal income tax, whether cash or noncash. An individual who receives less than $20 per month of tips while working one job does not have to report the tip income to his employer, but the income is still subject to federal income tax and must be reported on the taxpayer's Form 1040.

5. The answer is A. All of the disability benefits are excluded from taxable income. VA disability compensation is exempt from taxation if the veteran was terminated through separation or discharged under honorable conditions. The VA does not issue Form W-2, Form 1099-R, or any other tax-related document for veterans' disability benefits.

6. The answer is B. An employer-provided company car would be partially taxable if it was used for personal driving. The value of the personal use of the automobile must be added to the employee's wages. These valuation rules are covered in IRS Publication 15-B, *Employer's Tax Guide to Fringe Benefits.*

7. The answer is D. Adjusted gross income (AGI) is gross income (the sum of all income subject to taxation that the taxpayer receives during the year) minus certain allowable deductions or adjustments. AGI is calculated before exemptions, and the standard deduction or itemized deductions are taken.

8. The answer is C. Wage income is never considered self-employment income. The other examples listed are all types of self-employment income and subject to self-employment tax on Form 1040.

9. The answer is A. Meals furnished to Alida are not taxable because they are for the convenience of the employer. Meals that employers furnish to a restaurant employee during, immediately before or after the employee's working hours are considered furnished for the employer's convenience. Since Alida is a waitress who works during the normal breakfast and lunch periods, Foster can exclude from her wages the value of those meals. If Foster allowed Alida to have meals without charge on her days off, the value of those meals would be included in her wages.

10. The answer is A. Clergy members may exclude from gross income for income tax purposes, but not for self-employment tax purposes, the rental value of a home, or a rental allowance to the extent the allowance is used to provide a home, even if deductions are taken for home expenses paid with the allowance.

11. The answer is A. A de minimis fringe benefit is deductible by the employer but is not taxable to the employee. The IRS defines a de minimis benefit in this way: a benefit that, considering its value and the frequency with which it is provided, is so small as to make accounting for it unreasonable or impractical. For example, a de minimis fringe benefit might include occasional snacks, coffee, or doughnuts provided in a company's breakroom. The items in the other choices would be taxable to the employee.

12. The answer is B. If a taxpayer serves in a combat zone as an enlisted person for *any part* of a month, all of his pay received for military service that month is excluded from gross income. Since Salvador served for a few days in September, as well as January, all the income for those months is excluded as combat pay. Only October through December would be taxable.

13. The answer is C. Use of a company vehicle for commuting is not a qualified fringe benefit. Commuting expenses are not deductible. Use of a company van after normal working hours is personal use and not business use, so it would result in taxable income to the employee. The cell phone, reimbursements for business travel, and the occasional personal use of an office copy machine are noncash fringe benefits that are not taxable.

14. The answer is A. Under an accountable plan, employee reimbursements are not included in the employee's income. The employer can deduct the expenses as current expenses on its tax return. The employee is not required to be taxed on any amounts received in accordance with the terms of a qualified accountable plan; however, the employee cannot deduct any employment-related expenses that have been reimbursed to him by his employer.

15. The answer is C. Life insurance proceeds are not taxable to the recipient. Interest earned on life insurance proceeds is taxable. Faye must report the interest income in the year she receives it.

16. The answer is D. Travel reimbursements, if paid through an accountable plan, are not included in an employee's wages.

17. The answer is A. Brendan only has to include his wages on his tax return. The free flights offered on standby to airline personnel are considered no-additional-cost services and are not taxable to the employee. Reimbursements under an accountable plan and amounts paid for workers' compensation are nontaxable. Since

Brendan returned the unspent amounts to his employer, the travel reimbursements qualify under an accountable plan, and the amounts spent are not taxable to him.

18. The answer is C. Orval must pay self-employment tax on his earnings, regardless of how he and Rae choose to file. Taxpayers cannot combine both spouses' income or loss to determine their earnings subject to SE tax. However, if a taxpayer has more than one business, he must combine the net profit or loss from each to determine the total earnings subject to SE tax.

19. The answer is B. Elaine's commissions must be included in gross income, as well as advance payments in anticipation of future services ($10,000 + $1,000 =$11,000). The expense reimbursements from an accountable plan ($200) would not be included in her taxable income.

Unit 5: Interest and Dividend Income

For additional information read:
Publication 550, *Investment Income and Expenses*
FS Publication 51, *Using Savings Bonds for Education*

Taxpayers who lend or deposit cash or invest in securities such as stocks, bonds, and mutual funds may earn income from interest, dividends, and capital appreciation. This unit covers interest and dividend income. Other types of income from investments, such as capital gains resulting from sales, are covered later.

Interest Income

Interest is a form of income that may be earned from deposits, such as in bank and money market accounts, notes receivable, and investments in instruments such as bonds. Some interest income is taxable, and some is not.

Certain distributions, commonly referred to as dividends, are actually reported as taxable interest income. These include "dividends" on deposits or share accounts in cooperative banks, credit unions, domestic savings and loan associations, and mutual savings banks. A taxpayer can also have taxable interest from certificates of deposits (CDs) and other deferred interest accounts.

Interest income is generally reported to the taxpayer on Form 1099-INT by the financial institution or other payor if the amount of interest is $10 or more for the year. Even if a taxpayer does not receive Form 1099-INT from a payor, all taxable interest income must be reported. If taxable interest income exceeds $1,500, the taxpayer cannot file Form 1040EZ and must report the interest on Schedule B, *Interest and Ordinary Dividends*, and file Form 1040 or Form 1040A.

Example: Leona has five savings accounts in different banks. The total amount of interest earned from the accounts is $1,950. Leona will receive five Forms 1099-INT. She must list each payor and amount on Schedule B and file it with her tax return.

Example: Ina has two savings accounts. In 2016, she earns $6 in interest from the first savings account and $8 in interest from the second account. Because the amounts are below the reporting threshold, she does not receive a Form 1099-INT from either bank. The interest is still taxable income and must be reported on her return, assuming that she has a filing requirement for the year.

Interest on U.S. Treasury Bills, Notes, and Bonds

Interest on U.S. obligations, such as U.S. Treasury bills, notes, and bonds issued by any agency of the United States, is normally taxable for federal income tax purposes.

The **Series EE bond** is the most common type of U.S. savings bond. These bonds are issued at a discount, and the difference between the purchase price and the amount received when the bonds are later redeemed (or "cashed in") is interest income.

Series I bonds are issued at face value with a maturity period of 30 years. The face value and accrued interest are payable at maturity.

Individual taxpayers can generally report interest income from a Series EE or Series I savings bond either:

- When the bond matures or is redeemed (whichever occurs first), or
- Each year as the bond's redemption value increases.

However, a taxpayer must use the same reporting method for all the Series EE and Series I bonds he owns. When a taxpayer redeems savings bonds, he should receive a Form 1099-INT from the bank or other payer. To exclude interest earnings on Series EE and Series I bonds, a taxpayer must be at least 24 years old before the bond's issue date.

Series HH U.S. savings bonds are issued at face value and pay interest twice a year. Taxpayers must report the interest in the year it is paid.

Interest earned on other U.S. obligations, such as U.S. Treasury bills, notes, and bonds, is taxable when it is received.

Interest on Educational Savings Bonds

Taxpayers may purchase and eventually redeem certain Series EE or I bonds on a tax-free basis to pay qualified higher education expenses. The expenses must be for the taxpayer, his spouse, or dependents for whom an exemption is claimed.

The taxpayer must use both the principal and interest to pay for qualified education expenses. If the amount of savings bonds cashed during the year exceeds the amount of qualified educational expenses paid during the year, the amount of excludable interest is reduced.

Example: Molly is a full-time college student. She redeemed several education savings bonds in 2016 to pay for her college expenses. The total bond proceeds were $10,000 ($8,000 principal and $2,000 in interest). Molly's qualified educational expenses were only $8,000. She used the remaining $2,000 to make a down payment on a new car. Therefore, since Molly used only 80% of the bond proceeds for qualified expenses, she can only exclude 80% of the bond interest. The excludable portion would equal $1,600 (80% x $2,000 bond interest = $1,600). She would pay tax on the remaining $400 of bond interest.

Married taxpayers who file separately (MFS) do not qualify for the education savings bond interest exclusion. If a taxpayer cashes an education savings bond during the year, and then files MFS, all the interest would be taxable, regardless of whether or not the taxpayer had qualifying education expenses. For the purposes of this exclusion, qualified educational expenses include:

- College tuition and fees (such as lab fees and other required course expenses), except for expenses for any course or other education program involving sports, games, or hobbies that are not part of a degree program.
- Expenses paid for any course required as part of a degree or certificate program.
- The costs of room and board, as well as books, are not eligible expenses for this exclusion.

The amount of qualified expenses is reduced by the amount of any scholarships, fellowships, employer-provided educational assistance, and other forms of tuition reduction. The exclusion is calculated and reported on Form 8815, *Exclusion of Interest from Series EE and I U.S. Savings Bonds*

Issued After 1989. There are certain rules that must be followed in order for the educational exclusion to qualify:

- The bonds must be purchased by the owner. They cannot be a gift.
- Qualified higher education expenses must be reduced by certain tax-free benefits received and by expenses used to claim the American Opportunity and Lifetime Learning credits.
- The total interest received may be excluded only if the combined amounts of the principal and the interest received do not exceed the taxpayer's qualified higher education expenses.

Note: The costs of required textbooks are not qualified expenses for the purposes of the savings bond interest exclusion.[19] However, the cost of required textbooks *is* a qualified educational expense for the purposes of the Lifetime Learning Credit and the American Opportunity Credit.

Gift for Opening a Bank Account: If a taxpayer receives noncash gifts or services for making deposits or for opening an account in a savings institution, the value of the gift may have to be reported as interest. For deposits of less than $5,000, gifts or services valued at more than $10 must be reported as interest. For deposits of $5,000 or more, gifts or services valued at more than $20 must be reported as interest. The value of the gift is determined by the financial institution.

A cash bonus for opening a new checking or credit card account is also taxable interest. Similarly, reward points or airline miles that a bank offers as a gift to customers who open new accounts are taxable. However, cash back and reward points earned on credit and debit card purchases are not taxable interest income.

Interest Earned on a Certificate of Deposit

Interest earned on a certificate of deposit (CD) is generally taxable when the taxpayer receives it or is entitled to receive it without paying a substantial penalty.

The interest a taxpayer pays on funds borrowed from a financial institution to meet the minimum deposit required for a CD, and the interest a taxpayer earns on the CD are two separate items. The taxpayer must include the total interest earned on the CD in income. If the taxpayer itemizes deductions, he can deduct the interest paid as investment interest, up to the amount of net investment income.

Example: Sienna wanted to invest in a $10,000 six-month CD. She deposited $5,000 of her own money in a CD with a bank and borrowed an additional $5,000 from the same bank to make up the $10,000 minimum deposit required to buy the six-month CD. The certificate of deposit earned $575 at maturity in 2016, but Sienna actually received a net amount of $265 for the year after taking into account the $310 of interest paid to the bank. This represented the $575 Sienna earned on the CD, minus $310 interest charged on the $5,000 loan. The bank gives Sienna a Form 1099-INT for 2016 showing the $575 interest she earned. The bank also gives Sienna a statement showing that she paid $310 in investment interest during the year. Sienna must include the total interest amount that she earned, $575, in her gross income for 2016. She can deduct the interest expense of $310 only if she itemizes deductions on Schedule A.

---

[19] For more information on educational savings bonds, see FS Publication 0051, *Using Savings Bonds for Education*.

Tax-Exempt Interest

Interest earned on debt obligations of state and local governments (also commonly called *muni bonds* or *municipal bonds*) is generally exempt from federal income tax, but may be subject to income taxes by state and local governments. However, interest on federally-guaranteed state and local obligations is generally taxable. In addition, even if interest on an obligation is nontaxable, the taxpayer may need to report a capital gain or loss when the investment is sold.

The taxpayer's Form(s) 1099-INT may include both taxable and tax-exempt interest. Tax-exempt interest must be reported on Form 1040, even though it is not taxable.

Dividend Income

A dividend is a distribution of cash, stock, or other property from a corporation or a mutual fund. The payor will generally use Form 1099-DIV to report dividend income to taxpayers. If a taxpayer does not receive Form 1099-DIV from a payor, he must still report all taxable dividend income.

Generally, if a taxpayer's total dividend income is more than $1,500, it must be reported on Schedule B, *Interest and Ordinary Dividends*. Otherwise, it can be reported directly on Form 1040 or 1040A. Dividends are not subject to employment taxes.

Ordinary Dividends: Ordinary dividends are corporate distributions in cash (as opposed to property or stock shares) that are paid to shareholders out of earnings and profits. Unless they are qualified dividends, they are taxed at ordinary income rates rather than at lower long-term capital gain rates. Ordinary dividends are reported on Box 1a of Form 1099-DIV.

Nondividend Distributions: Distributions that are not paid out of earnings and profits are nondividend distributions. They are considered a recovery or return of capital and therefore are generally not taxable. However, these distributions reduce the taxpayer's basis in the stock of the corporation. Once the basis is reduced to zero, any additional distributions are capital gains and are taxed as such. Nondividend distributions are reported on Box 3 of Form 1099-DIV.

Qualified Dividends: Qualified dividends are reported to the taxpayer on box 1b of Form 1099-DIV. These are ordinary dividends that are given preferred tax treatment as long-term capital gains if specific criteria are met.

2016 Tax Rate on Qualified Dividends	
Tax Bracket (Ordinary Income)	Tax Rate (Qualified Dividends)
10%, 15% brackets	0%
25%, 28%, 33%, 35% brackets	15%
39.6% bracket	20%

In order for the dividends to qualify for these preferred tax rates, the following are the two most common requirements that must be met:

- The dividends must be paid by a U.S. corporation or a qualified foreign corporation,[20] and
- The taxpayer generally must have held the stock for more than 60 days during the 121-day period that begins 60 days before the ex-dividend date.

---

[20] A "qualified foreign corporation" for the purposes of this rule is generally a foreign corporation whose stock is traded on a U.S. stock exchange or if a tax treaty between the U.S. and the foreign country of the corporation allows for qualified dividend status.

When figuring the holding period for qualified dividends, the taxpayer may count the number of days he held the stock and include the day he disposed of the stock. The date the taxpayer acquires the stock is not included in the holding period. A longer holding period may apply for dividends paid on preferred stock.

Example: Israel bought 5,000 shares of Moonshine Corporation stock on July 9, 2016. Moonshine paid a cash dividend of 10 cents per share. The ex-dividend date was July 17, 2016. Israel's Form 1099-DIV from Moonshine shows $500 in dividends. However, Israel sold the 5,000 shares on August 12, 2016. Israel held his shares of Moonshine for only 34 days of the 121-day required holding period (34 days from July 17, 2016, to August 12, 2016), which began on May 18, 2016 (60 days before the ex-dividend date), and ended on September 15, 2016. Israel has no qualified dividends from Moonshine because he held the stock for less than the required 61 days. He does not qualify for the preferred tax treatment that is given to qualified dividends. Instead, his dividends will be taxed as ordinary income.

Definition: The **ex-dividend date** is the date a shareholder will no longer be entitled to receive the most recently declared dividend (typically the day following the record date).

Mutual Fund Distributions

A taxpayer who receives mutual fund distributions during the year should also receive Form 1099-DIV identifying the types of distributions received. Mutual fund distributions are reported based upon the character of the income source and may include ordinary dividends, qualified dividends, capital gain distributions, exempt-interest dividends, and nondividend distributions.

Capital gain distributions from a mutual fund are always treated as long-term, regardless of the actual period the mutual fund investment is held. Distributions from a mutual fund investing in tax-exempt securities are tax-exempt interest and retain their tax-exempt character for the payee. Even so, the taxpayer must report them on his tax return.

If a mutual fund or Real Estate Investment Trust (REIT) declares a dividend payable to shareholders in October, November, or December, but actually pays the dividend during January of the following year, the shareholder is considered to have received the dividend on December 31 of the prior tax year and must report the dividend in the year it was declared. Mutual fund distributions may be reported on Form 1040 or Form 1040A. This is a special rule that applies only to this type of dividend.

Stock Dividends

A stock dividend is a distribution of stock, rather than money, by a corporation to its own shareholders. A stock dividend is generally not a taxable event and does not affect the shareholder's income in the year of distribution, because he is not actually receiving any money and all shareholders increase their total number of shares pro rata.

When a stock dividend is granted, the total basis of the shareholder's stock is not affected, but the basis of individual shares is adjusted by the inclusion of the newly-issued shares.

Example: Razor Ball Corporation declares a year-end stock dividend. Scarlett is a shareholder in Razor Ball, and prior to the stock dividend she owns 100 shares. Her basis in the shares is $5,000, or $50 per share. Scarlett receives a stock dividend of 100 shares. After the dividend, Scarlett owns 200 shares. Her overall basis in the shares does not change (it is still $5,000), but her new basis in each individual share is $25 per share ($5,000/200 = $25 per share). Scarlett does not have any taxable income as a result of the stock dividend.

If a shareholder has the option to receive cash instead of stock, the stock dividend is taxable in the year it is distributed. The recipient of the stock must include the FMV of the newly-issued stock in his gross income, and that same amount is the basis of the shares received.

Example: The Arch Corporation declares a year-end stock dividend and gives its shareholders the option of receiving cash instead of stock. Therefore, the stock dividend becomes a taxable event. Prior to the dividend, Dale owns 1,000 shares in Arch Co., and his basis in the shares is $10,000, or $10 per share. Dale decides to take the stock instead of cash and receives an additional 100 shares. The FMV of the stock at the time of the distribution is $15 per share. Dale must recognize $1,500 of income ($15 FMV × 100 shares = $1,500), which also is his basis in the new shares.

Dividend Reinvestment Plans (DRIP): A dividend reinvestment plan allows a taxpayer to use dividends to purchase more shares of stock in a corporation instead of receiving dividends in cash. If the taxpayer uses his dividends to buy more stock at a price equal to its fair market value, he must still report the dividends as income.

Some plans also allow taxpayers to invest cash to buy shares of stock at a price less than fair market value. In this case, the taxpayer must report as dividend income the difference between the cash he invests and the FMV of the stock he purchases.

Example: Lois owns 100 shares of Barclift Corporation, which is currently trading at $50 a share on the open market. Through Barclift's DRIP, Lois buys 50 additional shares at a price of $40 per share. She must report $500 as dividend income ($10 per share difference between FMV and purchase price multiplied by 50 shares).

Constructive Distributions

Certain transactions between a corporation and its shareholders may be regarded as constructive distributions. They may be considered dividends or nondividend distributions and may be taxable to the shareholders. Examples of constructive distributions include:

- **Payment of personal expenses:** If a corporation pays personal expenses on behalf of an employee-shareholder, the amounts should be classified as a distribution, rather than expenses of the corporation.
- **Unreasonable compensation:** If a corporation pays an employee-shareholder an unreasonably high salary considering the services actually performed, the excessive part of the salary may be treated as a distribution.
- **Unreasonable rents:** If a corporation rents property from a shareholder and the rent is unreasonably higher than the shareholder would charge an unrelated party for the use of the

property, the excessive part of the rent may be treated as a distribution. Conversely, if a corporation rents property_to a shareholder and the rent is unreasonably low, the discounted portion of the rent could be treated as a distribution as well.

- **Cancellation of a shareholder's debt:** If a corporation cancels a shareholder's debt without repayment by the shareholder, the amount canceled may be treated as a distribution.
- **Property transfers for less than FMV:** If a corporation transfers or sells property to a shareholder for less than its FMV, the excess may be treated as a distribution.
- **Below market or interest-free loans:** If a corporation gives a loan to a shareholder on an interest-free basis or at a rate below the applicable federal rate, the uncharged interest may be treated as a distribution.

Example: Maureen's father owns 95% of Fallon Orthotics Corporation, and she and her siblings own the remaining 5%. Maureen performs secretarial duties on a part-time basis for the corporation and is paid a salary of $700,000 a year. The corporation also pays for various personal expenses Maureen incurs, such as monthly payments on the car she uses to commute to work. The IRS would likely consider Maureen's salary as unreasonably high based on the nature of her duties, meaning that a portion of the salary and the personal expenses would be reclassified as constructive distributions.

Unit 5: Study Questions

(Test yourself first, then check the correct answers at the end of this quiz.)

1. A taxpayer must generally have held stock for _____ in order for his dividend income to be considered qualified dividends.

A. More than 30 days during the 121-day period that begins 60 days before the ex-dividend date.
B. More than 60 days during the 121-day period that begins 60 days before the ex-dividend date.
C. More than 120 days.
D. More than one year.

2. Which of the following dividends are reported as interest income on a taxpayer's return?

A. Stock dividends.
B. Dividends earned on deposits in credit unions.
C. Preferred dividends.
D. Qualified dividends.

3. Six years ago, Derrick bought a U.S. Series EE savings bond and decided to report the interest earned each year until maturity. This year, he bought another Series EE savings bond. How should Derrick report the interest on this new bond?

A. He must wait until the second bond matures to report all the interest earned at that time.
B. He must report the interest earned each year until maturity.
C. He can use either method to report interest earned, as long as he makes the election on a timely filed return.
D. This type of interest is now exempt from federal income tax.

4. Alec received a Form 1099-DIV from his brokerage firm showing that he earned $1,200 of ordinary dividends in 2016. He received no other dividends during the year. How should this income be handled on Alec's tax return?

A. He must report the dividend income on Schedule B, but it is not taxable.
B. He must report the dividend income on Schedule B. It is taxable as ordinary income.
C. He can report the dividend income on page one of his Form 1040. It is taxable as ordinary income.
D. He does not have to report the dividend income until he sells the stock from the corporations that distributed the dividends.

5. In 2016, Remy had the following transactions from which she earned interest:

- Interest of $700 from a certificate of deposit that matured in September.
- Upon maturity of the first CD, she invested the proceeds in a second CD with a maturity in March 2017. As of December 31, 2016, this second CD had accrued interest of $400.
- She loaned $2,000 to a family member who repaid the loan and related interest of $120 with a check dated December 31, 2016, which Remy received on January 4, 2017.

What is the amount of taxable interest income that Remy must report for 2016?

A. $1,100
B. $1,220
C. $820
D. $700

6. Nondividend distributions are:

A. Considered a return of capital.
B. Never taxable.
C. Always taxable as ordinary income.
D. Both A and B.

7. Anand opened a savings account at his local bank and deposited $800. He received a $15 calculator as a gift for opening the account, and he earned $20 of interest in 2016. Anand also received $100 of municipal bond interest in his mutual funds account. How much taxable interest income must Anand report on his Form 1040?

A. $15
B. $20
C. $35
D. $135

8. Robert is a 5% employee-shareholder of a family-owned corporation. Which of the following would the IRS likely classify as a constructive distribution?

A. Use of a company copy machine for making occasional personal copies.
B. Payment of Robert's monthly gym membership by the corporation.
C. Dental benefits paid by the corporation through a cafeteria plan.
D. All of the above.

9. Toni files as head of household and has modified AGI of $72,000 in 2016. She owns a Series EE savings bond, which she purchased as an investment to help pay for her daughter Holland's education. She redeems the bond in 2016 and immediately uses all the funds to pay college tuition expenses for Holland. Toni claims Holland as a dependent. The bond's interest is reported on:

A. Toni's tax return, and it is 100% taxable.
B. Holland's tax return and it is 100% taxable.
C. Toni's tax return, and it is exempt from taxes.
D. Nowhere. It is not taxable and not required to be reported, as long as Toni uses all the funds to pay for qualified higher education costs.

10. All of the following statements about stock dividends are correct except:

A. When a stock dividend is granted, the basis of the stockholder's existing shares is adjusted to reflect issuance of the new shares.
B. A stock dividend occurs when a corporation distributes stock to its own shareholders.
C. A taxpayer generally recognizes income only when he sells the stock received in a stock dividend distribution.
D. A stock dividend is never taxable if a taxpayer has the choice to receive cash instead of stock.

11. Miguel deposited $4,000 of his own funds and also borrowed $12,000 from the bank to buy a six-month certificate of deposit for $16,000. The certificate earned $375 at maturity in 2016, and Miguel received $175, which represented the $375 he earned minus $200 of interest charged on the $12,000 loan. The bank gives Miguel a Form 1099-INT showing the $375 interest he earned. The bank also gives him a statement showing that he paid $200 of interest. How should Miguel report these amounts on his tax return?

A. He should report $175 of interest income.
B. He should report $375 of interest income. The $200 of interest he paid to the bank is not deductible.
C. He should report $375 of interest income and can deduct $200 on his Schedule A, subject to the net investment income limit.
D. He does not have to report any income from this transaction.

12. Araceli received $500 of interest from bonds issued by the state of New Jersey. How should she report this on her Form 1040?

A. It must be reported on her tax return, but it is not taxable income.
B. It must be reported as interest income, and it is 100% taxable.
C. She does not have to report the bond interest.
D. She must report the interest on her state tax return, but it does not have to be reported on her federal return.

13. Kent invested in a mutual fund in 2016. The fund declared a dividend, and Kent earned $19. He did not receive a Form 1099-DIV for the amount, and he did not withdraw the money from his mutual fund. Kent sold his investment in the mutual fund on January 2, 2017. Which of the following statements is correct?

A. The dividend is not reportable in 2016 because Kent did not receive the money yet.
B. The dividend is not reportable in 2016 because Kent did not receive a 1099-DIV.
C. The dividend is taxable and must be reported in 2016.
D. The dividend is taxable and must be reported in 2017.

14. Marcelo opened a savings account at his local bank and deposited $800. The account earned $20 interest in 2016. On his credit card account, Marcelo received $100 worth of reward points for charging $10,000 of purchases, which he used to pay a portion of his credit card bill. How much interest income must Marcelo report on his Form 1040?

A. $20
B. $75
C. $120
D. $900

15. All of the following statements about dividends are correct *except*:

A. A taxpayer will pay a higher tax rate on an ordinary dividend than on a qualified dividend.
B. A taxpayer will pay a higher tax rate on a qualified dividend than on an ordinary dividend.
C. The ex-dividend date is the date a shareholder will no longer be entitled to receive the most recently declared dividend (normally right after the record date).
D. When figuring the holding period for qualified dividends, the taxpayer may count the number of days he held the stock (starting the day after the stock was acquired) and include the day he disposed of the stock.

16. Constance is using educational savings bonds to help pay her college expenses. Which of the following is a qualified expense for the educational savings bond exclusion?

A. College tuition.
B. Room and board.
C. Required textbooks.
D. Student health fees.

17. To exclude interest earnings on Series EE and Series I bonds for qualifying educational purposes, the taxpayer must be at least _____ before the bond's issue date.

A. 18 years old.
B. 24 years old.
C. 17 years old.
D. 13 years old.

Unit 5: Answers

1. The answer is B. A taxpayer must generally have held stock for more than 60 days during the 121-day period that begins 60 days before the ex-dividend date. The ex-dividend date is the date a shareholder will no longer be entitled to receive the most recently declared dividend. When figuring the holding period for qualified dividends, the taxpayer may count the number of days he held the stock and include the day he disposed of the stock. The date the taxpayer acquires the stock is not included in the holding period. A longer holding period may apply for dividends paid on preferred stock.

2. The answer is B. The dividends earned on deposits in credit unions are reported and taxed as interest income.

3. The answer is B. Savings bond owners must use the same interest-reporting method for all the Series EE and Series I bonds they own.

4. The answer is C. Ordinary dividends are taxable as ordinary income in the year they are earned. Only amounts over $1,500 must be reported on Schedule B, so Alec can report the $1,200 of dividend income directly on page one of his Form 1040.

5. The answer is D. The interest earned on the first certificate of deposit was received upon maturity, and was, therefore, taxable in 2016. The accrued interest on the second certificate would have been subject to penalty if the certificate had been redeemed prior to maturity, and the accrued interest was therefore not taxable. Remy did not have constructive receipt of the interest paid on the loan until 2017, and so it was not taxable in 2016.

6. The answer is A. Nondividend distributions are not paid out of a corporation's earnings and profits. They are considered a recovery or return of capital and therefore are generally not taxable. However, these distributions reduce the taxpayer's basis. Once basis is reduced to zero, any additional distributions are taxed as capital gains.

7. The answer is C. A gift for opening a bank account is normally taxed as interest income. If no other interest is credited to Anand during the year, the Form 1099-INT he receives will include the fair market value of the calculator and show a total of $35 of interest for the year. The $100 of municipal bond interest is not taxable for federal tax purposes, but it must be reported on the return.

8. The answer is B. The payment of personal expenses on behalf of an employee-shareholder is treated as a constructive distribution. In this case, the payment of his monthly gym membership is likely to be reclassified as a taxable dividend to Robert or a nondividend distribution, depending upon whether the corporation has earnings and profits. Choice C is incorrect because dental and medical benefits paid by an employer are an allowable employee benefit. Answer A is incorrect because the use of a company copier is an allowable de minimis fringe benefit. See Publication 5137, *Fringe Benefit Guide,* for more information.

9. The answer is C. As the buyer and owner of the bond, Toni reports the interest on her tax return, but excludes the interest from her taxable income because she used the funds to pay for qualified higher education expenses for her dependent daughter in the same year.

122

10. The answer is D. If a taxpayer is given a choice between receiving cash or stock, a stock dividend is taxable in the year it is distributed.

11. The answer is C. Miguel must include the total amount of interest earned, $375, in his income. If he itemizes deductions on Schedule A, he can deduct $200 of interest expense, subject to the net investment income limit. He may not report the investment income and expenses on a net basis.

12. The answer is A. Interest earned on state and local bonds (muni bonds) are generally tax-exempt at the federal level. Although the interest is not taxable, it must still be reported on the taxpayer's federal return. Note that these bonds may be taxable at the state and local level, even if they are not taxable at the federal level.

13. The answer is C. Kent earned the dividends in 2016, and whether or not he received a 1099-DIV is irrelevant. Mutual fund dividends are taxable in the year declared regardless of whether the taxpayer withdraws the dividends or reinvests them, so Kent must report the earnings in 2016.

14. The answer is A. If no other interest is credited to Marcelo during the year, the Form 1099-INT he receives will show $20 of interest for the year. The IRS does not count reward points or cash back from a credit card as taxable interest income, so Marcelo does not have to report the $100 or pay tax on it.

15. The answer is B. Ordinary dividends are taxed at higher ordinary income rates than qualified dividends. If certain conditions are met, qualified dividends are given preferred tax treatment. Qualified dividends must have been paid by a U.S. corporation or a qualified foreign corporation, and the taxpayer generally must have held the stock for more than 60 days during the 121-day period that begins 60 days before the ex-dividend date.

16. The answer is A. The savings bond education tax exclusion permits qualified taxpayers to exclude from their gross income all or part of the interest paid upon the redemption of eligible Series EE and I Bonds. Eligible educational expenses include tuition and required fees. The costs of room and board, as well as books, are not eligible expenses.

17. The answer is B. To exclude interest earnings on Series EE and Series I bonds, a taxpayer must be at least 24 years old before the bond's issue date.

Unit 6: Basis of Assets

> **For additional information read:**
> Publication 551, *Basis of Assets*
> Publication 544, *Sales and Other Dispositions of Assets*

The tax treatment of an asset varies based on whether the asset is personal-use, business property, or investment property. When an asset is sold, the difference between the asset's basis and the selling price may be a taxable gain or loss. Sometimes, when an asset is disposed of or sold, no gain or loss is recognized until a later date. In order to correctly calculate gains and losses, you must first understand the concept of basis.

Study Note: Understanding basis and how it is applied to various types of property is critical to your success in passing Part 1 *and* Part 2 of the EA exam. You will be expected to calculate basis in multiple questions.

The initial basis of an asset is usually its cost. However, there are instances in which basis is determined based upon the fair market value of the asset when acquired by the taxpayer, rather than its cost, typically when property is acquired by inheritance and sometimes by gift. The cost basis of an asset may include:

- Sales taxes charged during the purchase
- Freight-in charges and shipping fees
- Installation costs and testing fees
- Delinquent real estate taxes that are paid by the buyer of a property
- Legal and accounting fees to transfer an asset

Example: Raoul purchases a new car for $15,000. The sales tax on the vehicle is $1,200. He also pays a delivery charge to have the car shipped from another dealership to his home. The freight charge is $210. Therefore, Raoul's basis in the vehicle is $16,410 ($15,000 + $1,200 + $210).

Example: Hilda is a self-employed writer. She purchases a new printer for her home office. The printer costs $540, with an additional $34 for sales tax. Therefore, Hilda's basis in the item is $574 ($540 + $34).

In order to correctly report a taxable gain or loss related to disposition of an asset, a taxpayer needs to identify:

- The asset's basis or adjusted basis:
  - o As described above, the initial basis of an asset is usually its purchase cost, including certain ancillary charges.
  - o Adjusted basis includes the original basis plus any increases or decreases resulting from events, transactions, or tax benefits that occur after the original purchase or acquisition by the taxpayer (such as subsequent improvements, depreciation deductions, casualty losses, rebates, and insurance reimbursements).
- The asset's holding period:
  - o Short-term property is held one year or less.
  - o Long-term property is held <u>more</u> than one year (at least a year, plus one day).
- The proceeds from the sale.

Example: Brian buys a house for $120,000. The following year, he paves the driveway, which costs $6,000. Brian's adjusted basis in the home is now $126,000 ($120,000 original cost + $6,000 for major improvements).

Example: Whitney purchases a commercial washing machine for her pet grooming business. The washer costs $1,230, with an additional $62 of sales tax and freight and installation charges of $96, all of which increase the basis. Whitney receives a manufacturer's rebate check for $300 several weeks later, which decreases the basis. Her basis in the washer is figured as follows:

Cost:	$1,230
Sales tax:	62
Professional installation:	96
Rebate:	(300)
Adjusted Basis:	**$1,088**

Depreciation

Depreciation is an income tax deduction that allows a business to recover the cost or basis of property used in the business over time. It is an annual allowance for the wear and tear, deterioration, or obsolescence of assets. The amount allowed as an annual depreciation deduction is intended to roughly approximate the reduction in the value of assets as they age. Property ceases to be depreciable when the business has fully recovered the property's cost, or when the taxpayer sells or retires it from service, whichever happens first.

Some types of property, such as land, cannot be depreciated. Most other types of tangible property, such as buildings, machinery, vehicles, furniture, and equipment, are depreciable.

Study Note: Depreciation is an important business concept, so it is tested most often on *Part 2: Businesses* of the EA exam. For Part 1 of the EA exam, test-takers must understand depreciation primarily in the context of rental property.

Basis of Real Property (Real Estate)

The basis of real estate usually includes a number of costs in addition to the purchase price. If a taxpayer purchases real property (such as land or a building), certain fees and other expenses are included in the cost basis. They may include real estate taxes the seller owed at the time of the purchase if the real estate taxes were paid by the buyer.

Example: Tara sells Lawrence a home for $100,000. She had fallen behind on her property tax payments, so Lawrence agrees to pay $3,500 of delinquent real estate taxes as a condition of the sale. Because a taxpayer is not allowed to deduct property taxes that are not his legal responsibility, Lawrence must add the property taxes paid to his basis. His basis in the home is $103,500 ($100,000 + $3,500).

If a property is constructed rather than purchased, the basis of the property includes the expenses of construction. This includes the cost of payments to contractors, building materials, and inspection fees.

Demolition costs and other costs related to the preparation of land prior to construction must be added to the basis of the land, rather than to any buildings constructed on it later.

> **Example:** Wanda pays $50,000 for an empty lot where she plans to build her home. She also pays $2,800 for the removal of tree stumps and $6,700 to demolish an existing concrete foundation on the lot. These costs must be added to the basis of the land, not to the basis of the house. Therefore, Wanda's basis in the land is $59,500 ($50,000 + $2,800 + $6,700).

Settlement Costs: Generally, a taxpayer must include settlement costs for the purchase of property in his basis. The following fees are some of the closing costs that can be included in a property's basis:

- Abstract fees
- Charges for installing utilities
- Legal fees (including title search and preparation of the deed)
- Recording fees
- Surveys
- Transfer taxes
- Owner's title insurance

Also included in a property's basis are any amounts the seller legally owes that the buyer agrees to pay, such as recording or mortgage fees, charges for improvements or repairs, and sales commissions. A taxpayer cannot include fees incidental to getting a loan in the basis of the property financed with proceeds from the loan.

Basis of Securities

A taxpayer's basis in securities (such as stocks or bonds) is usually the purchase price plus any additional costs (e.g., brokers' commissions).

When a taxpayer sells securities, his investment broker should provide Form 1099-B, *Proceeds from Broker and Barter Exchange Transactions,* by January 31 following the end of the tax year, showing the proceeds of the sale. The IRS also receives a copy of Form 1099-B. If Form 1099-B does not identify a taxpayer's basis, the taxpayer must keep track of this information. If a taxpayer cannot provide evidence of his basis in an asset sold, the IRS may deem the basis to be zero.

> **Note:** The IRS requires stockbrokers and mutual fund companies to report the basis for most stock purchased. The reporting is made to investors and to the IRS. You must understand how to calculate the basis of securities because this subject is tested frequently on Part 1 of the exam.

A taxpayer may own more than one block of shares in a particular company's stock. Each block may differ from the others in its holding period (long-term or short-term), its basis, or both. When directing a broker to sell stock, a taxpayer may specify which block, or part of a block, to sell; this is called *specific identification*. The specific identification method requires good recordkeeping; however, it simplifies the determination of the holding period and the basis of stock sold, and gives the taxpayer better control over the recognition of taxable income and losses when selling part of an investment.

If the taxpayer cannot identify a specific block at the time of sale, shares sold are treated as coming from the earliest block purchased. This method is called First In, First Out (FIFO).

Example: Tia bought 50 shares of stock of Yates Corp. in 2008 for $10 a share. In 2009, Tia bought another 200 shares of Yates Corp. for $11 a share. In 2011, she bought an additional 100 shares for $9 a share. In 2016, she sells 130 shares. She cannot identify the exact shares she sold, so she must use the stock FIFO method to determine the basis of the shares that she sold. Tia calculates her stock basis as follows:

Shares purchased:

Year Purchased	# of shares	Cost per share	Total cost
2007	50	$10	$500
2008	200	$11	$2,200
2010	100	$9	$900
Total shares:	**350**		

The basis of the stock sold is figured as follows:

50 shares (50 × $10) of stock bought in 2008	$500
80 shares (80 × $11) of stock bought in 2009	$880
Total basis of stock sold in <u>2016</u>	**<u>$1,380</u>**

Example: Amber buys two blocks of 400 shares of stock (800 shares total). She buys 400 on May 1, 2013, for $11,200, and an additional 400 shares two months later for $11,600. On September 10, 2016, she sells 400 shares for $11,500 without specifying which block of shares she is selling. The sold shares are therefore treated as coming from the earliest block purchased (those purchased in May 2013). Since the basis and holding period defaults to the original block of shares, Amber realizes a long-term capital gain of $300 ($11,500 - $11,200).

Events that occur after the purchase of stock can require adjustments (increases or decreases) to the basis per individual share.

For example, the original basis per share can be changed by events such as stock dividends and stock splits. Stock dividends and stock splits usually are not taxable events. However, a stock dividend may be taxable when shareholders have the option to receive cash or other property instead of stock.

- **Stock dividends** are additional shares a company grants to its shareholders in lieu of paying cash dividends. These additional shares increase the number of shares owned by an individual shareholder, so his original basis is spread over more shares, which decreases the basis per individual share. The total basis of all the shares remains the same.
- A **stock split** is similar to a stock dividend and occurs when a company issues additional shares of stock for every existing share an investor holds. Stock splits are a way for a company to

lower the market price of its stock. For example, in a 2-for-1 stock split, a corporation issues one share of stock for every share outstanding. This decreases a shareholder's basis per individual share by half. An original basis of $200 for 100 shares becomes $200 for 200 shares in a 2-for-1 stock split. However, the total basis in the stock remains the same even though the basis per share decreases.

> **Example:** Victoria pays $1,050 for 100 shares of stock, plus a broker's commission of $50. Her basis in the 100 shares is $1,100 ($1,050 original cost + $50 broker's commission), or $11 per share ($1,100/100). Victoria later receives ten additional shares of stock as a stock dividend. Her $1,100 basis must be spread over 110 shares (100 original shares plus the ten-share stock dividend). Her basis per share decreases to $10 ($1,100/110).

> **Example:** Sean buys 100 shares of WinPro Corp. for $50 per share. His cost basis is $50 × 100 shares or $5,000. In 2016, WinPro declares a 2-for-1 stock split, and Sean receives 100 additional shares of stock. Therefore, his new basis in each individual stock is $25 = ($5,000 ÷ [100+100]). His total basis in the shares remains $5,000.

Stock Options

A taxpayer may purchase options to buy or sell property, such as stocks or commodities, through an exchange or in the open market. He may realize a gain or loss from the sale or trade of an option itself, or he may exercise the option to buy or sell the underlying property and realize a gain or loss from disposition of that property.

In addition, companies may grant options to their employees, as compensation for their service and as an incentive that allows them to purchase the company's stock at a later date. If an employee receives stock options, he may have income when the options are granted, when he exercises them (to buy the company's stock), or when he sells or otherwise disposes of the options or the stock. In general, there are two types of stock options:

- **Incentive Stock Options (ISOs)**
- **Nonqualified Stock Options (NSOs)**

These options are treated very differently for tax purposes. In most cases, incentive stock options (ISOs) provide more a favorable tax treatment than nonqualified stock options (NSOs). In the next section, we will cover these two types of options and their taxable effect on individual taxpayers.

> **Note:** For Part 1 of the EA Exam, you must understand the concept of stock options from the perspective of the individual taxpayer *receiving* the options. For Part 2 of the EA Exam, you must understand stock options from the point of view of the corporation *issuing* the stock options.

The nature, timing and amount of income depend on whether the options are considered to be *statutory* or *nonstatutory* options.

Statutory Stock Options

There are two types of statutory stock options:

- **Incentive Stock Options (ISOs)** allow employees to purchase stock at a pre-established price (exercise price) that may be below the actual market price on the date of exercise.
- Stock options granted under **Employee Stock Purchase Plans (ESPPs)**.

For either of these types of options, the taxpayer must normally be an employee of the company granting the option, or a related company, at all times during the period beginning on the date the option is granted and ending three months before the option is exercised.

The tax advantage of a statutory stock option is that income is not reported when the option is granted or when it is exercised. Income is only reported once the stock is ultimately sold.

However, the bargain element of an ISO, representing the difference between the exercise price and the market value of the stock on the exercise date, is considered a tax preference item for purposes of the alternative minimum tax. The employee's basis in the stock is the actual amount paid at exercise plus any amounts paid for the option itself or in connection with the exercise of it. Thus, the employee may have taxable income or a deductible loss when he sells the stock he bought by exercising the option. The income or loss will generally be treated as capital gain or loss if the employee:

- Does not sell the stock until two years after the date of the grant of the option, and
- The stock is held by the employee for at least one year after the option is exercised. Otherwise, all or a portion may be treated as ordinary income or loss.[21]

> **Example:** The Bodysculpt Fitness Corporation has an employee stock purchase plan (ESPP). The option price is the lower of the stock price at the time the option is granted or at the time the option is exercised. The value of the stock when the option was granted was $25. Bodysculpt Fitness deducts $5 from Morgan's pay every week for 48 weeks (total = $240 [$5 × 48]). The value of the stock when the option is exercised is $20. Morgan receives 12 shares of Bodysculpt stock ($240 ÷ $20). Her holding period for all 12 shares begins the day after the option is exercised, even though the money used to purchase the shares was deducted from her pay on many different days. Morgan's basis in each share is $20.

Nonstatutory Stock Options

A nonstatutory or nonqualified stock option (NQSO) also allows an employee to purchase stock at a pre-established exercise price.

If the option is actively traded on an established market or its FMV is otherwise readily determinable, the employee must recognize compensation income, either at the date of grant, if there are no restrictions that affect its value to the employee, or at a later date when any restrictions no longer apply.

---

[21] IRC Section 422(a)

Note: A major difference between ISOs (Incentive Stock Options) and NQSOs (Nonqualified Stock Options) is that, with NQSOs, the difference between the strike price[22] and market price is included on the employee's Form W-2 in the year granted (the amounts are usually reported on Form W-2, Box 14 as code V). The ordinary income for ISOs isn't reported until the option is exercised.

Example: Patricia works for a company that grants her a nonstatutory stock option to buy 1,000 shares of stock at $5 per share. At the date of the grant, the stock is trading at $7.50 per share, and there are no restrictions on Patricia's ability to exercise the option or sell the shares, so she must recognize $2,500 of ordinary income (equal to the discount of $2.50 per share for each of the 1,000 shares). In year five, Patricia exercises her options and purchases 1,000 shares of stock at $5 per share. The ordinary income would be included in her Form W-2 in Box 14 (Code V). The stock is now worth $20 per share, and she sells all 1,000 shares at that price. She recognizes $12,500 as capital gain, the difference between the selling price ($20,000) and her basis in the stock of $7,500 (purchase price of $5,000 for the stock plus the gain of $2,500 recognized when her stock options were granted).

If the option's FMV is not readily determinable at the date of grant, the difference between the exercise price and the market value of the stock on the exercise date must be recognized as ordinary income in the year the option is exercised.

An employee's basis in stock is the market value of the stock at the time of grant or exercise plus any amount paid for the option itself.

Example: Basil works for a company that grants employees Incentive stock options. In 2016, Basil has the opportunity to buy 1,000 shares of company stock at $2 per share. The stock is not sold on the open market,[23] and its fair market value cannot be readily determined. Basil does not recognize income at the time the stock is granted. A few years later, the company has an initial public offering, and its stock sells for $10 per share. Basil exercises his stock options and purchases 1,000 shares of stock at $2 per share. Basil must recognize $8,000 as ordinary income.

Basis Other Than Cost

The following are examples of situations in which an asset's basis is determined by something other than purchase cost.

Property in Exchange for Services: If a taxpayer receives property in payment for services, he must include the property's FMV in income, and this becomes his basis in the property. If two people agree on a cost for services beforehand, the agreed-upon cost may be used to establish the amount included as income and as the asset's basis.

Example: Cassidy is a CPA who prepares tax returns for a long-time client named Katie. Katie loses her job and cannot pay Cassidy's bill, which totals $400. Katie offers Cassidy an antique vase in lieu of paying her invoice. The fair market value of the vase is approximately $525. Cassidy agrees to accept the vase as full payment on Katie's delinquent invoice. Cassidy's basis in the vase is $400, the amount of the invoice that was agreed upon by both parties.

---

[22] The "strike price" is the price at which the option holder can purchase the underlying security.
[23] Incentive stock options (ISOs) are a type of employee stock option that can be granted only to employees. ISOs are also sometimes referred to as incentive share options or Qualified Stock Options by the IRS.

Basis After Casualty Loss: If a taxpayer has a casualty loss, he increases the basis in the property by the amount spent on repairs that restore the property to its pre-casualty condition. However, he must also decrease the basis of the property by any related insurance proceeds.

> **Example:** Ira paid $5,000 for a car several years ago. It was damaged in a flood, so he spends $3,000 to repair it. He does not have flood insurance on the car. Therefore, his new basis in the car is $8,000 ($5,000 + $3,000).

Basis After Mortgage Assumption: If a taxpayer buys property and assumes an existing mortgage on it, the taxpayer's basis includes the amount paid for the property plus the amount owed on the mortgage. The basis also includes the settlement fees and closing costs paid to buy the property. However, fees and costs for obtaining a loan on the property (points) are not included in a property's basis.

> **Example:** Sondra buys a building for $20,000 cash and also assumes an existing mortgage of $80,000 on it. Therefore, her basis is $100,000.

Basis of Property Transferred from a Spouse: The basis of property transferred by a spouse (or former spouse if the transfer is due to divorce) is the same as the spouse's adjusted basis. Generally, there is no gain or loss recognized on the transfer of property between spouses (or between former spouses if the transfer is because of divorce). This rule applies even if the transfer was in exchange for cash, the release of marital rights, the assumption of liabilities, or other considerations.

> **Example:** Before they divorced, Margot and Zachary jointly owned a home that had a basis of $50,000 and an FMV of $250,000. When they divorced last year, Margot transferred her entire interest in the home to Zachary as part of their property settlement. Zachary's basis in the home is the same as their original joint basis of $50,000.

Basis of Inherited Property

The basis of inherited property is generally the FMV of the property on the date of the decedent's death, regardless of what the deceased person paid for the property. This means that if the property is sold by the beneficiary, gain will be calculated based on the change in value from the date of death.

This usually results in a beneficial tax situation for anyone who inherits property because the taxpayer generally gets an increased or "stepped up" basis. However, there are cases in which this rule can work against taxpayers. Although the value of most property such as stocks, collectibles, and bonds increases over time, there are also instances in which a property's value drops. This creates a "stepped down" basis.

Although the basis of an estate for estate tax purposes is usually determined on the date of death, a special rule allows the personal representative of the estate to elect a different valuation date of six months after the date of death. This is known as the alternate valuation date.

To elect the alternate valuation date, the estate's value and related estate tax must be less than they would have been on the date of the taxpayer's death. If the alternate valuation date has been elected for the estate, the basis for inherited assets is normally the fair market value of the assets six months after the date of death.

However, if any assets are received from the estate less than six months after the date of death, the basis in these inherited assets is the fair market value as of the date the asset was distributed to the heir.

Example #1: Sasha's uncle bought 300 shares of stock many years ago for $500. Sasha inherited the stock when her uncle died. On the date of his death, the stock was valued at $9,000, so Sasha's basis is $9,000. She later sells the stock for $11,000. She has a gain of $2,000 ($11,000 - $9,000).

Example #2: With the same facts, if Sasha were to sell the stock for $8,000, she would have a loss of $1,000 ($9,000 - $8,000).

Example #3: Sasha's aunt also bought 100 shares of stock many years ago for $10,000. Sasha inherited the stock when her aunt died. On the date of her aunt's death, the value of the stock was $500, meaning Sasha's basis in the stock is stepped down for tax purposes to $500. She later sells the stock for $500. She cannot report a loss on the stock.

If a federal estate tax return (Form 706) is not filed for the deceased taxpayer, the basis in the beneficiary's inherited property is the FMV value at the date of death, and the alternate valuation date does not apply.

Basis of Gifted Property

The basis of property received as a gift is determined differently than property that is purchased. The taxpayer must know the donor's adjusted basis in the property when it was gifted, its fair market value on the date of the gift, and the amount of gift tax the donor paid on it, if any.

Generally, the basis of gifted property for the donee is equal to the donor's adjusted basis. This is called a "transferred basis". For example, if a taxpayer gives his son a car and the taxpayer's basis in the car is $2,000, the basis of the vehicle remains $2,000 for the son. The holding period of the gift would also transfer to the donee.

Example: Alicia's father gives her 50 shares of stock that he purchased ten years ago. Her father has an adjusted basis in the stock of $500. Alicia's basis in the stock, for purposes of determining gain on any future sale, is also $500 (this is a "transferred basis"). Alicia is also considered to have "held" the stock for ten years, the same amount of time that her father held the stock.

In situations where the fair market value of the property on the date of the gift is less than the transferred basis, the donee's basis for gain is the transferred basis. However, if the donee reports a loss on the sale of gifted property, his basis is the lower of the transferred basis or the FMV of gifted property on the date of the gift.

The sale of gifted property can also result in no gain or loss. This happens when the sale proceeds are greater than the gift's FMV but less than the transferred basis.

Example: Benny's Aunt Roberta bought 100 shares of IBM stock when it was at $92 per share. Roberta's basis for the 100 shares is $9,200. Roberta gives the stock to Benny when it is selling at $70 and has an FMV of $7,000. In this case, Benny has a dual basis in the stock. He has one basis for purposes of determining a gain, and a different basis for determining a loss. Here are three separate scenarios that help illustrate how the gain or loss would be calculated when Benny sells the gifted stock:

Scenario #1: If Benny sells the stock for more than his aunt's basis, he will use her basis to determine his amount of gain. For example, if he sells the stock for $11,000, he will report a gain of $1,800 ($11,000 - $9,200).

Scenario #2: If Benny sells the stock for less than the FMV of the stock at the time of the gift ($7,000 in the example), he will use as his basis the FMV at the time of the gift to determine the amount of his loss. For example, if the stock continues to decline and Benny eventually sells it for $4,500, he can report a loss of $2,500 ($7,000 - $4,500).

Scenario #3: If Benny sells the stock for an amount between the FMV and the donor's basis, no gain or loss will be recognized. For example, if Benny sells the stock for $8,000, there will be no gain or loss on the transaction (his basis will be deemed to be $8,000, the same as his sales price).

Unit 6: Study Questions

(Test yourself first, then check the correct answers at the end of this quiz.)

1. Stephen purchases a truck for $15,000 to use in his carpentry business. He pays $5,000 in cash and finances the remaining $10,000 with a five-year loan. He also pays taxes and delivery costs of $1,300 and $250 to install a protective bedliner. What is Stephen's basis for depreciation of the truck?

A. $6,550
B. $10,000
C. $16,550
D. $16,300

2. On June 1, 2016, Pham Software Corporation granted 500 Incentive Stock Options to one of their executives, Wesley. The stock had an option price of $25. On December 31, 2016, Wesley exercised all of his options when the market price per share was $50. What is the basis of his stock and how much should be included on his Form W-2 as income for 2016?

A. Basis $12,500; income $0
B. Basis $0; income $0
C. Basis $12,500; income $12,500
D. Basis $12,500; income $25,000

3. Which of the following is not added to the basis of a property?

A. Legal and accounting fees.
B. Points on a loan.
C. Sales tax.
D. Freight-in charges.

4. The basis of inherited property is generally:

A. The adjusted basis to the decedent.
B. The fair market value of the property on the date of the decedent's death.
C. The purchase price that the decedent paid.
D. Determined nine months after the death of the decedent.

5. On February 11, 2016, Henry bought 1,000 shares of stock for $4 per share and paid an additional $70 for his broker's commission. What is Henry's basis in the stock?

A. $1,000
B. $4,000
C. $4,070
D. None of the above

6. Mackenzie purchases an empty lot at auction for $50,000. She pays $15,000 in cash and finances the remaining $35,000 with a bank loan. The lot has a $4,000 lien against it for unpaid property taxes, which she also agrees to pay. Which of the following statements is correct?

A. Her basis in the property is $50,000, and she can deduct the property taxes on her Schedule A as property taxes paid.
B. Her basis in the property is $19,000.
C. Her basis in the property is $54,000.
D. Her basis in the property is $46,000.

7. On January 3, 2016, Brigit purchased 1,000 shares of stock at a cost of $5,100, including the broker's commission. On August 14, 2016, she sold 500 shares for $3,300. What is the adjusted basis of the stock she sold?

A. $5,100
B. $2,550
C. $3,300
D. $3,255

8. Which statement is not correct about the basis of assets?

A. The basis of an asset is always equal to its cost.
B. The basis of purchased stocks or bonds is the acquisition price plus any additional costs, such as brokers' commissions.
C. The adjusted basis of a property must be determined before figuring gain or loss on the sale or exchange of the property.
D. The cost basis of an asset includes sales tax and other expenses connected with the purchase.

9. Two years ago, Arnold paid $1,050 for 100 shares of Kirkner Corporation stock, plus a broker's commission of $50. During the year, Arnold received ten additional shares of Kirkner stock as a nontaxable stock dividend. What is the adjusted basis of Arnold's stock at the end of the year?

A. $9 per share
B. $10 per share
C. $11 per share
D. $25 per share

10. Julian owned one share of common stock that he bought for $45. The corporation distributed two new shares of common stock for each share held. Julian then had three shares of common stock. What is Julian's basis for each share?

A. $5
B. $45
C. $15
D. $135

11. If a taxpayer cannot determine his basis in a property and the property is sold, the IRS will deem the basis to be:

A. Zero.
B. Fair market value.
C. Actual cost.
D. Average cost.

12. During the year, Clementine bought 52 total shares of GRE Corporation for $624. That cost included a $40 broker commission. Later, in the year, GRE Corporation issued a 2-for-1 stock split. What is her basis per share after the split?

A. $12 per share
B. $6 per share
C. $24 per share
D. $26 per share

13. Which of the following must be added to the basis of a property, rather than deducted as a current expense on a taxpayer's return?

A. Casualty loss.
B. The cost of demolishing a building.
C. Personal property tax based on the value of a car.
D. Investment interest expense.

14. David wishes to sell a home that he inherited from his mother last year. His mother had paid $45,000 for the home ten years ago. She put a new roof on the property two years ago at a cost of $10,500. The fair market value of the home on the date of his mother's death was $120,000. An estate tax return was not required for his mother's estate, and the alternate valuation date was not elected. What is David's basis in the home?

A. $45,000
B. $55,500
C. $34,500
D. $120,000

15. Esteban installs artificial turf at a client's home and bills the client $1,500. After the installation, his client, Alice, receives a foreclosure notice and is unable to pay Esteban's bill. Alice has a golden-doodle show dog that just had puppies. The FMV of each puppy is $1,800. Esteban loves animals and decides to take one of the puppies as full payment on Alice's delinquent bill. What is Esteban's basis in his new dog?

A. $0
B. $300
C. $1,500
D. $1,800

16. On April 1, 2016, Miletech Corporation granted 1,000 Nonqualified Stock Options to Gary, (an employee). The exercise price on the shares was $23 per share. On December 31, 2016, Gary exercised all of his options when the market price per share was $43. What is the basis of his stock, and what amount should be included on Gary's Form W-2 as wage income in 2016?

A. Basis $23,000; income $0
B. Basis $43,000; income $20,000
C. Basis $0; income $0
D. None of the above

17. Flora gave Clifford a rental property. She had purchased the property ten years ago for $120,000 and claimed $18,000 in depreciation. The fair market value of the rental house on the day of transfer was $144,000. Assuming no gift tax was paid, what is Clifford's basis in the property?

A. $102,000
B. $120,000
C. $126,000
D. $144,000

18. Claire owned two shares of common stock. She bought one for $30 in 2008 and the other for $45 in 2011. In 2016, the corporation distributed two new shares of common stock for each share held. Claire had six shares after the distribution. How is the basis allocated between these six shares?

A. All six shares now have a basis of $12.50.
B. Three shares have a basis of $10 each and three have a basis of $15 each.
C. The shares are valued at $45 each.
D. None of the above.

19. Which of the following does not decrease the basis of an asset?

A. Depreciation.
B. Manufacturers' rebates.
C. Theft losses.
D. Assessments for local improvements.

20. Becky owns a piece of land she purchased several years ago for $25,000. The land is now worth $75,000. During the year, she borrows $50,000 from the bank to improve the property. She uses $46,000 of the loan to demolish an existing foundation on the property and clear it for construction, which will begin next year. What is Becky's basis in the land after the demolition is completed?

A. $0
B. $30,000
C. $71,000
D. $75,000

Unit 6: Answers

1. The answer is C. Stephen's basis in the truck includes the cost of acquiring the property (including any taxes associated with the purchase and delivery charges) and preparing it for use (in this case, installing the bedliner). Therefore, his basis is as follows: ($15,000 + $1,300 + $250) = $16,550. Any funds that are borrowed to pay for an asset are included in the basis.

2. The answer is A. For Incentive Stock Options (ISOs), the basis in the stock is the actual price per share paid upon exercise of the options. In this case, the executive's basis is 500 × $25 = $12,500. The bargain element attributable to the difference between the exercise price and the value at the date of exercise ([$50 - $25] × 500 shares = $12,500) is not recognized by the taxpayer until the stock is sold. However, the taxpayer may need to make an adjustment for alternative minimum tax (AMT) purposes for the bargain element. When the stock is sold, income will be recognized for the difference between his basis and the net proceeds of the sale. Note that the rules are different for Incentive Stock Options (ISOs) and Nonqualified Stock Options (NSOs). They are treated very differently for tax purposes.

3. The answer is B. Points related to a loan used to acquire property may be deductible in the year they are paid or amortizable over the term of the loan. They are not added to the basis of the property.

4. The answer is B. The basis of inherited property is generally the FMV of the property on the date of the decedent's death, regardless of what the deceased person paid for the property.

5. The answer is C. Henry's basis in the stock is $4,070 ([1,000 × $4] = $4,000 + $70).

6. The answer is C. Mackenzie's basis is determined as follows: ($50,000 + $4,000 = $54,000). She cannot deduct the delinquent property taxes on her Schedule A. Any obligations of the seller assumed by the buyer increase the basis of the asset and are not currently deductible. Since Mackenzie did not owe the property taxes, but she still agreed to pay them, she must add the property tax to the basis of the property.

7. The answer is B. Brigit's original basis in the total stock was $5,100, which is $5.10 per share, so her basis in the 500 shares she sold is 500 × $5.10, or $2,550.

8. The answer is A. In many situations, the initial basis of an asset is its cost, including any sales tax or brokers' commissions paid. However, there are many other times when cost cannot be used to determine basis, such as when an asset is inherited or received as a gift.

9. The answer is B. Arnold's original basis per share was $11 ([$1,050 + $50 broker's commission = $1,100] ÷ 100). After the stock dividend, his $1,100 basis must be spread over 110 shares (100 original shares plus the additional 10 shares). Therefore, if Arnold's basis in the stock was $1,100 for 100 shares, the ten additional shares mean Arnold's basis per share decreased to $10 per share ($1,100 ÷ 110).

10. The answer is C. Julian's basis in each share is $15 ($45 ÷ 3). If a taxpayer receives a nontaxable stock dividend, he divides the adjusted basis of the stock by the total number of shares of stock (old and new). The result is the taxpayer's basis for each share of stock.

11. The answer is A. In order to compute gain or loss on a sale, a taxpayer must determine his basis in the property sold. If he cannot determine his basis in the property, the IRS will deem the basis to be zero.

12. The answer is B. The stock is $6 per share after the stock split. Figure the answer as follows:

Initial purchase: 52 shares=$624 ($40 broker commission already included in the price)
2-for-1 stock split doubles the shares to 104 total shares, so $624 (original basis) ÷ 104 shares = **$6 per share**.

13. The answer is B. Demolition costs are not deductible. They must be added to the basis of the land on which the building was located.

14. The answer is D. David's basis in the home is $120,000, the FMV on the date of his mother's death. Heirs can generally use a stepped-up basis for inherited property, regardless of what the deceased person actually paid for the asset. The basis of inherited property is generally the FMV of the property on the date of the decedent's death. When the property is ultimately sold, the beneficiary's gain or loss will be calculated based on the change in value from the date of death.

15. The answer is C. If a taxpayer receives property as payment for services, he must include the property's FMV in income, and this becomes his basis. However, if the two parties agree on a cost beforehand, the IRS will usually accept the agreed-upon cost as the asset's basis.

16. The answer is B. The options were issued at an exercise price of $23, which means that $20,000 ($43 - $23 = $20 × 1,000), representing the difference between his exercise price and the stock's value at exercise, must be included in his W-2 for 2016. The basis of the stock would be the value on December 31, 2016 ($43,000), which includes the amount paid for the stock ($23,000) and the amount of taxable income recognized ($20,000). When the stock is later sold, the taxpayer would recognize gain or loss equal to the difference between his sales proceeds and his $43,000 basis in the stock. Note that the rules are different for Incentive Stock Options (ISOs) and Nonqualified Stock Options (NSOs). They are treated very differently for tax purposes.

17. The answer is A. The basis of gifted property for the donee is generally equal to the donor's adjusted basis, which is called a transferred basis. ($120,000 minus $18,000 depreciation = $102,000). If the fair market value of the property on the date of the gift is less than the transferred basis, the donee's basis for gain is the transferred basis. However, if the donee reports a loss on the sale of gifted property, his basis is the lower of the transferred basis or the FMV of gifted property on the date of the gift.

18. The answer is B. The shares now are valued as follows: three with a basis of $10 each ($30 ÷ 3), and three with a basis of $15 each ($45 ÷ 3). If a taxpayer receives a nontaxable stock dividend, she must divide the adjusted basis of the old stock by the number of shares of old and new stock. The result is the taxpayer's basis for each share of stock.

19. The answer is D. The basis of property must be increased for tax assessments the taxpayer is required to pay in order to finance local improvements, such as paving roads and building ditches. Basis is decreased for depreciation deductions and manufacturers' rebates received, and when the taxpayer incurs theft or other casualty losses.

20. The answer is C. Becky's basis in the land is calculated as follows: $25,000 (cost basis) + $46,000 (demolition costs) = $71,000. The loan amount is irrelevant because the act of borrowing does not increase basis; the amount spent on the improvement of the property increases its basis.

Unit 7: Capital Gains and Losses

For additional information read:
Publication 550, *Investment Income and Expenses*
Publication 523, *Selling Your Home*
Publication 544, *Sales and Other Dispositions of Assets*

Many of the items a taxpayer owns and uses for personal or investment purposes are capital assets. The net gains that result from their disposition may be subject to tax at favorable capital gains tax rates. Examples include:

- A main home or vacation home
- Furniture, a car, or a boat
- Antiques
- Stocks, bonds, and mutual funds (except when held for sale by a professional securities dealer)

Note: Losses from the sale of personal-use property, such as a main home, furniture, or jewelry, are not deductible.

Note: Do not confuse "personal-use property" with "personal property". "Personal property" is a legal term that is used by the IRS as well as legal and accounting professionals. The legal definition of "personal property" describes assets *other* than real estate, land, or buildings.

Example: Liam owns a station wagon that he uses to commute to work, run errands, and take on weekend ski trips. He purchased the car four years ago for $21,000. In 2016, he sells the car for $13,000. Liam cannot claim a loss from the sale of the car since it is his personal-use vehicle.

Example: Mason sold his personal computer to his friend for $750. Mason paid $5,000 for the computer five years ago. Mason used the computer to play games, surf the Internet, and pay bills on-line. He did not use the computer for business. Mason cannot deduct a loss on the sale of his personal computer.

Example: Priscilla collects antique coins as a hobby. She is not a professional coin dealer. Two years ago, Priscilla purchased an antique Roman coin at an estate sale for $50. In 2016, she is offered $1,000 for the coin, and she promptly sells it. Priscilla has a taxable capital gain that she must report on her tax return.

Although losses on personal-use property are not deductible, the gains on the sale of personal-use property may be taxable, subject to certain exclusions.

The applicable capital gains tax rate depends on the holding period, the type of asset, and the taxpayer's ordinary income tax bracket.

Noncapital Assets

Assets held for business-use or created by a taxpayer for purposes of earning revenue (author's writings, copyrights, inventory, etc.) are considered noncapital assets. Gains and losses from the sale of business property are reported on Form 4797, *Sales of Business Property*, and in the case of individual taxpayers, the amounts flow through to Form 1040, Schedule D, *Capital Gains and Losses.*

Example: Tony is the sole proprietor of a health club. In 2016, he sells used fitness equipment to make room for new equipment. Since the equipment was business property, Tony reports the sale on Form 4797. Also during the year, Tony sells some stock at a substantial profit. He has a capital gain on the stock that he reports on Schedule D.

The following assets are noncapital assets:

- Inventory or any similar property held for sale to customers
- Depreciable property used in a business, even if it is fully depreciated
- Real property used in a trade or business, such as a commercial building or a residential rental
- Self-produced copyrights, transcripts, manuscripts, drawings, photographs, or artistic compositions
- Accounts receivable or notes receivable acquired by a business
- Stocks and bonds held by professional securities dealers
- Business supplies
- Commodities and derivative financial instruments

Unlike capital assets, the costs of many noncapital assets may be deducted as business expenses when they are sold.

Example: Michael is a self-employed fisherman who reports his income and expenses on Schedule F. In 2016, he sells some of his commercial fishing equipment. The fishing equipment is a noncapital asset, and the sale must be reported on Form 4797, *Sales of Business Property.* Also during the year, Michael sells his vacation home at a substantial loss. Unlike the fishing equipment, the vacation home is a capital asset, but since it is personal-use property, he cannot deduct the loss.

Holding Period (Short-Term or Long-Term)

When a taxpayer disposes of investment property, his holding period affects the tax treatment of his capital gain or loss. This is important because long-term capital gains are taxed at lower rates than short-term gains.

If a taxpayer holds investment property for more than one year, any capital gain or loss is long-term capital gain or loss. If a taxpayer holds investment property for one year or less, any capital gain or loss is short-term capital gain or loss.

Long-term = <u>more</u> than one year (at least a year and a day)
Short-term = one year or less

To determine how long a taxpayer has held an investment property, he must begin counting on the date after the day he acquires the property. The day the taxpayer disposes of the property is part of the holding period.

Example: Nicky bought 50 shares of stock on February 5, 2015, for $10,000. She sells all the shares on February 5, 2016, for $20,500. Nicky's holding period is not more than one year, and so she has a short-term capital gain of $10,500. The short-term gain is taxed at ordinary income tax rates. If Nicky had waited one more day, she would have received long-term capital gain treatment on her gain, and been taxed at a lower rate.

> **Example:** Stuart bought 100 shares of stock on October 1, 2015, for $1,200. To determine his holding period, Stuart must start counting his holding period on October 2, 2015 (the day *after* the purchase). He sells all the stock on October 2, 2016, for $2,850. Stuart's holding period has been more than one year, and therefore, he will recognize a long-term capital gain of $1,650 in 2016 ($2,850 - $1,200).

Stock shares acquired as a result of a nontaxable stock dividend or stock-split have the same holding period as the original shares owned.

> **Example:** On September 10, 2014, Nathan bought 500 shares of Felton Software stock for $1,500, including his broker's commission. On June 6, 2016, Felton Software distributes a 2% nontaxable stock dividend (10 additional shares). Three days later, Nathan sells all his Felton Software stock for $2,030. Although Nathan owned the 10 shares he received as a nontaxable stock dividend for only three days, a long-term holding period applies to all of his shares in the stock. Because he bought the stock for $1,500 and then sold it for $2,030 more than a year later, Nathan has a long-term capital gain of $530 on the sale of the 510 shares.

The holding period for a gift is treated differently than the holding period for purchased property. If a taxpayer receives a gift of property, his holding period normally includes the donor's holding period. This concept is known as *tacking on* the holding period.

> **Example:** Florence gives her niece, Marian, an acre of land. At the time of the gift, the land had an FMV of $23,000. Florence's adjusted basis in the land was $20,000. Florence held the property for six months. Marian holds the land for another seven months. Neither held the property for over a year. Regardless, Marian may "tack on" her holding period to her aunt's holding period. Therefore, if Marian were to sell the property, she would have a long-term capital gain or loss, because jointly they held the property for 13 months or more than one year.

If a taxpayer inherits property, he is considered to have held the property long-term, regardless of how long he actually held it.

Determining Capital Gain or Loss

A taxpayer determines gain or loss on a sale or trade of stock or property by comparing the amount realized with the adjusted basis of the property.

> **Example:** Corbin receives Form 1099-B showing a net sales price of $1,200 on the sale of 600 shares of LeGrand Corporation. He bought the stock six years ago and sold it on September 25, 2016. His basis in LeGrand, including commissions paid, is $1,455. He will report a $255 loss on Schedule D.

A disposition of stock, and the related income or loss must be reported in the year of sale, regardless of when the taxpayer receives the proceeds. Capital losses are netted against capital gains.

A taxpayer can deduct up to $3,000 ($1,500 for MFS) of net capital losses against ordinary income in a tax year. Unused losses in excess of this limit are carried over to later years. The carryover losses are combined with gains and losses that occur in the next year.

Amounts carried over retain their character as either long-term or short-term and are reported on Schedule D. Thus, a long-term capital loss carried over to the next tax year will reduce that year's long-term capital gains before it reduces that year's short-term capital gains.

Example: Nadine purchased 50 shares of Hanson stock five years ago for $5,000. Two years ago, she purchased 750 shares of Sherwin stock for $8,200. In 2016, Nadine sells all her stock. Her Hanson stock sells for $2,000, and her Sherwin stock sells for $13,000. Nadine's gain and loss are both long-term because she held both stocks for more than one year. Her long-term loss and long-term gain are netted against each other, resulting in a net long-term capital gain, as follows:

Stock	Basis	Sale Price	Gain (Loss)
Hanson	$5,000	$2,000	($3,000)
Sherwin	$8,200	$13,000	$4,800
Net Long-term Capital Gain			**$1,800**

Example: Arthur purchased stock three years ago for $16,000. The stock declines in value, and he sells it in 2016 for $12,000. Arthur has a $4,000 long-term capital loss on the stock sale. He also has $60,000 of wages in 2016. He can claim $3,000 of his long-term capital loss against his ordinary income, thereby lowering his gross income to $57,000 ($60,000 - $3,000). The remainder of the long-term capital loss ($1,000) must be carried forward to the following tax year.

Note: Married taxpayers are actually at a disadvantage when deducting capital losses. On a joint return, the capital loss limit is $3,000, which is the same limit for single taxpayers. MFS filers only get half of that (a $1,500 capital loss limit).

Example: Judy and Paul are married and file separate returns (MFS). In 2016, Judy sells some stock and incurs a $5,000 capital loss. Paul also sells some stock and has a $12,500 capital gain. Judy can only claim $1,500 of her loss on her tax return because she is filing MFS. Paul must pay tax on the entire gain on his separate tax return.

A capital loss can be carried over indefinitely during the taxpayer's life. However, once a taxpayer dies, the capital losses not used on the final return cannot be carried over to a beneficiary or an heir. Capital losses always belong to the decedent. Any capital loss carryovers that are not used on the taxpayer's final return are essentially lost.

Worthless Securities

A taxpayer may choose to "abandon" a security that has lost its entire value in order to take advantage of the loss for tax purposes rather than retaining ownership. Stocks, stock rights, and bonds (other than those held for sale by a securities dealer) that became worthless during the tax year are treated as though they were sold for zero dollars on the last day of the tax year. To abandon a worthless security, a taxpayer must permanently surrender all rights to it and receive no consideration in exchange.

Example: Reginald owned 500 shares of WorldCom stock. The company files for bankruptcy and the bankruptcy court extinguishes all rights of the former shareholders. Reginald learns of the bankruptcy court's decision in December 2016. Rather than wait for a formal notice from the court, he chooses to abandon his WorldCom securities, knowing that his shares are essentially worthless. He takes a capital loss on his 2016 tax return, reflecting the value of his worthless shares as "zero."

A loss from worthless securities receives special tax treatment. Unlike other losses, a taxpayer is allowed to amend a tax return for up to seven years in order to claim a loss from worthless securities. This is more than double the usual three-year statute of limitations for amending returns.

Capital Gains from Mutual Funds

A mutual fund is a regulated investment company generally created by pooling funds of investors to allow them to take advantage of a diversity of investments and professional management. Two different types of transactions may result in taxable capital gains reporting by a taxpayer who invests in mutual funds.

First, profits resulting from investments made by the fund itself are reported to its own shareholders as capital gain distributions on Form 1099-DIV. The capital gain distributions are always taxed at long-term capital gains tax rates, without regard to how long a taxpayer has owned shares in the mutual fund.

In addition, if a taxpayer disposes of shares that represent all or a portion of his investment in the mutual fund itself, Form 1099-B will be issued. The taxable gain or loss that results from the sale or exchange of the taxpayer's shares in the mutual fund is reported on Form 1040, Schedule D. Brokers are now required to include the basis of mutual funds on Form 1099-B.

Wash Sales

A wash sale occurs when an investor sells a security to claim a capital loss, only to repurchase it again very soon thereafter. A taxpayer cannot deduct a loss on the sale of an investment if an identical investment was purchased within 30 days before or after the sale.

A wash sale is considered to have occurred when a taxpayer sells a security and, within 30 days:
- Buys the identical security,
- Acquires a substantially identical security in a taxable trade, or
- Acquires a contract or option to buy the identical security.

If a taxpayer's loss is disallowed because of the wash sale rules, he must add the disallowed loss to the basis of the new stock or securities.

The result is an increase in the taxpayer's basis in the new stock or securities. This adjustment postpones the loss deduction until the disposition of the new stock or securities.[24]

It is considered a wash sale if a taxpayer sells stock and his spouse then repurchases identical stock within 30 days, even if the spouses file separate tax returns.

---

[24] Wash sale rules do not apply to trades of commodity futures contracts and foreign currencies. The rules also do not apply to dealers in stocks or securities.

Example: Carlos sells 800 shares of Granger Corporation stock on December 4, 2016, resulting in a loss of $3,200. He regrets selling the stock, so on January 2, 2017, he repurchases 800 shares of Granger stock on the open market. Because of the IRS wash sale rules, all of the $3,200 loss is disallowed, and he must add the disallowed loss to the basis of the newly-purchased shares. He cannot take the loss until he finally sells the repurchased shares at some later time.

For purposes of the wash sale rules, securities of one corporation are not considered identical to securities of another corporation. This means that a person can sell shares in one corporation and then purchase shares in a different corporation and this will not trigger a wash sale. Similarly, preferred stock of a corporation is not considered identical to the common stock of the same corporation.

Home Sale Gain or Loss

The following are used to figure the gain or loss on the sale of a home:

- Selling price
- Amount realized
- Basis
- Adjusted basis

Selling Price: The selling price is the total amount the taxpayer received for his main home. It includes money, all notes, mortgages, or other debts taken over by the buyer as part of the sale, and the fair market value of any other property or services that the seller received. Real estate sales proceeds are reported on Form 1099-S, *Proceeds From Real Estate Transactions*. If a taxpayer does not receive a Form 1099-S, he must rely upon sale documents and other records.

Amount Realized: The amount realized is the selling price minus selling expenses, which include commissions, advertising fees, legal fees, and loan charges paid by the seller, such as points.

Basis: The basis in a home is determined by how the taxpayer obtained the home. For example, if a taxpayer purchases a home, the basis is the cost of the home. If a taxpayer builds a home, the basis is the building cost plus the cost of land. If a taxpayer receives a home through inheritance or gift, the basis is either its FMV or the decedent's or donor's adjusted basis.

Example: Eve is single. She sells her home for $350,000. She purchased the home 20 years ago for $50,000 and had lived in it continuously since then. She pays $4,000 in seller's fees to sell the home. Her amount realized in the sale is $346,000 ($350,000 - $4,000 = $346,000). Her basis is subtracted from her amount realized in order to figure her gain: ($346,000 - $50,000 basis) = $296,000.

If the taxpayer inherited the home, the basis is generally its FMV on the date of the decedent's death, or the later alternate valuation date chosen by the representative for the estate.

Adjusted Basis: The adjusted basis is the taxpayer's basis in the home increased or decreased by certain amounts. Increases include additions or improvements to the home that have a useful life of more than one year. Repairs that simply maintain a home in good condition are not considered improvements and should not be added to the basis of the property. Decreases to basis include deductible casualty losses, credits, and product rebates. Depreciation reduces basis for business assets, such as rental property, but is never taken on personal-use property.

Formula for figuring adjusted basis:
Basis + Increases - Decreases = Adjusted Basis
Example: Immanuel purchased his home ten years ago for $125,000. In 2016, he added another bathroom to the property at a cost of $25,000. Immanuel's adjusted basis in the home is therefore $150,000 ($125,000 purchase price + $25,000 addition).

If the amount realized on the sale of a home is less than the adjusted basis, the difference is a loss. A loss on the sale of a primary residence can never be deducted.

If the amount realized is more than the adjusted basis of the property, the difference is a gain. As described in detail later, the taxpayer may be able to exclude all or part of the gain. If not excluded and the taxpayer owns a home for one year or less, the gain is reported as a short-term capital gain. If the taxpayer owns the home for more than one year, the gain is reported as a long-term capital gain.

There are special rules regarding the sale of a taxpayer's primary residence. We will go over those rules later, in the chapter dedicated to nonrecognition property transactions (Unit 8).

Related Party Transaction Rules

Special rules apply to related party transactions, which are between two parties who are joined by a special relationship. If a taxpayer sells an asset to a close family member or to a business entity that the taxpayer controls, he may not receive all the benefits of the capital gains tax rates, and he may not be able to deduct his losses. The rules were made to prevent related persons and entities from shuffling assets back and forth and taking improper losses.

50% Control Rule: If a taxpayer controls more than 50% of a corporation or partnership, any property transactions between the taxpayer and the business are subject to related party transaction rules.

In general, a loss on the sale of property between related parties is not deductible. When the property is later sold to an unrelated party, gain is recognized only to the extent it is more than the disallowed loss. If the property is later sold at a loss, the loss that was disallowed to the related party cannot be recognized.

If a taxpayer sells or trades property at a loss (other than in the complete liquidation of a corporation), the loss is not deductible if the transaction is between the taxpayer and the following related parties:

- Members of immediate family, including a spouse, siblings, ancestors, or descendants (children, grandchildren, etc.).
- A partnership or corporation that the taxpayer controls. A taxpayer "controls" an entity when he has more than 50% ownership in it. This also includes partial ownership by other family members.
- A tax-exempt or charitable organization controlled by the taxpayer or a member of his family.
- Losses on sales between certain closely related trusts or business entities controlled by the same owners.

> **Note:** For purposes of this rule, the following are not considered related parties: uncles, aunts, nephews, nieces, cousins, stepchildren, stepparents, in-laws, and ex-spouses.

> **Example:** Aida buys stock from her brother, Clyde, for $7,600. Clyde's cost basis in the stock is $10,000. He cannot deduct the loss of $2,400 because of the related party transaction rules. Later, Aida sells the same stock on the open market for $10,500, realizing a gain of $2,900. Aida's reportable gain is $500 (the $2,900 gain minus the $2,400 loss not allowed to her brother).

> **Example:** Vicky purchases stock from her father for $8,600. Her father's basis in the stock is $11,000. Vicky later sells the stock on the open market for $6,900. Her recognized loss is $1,700 (her $8,600 basis minus $6,900). Vicky cannot deduct the loss that was disallowed to her father.

> **Example:** Tran sells 100 shares of stock to her step-brother, Thai. She recognizes a $3,000 capital loss on the transaction. Since a step-brother is not considered a related party for IRS purposes, she is allowed to take the loss on her tax return.

In the case of a related party transaction, if a taxpayer sells multiple pieces of property and some are at a gain while others are at a loss, the gains will generally be taxable while the losses cannot be used to offset the gains.

Installment Sales

An installment sale is a sale of property in which at least one payment is expected to be received after the tax year in which the sale occurs. If a taxpayer sells property and receives payments over multiple years, he may use the installment method in order to defer tax by only reporting a portion of his gain as each installment is received.

A taxpayer's gain, or gross profit, is the amount by which the selling price exceeds the adjusted basis in the property sold. A gross profit percentage is calculated by dividing the gross profit from the sale by the selling price.

> **Study Note:** Test-takers may be required to determine gross profit percentage on an installment sale for either Part 1 or Part 2 of the EA exam.

Each payment received on an installment sale typically consists of the following three parts:
- Interest income
- Return of the adjusted basis in the property
- Gain on the sale (determined by applying the gross profit percentage to the amount of the payment received minus the interest portion)

In each year the taxpayer receives a payment, he must report the interest income and the portion that relates to his gain on the sale. The taxpayer does not include in income the part that is the return of his basis in the property. A taxpayer would normally calculate his installment sale income using the following formula: (next)

Calculating Gross Profit Percentage

1. Enter the selling price for the property: _____

2. Enter the adjusted basis for the property: _____

3. Enter the selling expenses: _____

4. Enter any depreciation recapture: _____

5. Add lines 2, 3, and 4. This is the adjusted basis for installment sale purposes: _____

6. Subtract line 5 from line 1. This is the gross profit: _____. (If zero or less, there is no gain, and a taxpayer would not use the installment method.)

7. Divide line 6 by line 1. This is the gross profit percentage: _____

8. Multiply line 7 by amount of the current year installment payment (exclusive of interest income). This is the installment gain recognizable for the year: _____

Definition: When a taxpayer disposes of certain types of property that have been depreciated, the property may be subject to **depreciation recapture**, which requires that the taxpayer report all or a portion of the prior depreciation deductions as ordinary income in the year of the sale.

Example: In 2016, Chloe sells an empty lot with a basis of $40,000 for $100,000. Her gross profit is $60,000 ($100,000 - $40,000) for a gross profit percentage of 60%. She receives a $20,000 down payment and the buyer's note for $80,000. In 2016, Chloe must report $12,000 gain allocated from the down payment she received. The note provides for four annual payments of $20,000 each, plus 8% interest, beginning in 2017. Exclusive of the interest income, she must report $12,000 of her installment gain for each $20,000 payment received ($20,000 × .60 = $12,000).

The selling price includes the cash and any other property to be received from the buyer, any existing mortgage or debt the buyer pays or assumes, and any selling expenses the buyer pays.

However, if the buyer assumes or pays off a mortgage or other debt on the property sold, the calculation of gross profit percentage is affected. The mortgage assumption is considered a recovery of basis in the year of sale and is subtracted before calculating the gross profit percentage, except to the extent that it exceeds the adjusted basis of the property for installment sale purposes.

In contrast, if the property is sold to a buyer who holds a mortgage on it and the mortgage is canceled rather than assumed, the cancellation is treated as a payment received in the year of the sale and is not subtracted in calculating the gross profit percentage.

Example: Ernesto sells property in an installment sale for $6,000. His gross profit is $1,500. The gross profit percentage on the sale is 25% ($1,500 ÷ $6,000). After subtracting interest, Ernesto reports 25% of each payment, including the down payment, as installment sale income in the year received. The remainder of each payment is the tax-free return of the property's basis.

If installment payments are made according to a schedule other than what was originally agreed, income is recognized according to the actual payments received. However, if the parties subsequently agree to adjust the selling price, the gross profit percentage must be recalculated, and income from future installments must be recognized based upon the adjusted gross profit.

If a taxpayer decides not to use the installment method, he must report all the gain in the year of the sale. Installment sale rules do not apply to property that is sold at a loss.

The installment method cannot be used for publicly traded securities, such as stocks and bonds. A taxpayer must report gain on the sale of securities in the year of the sale, regardless of whether the proceeds are received in the following year.

> **Example:** Dillon owns 500 shares of stock, which he sells at a gain on December 29, 2016. Dillon does not receive the proceeds until January 15, 2017. Dillon is required to report the capital gain on the sale of the stock on his 2016 tax return. He cannot delay reporting the gain, and the sale is not considered an installment sale.

Installment sales to related persons are generally allowed. However, if a taxpayer sells property to a related person who then sells or disposes of the property within two years of the original sale, the taxpayer will lose the benefit of installment sale reporting.

> **Example:** Lou sells a plot of land to his daughter, Melanie. The sale price is $25,000, and Lou realizes a profit on the sale of $10,000. Melanie agrees to pay in five installments of $5,000. A year later, Melanie decides she no longer wants the property and she sells the land to another person. Lou must report the entire profit of $10,000 on the sale, even though he may not have received all the installment payments. The installment sale method is disallowed on the related party sale because the property was disposed of during the two-year holding period.

Installment sales are reported on Form 6252, *Installment Sale Income*, which is attached to Form 1040. A taxpayer may also be required to complete Schedule D or Form 4797.

Reporting Asset Sales

Capital gains and losses are typically reported on these two forms:

- Schedule D, *Capital Gains and Losses*, and
- Form 8949, *Sales and Other Dispositions of Capital Assets.*

Taxpayers who must file Form 8949 and Schedule D will not be able to use either the 1040A or the 1040EZ form; they must file Form 1040.

Schedule D is used to report gain or loss on the sale of investment property and most capital gain (or loss) transactions. However, before the taxpayer can calculate their net gain or loss on Schedule D, he may also have to complete Form 8949, *Sales and Other Dispositions of Capital Assets.* Form 8949 reports the details about each stock trade the taxpayer makes during the year.

The totals from certain transactions can be reported directly on Schedule D without needing to report them on Form 8949. A taxpayer can skip filing Form 8949 if both of the following are true:

- He received a Form 1099-B that shows basis was reported to the IRS and does not show a nondeductible wash sale loss in box 5, and
- He does not need to make any adjustments to the basis or type of gain or loss (short-term or long-term) reported on Form 1099-B, or to his gain or loss.

Example: Eugene receives a Form 1099-B reporting the sale of stock he had held for five years. It shows gross proceeds of $8,000 and cost basis of $3,000. Box 6b is checked, meaning that his basis was reported to the IRS. Eugene does not need to make any adjustments to the amounts reported on Form 1099-B. He does not report the amounts on Form 8949. Instead, he enters the amounts directly onto his Schedule D.

There are two parts to Form 8949. The first is for short-term assets, and the second part is for long-term assets. Form 8949 is used to report the following:

- The sale or exchange of capital assets
- Gains from involuntary conversions (other than from casualty or theft)
- Nonbusiness bad debts and worthless securities

The information reported on Form 8949 describes all sales and exchanges of capital assets, including stocks, bonds, and mutual funds. This form must be filed along with Schedule D, which contains the summary of all capital gains and losses.

Example: In 2016, Amadeo received the following information statements regarding various investments:

- **Form 1099-DIV** showing a capital gain distribution of $170.
- **Form 1099-B** that shows a net sales price of $1,200 on the sale of 600 shares of Historic Group, Inc., but it does not show his basis in the stock.

He held the stock for over 2 years. His basis in the stock including commission is $1,455. Amadeo must use Form 8949 and Schedule D to report these transactions.

Unit 7: Study Questions

(Test yourself first, then check the correct answers at the end of this quiz.)

1. Lily bought shares in the Vanest Mutual Fund in 2013 for $8 a share. Since then, she received the following nondividend distributions:

- 2013: $2 per share
- 2014: $2 per share
- 2015: $3 per share
- 2016: $3 per share

What is Lily's basis in the stock and what amount of gain, if any, must she report in 2016?

A. $0 basis; $6 gain.
B. $14 basis; $0 gain.
C. $0 basis; $2 gain.
D. $8 basis; $3 gain.

2. What is the maximum number of years a taxpayer can carry over an unused capital loss?

A. One year.
B. Two years.
C. Five years.
D. As many years as required to utilize the entire deduction.

3. Five years ago, Marsha bought 100 shares of stock. Her sale date was March 10, 2016. Marsha's original cost for the stock was $10,110, plus an additional $35 of broker's fees. When she sold the stock, she received gross proceeds of $8,859. What is the net gain or loss from this transaction?

A. $1,286 long-term capital loss.
B. $1,286 short-term capital loss.
C. $1,251 long-term capital loss.
D. $1,251 long-term capital gain.

4. Which of the following losses is deductible?

A. A loss on the sale of a primary residence.
B. A loss on the sale of a vacation home.
C. A loss on the sale of a personal-use mobile home.
D. A loss on the sale of rental property.

5. Oliver operates an electronics repair business as a sole proprietorship. In 2016, Oliver sold property that was acquired for use in the business for $15,000. The purchase price of the property was $12,000, and Oliver had claimed depreciation of $3,000 related to the property. He accepted a down payment of $5,000 from the buyer, along with a note requiring additional payments of $2,500 plus interest in each of the next four years. Based upon the information provided, what amount of taxable income will result in 2016 if Oliver uses the installment method to report the sale of this property?

A. Capital gain of $5,000 and ordinary income of $1,000.
B. Capital gain of $1,000 and ordinary income of $3,000.
C. Capital gain of $2,000.
D. Capital gain of $1,000 and ordinary income of $1,000.

6. Nikhil's adjusted basis in 500 shares of Edico Corporation was $2,550. He owned the shares for three months. If he sold 500 shares for $3,300, what is the resulting gain or loss?

A. $750 short-term gain.
B. $700 short-term gain.
C. $750 long-term gain.
D. $750 long-term loss.

7. Ruben bought 100 shares of stock on October 1, 2015, when the share price was $26. He sold the stock for $20 a share on October 1, 2016. How should this trade be reported, and what is the nature of Ruben's gain or loss?

A. Short-term capital loss of $600.
B. Long-term capital loss of $600.
C. This is a wash sale, and there is no gain or loss.
D. Short-term capital loss of $500.

8. When trying to determine the holding period for investment property, which of the following is important?

A. The cost of the property.
B. In the case of gifted property, the amount of the gift.
C. The date of acquisition.
D. The amount realized in the transaction.

9. Gianna purchased 200 shares of stock on January 26, 2016, for $1,000. She sold all the shares on December 31, 2016, for $2,500. On January 9, 2017, the shares were delivered and payment was submitted to Gianna's account. How should this sale be reported?

A. $1,500 long-term gain on her 2016 return.
B. $1,500 short-term gain on her 2016 return.
C. $1,500 long-term gain on her 2017 return.
D. $1,500 short-term gain on her 2017 return.

10. Fred bought ten shares of Jixi Corporation stock on May 2, 2015. He sold them for a $7,000 loss on May 2, 2016. He has no other capital gains or losses. He also has $20,000 of wage income. How must Fred treat this transaction on his tax return?

A. He can deduct the $7,000 as a long-term capital loss on his 2016 return.
B. He can deduct the $7,000 as a short-term capital loss on his 2016 return.
C. He can deduct $3,000 as a short-term capital loss to offset his wage income on his 2016 return. The remaining amount, $4,000, must be carried over to future tax years.
D. He cannot deduct any of the capital loss; it must be carried over to future tax years.

11. Norma sells an empty lot with an adjusted basis of $20,000. Her buyer assumes an existing mortgage on the property of $15,000 and agrees to pay Norma $10,000, with a cash down payment of $2,000 and then $2,000 every year (plus 12% interest) in each of the next four years. What is Norma's gross profit and gross profit percentage on the installment sale?

A. The gross profit is $5,000, and the gross profit percentage is 20%.
B. The gross profit is $10,000, and the gross profit percentage is 100%.
C. The gross profit is $15,000, and the gross profit percentage is 20%.
D. The gross profit is $5,000, and the gross profit percentage is 50%.

12. Mario purchased his home five years ago for $150,000. He sold it at a loss for $115,000 in 2016. Which of the following statements is correct?

A. If he itemizes deductions, Mario can claim a loss of $35,000 on his 2016 tax return.
B. Mario can claim a loss of $3,000 in 2016, but must carry over the remainder to future years until the loss is completely deducted.
C. Mario can claim a loss of $35,000 because the home sale was an involuntary conversion.
D. Mario cannot claim a loss for the sale of his home.

13. Tahir purchased 100 shares in Foresthill Mutual Fund in April 2016 for $750. He received a capital gain distribution of $120 in 2016. The $120 was reported to him on Form 1099-DIV. How should this be reported on his tax return?

A. He must reduce his stock's basis by $120.
B. He must report the $120 as interest income.
C. He must report the $120 as a long-term capital gain.
D. He must report the $120 as a short-term capital gain.

14. Melissa purchased 1,000 shares of Devil Foods Company stock in 2012 at $10 per share. She sold 900 shares on January 15, 2016, at $9 per share, resulting in a $900 loss. Melissa's husband, Alex, purchased 900 shares of Devil Foods Company stock on February 10, 2016. Alex and Melissa keep their finances separate and will file MFS in 2016. Which of the following statements is correct?

A. Melissa can deduct the $900 capital loss on her tax return.
B. Melissa has a wash sale, and her loss is not deductible.
C. Alex can deduct the loss on his separate tax return.
D. None of the above.

15. Phil and Sharon owned a vacation home for 14 months before selling it for $254,000. Their adjusted basis in the home was $232,000, and they incurred $12,500 of selling expenses. Prior to the sale, they did not rent the home. What is the nature and amount of their gain?

A. $22,000 long-term capital gain.
B. $9,500 long-term capital gain.
C. $9,500 short-term capital gain.
D. $34,500 long-term capital gain.

16. Conrad purchased Blue-Chip Corporation stock in 2010 and sold it in 2016. Also in 2016, he traded in a copy machine that he used in his business since 2009 for a new model. On December 15, 2016, Conrad's mother gave him 35 shares of Energy Corporation stock that she had held for five years, and the fair market value of the stock was more than her basis in the stock at the time of the gift. Conrad sold the gifted stock two weeks after he received it from his mother. What is the holding period for all these assets?

A. All are short-term.
B. Blue-Chip stock and copy machine are long-term, and Energy Corporation stock is short-term.
C. All the stocks are long-term; the copy machine is short-term.
D. All are long-term.

17. Consuela purchased 1,000 shares of Hometown Mutual Fund on February 15, 2012, for $15 per share. On January 31, 2016, she sold all her shares for $3.75 per share. She also earned $45,000 of wages in 2016. She has no other transactions during the year. How should this transaction be reported on her tax return?

A. She has a capital loss of $11,250 that she can deduct against her wage income.
B. She must carry over the losses to a future tax year and offset future capital gains.
C. She can deduct a $3,000 capital loss on her 2016 tax return and the remainder of the losses will carry forward to subsequent years.
D. She can deduct a $5,000 capital loss on her 2016 tax return and the remainder of the losses will carry forward to subsequent years.

18. Noah bought two blocks (each of 400 shares) of Acme Corporation stock. He purchased the first block in April 2009 for $1,200 and the second block in March 2016 for $1,600. In June of 2016, he sold 400 shares for $1,500 but is unable to specify which block of stocks he sold. Noah's stock sale results in a:

A. Short-term loss of $100.
B. Short-term gain of $300.
C. Long-term loss of $100.
D. Long-term gain of $300.

19. Colin purchased 100 shares of Entertainment Digital Media stock for $1,000 on December 1, 2015. He sold these shares for $750 on December 22, 2016. Colin has seller's remorse, and on January 19, 2017, he repurchases 100 shares of Entertainment Digital for $800. Which of the following statements is correct?

A. Colin can report a $250 capital loss in 2016.
B. Colin can report a loss in 2016 and a taxable gain in 2017.
C. Colin cannot deduct his stock loss of $250 and must add the disallowed loss to his basis.
D. Colin can report a $250 capital loss in 2017.

20. All of the statements are correct about related party transactions except:

A. If a taxpayer controls more than 50% of a corporation or partnership, any property transactions between the taxpayer and business would be subject to the related party transaction rules.
B. Typically, a loss on the sale of property between related parties is not deductible.
C. The related party transaction rules apply to step-parents and step-siblings.
D. Related party transaction rules are designed to prevent improper deductions between two parties joined by a special relationship.

Unit 7: Answers

1. The answer is C. The first $8 of nondividend distributions per share reduces Lily's basis to zero. In 2016, the final $2 of nondividend distribution must be reported as capital gain.

2. The answer is D. Unused capital losses may be carried over indefinitely until they are utilized. There is no limit to how many years the taxpayer can claim the losses.

3. The answer is A. The answer is calculated as follows: The original basis is increased by the broker's commission. Therefore, Marsha's adjusted basis is $10,145 ($10,110 + $35). The gross proceeds from the sale are $8,859, which is subtracted from the basis, resulting in a long-term capital loss of $1,286 ($8,859 - $10,145) because she held the stock for more than one year.

4. The answer is D. Losses on the sale of personal-use property, including a loss on the sale of a primary residence or a vacation home, are not deductible. Only losses associated with business property and investment property (such as stocks and bonds or rental property) are deductible.

5. The answer is B. The amount of depreciation deducted for the property ($3,000) is recaptured and reported in 2016 as ordinary income. This amount is added back to the adjusted basis of $9,000 to determine the adjusted basis for the installment sale ($12,000). This amount is subtracted from the total proceeds of the sale ($15,000) to determine the gross profit of $3,000, which derives a gross profit percentage of 20%. This percentage is applied to the portion of proceeds received in 2016 ($5,000) to determine the amount of capital gain recognizable this year.

Original purchase price	$12,000
Minus depreciation deductions	(3,000)
Adjusted basis at date of sale	9,000
Depreciation recapture	3,000
Adjusted basis for installment sale	(12,000)
Proceeds of sale	15,000
Gross profit percentage	20%
Proceeds in 2016	5,000
Capital gain to be recognized	**$1,000**

6. The answer is A. The sales price is $750 more than the adjusted basis of the shares. The gain is short-term since Nikhil did not own the shares for more than one year.

7. The answer is A. Ruben has a short-term capital loss of $600 = (100 shares × $26) - (100 shares × $20). Ruben's holding period was not more than one year, which means that the loss must be treated as short-term. To determine holding period, begin counting on the day after the date the taxpayer acquires the property.

8. The answer is C. To determine the holding period; a taxpayer must begin counting on the day *after* the acquisition date. If a taxpayer's holding period is not more than one year, the taxpayer will have a short-term gain or loss. The amount realized in the transaction has no bearing on the holding period.

9. The answer is B. The sale and income must be reported in the year the security is sold, regardless of when the proceeds were received. She held the shares for less than one year, so Gianna has a short-term gain that must be reported on her 2016 tax return.

10. The answer is C. Fred has a short-term capital loss because he did not hold the stock for more than one year. He can deduct $3,000 of the loss in 2016, netting against his wage income. The remaining amount, $4,000, must be carried over to future tax years. A capital loss carryover retains its character as either long-term or short-term.

11. The answer is D. Norma's gross profit is $5,000, and the gross profit percentage is 50%. Her selling price is $25,000 ($2,000 down payment + $8,000 to be paid over four years + $15,000 for buyer's assumption of mortgage). Therefore, Norma's gross profit is $5,000 ($25,000 – $20,000 adjusted basis). If the entire selling price were payable in cash, her gross profit percentage would have been 20% ($5,000/$25,000). However, if a buyer assumes or pays off a mortgage or other debt on a property, the calculation of the installment sale gross profit percentage is affected. The mortgage assumption is subtracted before calculating the gross profit percentage, except to the extent that it exceeds the adjusted basis of the property for installment sale purposes, to derive what the IRS calls "contract price," rather than selling price. The mortgage assumption is considered a recovery of the seller's basis in the year of sale. Although the mortgage assumption is considered a payment, none of the gross profit is recognized in connection with the assumption. Instead, in this case, the contract price is considered to be $10,000 ($25,000 selling price - $15,000 mortgage assumption). Therefore, Norma's gross profit percentage is 50% ($5,000 ÷ $10,000). Norma must report half of each payment received as gain from the sale. She must also report all interest received as ordinary income.

12. The answer is D. Losses on the sale of personal-use property, including residences, are never deductible.

13. The answer is C. Mutual funds frequently distribute capital gains to shareholders. Capital gain distributions for mutual funds are always taxed as long-term capital gains, no matter how long a taxpayer has actually held the mutual fund shares.

14. The answer is B. The loss is disallowed. Melissa has a wash sale because her spouse repurchased identical securities within 30 days. It does not matter if they file separate returns. If a taxpayer sells stock and her spouse then repurchases identical stock within 30 days, the taxpayer has a wash sale. The fact that the taxpayers file MFS is irrelevant—the wash sale rules still apply.

15. The answer is B. The sale of a second home is a taxable event. Since Phil and Sharon owned the property for longer than one year, their gain is long-term. The gain is calculated as follows:

Sale price	$254,000
Minus selling expenses	(12,500)
Net proceeds	241,500
Minus adjusted basis in the property	(232,000)
Taxable gain on the sale	$9,500

16. The answer is D. All the property is long-term property. Generally, if a taxpayer holds investment property for more than one year, any gain or loss is a long-term gain or loss. If the taxpayer holds a property for one year or less, any gain or loss is a short-term gain or loss. However, if a taxpayer receives a gift of property, his holding period includes the donor's holding period if the fair market value of the gift was more than the donor's basis. Since Conrad's mother had held the stock for a few years, Conrad's disposition would receive long-term treatment.

17. The answer is C. Consuela cannot deduct all her stock losses in the current year. She can claim a $3,000 capital loss on her 2016 tax return and the remainder of the losses will carry forward to subsequent years.

18. The answer is D. Noah realized a long-term gain of $300 because the basis and holding period would automatically default to the oldest block of shares. A FIFO method is used if the taxpayer cannot specifically identify the shares sold.

19. The answer is C. Because Colin bought substantially identical stock, this is considered a wash sale and he cannot deduct his loss of $250 on the sale. Instead, he must add the disallowed loss to the cost of the new stock to obtain his adjusted basis in the new stock.

20. The answer is C. Related party transaction rules do not apply to uncles, aunts, nieces, nephews, cousins, stepchildren, stepparents, or in-laws.

Unit 8: Nonrecognition Property Transactions

> **For additional information read:**
> Publication 544, *Sales and Other Dispositions of Assets*
> Publication 523, *Selling Your Home*

For some transactions in which a taxpayer sells or exchanges property, gains may be nontaxable, partially taxable, or deferred. Three of the most common types of nonrecognition transactions involve:

- **Sale of a main home** (section 121, excluded gain)
- **Like-kind exchanges** (section 1031 exchange)
- **Involuntary conversions** (section 1033 exchange)

> **Note:** For Part 1 of the EA Exam, you will be tested primarily on the sale of a main home, involuntary conversions of personal-use property, and like-kind exchanges of residential rental property (Form 1040, Schedule E). For Part 2 of the EA exam, you will be tested on nonrecognition property transactions, but exclusively with business or rental property.

Sale of Main Home (Section 121)

In many cases, a taxpayer may exclude the gain from the sale of a main home. Up to $250,000 of gain may be excluded by single filers and up to $500,000 by joint filers. Generally, if the taxpayer can exclude all of the gain, it is not even necessary to report the sale. However, if part of the gain is taxable, the sale must be reported on Schedule D. Gain from the sale of a home that is not the taxpayer's main home must be reported as income.

The section 121 exclusion applies only to a "main home" and not to rental properties, vacation homes, or second homes. A taxpayer's main home is the residence where he lives most of the time. It does not have to be a traditional house. The main home can be a house, houseboat, mobile home, cooperative apartment, or condominium. To qualify as a home, it must have sleeping, kitchen, and bathroom facilities.

> **Example:** Wayne owns and lives in a house in Detroit. He also owns a lake cottage, which he uses only during the summer. The house in Detroit is his main home; the lake cottage is not. Wayne sells the lake cottage and has $100,000 of gain. The gain cannot be excluded because the cottage is not his main home. He must pay tax on the entire gain.

If the home was used for business purposes or as rental property, the gain is reported on Form 4797, *Sales of Business Property.* If a taxpayer took depreciation deductions because he used his home as a rental or for other business purposes, he cannot exclude the part of the gain equal to any deductible depreciation. Section 121 applies only to the nonbusiness portion of a home.

> **Example:** Erica lives in one-half of a duplex she owns and lets her daughter live in the other unit of the duplex rent-free. She purchased the duplex ten years ago for $200,000. In 2016, Erica sells the duplex for $340,000, a gain of $140,000. Since only half of the duplex counts as her main home, Erica may exclude only half of the gain ($70,000). She must report the other $70,000 as long-term capital gain.

Eligibility Requirements for Section 121

To be eligible for the section 121 exclusion, a taxpayer must:

- Have sold his main home
- Meet ownership and use tests
- Not have excluded gain in the two years prior to the current sale of a home

Ownership and Use Tests: During the five-year period ending on the date of the sale, the taxpayer must have:

- Owned the home for at least two years (the ownership test), and
- Lived in the home as his main home for at least two years (the use test).

Example: For the past six years, Lindsay lived with her parents in the home her parents owned. On September 1, 2015, she bought the house from her parents. She continued to live there until December 14, 2016, when she sold it because she wanted a bigger house. Lindsay does not meet the requirements for exclusion. Although she *lived* in the property as her main home for more than two years, she did not *own* it for the required two years. Therefore, she does not meet both the ownership and use tests.

A taxpayer meets the tests if he owned and lived in the property as his main home for either 24 full months or 730 days (365 × 2) during the five-year period.

Example: Irene bought a house in September 2011. After living there for ten months, she moved in with her boyfriend and kept her house vacant. They broke up and she moved back into her own house in 2015. She lived there for 16 months until she sold it in September 2016. Irene meets the ownership and use tests because, during the five-year period ending on the date of sale, she owned the house for four years and lived in the house a total of 26 months.

Note: The required two years of ownership and use do not have to be continuous. Further, ownership and use tests can be met during different two-year periods.

Short, temporary absences, even if the property is rented during those absences, are still counted as periods of use. Short absences include vacations and other seasonal absences. Longer breaks, such as a one-year sabbatical, are not included.

Example: In 2008, Carter began living in an apartment he rented. The apartment was converted to a condominium, which he purchased on December 1, 2013. In 2014, Carter became seriously ill, and on April 14 of that year, he moved into his daughter's home. On July 10, 2016, while still living in his daughter's home, Carter sold his condo. He can exclude all the gain on the sale because he meets the ownership and use tests. His five-year "lookback" period is from July 11, 2011, to July 10, 2016 (the date he actually sold the condo). He *owned* the condo from December 1, 2013, until July 10, 2016 (more than two years). He lived there from 2008 until April 14, 2014 (more than two years), so he would qualify to exclude all the gain, even though his ownership and use periods do not always overlap.

> **Example:** Katarina bought her home on February 1, 2013. Each year, she left her home for a four-month vacation in Ecuador. Katarina sold the house on March 1, 2016. She may exclude up to $250,000 of gain. Her vacations are considered short temporary absences and are counted toward her periods of use.

Different Rules for Married Homeowners

The ownership and use tests are applied differently to married homeowners. Married homeowners can exclude gain of up to $500,000 if they meet all of the following conditions:

- They file a joint return.
- Either spouse meets the ownership test (only one is required to own the home).
- Both spouses meet the use test.
- Neither spouse has excluded gain in the two years before the current sale of the home.

If they do not satisfy these requirements, the couple cannot claim the maximum $500,000 exclusion.

> **Example:** Leigh owns her home and has lived in it continuously for the last seven years. She meets William and marries him in September 2016. They move in together, but William doesn't like Leigh's house, and he convinces her to sell it a few months later. Leigh sells the home on December 10, 2016, and has $350,000 of gain. Leigh meets the ownership and use tests, but William does not meet the use test because he only lived in the house for a few months. Leigh can exclude up to $250,000 of gain on her 2016 tax return, whether she files MFJ or MFS. The $500,000 exclusion for joint returns does not apply.

> **Example:** Robert owns a home that he has lived in continuously for five years. In June 2013, he marries Annabel. She moves in, and they both live in the house together until December 1, 2016, when the house is sold. Robert meets the ownership test and the use test. Annabel does not own the home because Robert is listed as the sole owner of the property. However, she meets the "use test" because she lived in the home for at least two years. Therefore, on a jointly filed return, they can claim the maximum $500,000 exclusion.

Legally married same-sex spouses are eligible for the maximum $500,000 exclusion from gain on their jointly-filed returns.

> **Example:** Brandon and Max were legally married in Vermont two years ago. In 2016, they sell the house they had co-owned and lived in together for ten years. The house sold for $575,000 more than they paid for it. Brandon and Max may receive the maximum $500,000 exclusion for married couples when they file jointly in 2016. The remaining $75,000 of gain is taxable as long-term capital gain.

Unrelated Individuals: An unmarried couple or other taxpayers who own a home and live together may take the $250,000 exclusion individually on their separate returns if they meet the use and ownership tests.

Example: Greta and Carolyn are sisters. They are both widowed in 2016 and decided to purchase a home and live together. If they later sell the home, the ownership and use tests would apply to them individually. Each could claim an exclusion of up to $250,000 for her portion of the sale on her individual return.

Deceased Spouse: When a taxpayer's spouse dies, the taxpayer is considered to have owned and lived in a home during any period of time that the spouse owned and lived in it as a main home (provided that the taxpayer did not remarry before the date of sale). In effect, the holding period of the deceased spouse is tacked on for surviving spouses. As a result, the surviving spouse may exclude up to $500,000 of gain even if he sells the home within two years from the date of death of the deceased spouse.

Example: Alice owned and lived in her home for seven years. She married Stanley in April 2016, and he moved into the home with her. Alice died six months later, and Stanley inherited the property. He did not remarry. Stanley decides to sell the home on December 1, 2016. Even though he did not own or live in the house for two years, he meets the test requirements because his period of ownership and use includes the period that Alice owned and used the property before her death. Stanley may exclude up to $500,000 of the gain under the special rule that applies to deceased spouses.

Note: This "special rule" also applies to a home that is transferred by a spouse in a divorce. The receiving spouse is considered to have owned the home during any period of time that the transferor owned it.

Military Personnel Exception: Members of the armed forces are often required to move and might have difficulty meeting the tests for ownership and use within the five-year period prior to the sale of a home. The five-year period can be suspended for up to ten years for military and Foreign Service personnel, Peace Corps workers, and intelligence officers that are on official extended duty. This provides the taxpayer a better opportunity to meet the two-year use test even if he and/or his spouse did not actually live in the home during the normal five-year period required of other taxpayers.

Disability Exception: There is an exception to the use test if, during the five-year period before the sale of the home, a taxpayer becomes physically or mentally unable to care for himself, but he has owned and lived in the home for at least one year. The taxpayer is considered to have lived in the home during any time that he is forced to live in a licensed facility, including a nursing home. The taxpayer must still meet the two-year ownership test.

Reduced Exclusions

A taxpayer who owned and used a home for less than two years (and therefore does not meet the ownership and use tests) or who has used the home sale exclusion within the prior two-year period may be able to claim a reduced exclusion under certain conditions.

This may apply if a home sale has occurred primarily because of "unforeseen circumstances" during the taxpayer's period of use and ownership. Unforeseen circumstances include the following:

- Death, divorce, or legal separation.

- Certain health reasons related to care for the taxpayer, a spouse, a child, or certain other related persons. The related person does not have to be a dependent in order for the reduced exclusion to apply.
- Unemployment or a job change. The job-related exclusion applies if a new job is at least 50 miles farther from the old home than was the former place of employment. If there was no former place of employment, the distance between the new place of employment and the old home must be at least 50 miles.
- Multiple births resulting from the same pregnancy.
- Damage to the residence resulting from a disaster, an act of war, or terrorism.
- Involuntary conversion of the property.

The circumstances may involve the taxpayer, his spouse, a co-owner, or a member of the taxpayer's household. The IRS also has the discretion to deem other circumstances as unforeseen.

> **Example:** Justin purchased his new home in Mississippi in June 2015, but he lost his job shortly after he moved in. He found a new job in North Carolina and sold his house in April 2016. Because the distance between Justin's new place of employment and his former home is at least 50 miles, the sale satisfies the distance requirement. Justin's sale of his home is due to a change in place of employment, and he is entitled to claim a reduced exclusion on his gain from the sale.

Calculating the Reduced Exclusion

The reduced exclusion amount equals the full $250,000 (or $500,000 for married couples filing jointly) multiplied by a fraction. The numerator is the shorter of:

- The period the taxpayer owned and used the home as a principal residence during the five-year period ending on the sale date, or
- The period between the last sale for which the taxpayer claimed the exclusion and the sale date for the home currently being sold.

The denominator is two years or the equivalent in months or days. Thus, the amount of the reduced exclusion is figured by multiplying the full exclusion amount by the number of days or months the taxpayer owned and used the property, and dividing by either 730 days or 24 months.

> **Example:** Sabrina, a single taxpayer, lived in her principal residence for one full year (365 days) before selling it at a $400,000 gain in 2016. She qualifies for the reduced exclusion because she is pregnant with triplets (multiple births exclusion). Sabrina can exclude $125,000 of gain ($250,000 × [365 ÷ 730]).

> **Example:** Carrie purchased her home on January 1, 2016, for $350,000. Her mother is diagnosed with cancer, and Carrie must move to care for her. Even though Carrie does not claim her mother as a dependent, the move still qualifies as an unforeseen circumstance. Carrie sells her home on May 1, 2016, for $430,000, realizing a gain of $80,000. She qualifies for the reduced exclusion, so part of her gain is nontaxable. She owned and occupied the home for 121 days (January 1 to May 1). She may exclude $41,438 ($250,000 × [121 days ÷ 730 (365 X 2 years)]). Therefore, Carrie's taxable gain is $38,562 ($80,000 - $41,438). This amount is a short-term capital gain since she owned the house for less than one year.

Land Sales: If a taxpayer sells the land on which his main home is located but not the house itself, he cannot exclude the gain. Similarly, the sale of a vacant plot of land with no house on it does not qualify for the section 121 exclusion.

> **Example:** Theresa purchased an empty lot in 2013 for $90,000, planning to build her dream home. Construction was delayed and her house was never completed. In December 2016, Theresa sells the land for $150,000. She owned the property for more than a year, so she has $60,000 of long-term capital gain. None of the gain can be excluded from income because there is no residence on the property. Section 121 only applies to homes, not to empty land.

If a taxpayer sells a vacant lot that is adjacent to his main home, he may be able to exclude the gain from the sale under certain circumstances. Gain from the sale of vacant land that was used in connection with a principal residence may be excluded if the land sale occurs within two years before or after the sale of the home. The sale of the land and the sale of the home are treated as one sale for purposes of the exclusion.

Like-Kind Exchanges (Section 1031 Exchange)

A section 1031 *like-kind exchange* occurs when a taxpayer exchanges business or investment property for similar property. If the exchange qualifies under section 1031, the taxpayer does not recognize any resulting gain and cannot deduct any losses until he later disposes of the property received. To qualify for nonrecognition treatment, the exchange must meet all of the following conditions:

- The property must be held for investment or for productive use in a business. Property held for personal use, such as a personal residence, does not qualify.
- The property must not be "held primarily for sale" (such as inventory).
- There must be an actual exchange of two or more assets or properties (the exchange of cash for property is treated as a sale, not as an exchange).
- For instances in which a property is transferred in exchange for like-kind property to be received later (known as a deferred exchange), the property to be received must be identified in writing (or actually received) within 45 days after the date of transfer of the property given up.

Further, the replacement property in a deferred exchange must be received by the earlier of:

- The 180th day after the date on which the property given up was transferred, or
- The due date, including extensions, of the tax return for the year in which the transfer of that property occurs. The IRS is very strict about these deadlines.

Taxpayers report like-kind exchanges on Form 8824, *Like-Kind Exchanges*.

Qualifying Exchanges: To qualify under section 1031, an exchange must involve like-kind property, such as the trade of real property for real property or personal property for personal property.

> **Definition:** The accounting term **"personal property"** does not refer to items used for personal use but rather to assets used in a business that is not classified as real property (real estate).

An exchange of real property generally qualifies more easily as like-kind, regardless of how each property is used or whether each property is improved or unimproved. For instance, the exchange of a building for farmland would qualify, as would the exchange of an apartment complex for an office building. However, the exchange of factory machinery (personal property) for a factory building (real property) is not a qualifying exchange.

In contrast, an exchange of personal property must involve items that are at least similar enough to both be categorized within one of several asset classes established by the IRS. For example, the exchange of a panel truck for a pickup truck may qualify as a trade of like-kind property, but the exchange of a pickup truck for a semi-truck likely would not.

Example: Casey exchanges a private jet with an adjusted basis of $400,000 for an office building valued at $375,000. The exchange of personal property (an airplane) for real property (the building) does not qualify for section 1031 treatment, so gain (or loss) must be recognized on this transaction.

Nonqualifying Exchanges: The exchange of equipment or business assets that are used within the United States for similar items used outside the United States would not be considered an exchange of qualifying like-kind property. Similarly, real estate within the United States and real estate outside the United States is not "like" property, and an exchange would not qualify for section 1031 treatment.

Other exchanges that do not qualify for section 1031 treatment include the following types of property:

- Livestock of different sexes
- Securities, bonds, stocks, currency, or notes
- Partnership interests

Taxable Exchanges: If a taxpayer receives property in exchange for other property that is not similar or related in use to the property exchanged, he may need to recognize gain if the fair market value of the property received is greater than the adjusted basis of the property exchanged. His basis in the property received is generally its FMV at the time of the exchange.

Example: Tyler trades an empty lot with an adjusted basis of $10,000 for an SUV to use in his pest control business. The SUV's fair market value is $15,000. Since the exchange does not qualify for section 1031 treatment, Tyler must report $5,000 of capital gain. The SUV's basis is $15,000.

Boot: Although the Internal Revenue Code itself does not use the term "boot," it is frequently used to describe cash or other property added to an exchange in order to compensate for a difference in the values of properties traded.

An exchange that includes "boot" may still be valid under section 1031, but the taxpayer who receives boot may have to recognize taxable gain to the extent of the cash and the FMV of unlike property received. The amount considered boot would be reduced by qualified costs paid in connection with the transaction.

Example: Sloan wishes to exchange his rental property in a 1031 exchange. The relinquished rental property has an FMV of $60,000 and an adjusted basis of $30,000. The replacement property Sloan receives has an FMV of $50,000, and he also receives $10,000 of cash as part of the exchange. Sloan, therefore, has a gain of $30,000 on the exchange (combined value of $60,000 received minus his basis of $30,000 in the property exchanged). He is required to pay tax on only $10,000, the cash (boot) received in the exchange. The rest of his gain is deferred until he disposes of the property at a later date.

When an exchange involves property that is subject to a liability, assumption of the liability is treated as if it was a transfer of cash and thus considered boot by the party who is relieved of the liability. If each property in an exchange is transferred subject to a liability, a taxpayer is treated as having received boot only if he is relieved of a greater liability than the liability he assumes.

Basis of Property Received in a Like-Kind Exchange

The basis of the property received is generally the adjusted basis of the property transferred.

Example: Judy has a rental house with an adjusted basis of $70,000. In 2016, she trades the rental house for an empty lot with an FMV of $150,000. Judy's basis in the lot is $70,000, equal to the adjusted basis of the property she exchanged.

If a taxpayer trades property and also pays money as part of the exchange, the basis of the property received is the basis of the property given up, increased by any additional money paid.

Example: Jorge trades a plot of land with an adjusted basis of $30,000 for a different plot of land in another town with an FMV of $70,500. He pays an additional $4,000 of cash. Jorge's basis in the new land is $34,000: his $30,000 basis in the old land plus the $4,000 cash.

Example: Peyton bought a new diesel truck for use in her catering business. She received a credit of $13,600 for trading in her old truck and also paid $43,000 of cash. The old truck cost $50,000 two years ago, and Peyton had taken depreciation deductions of $39,500 on it. She has a $3,100 gain on the exchange ($13,600 trade-in allowance minus her $10,500 adjusted basis for the old truck), but recognition of the gain is postponed under the rules for like-kind exchanges.

If a taxpayer receives boot in connection with an exchange and recognizes gain, the basis of the property received is equal to the basis of the property given up plus the amount of gain recognized.

Example: Cole exchanges a tractor with an adjusted basis of $50,000 for a harvester with an FMV of $60,000. He receives cash of $10,000 in connection with the exchange and must recognize gain to the extent of the boot received. His basis in the harvester is $60,000 ($50,000 basis in the old tractor plus $10,000 recognized gain).

Related Party Transactions: Like-kind exchanges are allowed between related parties. However, if either party disposes of the property within two years after a 1031 exchange, the exchange is disqualified from nonrecognition treatment; any gain or loss that was deferred in the original transaction must be recognized in the year the disposition occurs. For purposes of this rule, a related person includes a close family member (such as a spouse, sibling, parent, or child). It also includes a corporation or partnership in which a taxpayer holds ownership or interests of more than 50%.

The two-year holding period rule does not apply:

- If one of the parties involved in the exchange dies
- If the property is subsequently converted in an involuntary exchange (such as a fire)
- If it can be established to the satisfaction of the IRS that the exchange and subsequent disposition were not done mainly for tax avoidance purposes

The IRS gives close scrutiny to exchanges between related parties because they can be used by taxpayers to evade taxes on gains.

Involuntary Conversions (Section 1033)

An involuntary conversion occurs when a taxpayer's property is lost, damaged, or destroyed, and the taxpayer receives an award, insurance money, or some other type of payment, as a result of:

- Casualty, disaster, or theft,
- Condemnation (or threat of condemnation).

Involuntary conversions can occur with business property as well as personal-use property, but the rules differ for each. Gain or loss from an involuntary conversion is usually recognized for tax purposes unless the property is a main home. A taxpayer reports the gain or deducts the loss in the year the gain or loss is realized. A taxpayer cannot deduct a loss from an involuntary conversion of personal-use property unless the loss resulted from a casualty or theft.

However, under section 1033, a taxpayer can elect to defer reporting gain on an involuntary conversion if he receives proceeds from insurance or another source and invests in property that is similar to the converted property.

Example: A hurricane destroys Denise's residential rental property that had an adjusted basis of $50,000. The insurance company gives Denise a check for $100,000, which is the FMV of the home. Denise buys a replacement rental property six months later for $100,000. Her gain on the involuntary conversion is $50,000 ($100,000 insurance settlement minus her $50,000 basis). However, Denise does not have to recognize any taxable gain because she reinvested all her insurance proceeds in another, similar property under a qualified 1033 exchange.

Replacement Period: The replacement period for an involuntary conversion generally ends two years after the end of the first tax year in which any part of the gain is realized.

Real property that is held for investment or used in a trade or business is allowed a three-year replacement period. The replacement period is four years for livestock that is involuntarily converted because of weather-related conditions.

Example: Barney owns a drywall repair business. On September 1, 2016, a flood destroys a storage shed filled with his supplies. Barney's insurance company reimburses him for the loss on October 26, 2016. He has until December 31, 2018 (two years) to replace the shed and supplies using the insurance proceeds. Barney is not required to report the insurance proceeds on his 2016 tax return. If he reinvests all the proceeds in a replacement property, he will not have any taxable gain.

Example: Lane and Candace are married and file jointly. They paid $100,000 for their home ten years ago. They receive an insurance payment of $700,000 after their home is destroyed in a mudslide, for a $600,000 gain on the conversion. They may exclude $500,000 of the gain under section 121, leaving $100,000 as taxable long-term capital gain. If they reinvest the insurance proceeds in a new home, under the rules for involuntary conversions, they may defer the remainder of the gain. If they choose not to reinvest the insurance proceeds, then they will be required to pay capital gains on $100,000.

If a main home is damaged or destroyed and is in a federally-declared disaster area, the replacement period is extended to four years. A five-year replacement period has been applied to certain extreme disaster areas, but only if the replacement property is purchased in the same area.

Property Type	Replacement Period
Most property except those noted below	Two years
Real property (real estate) that is held for investment or business use, such as residential rentals and office buildings	Three years
Sale of livestock due to weather-related conditions	Four years
Main home in federally-declared disaster area	Four to five years

If a taxpayer reinvests in replacement property similar to the converted property, the replacement property's basis is the same as the converted property's basis on the date of the conversion, subject to the following adjustments:

The basis is **decreased** by the following:

- Any loss a taxpayer recognizes on the involuntary conversion
- Any money a taxpayer receives that he does not spend on similar property

The basis is **increased** by the following:

- Any gain a taxpayer recognizes on the involuntary conversion
- Any additional costs of acquiring the replacement property

Example: Franco owns an apartment building in Texas with a basis of $250,000. He receives an insurance settlement of $400,000 after the building is destroyed by a tornado. A year later, Franco purchases another apartment building in Wisconsin for $380,000. Franco's realized gain on the involuntary conversion is $150,000 ($400,000 - $250,000 basis). He must recognize $20,000 of gain because he received an insurance payment of $400,000 but only spent $380,000 on the replacement property ($400,000 - $380,000). His basis in the new property is $250,000, which is calculated as the cost of the new property in Wisconsin minus the deferred gain ($380,000 - $130,000 = $250,000). If Franco had used all the insurance proceeds and invested it in the new property, he would not have to report any taxable gain.

Example: Paula paid $100,000 for a rental property five years ago. After factoring in her depreciation deductions, her adjusted basis in the property is $75,000 at the beginning of 2016. The property is insured for $300,000 and is destroyed by fire in June 2016. On December 15, 2016, Paula receives a $300,000 payment from her insurance company. Paula reinvests all the insurance proceeds, plus $5,000 more of her own savings, into a new rental property. She qualifies to defer all of her gain. Her basis in the new property is $80,000 ($75,000 + $5,000 of her additional investment).

Condemnations

A condemnation is a type of involuntary conversion. Condemnation is the process by which private property is taken from its owner for public use. The property may be taken by the government or by a private organization that has the legal power to seize it.

The owner generally receives a condemnation award (money or property) in exchange for the property that is taken. A condemnation is like a forced sale, with the owner being the seller and the government or other third party being the buyer.

Example: The local government informs Trevor that his farmland is being condemned to create a public park. Although Trevor does not want to sell his land, the government forces the sale and issues a condemnation award to Trevor, paying him the property's fair market value of $400,000. Trevor's basis in the farmland was $80,000. Trevor decides not to purchase replacement farmland. Therefore, he has a taxable event, and he must recognize $320,000 as income ($400,000 - $80,000 = $320,000). However, if Trevor were to purchase replacement property with the condemnation award, he would have a nontaxable section 1033 exchange.

Amounts taken out of a condemnation award to pay debts on the property are considered paid to the taxpayer and are included in the amount of the award.

Example: The state condemned Nhan's property in order to build a light rail system. The court award was set at $200,000. The state paid him only $148,000 because it paid $50,000 to his mortgage company and $2,000 in accrued real estate taxes. Nhan is considered to have received the entire $200,000 as a condemnation award.

The time period for replacing condemned property is the same as other qualified section 1033 exchanges, two years after the end of the first tax year in which any part of the gain on the condemnation is realized. For real property held for business use or investment, the replacement period is three years instead of two.

Example: Joel owns a pool hall. In February 2016, the building is condemned by the city because asbestos is discovered in the ceiling. He receives his condemnation award from his insurance company in May 2016. He has until December 31, 2019, to replace the condemned pool hall with a similar building. This is because the pool hall is business-related real estate, so Joel has three full years to reinvest the proceeds.

Condemnation of a Main Home: If a taxpayer has a gain because his main home is condemned, he can generally exclude the gain as if he had sold the home under the section 121 exclusion. Single filers can exclude up to $250,000 of the gain and joint filers up to $500,000. Any excess gains above these amounts may be potentially excludable under section 1033.

Unit 8: Study Questions

(Test yourself first, then check the correct answers at the end of this quiz.)

1. Christy exchanged a rental duplex with an adjusted basis of $160,000 for a rental house. The fair market value of the rental house she received was $200,000. She also received $10,000 of cash and paid $5,000 of exchange expenses. What is her recognized (taxable) gain on the transaction, if any?

A. $0
B. $5,000
C. $10,000
D. $45,000

2. Isaiah has lived in and owned his home for 15 months when he decides to move in with his girlfriend, so he sells his home for $285,000. His adjusted basis in the home is $160,000. What is the amount and nature of his taxable gain on the sale?

A. $0
B. $35,000 long-term capital gain.
C. $125,000 long-term capital gain.
D. $125,000 short-term capital gain.

3. Heather is single and bought her first home five years ago for $350,000. She lived continuously in the house until she sold it in 2016 for $620,000. Which of the following statements is correct?

A. She may exclude $250,000 of gain and report the remaining amount as a long-term capital gain.
B. She may exclude the entire gain. There is no amount that needs to be reported.
C. She may not exclude the gain.
D. She may exclude $250,000 of gain. The remaining amount must be reported as a short-term capital gain.

4. Which of the following transactions cannot qualify for a section 1031 like-kind exchange?

A. An exchange of a building in Manhattan for 20 acres of empty farmland.
B. An exchange of an apartment building in New Mexico for an office building in Alaska.
C. An exchange of a business computer for a business printer.
D. An exchange of inventory for different inventory.

5. Bob and Grace were married in January 2010. They purchased their first home together in March 2010 for $150,000. In February 2016, Bob and Grace legally separated, and the court granted Grace ownership of the home as part of the divorce settlement. The divorce became final in June 2016, and the fair market value of the home was $370,000 when ownership was transferred to Grace. She sells the house on December 23, 2016, for $480,000. What is Grace's taxable gain in the transaction?

A. $0
B. $80,000
C. $120,000
D. $210,000

6. Which of the following would not be an acceptable "unforeseen circumstance" for a taxpayer to take a reduced exclusion on the sale of his primary residence?

A. The home is condemned by the city.
B. A legal separation.
C. The birth of twin girls.
D. Moving to another state to be closer to grown children.

7. Lucille owns a home in the Vail ski area. She stays at the ski home most weekends and spends the entire months of December, January, and February there. When she is not at the ski home, she lives in a four-room apartment that she rents in Denver. What is Lucille's main home for purposes of the section 121 exclusion?

A. Her ski home in Vail.
B. Her apartment in Denver.
C. She is considered a transient for tax purposes.
D. None of the above.

8. Bailey exchanges his residential rental property with an adjusted basis of $50,000 and an FMV of $80,000 for a different rental property with an FMV of $70,000. What is Bailey's basis in the new property?

A. $50,000
B. $70,000
C. $80,000
D. $100,000

9. Aiden exchanges a residential rental property in Las Vegas with a basis of $100,000 for an investment property in Miami Beach valued at $220,000. Aiden also received $15,000 of cash boot in the exchange. What is Aiden's taxable gain on the exchange, if any, and what is his basis of the new property in Miami Beach?

A. Taxable gain: $15,000; basis: $115,000.
B. Taxable gain: $0; basis: $235,000.
C. Taxable gain: $15,000; basis: $135,000.
D. Taxable gain: $15,000; basis: $220,000.

10. Geoff sold his main home in 2016 at a $29,000 gain. He meets the ownership and use tests to exclude the gain from his income. However, he used one room of the home for business in 2014 and 2015. His records show he claimed $3,000 of depreciation for a home office. What is Geoff's taxable gain on the sale, if any?

A. $0
B. $1,000
C. $2,000
D. $3,000

11. A tornado destroyed Bryant's home on July 15, 2016. He wants to replace the home using a section 1033 exchange for involuntary conversions. What is the latest that Bryant can replace the property in order to defer any gain from his insurance reimbursement that was paid to him on August 23, 2016?

A. December 31, 2018
B. July 15, 2017
C. August 23, 2018
D. December 31, 2017

12. Jonah exchanged an empty lot that he held for investment for a rental building. The original cost of the empty lot was $16,000, and he had made $10,000 of improvements (such as permanent fencing) prior to the exchange. The fair market value of the rental building at the time of the exchange was $36,000. Jonah did not recognize any gain from the exchange. What is his basis in the new property?

A. $10,000
B. $16,000
C. $26,000
D. $36,000

13. Mitchell and Kay are married and file jointly. They owned and used their house as their main home for 15 months. Mitchell got a new job in another state, and they sold their home. What is the maximum amount they can exclude from income under the rules regarding a reduced exclusion?

A. $22,727
B. $250,000
C. $312,500
D. $500,000

14. Allen is a flight instructor. He trades in a small plane (adjusted basis $300,000) for another, larger plane (FMV $750,000) and pays $60,000 of cash in addition. He uses the plane 100% in his flight instruction business. What is his basis in the new plane?

A. $300,000
B. $360,000
C. $690,000
D. $750,000

15. Gino bought a house for $189,000 in July 2012. He lived there continuously for 13 months and then moved in with his girlfriend. They later separated, and Gino moved back into his own house and lived there for 12 months until he sold it in July 2016 for $220,000. What is the amount and nature of his gain?

A. Gino has no taxable gain because the sale qualifies for section 121 exclusion.
B. $31,000 long-term capital gain.
C. $31,000 short-term capital gain.
D. $30,000 long-term capital gain.

16. Katherine owns a yacht that she rents out for parties. Her purchase price was $150,000. A typhoon destroys the yacht in 2016. Katherine collects $175,000 from her insurance company and promptly reinvests all the proceeds in a larger, new yacht, which costs her $201,000. What is her basis in the new yacht?

A. $175,000
B. $176,000
C. $201,000
D. $226,000

17. Annalise sold her primary residence in Utah and moved to Iowa. She had purchased the house in 2001 for $200,000, and she sold it in 2016 for $550,000, net of selling expenses. During the time she lived in the house, she paid $25,000 for major improvements and $15,000 for general repairs. Assuming that Annalise utilizes the maximum available exclusion, what amount would she report as taxable gain?

A. $0
B. $60,000
C. $75,000
D. $100,000

18. Christian owned an office building with an adjusted basis of $400,000. The building was destroyed by a fire in 2016, and Christian received an insurance reimbursement of $600,000. He purchases a new office building for $450,000 and invests the rest of the insurance proceeds in stocks. Which of the following statements is correct?

A. He has $200,000 of taxable gain he must recognize on his tax return.
B. He has $150,000 of taxable gain he must recognize on his tax return.
C. He does not have a taxable gain.
D. He has $50,000 of taxable gain he must recognize on his tax return.

19. Shane and Phyllis moved after living in their home for 292 days because Phyllis became pregnant with triplets and they needed a larger home. The gain on the sale of the home is $260,000. Since they lived there for less than two years but meet one of the exceptions, what is the actual amount of their reduced exclusion? (Two years = 730 days).

A. $60,000
B. $200,000
C. $260,000
D. $500,000

20. Clayton trades farm land with an adjusted basis of $44,000 for a tractor with a fair market value of $77,000. What is the basis of the tractor and how much taxable gain, if any, must Clayton report?

A. $0 gain; $33,000 basis
B. $0 gain; $77,000 basis
C. $33,000 gain; $44,000 basis
D. $33,000 gain; $77,000 basis

Unit 8: Answers

1. The answer is B. Although the total gain on the transaction is $45,000, the recognized gain is only $5,000. The answer is calculated as follows:

FMV of like-kind property received	$200,000
Cash	10,000
Total received	210,000
Subtract: Exchange expenses paid	(5,000)
Amount realized	205,000
Subtract: Adjusted basis of property transferred	(160,000)
Realized Gain	$45,000
Cash received (boot)	$10,000
Subtract: Exchange expenses paid	(5,000)
Recognized (taxable) gain	**$5,000**

2. The answer is C. His gain is $125,000, the result of subtracting the adjusted basis in the home from the amount realized ($285,000 - $160,000 = $125,000). Since he does not meet the ownership or use tests or qualify for a reduced exclusion, he cannot exclude any of his gain under section 121, (because he hasn't lived in the house for 2 out of the last 5 years). He owned the property for more than a year, so the gain is taxed as a long-term capital gain.

3. The answer is A. As a single taxpayer; Heather may exclude a maximum gain amount of $250,000 from the sale of her home. Her gain is $270,000 ($620,000 - $350,000). Her taxable gain is $20,000 ($270,000 gain - $250,000 exclusion), which must be reported as a long-term capital gain.

4. The answer is D. Inventory never qualifies for like-kind exchange treatment. The property must not be held "primarily for sale", such as merchandise, retail stock, or inventory. Generally, real property exchanges will qualify for like-kind treatment, even though the properties themselves might be dissimilar. Business computers and printers are in the same asset class, so that exchange is valid.

5. The answer is B. Grace meets the ownership and use tests, and the basis in the property remains the same. Property transfers related to a divorce are nontaxable, and the FMV of the property at the time of the divorce has no bearing on the taxable outcome. Since she owned the property for longer than one year, the taxable portion of Grace's gain would be reported as a long-term capital gain. The gain is calculated as follows:

Original cost	$150,000
Sale price	480,000
Total realized gain	330,000
Section 121 exclusion	-250,000
Taxable gain	$80,000

6. The answer is D. The move to be closer to grown children would not qualify. All of the following events would be qualifying events in order to claim a reduced exclusion from a premature sale:

- A divorce or legal separation
- A pregnancy resulting in multiple births or serious health issues
- The home is sold after being seized or condemned
- A move due to a new job or new employment

If any of these exceptions apply, the taxpayer may figure a reduced exclusion based on the number of days he owned and lived in the residence.

7. The answer is B. Lucille's main home is her rental apartment in Denver because she lives there most of the time. If she were to sell the ski home, she would not qualify for the section 121 exclusion on the sale because it is a vacation home and not her primary residence.

8. The answer is A. His basis in the new property is the same as the basis of the property given up: $50,000.

9. The answer is A. Aiden's total gain on the exchange is $135,000 ($220,000 value of new property + $15,000 cash - $100,000 basis in the old property). However, only the cash boot received is taxable. Aiden's basis in the new building is $115,000 (the original basis in the property he gave up plus the gain recognized as a result of the boot received).

10. The answer is D. Geoff can exclude $26,000 ($29,000 - $3,000) of his gain. He has a taxable gain of $3,000. He must report the depreciation recapture as ordinary income. If a taxpayer took depreciation deductions because he used his home for business purposes or as a rental property, he cannot exclude the part of the gain equal to any depreciation allowed as a deduction.

11. The answer is A. Bryant must acquire qualifying replacement property by December 31, 2018 (*two* years from the *end* of the tax year during which any part of the gain is realized.) Since Bryant received the reimbursement check in 2016, he has 2 years from December 31, 2016, to acquire replacement property. Different types of property have different replacement periods. For example, if Bryant's main home had been located in a federally-declared disaster area, he could have had four years to replace the property.

12. The answer is C. The basis in the new building is the same as his basis in the empty lot. The $10,000 spent on improvements is added to the $16,000 cost, so the adjusted basis of the relinquished empty lot was $26,000. Therefore, this is his basis in the new property, as well. The fair market value is irrelevant in this calculation.

13. The answer is C. A reduced exclusion is available, even though the taxpayers did not live in the home for two full years. They qualify for a reduced exclusion because they are moving for a change in Mitchell's employment. Their maximum reduced exclusion is $312,500 ($500,000 × [15 months/24 months]). The reduced exclusion applies when the premature sale is primarily due to a move for employment in a new location.

14. The answer is B. Allen's basis is $360,000: the $300,000 basis of the old plane plus the $60,000 cash paid. The fair market value of the property has no bearing on Allen's basis in the new property.

15. The answer is A. This sale qualifies for section 121 treatment. Gino meets the ownership and use tests because, during the five-year period ending on the date of sale, he owned the house for three years and lived in it for a total of 25 months (over 2 years). The gain is not taxable and does not need to be reported.

16. The answer is B. Since Katherine purchased replacement property, the basis of the replacement property is the cost of the new yacht ($201,000) minus her deferred gain ($25,000), or $176,000. The deferred gain of $25,000 is calculated as follows: Insurance proceeds of $175,000 minus the cost of the old yacht of $150,000. Alternatively, the basis of the replacement property could be determined as follows: Basis of the old yacht ($150,000) plus cash paid in excess of insurance proceeds ($201,000 - $175,000 = $26,000).

17. The answer is C. Annalise's adjusted basis in the house would be the total of her original purchase price of $200,000 and the $25,000 cost of improvements. The cost of repairs would not be considered in determining her adjusted basis. Therefore, her gain on the sale would be $325,000, or the excess of her net proceeds over her adjusted basis. Since she met the requirements for ownership and use of the house as her primary residence, she qualifies for the maximum exclusion of $250,000 available to a single taxpayer, and the taxable portion of her gain would be $75,000.

Purchase price of house	$200,000
Cost of improvements	25,000
Adjusted basis	225,000
Net proceeds of sale	$550,000
Gain on sale	325,000
Exclusion for single taxpayer	(250,000)
Taxable gain	$75,000

18. The answer is B. Christian's realized gain is $200,000 ($600,000 - $400,000) and his taxable gain is $150,000. He purchased another building for $450,000, so he may defer $50,000 of the gain under section 1033 for involuntary conversions. The remainder of the gain, $150,000 ($600,000 - $450,000), must be recognized because he did not reinvest the remaining proceeds in like-kind property. If Christian had reinvested all the proceeds in the new building, his entire gain would have been deferred.

19. The answer is B. The couple has a reduced exclusion of $200,000 (292/730 multiplied by the $500,000 maximum exclusion available for married taxpayers). The remaining $60,000 would be considered taxable capital gain income and would be reported on Schedule D. This move qualifies for the reduced exclusion because multiple births from the same pregnancy are considered an unforeseen circumstance.

20. The answer is D. This is a taxable exchange of property that is not similar. Clayton must report $33,000 of gain, the difference between the adjusted basis of the farmland and the FMV of the tractor ($77,000 minus $44,000). The basis of property received in a taxable exchange is generally its FMV at the time of the exchange.

179

Unit 9: Rental and Royalty Income

> **For additional information read:**
> Publication 527, *Residential Rental Property*
> Publication 946, *How to Depreciate Property*
> Publication 525, *Taxable and Nontaxable Income*

Rental income is any payment received for the use or occupation of property. In most cases, taxpayers must include amounts received as rent in their gross income.

Property owners can deduct the expenses of managing, conserving, and maintaining their rental properties. Common rental expenses include:

- Mortgage interest and property taxes
- Maintenance, repairs, and cleaning fees
- Advertising
- Utilities
- Insurance
- Depreciation

Advance Rent: Taxpayers must report rental income when it is constructively received, i.e. available without restrictions. This includes advance rent, which is any amount received before the period that it covers. Thus, a taxpayer must include advance rent in income in the year he receives it, regardless of the period covered or the accounting method used.

> **Example:** Gene rents out a duplex. On December 20, 2016, his tenant pays two months of rent in advance for January and February because she is leaving town on vacation. Gene cannot delay reporting of the income. He must report all the advance rent as taxable income in 2016 (when he received it), not in 2017.

Lease Cancellation: If a tenant pays to cancel a lease, the amount received for the cancellation is rental income. The payment is included in the year received regardless of the taxpayer's accounting method.

Security Deposits: A security deposit is not considered income upon initial receipt if the deposit is refundable to the tenant at the end of the lease. However, if the taxpayer keeps the security deposit because the tenant did not live up to the terms of the lease or because he damaged property, the deposit amount is recognized as income in the year it is forfeited by the tenant.

Insurance Premiums Paid in Advance: If a cash-basis taxpayer pays an insurance premium for more than one year in advance, he can deduct only the part of the premium payment that applies to that year. He cannot deduct the total premium in the year he pays it.

Local Benefit Taxes: In most cases, a taxpayer cannot deduct charges for local taxes that increase the value of a rental property, such as assessments for streets, sidewalks, or water and sewer systems. These charges are nondepreciable capital expenditures that must be added to the basis of the property. Only taxes to maintain or repair such infrastructure, or to pay interest charges related to financing its construction, can be deducted.

Property or Services in Lieu of Rent: If a taxpayer receives property or services as payment for rent instead of cash, the fair market value must be recognized as rental income. If the tenant and landlord agree in advance to a price, the agreed-upon price is deemed the fair market value unless there is evidence to the contrary.

> **Example:** Beth owns an apartment complex. Beth's tenant, Chris, is a professional chimney sweep. Chris offers to clean all of Beth's chimneys in her apartment building instead of paying three months' rent in cash. Beth accepts Chris's offer. Beth must recognize income for the amount Chris would have paid for three months' rent. However, Beth can deduct that same amount as a business expense for maintenance of the property.

If a tenant pays expenses on behalf of the landlord, the landlord must recognize the payments as rental income. The landlord can deduct the expenses as rental expenses.

> **Example:** Rosetta owns an apartment building. While she is out of town, the furnace in the apartment building breaks down. Kerry, Rosetta's tenant, pays for the emergency repairs out-of-pocket and deducts the furnace repair bill from his rent payment. Rosetta must recognize as rental income both the actual amount of rent received in cash from Kerry and the amount he paid for the repairs. Rosetta can deduct the cost of the furnace repair as a rental expense.

Vacant Property: A taxpayer cannot deduct any loss of rental income for the period a property is vacant. However, if the taxpayer is actively trying to rent the property, he can deduct ordinary and necessary expenses as soon as the property is made available for rent.

> **Example:** Rodrigo purchased a rental property and made the property available for rent on March 1, 2016, by advertising it in the local newspaper. He found a tenant who moved in on June 1, 2016. Even though the rental was unoccupied from March through May, Rodrigo can still deduct the mortgage interest and other expenses related to the property during that period, because the property was available and advertised to rent.

Depreciation of Rental Property: A taxpayer begins to claim deductions for depreciation of a rental property when he places it in service for the production of income. Rental property is considered "placed in service" when it is ready and available for rent. Depreciation ends when a taxpayer has either fully recovered his cost or other basis, or when the property is retired from service, whichever happens first.

Three basic factors determine how much depreciation a taxpayer can deduct:

- Basis
- Recovery period for the property
- Depreciation method used, including certain conventions

The cost of land is never depreciated because land does not wear out, become obsolete, or get used up. For a personal residence that is later converted to rental property, the depreciable basis is the lower of:

- The taxpayer's adjusted basis in the property, or
- The fair market value of the property at the time of conversion.

Example: Five years ago, Lance purchased a home for $180,000. On the date of purchase, the assessed value of the land was $30,000. After living in the home for five years, Lance converted it to a rental property on April 1, 2016. Since land is not depreciable, Lance includes only the cost of the house when calculating his basis for depreciation. The allocated cost of the house is $150,000 ($180,000 - $30,000). In 2016, the county assessor's office assigned the home an FMV of $185,000, of which $40,000 was for land and $145,000 for the house. The basis for depreciation of the house is the FMV on the date of conversion ($145,000) because it is less than Lance's allocated cost ($150,000). Lance uses $145,000 to calculate depreciation, which is reported on Schedule E, *Supplemental Income and Loss (From rental real estate, royalties, partnerships, S corporations, estates, trusts, REMICs, etc.).*

Most residential rental buildings are depreciated over 27.5 years, and nonresidential buildings are generally depreciated over 39 years.

Example: In 2016, Shannon buys a rental property for $200,000. It has an assessed value of $160,000, of which $136,000 is for the house, and $24,000 is for the land. Shannon can allocate 85% ($136,000 ÷ $160,000) of the purchase price to the house and 15% ($24,000 ÷ $160,000) of the purchase price to the land. Therefore, her basis in the house is $170,000 (85% of $200,000) and her basis in the land is $30,000 (15% of $200,000). Shannon may use $170,000 as her basis for depreciation on the property.

Example: A residential rental building with a cost basis of $137,500 would generate depreciation of $5,000 per year ($137,500/27.5 years).

Repairs vs. Improvements to Rental Property

A taxpayer can currently deduct the cost of repairs to rental property, but cannot currently deduct the cost of improvements. Instead, the taxpayer must recover the cost of an improvement by taking depreciation deductions over its applicable recovery period.

A repair generally keeps an asset or property in good working condition, but does not add to the value of the asset or substantially prolong its life. Repainting, fixing leaks, and replacing broken windows are examples of repairs.

Example #1: Keith owns a rental home. A baseball broke a window, so he replaced it with an upgraded model, an insulated double-pane window that helps control heating and cooling costs. Even though this window is a substantial upgrade from the previous one, it is still considered a repair, because the old window was broken and needed to be replaced. If Keith were to replace all the windows in the house, the upgrade would be considered an improvement, and he would be required to capitalize the cost and claim depreciation deductions over a period of years.

Example #2: Keith also replaces the entire roof at the cost of $17,000. This is considered a substantial improvement, and the cost of the roof must be depreciated over time rather than deducted against current income.

Note: In September 2013, the IRS released its final tangible property regulations, a highly complex set of rules governing repairs and capitalization that affect all taxpayers who use tangible property in their businesses. These rules change the way businesses treat expenditures for tangible property. For the EA exam, most of the specific details of these regulations will likely not be tested. However, you should have a general understanding of the concept that a business may recover the costs of property either through current deductions or through periodic depreciation deductions for items required to be capitalized.

Under a safe harbor rule of the tangible property regulations,[25] materials and supplies costing no more than $2,500[26] are generally deductible in the year they are used or consumed.

An improvement is anything that results in the betterment of a property, restoration of a property, or adaptation of a property to a new or different use. Examples include:

- Additions of an extra bedroom, bathroom, deck, or garage
- The installation of a new roof
- Installation of central air conditioning, new plumbing, wall-to-wall carpeting, or upgraded wiring
- Construction of a retaining wall, fence, or swimming pool

Example: Glenna owns a rental property. In 2016, she spent $8,000 to replace the carpet, $6,540 to pave the driveway, and $175 to repair a couple of broken gutters. Only the gutter repair ($175) can be expensed on her 2016 tax return. The costs of the new carpet and the new driveway must be capitalized and depreciated over time.

The capitalized cost of an improvement is depreciated separately from the original cost of the asset or property that is being improved.

Rental Rules

The tax treatment of rental income, expenses, and losses depends on several factors: whether a taxpayer is a real estate professional or actively manages a property; whether there is any personal use of the rental property, and if so, whether the dwelling is considered a home; and whether the rental activity is for profit. We will briefly review the rules related to each of these situations next.

The Special $25,000 Loss Allowance for Rental Activity

The deductibility of losses from passive activities is limited, and a taxpayer usually cannot deduct losses from passive activities to offset his nonpassive income (such as wages). In general, a trade or business activity is considered a passive activity if the taxpayer does not *materially participate* in it. A taxpayer materially participates in an activity if he is involved in the operation of that activity on a regular, continuous, and substantial basis.

---

[25] The tangible property regulations are covered in more detail in Book 2, *Businesses*. For Part 1 of the exam, you may have to know how these new regulations apply to rental property.
[26] Effective for taxable years beginning on or after January 1, 2016, the Internal Revenue Service in Notice 2015-82 increased the de minimis safe harbor threshold from $500 to $2,500 per invoice or item for taxpayers without applicable financial statements.

Generally, losses from passive activities that exceed income from passive activities in the same year are disallowed. The disallowed losses are carried forward to the next taxable year and can be used to offset future income from passive activities.

The passive activity loss rules for taxpayers involved in rental activities are an exception, as most rental activities are considered passive activities, even if the taxpayer does materially participate in them. However, when a taxpayer *actively participates* in a rental real estate activity, he may be able to deduct up to $25,000 of losses against his nonpassive income. It should be noted that active participation is a different, and less stringent, standard than material participation.

> **Note:** Active participation is not the same thing as material participation. Material participation is a much stricter standard. For example, the owner of a rental property will generally be treated as actively participating if he makes management decisions such as approving new tenants, deciding rental contracts, approving repairs, and other similar management decisions.

In order to actively participate, a taxpayer must own at least 10% of the rental property and must make management decisions in a significant and bona fide way, such as approving new tenants and establishing the rental terms.

> **Example:** Theodore owns a residential rental property in San Diego, California. He also lives in San Diego and has a regular job that he works full time. Theodore actively manages his rental by choosing his own tenants, hiring workers to do any required repairs, and collecting the rent. Theodore is actively participating in this rental activity.

> **Note:** If the IRS determines a taxpayer has not actively participated, rental losses are not currently deductible, and he is not eligible for the special $25,000 loss allowance.

> **Example:** Toni owns a rental property in Hawaii. She lives in Nevada. Toni hired a management company to manage the property and screen new tenants. The management company handles all the repairs and collects the rent. The management company charges a fee for its services and then remits the net proceeds to Toni monthly. It has been several years since Toni has visited the property. Toni is not actively participating in this rental activity. She is not eligible for the special $25,000 loss allowance.

The full $25,000 allowance is available for taxpayers, whether single or MFJ, whose modified adjusted gross income (MAGI) is $100,000 or less. If a taxpayer is married and files a separate return, but lived apart from his spouse for the entire tax year, the taxpayer's special allowance for rental losses cannot exceed $12,500; this full allowance would be available if his MAGI is $50,000 or less. However, if the taxpayer lived with his spouse at any time during the year and is filing MFS, the taxpayer cannot use any of his passive rental losses to offset nonpassive income.

Rental losses that cannot be deducted due to the limitations described above can be carried forward indefinitely and used in subsequent years, subject to the same limitations.

> **Definition:** MAGI is a taxpayer's adjusted gross income with certain deductions added back in. These may include IRA contributions, rental losses, student loan interest, and qualified tuition expenses, among others. A taxpayer's MAGI is used as a basis for determining whether he qualifies for certain tax deductions.

Example: Kendrick owns a rental property in San Francisco. He actively participates in the rental activity. In the previous tax year, he incurred $9,000 in losses on his rental. Kendrick's modified adjusted gross income was $150,000 in that year. Because of his income threshold, Kendrick's rental losses are suspended, and he is not allowed to deduct any rental losses. The following year, (2016) Kendrick had $5,000 in losses from his rental activity. However, he also changed jobs in the middle of the year, and now his AGI is lower. In 2016, Kendrick's AGI is $85,000, so his rental losses are now allowable. His suspended rental losses from the prior year ($9,000) and his current year losses ($5,000) will be allowed on his 2016 tax return, for a total deduction of $14,000.

Example: Philip and Susanne own a residential rental property that they manage themselves. In 2016, they have wages of $98,000 and a rental loss of $26,800. Because they meet both the active participation and the MAGI tests, they are allowed to deduct $25,000 of the rental loss as an offset to their nonpassive income (wages). The remaining amount over the $25,000 limit ($1,800) that cannot be deducted in the current year is carried forward and may be used in the following year.

For every $2 by which a taxpayer's MAGI exceeds $100,000, the allowance is reduced by $1. If MAGI is $150,000 or more (or $75,000 or more if married filing separately), the $25,000 allowance is fully phased out.

Example: Hal and Lorena file jointly and have MAGI of $140,000. They have $25,000 of losses from the residential rental property that they actively manage. Because they actively manage the property, they potentially qualify to deduct up to $25,000 of losses against their nonpassive income. However, because their joint income is over $100,000, they are subject to the phase-out. Therefore, Hal and Lorena's deduction for rental losses is reduced by $20,000 (0.5 × ($140,000 - $100,000). They can deduct $5,000 ($25,000 - $20,000) against their nonpassive income. The additional $20,000 of losses is carried forward to the following year.

Exception for Real Estate Professionals

If a taxpayer qualifies as a real estate professional, losses from rental real estate activities in which he materially participates are not considered passive activity losses and are fully deductible.[27] If the tests for material participation are not met, rental losses are considered passive and are normally deductible only up to $25,000, based upon the passive activity rules outlined previously.

In most instances, if a property owner provides only basic services to tenants, such as trash collection, he reports rental income and expenses on Schedule E, Form 1040. It is not subject to self-employment tax.

In contrast, owners of property who provide significant services to the renter, such as maid cleaning and housekeeping services, are generally required to report revenue and expenses related to the property on Schedule C, *Profit of Loss from Business,* and any net profit is subject to self-

---

[27] The determination of whether someone is a "real estate professional" is based on a number of factors. In general, a taxpayer qualifies as a real estate professional if he performs more than 750 hours of services during the taxable year in real property trades or businesses in which he materially participates and more than one-half of the total personal services performed in trades or businesses by the taxpayer during the year are performed in real property trades or businesses in which the taxpayer materially participates.

employment tax. The most common examples of taxpayers who report their rental activities on Schedule C, instead of on Schedule E, are hotel owners and motel operators.

> **Example:** Joseph owns two residential rental properties and provides basic services to his tenants. He manages them and collects rents. He also has a full-time job as a restaurant manager. He is not a real estate professional. Joseph must report his rental income and losses on Schedule E. His rental income is considered passive activity income, and it is not subject to self-employment tax.

> **Example:** Sabi owns a small motel in downtown Cincinnati. Sabi does not offer long-term rentals. The hotel offers full maid service, cleaning, and breakfast daily. Since she provides "significant services" as a motel owner, the income would be treated as self-employment income, rather than rental income. Sabi would report her income on Schedule C.

Not Rented for Profit

A taxpayer who does not rent his property to make a profit can deduct rental expenses only up to the amount of his rental income. The IRS calls this a "not-for-profit rental." He cannot deduct a loss or carry forward to the next year any rental expenses that are more than his rental income for the year. The taxpayer reports the rental income on Form 1040; if he itemizes deductions, he can deduct expenses for mortgage interest and real estate taxes on Schedule A. He can also report his other rental expenses as miscellaneous itemized deductions on Schedule A, but the deductibility is subject to the 2% floor.

The IRS will presume a taxpayer is renting property to make a profit if his rental income is greater than his rental expenses for at least three out of five years.

If a taxpayer is just starting his rental activity and does not have three years showing a profit, he can elect to postpone the determination of whether the rental is for profit by filing Form 5213, *Election to Postpone Determination as to Whether the Presumption Applies that an Activity is Engaged in for Profit.* This gives the taxpayer five years to determine whether his rental is for profit or not for profit.

Renting Part of Property

A taxpayer who rents part of a property must divide certain expenses between the part of the property used for rental purposes and the part used for personal purposes, as though there were actually two separate pieces of property. Expenses related to the part of the property used for rental purposes can be deducted as rental expenses on Schedule E. This includes a portion of expenses that normally are nondeductible personal expenses, such as painting the outside of a house. If an expense applies to both rental use and personal use, such as a heating bill for the entire house, the taxpayer must divide the expense between the two. The two most common methods for dividing such expenses are based on:
- The number of rooms in the house, and
- The square footage of the house.

Example: Pablo rents out a bedroom in his house. The room is 12 × 15 feet or 180 square feet. Pablo's entire house, including this room, is 1,800 square feet. Pablo can deduct as a rental expense 10% of any expense that must be divided between rental use and personal use. Pablo's 2016 heating bills for the entire house totaled $600, and therefore $60 ($600 × .10) can be considered a deductible rental expense. The balance, $540, is a personal expense that Pablo cannot deduct.

A common situation involves a duplex in which the landlord lives in one side and rents out the other. Certain expenses, like mortgage interest and real estate taxes, apply to the entire property and must be split to determine rental and personal expenses.

Example: Gillian owns a duplex with two units of the same size. She lives in one side and rents out the other. In 2016, Gillian paid $12,000 of mortgage interest and $4,000 of real estate taxes for the entire property. Gillian can deduct $6,000 of mortgage interest and $2,000 of real estate taxes on Schedule E. She can claim the other $6,000 of mortgage interest and $2,000 of real estate taxes attributable to her personal use on Schedule A as itemized deductions.

If a taxpayer owns a partial interest in rental property, he can deduct expenses paid according to the percentage of ownership.

Personal Use of Dwelling Unit

When a taxpayer has a residence (whether a main home or a second home) that is used personally at certain times and rented out at other times, he must divide his expenses between rental use and personal use. Rental expenses generally will be no more than a taxpayer's total expenses multiplied by the following fraction: the denominator is the total number of days the dwelling is used, and the numerator is the total number of days actually rented at a fair rental price.

Any day the unit is rented at a fair rental price is a day of rental use. Any day the unit is available for rent but not actually rented is not a day of rental use.

Example: Carol owns a vacation home in Hawaii that she rented for 90 days in January, February, and March. She can deduct the rental expenses on Schedule E only for those 90 days. However, she can deduct expenses for mortgage interest and real estate taxes for the other 275 days of the year on her Schedule A.

If a taxpayer uses a property for both rental and personal purposes, the tax treatment of expenses depends on whether his personal use is considered to be usage as a "home". It is considered usage as a home if he uses the property for personal purposes during the year for more than the greater of fourteen days, or 10% of the total days it is rented at a fair rental price. Days of personal use are counted when:

- A member of the taxpayer's family uses the property without paying a fair rental price.
- Anyone uses the property at less than fair rental price.
- Use of the property is donated to a charitable organization.

However, any day the taxpayer spends working on repairs and maintaining the property is not counted as personal use, even if his family is also staying there.

> **Example:** Mike owns a mountain cabin at Lake Tahoe that was used as follows in 2016: He rented it for 60 days during the ski season, spent a week at the cabin cleaning and making repairs before the rental period began, and donated a week of rental use to a local charity. In apportioning expenses:
> - 7/67 days would be treated as personal use (for use by the charity); expenses such as mortgage interest and property taxes would be deductible in this ratio on Schedule A.
> - The remaining 60/67 days would be treated as rental use, and this fraction of total expenses incurred would be deductible on Schedule E.
> - The seven days cleaning and making repairs would not count as either personal or rental use for purposes of allocating expenses.
>
> Mike's cabin is not considered a "home" because his personal use was less than 14 days and less than 10% of the total days it was rented.

Renting a dwelling unit that is also used by the taxpayer for personal purposes during the year is not considered a passive activity. If a taxpayer's rental expenses are more than his rental income, he cannot use the excess expenses to offset income from other sources. However, excess deductions may be carried forward to the next year and treated as rental expenses for the same property, subject to the same limits.

> **Example:** Jack owns a condo on Hilton Head Island. He uses it as a personal residence four months out of the year and rents it out to tenants the rest of the year. Jack's rental income is $8,000 in 2016, and his rental expenses are $10,000. Jack cannot deduct the full $10,000 of rental expenses, but he can carry over the remaining $2,000 and deduct that amount from future rental income on the condo.

Minimal Rental Use (15 Day Rule)

If a taxpayer rents a main home or vacation home for fewer than 15 days, he does not have to recognize any of the income as taxable. He also cannot deduct any rental expenses. This is called the "15-day rule."

> **Example:** Brynn owns a condo on the Gulf Coast which is her personal residence. While she was away on vacation, she rented her condo for 11 days, charging $100 per day for a total of $1,100. She also had $320 of rental expenses during that time. Brynn does not report any of the income or expenses based on the exception for minimal rental use.

Converting to Rental Use: If a taxpayer changes a main home or second home to rental use at any time other than the beginning of a tax year, he must divide his expenses between rental use and personal use. He can deduct as rental expenses only the portion that is for the part of the year the property was used or held for rental purposes.

For depreciation purposes, the property is treated as being placed in service on the conversion date. When a taxpayer converts property held for personal use to rental use, the basis for depreciation will be the lesser of fair market value or his adjusted basis on the date of conversion.

Royalty Income

Like rental income, royalty income is reported on line 17 of Form 1040. Royalties from copyrights, patents, and oil, gas, and mineral properties are taxable as ordinary income.

In many cases, a taxpayer reports details of royalties on Schedule E, *Supplemental Income and Loss*. However, self-employed writers, musicians, and inventors report income on Schedule C, *Profit or Loss from Business,* and are subject to self-employment tax.

Example: In 2016, Don's brother died. Don inherited a copyright from his brother, who had written an instruction manual for woodworking. Don then leased the copyrighted material to schools and colleges for their use. Since he had not created the copyright himself, Don will report the royalty income on Schedule E.

Royalties from copyrights on literary, musical, or artistic works, or from patents on inventions, are paid to a taxpayer for the right to use his work over a specified period of time. Royalties are often based on the number of units sold, such as the number of books, tickets to a performance, or machines sold.

Example: Marisa is the self-employed author of a popular series of books for young children. She receives royalties from her publisher based on the number of books she has sold over a certain period of time. Marisa must report these royalties as taxable income on her Schedule C.

A taxpayer is required to issue Form 1099-MISC, *Miscellaneous Income,* to each person to whom he has paid at least $10 of royalties for the year.

Unit 9: Study Questions

(Test yourself first, then check the correct answers at the end of this quiz.)

1. Ian signs a three-year lease to rent a building he owns. In December 2016, he receives $12,000 for the first year's rent and $12,000 as rent for the last year of the lease. He also receives a $1,500 security deposit that is refundable at the end of the lease. How much rental income must Ian include in his 2016 tax return?

A. $1,500
B. $12,000
C. $24,000
D. $25,500

2. In 2016, Jane is single and has $40,000 of wages, $2,000 of passive activity income from a limited partnership, and $3,500 of passive activity loss from a rental real estate activity in which she actively participated. Which of the following statements is correct?

A. The first $2,000 of Jane's $3,500 passive loss offsets her passive income. Jane can deduct the remaining $1,500 loss to reduce taxation of her wages.
B. Jane cannot deduct the passive loss to reduce taxation of her wages.
C. Jane cannot offset the rental loss against the passive income from the partnership because it is not the same type of passive activity.
D. Jane must carry over her loss to the subsequent tax year.

3. Rosemary's home is used exclusively as her residence all year, except for 13 days. During this time, Rosemary rents her home to alumni while the local college has its homecoming celebration. She made $3,000 of rental income and had $500 of rental expenses during this 13 day period. Which of the following statements is correct?

A. All of the rental income may be excluded.
B. Rosemary can exclude only $2,500 of the rental income.
C. Rosemary can deduct her rental expenses when she reports her rental income on Schedule E.
D. Rosemary must recognize all $3,000 of rental income, and she can deduct the $500 in expenses on Schedule E.

4. Pam ordered a heating, ventilating, and air conditioning (HVAC) unit for her rental property on November 15, 2016. It was delivered on December 28, 2016, and was installed and ready for use on January 2, 2017. She paid for the unit using a credit card and paid off the card on February 2, 2017. In which month should the HVAC unit be considered placed in service for depreciation purposes?

A. November 2016
B. December 2016
C. January 2017
D. February 2017

5. Reba converted her primary residence to rental use during the year. Her original cost was $189,000, of which $13,200 was allocated to the land and $175,800 was to the house. On the date of the conversion, the property had a fair market value of $158,000, of which $11,000 was allocable to the land and $147,000 to the house. What is Reba's basis for depreciation on Schedule E?

A. $147,000
B. $189,000
C. $175,800
D. $158,000

6. Nicklaus decides to convert his residence to rental property. He moves out of his home in May 2016 and starts renting it on June 1, 2016. He has $12,000 of mortgage interest for the year. How should Nicklaus report his mortgage interest expense?

A. Report the entire $12,000 on Schedule E.
B. Report the entire $12,000 on Schedule A.
C. Report $7,000 on Schedule E as interest expense and $5,000 on Schedule A as mortgage interest.
D. Report $8,000 on Schedule E as interest expense and $4,000 on Schedule A as mortgage interest.

7. Which of the following costs related to rental property should be classified as a capital improvement and depreciated rather than being expensed currently?

A. Replacing an entire deck.
B. Repairing a broken toilet.
C. Painting the family room.
D. Patching a hole in the wall.

8. Which of the following describes depreciation?

A. A business expense that applies only to rental properties.
B. An improvement to an asset that must be capitalized.
C. A common type of accounting method used by most partnerships.
D. An annual tax deduction that accounts for the reduction in the value of an asset as it ages.

9. Tina owns a residential rental house. Last year, she paid $968 to repair a broken window. The cost of the labor was $468, and the cost of the replacement window was $500. She replaced the broken window with a premium energy-saving window. What is the correct treatment of this expense?

A. She cannot deduct the cost since it was an improvement; she must add it to the basis of the property.
B. She can deduct $468 as a rental expense on Schedule E (the labor cost). The cost of the actual window ($500) must be capitalized and depreciated.
C. She can deduct the entire $968 as a rental expense on Schedule E.
D. She can deduct $968 on Schedule A as an itemized deduction.

10. In 2016, Travis and Brittany moved to Florida. They decided to rent their house in California instead of selling it. They had purchased the home five years ago for $500,000 and had paid $80,000 for various improvements through the years. The purchase price of $500,000 was attributable to fair market values of $100,000 for the land and $400,000 for the house. Their new tenant paid a refundable security deposit of $6,000 and moved in on July 1, 2016. The FMV of the property on July 1 was $525,000, comprised of $105,000 for the land and $420,000 for the house. The tenant then paid rent of $3,000 each month from July through December of 2016. Travis and Brittany incurred the following expenses in 2016 related to the house:

- Mortgage interest: $10,000
- Property taxes: $10,000
- Casualty insurance: $1,000

In addition, they paid $500 for repairs during December. Exclusive of depreciation expense, what was Travis and Brittany's taxable rental income?

A. $1,500
B. $7,000
C. $7,250
D. $13,000

11. Based upon the information in the previous question, what is the amount of basis on which depreciation should be calculated for the rental period?

A. $400,000
B. $480,000
C. $580,000
D. $420,000

12. Matt and Diane are legally separated and have lived in separate residences for three years. They file separate tax returns (MFS). They own a rental property jointly, actively participate in the rental activity, and share income and losses equally. The rental property had $30,000 of losses during the year. Matt has wage income of $48,000 in 2016. He has no other items of income or loss. What is the maximum amount of rental losses that Matt can claim on his separate return?

A. $0
B. $12,500
C. $15,000
D. $25,000

13. All of the following statements about not-for-profit rentals are correct except:

A. Rental losses cannot be carried forward to the next year.

B. A taxpayer with a not-for-profit rental can deduct rental expenses only up to the amount of his rental income.

C. Profit is determined when rental income is greater than rental expenses for four out of five years.

D. A taxpayer with a new rental may elect to postpone the determination of whether the activity is for profit or not for profit for five years.

14. Shin acquired a multi-unit residential rental property in 2016 for $800,000 and paid an additional $35,000 to replace the roof in the same year. After acquiring the property and renting out the property for some time, he also incurred $40,000 for general repairs. The purchase price of the property was determined to be allocable as follows: 80% to the building and 20% to the land. Based upon the information provided, what is Shin's basis for depreciation on this rental property in 2016?

A. $800,000
B. $675,000
C. $640,000
D. $715,000

Unit 9: Answers

1. The answer is C. Ian must include $24,000 in his income in the first year. He must recognize all the advance rent as income in the year of receipt. The security deposit does not have to be recognized as income because it is refundable to the tenant.

2. The answer is A. Jane can use $2,000 of her rental loss to offset the passive activity income from the limited partnership. The remaining $1,500 loss can be offset against her $40,000 of wages. A taxpayer can deduct up to $25,000 per year of losses for rental real estate activities in which she actively participates, so long as their modified AGI does not exceed a certain amount. This special allowance is an exception to the general rule disallowing losses in excess of income from passive activities against non-passive income.

3. The answer is A. All the rental income may be excluded under the "15-day rule." The home is primarily for personal use, and a rental period of less than 15 days is disregarded, which means the IRS does not consider it a rental. The rental income is not taxable, but the rental expenses (such as utilities or maintenance costs) are not deductible.

4. The answer is C. Depreciation begins on the placed-in-service date when an asset becomes available for use. Typically, the placed-in-service date and the purchase date are the same, but that is not always necessarily the case. Since Pam did not have the HVAC unit ready for use until January 2, 2017, she must wait until 2017 to begin depreciating the unit. The fact that the unit was paid for with a credit card is irrelevant (it is treated the same as if it was paid by check or cash).

5. The answer is A. When a taxpayer converts property held for personal use to rental use (for example, the rental of a former home), the basis for depreciation will be the lesser of fair market value or adjusted basis on the date of conversion. The basis for depreciation on the house is its fair market value on the date of the conversion ($147,000) because the FMV on the date of conversion is less than the amount of her original cost that was allocable to the house ($175,800).

6. The answer is C. Nicklaus must allocate his expenses between personal use and rental use. He can deduct as rental expenses seven-twelfths (7/12) of annual expenses, such as taxes and insurance. Starting in June, he can deduct as rental expenses the amounts he paid for items generally billed monthly, such as utilities. When figuring depreciation, he should treat the property as placed in service on June 1.

7. The answer is A. The replacement of the deck would be considered a depreciable improvement. The other choices are repairs and may be deducted as current expenses.

8. The answer is D. Depreciation is an income tax deduction that allows a business to recover the cost or basis of property it uses over time. It is an annual allowance for the wear and tear, deterioration, or obsolescence of assets.

194

9. The answer is C. Generally, the expenses of renting a property, such as maintenance, insurance, taxes, and interest, can be deducted from rental income. This cost is a repair, not an improvement because the window was broken. If all the windows had been replaced with energy-efficient windows, the cost would have been considered an improvement and added to the property's basis.

10. The answer is B. They must report six months of rental income at $3,000 per month, or $18,000, but the security deposit of $6,000 is refundable and therefore not recognized as income in 2016. They can deduct 6/12 of the amounts incurred for mortgage interest, property taxes, and casualty insurance, or $10,500, plus the $500 cost of repairs while the house was rented. Thus, their reportable net rental income before considering depreciation would be $7,000.

Taxable rental income:	
Six months of rent (at $3,000)	$18,000
Minus deductible expenses:	
Mortgage interest (for six months)	5,000
Property taxes (for six months)	5,000
Casualty insurance (for six months)	500
Repair cost	500
Expenses before depreciation	(11,000)
Rental income before depreciation	**$7,000**

11. The answer is D. The basis for depreciation is the lesser of fair market value or the taxpayer's adjusted basis on the date the property was converted to rental use. The adjusted basis of the house on July 1, 2016, was $480,000 (original cost of $400,000 plus improvements of $80,000), but the FMV of $420,000 on the same date was lower. The basis of the land is not subject to depreciation and not included in the calculation.

Adjusted basis of house:	
Cost	$400,000
Improvements	80,000
Total adjusted basis	480,000
FMV on July 1, 2016	**$420,000**

12. The answer is B. Matt is allowed to claim a maximum of $12,500 of losses on his separately filed return. If a taxpayer actively participated in a passive rental real estate activity that produced a loss, he can deduct the loss to offset his nonpassive income, up to $25,000. However, married persons filing separate returns who lived apart during the year are each allowed a maximum of $12,500 for losses from passive real estate activities. Married persons who file separate returns but lived together during the year are not allowed to take losses on rental real estate activity. Instead, the losses are suspended and must be carried over until the property produces income, or the property is disposed of.

13. The answer is C. The determination of whether a rental is for profit or not for profit is made when rental income exceeds rental expenses for three out of five years, not for four out of five years.

14. The answer is B. The depreciable basis for the property is the sum of the purchase price minus the portion attributable to non-depreciable land, or $640,000 ($800,000 X 80%), plus the cost of major improvements ($35,000 roof), for a total of $675,000. The cost of repairs ($40,000) is deductible as a current expense and does not affect the calculation of basis or the depreciation calculation.

Purchase price (minus land value $800,000 X 80%)	$640,000
Improvements (roof replacement)	$35,000
Depreciable basis	$675,000

Unit 10: Other Taxable Income

For additional information read:
Publication 525, *Taxable and Nontaxable Income*
Publication 4681, *Canceled Debts, Foreclosures, Repossessions, & Abandonments*
Publication 504, *Divorced or Separated Individuals*

In this unit, we discuss a number of other types of taxable income that must be reported on Form 1040.

Taxable Recoveries

A recovery is a return of an amount a taxpayer deducted or took a credit for in an earlier year. The most common recoveries are refunds, reimbursements, and rebates of deductions itemized on Schedule A. A taxpayer must include a recovery in income in the year he receives it, to the extent the deduction or credit reduced his tax in the earlier year.

Example: In the prior year, Perla paid $2,700 for medical expenses. She subtracted $2,500, which was 10% of her adjusted gross income, to determine her medical expense deduction of $200. In 2016, Perla's medical insurance reimbursed $500 of her prior year medical expenses. The only portion of the $500 reimbursement she must include in her income for 2016 is $200, the amount she actually deducted.

State and local income tax refunds are reported as taxable income in the year received only if the taxpayer itemized deductions in the prior year in which those taxes were overpaid. The payer should send Form 1099-G, *Certain Government Payments*, to the taxpayer by January 31, and also send a copy to the IRS.

Example: Wally claimed the standard deduction on his prior year federal tax return. In 2016, he received a refund of $600 for state income taxes he paid during the prior year. The state tax refund is not taxable in 2016, as Wally received no federal tax benefit from his state tax payments because he did not itemize deductions in the previous year.

Refunds of federal income taxes are not included in a taxpayer's income because they are never allowed as a deduction.

Alimony Received

Alimony is taxable income to the recipient and deductible by the payer. In contrast, child support is not taxable income to the receiver and not deductible by the payer because it is viewed as a payment a parent makes simply to support his or her own child.

Alimony *received* is taxable income to the payee and reported on line 11 of Form 1040. Alimony *paid* is an adjustment to income for the payor. The payor does not have to itemize in order to deduct alimony payments made.

Example: Mark and Sibba are divorced. Their divorce decree requires Mark to pay Sibba $200 per month as child support and $150 per month as alimony. Mark makes all of his child support and alimony payments on time. Therefore, in 2016, he can deduct $1,800 ($150 × 12 months) as alimony paid, and Sibba must report $1,800 as alimony received as taxable income. The amount paid as child support, $2,400 ($200 × 12), is not deductible by Mark and is not reported as income by Sibba.

The alimony paid is listed on the first page of Form 1040 on line 31a. Form 1040A or Form 1040EZ cannot be used by a taxpayer who takes a deduction for alimony.

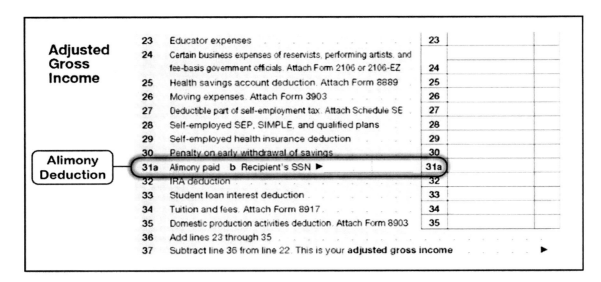

If a divorce agreement specifies payments of both alimony and child support and only partial payments are made by the payer, the partial payments are considered child support until that obligation is fully paid. Any additional amounts paid are then treated as alimony.

Example: Elsa and Jessie are divorced. Their divorce decree requires Jessie pay Elsa $2,000 a month ($24,000 [$2,000 × 12] a year) as child support and $1,500 a month ($18,000 [$1,500 × 12] a year) as alimony. Jessie falls behind on his payments and pays only $36,000 during 2016. In this case, the first $24,000 paid is considered child support and only the remaining amount of $12,000 ($36,000 - $24,000) is considered alimony. Jessie can deduct $12,000 as alimony paid. Elsa must report $12,000 as alimony income received.

If an alimony payment is subject to reduction based on a contingency relating to a child (e.g., attaining a certain age, marrying), the amount subject to reduction is treated as child support. If alimony payments continue after the receiving spouse dies, they will automatically be considered child support, not alimony. In order for a payment to qualify as alimony:

- The divorce agreement may not include a clause indicating that the payment is something else (such as child support or repayment of a loan).
- If the spouses are legally separated, they cannot live together when the alimony payments are made, or the IRS will not consider the payments to be alimony.

- The payor must have no liability to make any payment (in cash or property) after the death of the former spouse.

  Alimony does not include:

- Payments that are a former spouse's share of income from community property
- Payments to keep up the payer's property
- Free use of the payer's property
- Noncash property settlements

Note: Property settlements are simply a division of property and are not treated as alimony. In general, property transferred to an ex-spouse as part of a divorce proceeding is not a taxable event.

Example: Olga and Phillip divorce in 2016. As part of their divorce agreement, Olga must transfer a portion of her IRA account to Phillip. The IRA transfer is properly outlined in their property settlement agreement. On October 1, 2016, their divorce becomes final. Two days later, the IRA transfer is completed, and $12,000 is transferred directly from Olga's IRA to Phillip's IRA. The transfer is considered a division of marital assets and is not alimony. It is also not subject to an early withdrawal penalty.

Payments made to a third party can be considered alimony in some cases. For example, if, under the terms of a divorce agreement, a spouse pays the medical bills of his ex-wife, a cash payment to the hospital can count as alimony. For a jointly owned home, half of the mortgage payments and real estate taxes may be deducted as alimony, assuming the divorce decree or separation agreement requires a taxpayer to pay these expenses for his ex-spouse. The ex-spouse must include the payments as alimony received.

Government Benefits

Most government welfare benefits, including food stamps, heating assistance programs, and non-federal assistance benefits from states or local agencies are exempt from federal taxation. Worker's compensation, which provides wage replacement and medical benefits to injured workers, is not taxable income. In contrast, unemployment compensation is taxable.

Example: Wilma was laid off from her job in 2016. She received $300 a week of unemployment compensation for 26 weeks. When she was unable to find another job, she began receiving benefits from her state's WIC program, which provided vouchers for food for her and her toddler. The unemployment compensation would be taxable income, but the welfare (WIC) benefits would not be taxable.

Social Security Income

Social Security income is reported to the taxpayer on Form SSA-1099, and these benefits are taxable in certain cases, depending upon a taxpayer's income and the amount of benefits received for the year. To determine if any percentage of his Social Security benefits is taxable, a taxpayer must compare the base threshold amount for his filing status with the total of:

- One-half of his benefits, plus
- All of his other income, including tax-exempt interest.

If the sum is less than the base amount for his filing status, none of the Social Security is taxable. If the sum is more than the base amount for his filing status, a percentage of the Social Security is taxable.

Base Amounts for Calculating Taxability of Social Security

MFJ: $32,000

Single, HOH, QW, or MFS (and lived apart from his/her spouse all year): $25,000

MFS (if lived with spouse at any time during the year): $0

The taxpayer calculates the taxable portion on a worksheet in the *Instructions for Form 1040*, or Publication 915, *Social Security and Equivalent Railroad Retirement Benefits*. The taxable portion of Social Security benefits is never more than 85% and, in most cases, is less than 50%. Spouses who file jointly must combine their incomes and Social Security benefits when figuring the taxable portion of their benefits, even if one spouse did not receive any benefits.

Example: Bo and Yvonne are both over 65. They file jointly, and both received Social Security benefits during 2016. At the end of the year, Bo received a Form SSA-1099 showing net benefits of $7,500. Yvonne received a Form SSA-1099 showing net benefits of $3,500. Bo also received wages of $20,000 and taxable interest income of $500. He did not have any tax-exempt interest.

1. Total Social Security benefits	$11,000
2. Enter one-half of SS	$5,500
3. Enter taxable interest and wages	$20,500
4. Sum ($5,500 + $20,500)	$26,000

Bo and Yvonne's benefits are not taxable for 2016 because the total above is not more than the base amount ($32,000) for married filing jointly.

Other Income (Line 21)

"Other income" includes items that do not have separately identified lines on Form 1040. This line is the catch-all for all other types of taxable income that is not reportable on another schedule or area of Form 1040. Examples, which we cover in detail next, include:

- Gambling winnings
- Cancellation of debt income
- Hobby income
- Certain types of court awards
- Prizes and awards
- Taxable distributions from a Coverdell education savings account or a qualified tuition program if they are more than the qualified higher education expenses for a designated beneficiary

---

Note: Remember, taxpayers are required to report all taxable income, whether or not the taxpayer receives a document from the payer reporting the amount paid.

Gambling Winnings

Gambling income may include winnings from lotteries, raffles, horse races, and casinos. Gambling winnings should be reported to a taxpayer on Form W-2G if he wins:

- $600 or more from gambling
- $1,200 or more from bingo or slot machines
- $1,500 or more from keno
- Any amounts subject to federal income tax withholding

A taxpayer must report and pay tax on all gambling winnings, regardless of whether he receives a Form W-2G. Gambling losses are deductible on Schedule A as a miscellaneous deduction that is not subject to the 2% limit, but the deduction is limited to the amount of gambling winnings.

> **Example:** Yolanda had $1,000 of gambling winnings and $3,000 of gambling losses in 2016. Her deduction for gambling losses cannot exceed $1,000, the amount of her gambling winnings. In order to claim the deduction for her losses, Yolanda must itemize and list her gambling losses on Schedule A, Form 1040.

The taxpayer must keep an accurate diary or similar record of gambling winnings and losses, along with tickets, receipts, canceled checks, and other documentation. He is not required to include these supporting records with his tax return, but they should be retained in case of an audit.

Cancellation of Debt Income

Generally, if a taxpayer's debt is canceled or forgiven, the taxpayer must include the debt forgiveness or cancellation of debt (COD) in his gross income. If a lender cancels a debt and issues Form 1099-C, the lender will indicate on the form if the borrower was personally liable for repayment of the debt. The tax impact depends on the type of debt: whether the loan is recourse or nonrecourse. A recourse debt holds the borrower personally liable. All other debt is considered nonrecourse.

Cancellation of debt may include any indebtedness for which a taxpayer is personally liable or which attaches to the taxpayer's property, such as an auto loan, credit card debt, mortgage, or home equity loan.

> **Note:** A nonrecourse loan does not allow the lender to pursue anything other than the collateral. For example, if a borrower defaults on a nonrecourse home loan, the bank can only foreclose on the home. The bank cannot take further legal action to collect the money owed on the debt. Whether a debt is recourse or nonrecourse may vary from state to state, depending on state law. If a lender forecloses on property subject to a recourse debt and cancels the portion of the debt in excess of the FMV of the property, the canceled portion is treated as ordinary income. This amount must be included in gross income unless it qualifies for an exception or exclusion.[28]

If the debt is a nonbusiness debt, the canceled debt amount is reported as "other income" on line 21 of a taxpayer's Form 1040. The taxpayer must generally report two transactions:

1. The cancellation of debt income

---

[28] There is no taxable income from a canceled debt if it is intended as a gift (for example, if a taxpayer owes his parents money, but they choose to forgive the debt).

2. Gain or loss on the sale or repossession, generally equal to the difference between the FMV of the property at the time of the foreclosure and the taxpayer's adjusted basis in the property

If a personal asset such as a vehicle is repossessed, the repossession is treated as a sale for tax purposes, and a gain or loss must be computed. A loss related to a personal asset would be nondeductible.

> **Example:** Zach lost his sailboat because he could no longer make his payments. At the time of repossession, he owed a balance of $170,000 to the lender, and the FMV of the sailboat was $140,000. Zach is personally liable for the debt (recourse loan), so the abandonment is treated as a sale. The "selling price" from the repossession is $140,000, and Zach must recognize $30,000 in debt forgiveness income ($170,000 - $140,000).

> **Example:** Doreen bought a new car for $15,000. She made a $2,000 down payment and borrowed the remaining $13,000 from her bank. Doreen is personally liable for the car loan (recourse debt). The bank repossessed her car because she stopped making payments. The balance due on the loan at the time of the repossession was $10,000. The FMV of the car when repossessed was only $9,000. Since repossession is treated as a sale for tax purposes, the gain or loss must be computed. Doreen compares the amount realized ($9,000) with her adjusted basis ($15,000) to determine that she has a $6,000 nondeductible loss. She also has ordinary income from cancellation of debt. That income is $1,000 ($10,000 canceled debt – $9,000 FMV). Doreen must report the canceled debt as income on line 21 of her Form 1040.

> **Definition:** A **nonrecourse debt** is a type of loan that is secured by collateral in which the borrower does not have personal liability for the loan. The most common type of nonrecourse debt is a home mortgage.

Many home mortgages are nonrecourse. This means that if the borrower defaults, the lender can seize the home, but cannot seek out the borrower for any further compensation, even if the FMV of the home does not cover the remaining loan balance. If the taxpayer abandons property that secures debt for which the taxpayer is not personally liable (a nonrecourse loan), the abandonment is treated as a sale or exchange.

If a loan is nonrecourse and the borrower does not retain the asset, the borrower does not have to recognize cancellation of debt income. However, there is a deemed sales price based on the amount of the nonrecourse loan at the time of the abandonment or foreclosure.

> **Example:** Felix lost his home to foreclosure because he lost his job and could no longer make his mortgage payments. At the time of the foreclosure, Felix owed a balance of $170,000 to his mortgage lender, and the fair market value of the home was $140,000. The mortgage is a nonrecourse loan. Since Felix is not personally liable for the debt (nonrecourse loan), Felix abandons the property, and the bank forecloses. The abandonment is treated as a sale (for tax purposes) and the "selling price" would be $170,000, which is the balance of the loan.

A taxpayer may question the taxability of canceled debt because it can apply in a tax year in which cash is not received. In a situation where property is surrendered or repossessed, such as a foreclosure, the taxpayer may feel that by giving up the property, he should be relieved from any further obligation.

> **Example**: Phoebe borrows $10,000 to take a vacation and defaults on the loan after paying back only $2,000. She has the ability to pay back the loan but chooses not to. The lender writes off the remaining balance of the loan instead of pursuing Phoebe for the balance of the loan. Therefore, there is a cancellation of debt of $8,000, which is taxable income to Phoebe.

Not Taxable Canceled Debt

There are several circumstances in which canceled debt is not taxable.

Insolvency: A taxpayer is insolvent when his total debts are more than the FMV of his total assets. If a taxpayer is insolvent when the debt is canceled, the canceled debt is not taxable, but only to the extent of the insolvency (i.e., by how much his debts exceed his assets). For this purpose, the taxpayer's assets include the value of everything he owns, including pensions and retirement accounts.

> **Example:** In 2016, Darla had $5,000 of credit card debt, which she did not pay. The bank decided to cancel the entire $5,000 credit card balance. She received a Form 1099-C from her credit card company showing canceled debt of $5,000. Immediately before the cancellation, Darla's total liabilities were $15,000 and the FMV of her total assets was $7,000. Therefore, at the time the debt was canceled, Darla was insolvent to the extent of $8,000 ($15,000 total liabilities minus $7,000 FMV of her total assets). Darla can exclude the entire $5,000 canceled debt from income.

Bankruptcy: Debts discharged through bankruptcy court in a Title 11 bankruptcy case are not considered taxable income. The taxpayer must attach Form 982, *Reduction of Tax Attributes Due to Discharge of Indebtedness,* to his federal income tax return to report debt canceled in bankruptcy.

Home Mortgage Debt: Normally, when a bank forecloses on a home and sells it for less than the borrower's outstanding mortgage, the bank forgives the unpaid mortgage debt, and the canceled debt is taxable income to the homeowner. However, a taxpayer may exclude income realized as a result of loan modification or foreclosure of a taxpayer's principal residence. The principal residence is the home where the taxpayer ordinarily lives most of the time. This exclusion does not apply to second homes or vacation homes. Further, the exclusion does not apply unless it is directly related to a decline in the home's value or the taxpayer's financial condition. This provision for exclusion of home mortgage debt from a primary residence was extended by the PATH Act.

Qualified principal residence indebtedness (QPRI) is a mortgage secured by a taxpayer's principal residence that was taken out to buy, build, or substantially improve that residence and may also include debt from refinancing. QPRI cannot be more than the cost of the home plus improvements. The maximum amount that can be treated as QPRI is $2 million ($1 million if MFS).

If only part of a loan is qualified principal residence indebtedness, the exclusion from income for QPRI applies only to the extent the amount canceled exceeds the amount of the loan that is not QPRI.

However, the remaining part of the loan may qualify for a different exclusion (such as the exclusion for insolvency).

> **Example:** Ken incurred a mortgage debt of $800,000 when he purchased his home for $880,000. He made a down payment of $80,000 and financed the rest through his bank. When the FMV of the property was $1 million, Ken refinanced the debt for $850,000. At the time of the refinancing, the balance of the original loan was $740,000. Ken used the $110,000 he obtained from the refinancing ($850,000 minus $740,000) to buy a luxury car and take a vacation to the Bahamas. Two years after the refinancing, Ken lost his job. Ken's home declined in value to $750,000. Based on Ken's circumstances, the lender agreed to a short sale of the property for $735,000, and cancellation of the remaining $115,000 of the $850,000 debt. Ken can exclude only $5,000 of the canceled debt from his income using the exclusion for canceled QPRI ($115,000 canceled debt minus the $110,000 amount of the debt that was not QPRI). Ken must include the remaining $110,000 of canceled debt in income.

The taxpayer must report the amount of debt forgiven on his return by completing Form 982, *Reduction of Tax Attributes Due to Discharge of Indebtedness.*

> **Example:** Adam's home is subject to a $320,000 recourse mortgage. Adam's mortgage lender forecloses on the home in January 2016. The residence is later sold by the bank for $280,000 in December 2016. Adam has $40,000 of income from discharge of indebtedness and can claim the exclusion by filing Form 982 with his 2016 tax return.

Cancellation of Student Loans: Certain student loans contain a provision that all or part of the debt incurred to attend a qualified educational institution will be canceled if the student later works for a specified period of time in certain professions. The canceled debt does not have to be recognized as income on a taxpayer's return.

> **Example:** Tatum is a medical student completing her residency. In return for forgiveness of her student loans, she agrees to work for four years as a pediatrician in a state program in Minnesota that serves rural and poor communities. The canceled debt does not have to be recognized as income.

Qualified Farm Indebtedness: If a taxpayer incurred the canceled debt in a farming business, it is generally not considered taxable income.

Canceled Debt that is Otherwise Deductible: If a taxpayer uses the cash method of accounting, he should not recognize canceled debt income if payment of the debt would have otherwise been a deductible expense.

> **Example:** Jiao is a self-employed interior designer. A CPA firm agrees to file her business tax return and bill her at a later date. Jiao receives $2,200 of tax preparation and bookkeeping services for her business on credit. Later, Jiao loses a major account and has trouble paying her debts, so her CPA forgives the amount she owes. Jiao does not include the canceled debt in her gross income because payment of the debt would have been deductible as a business expense had it been paid.

Hobby Income

A hobby is an activity typically undertaken primarily for pleasure. Even though it may produce income, a hobby is not considered a business because it is not carried on to make a profit.

The IRS presumes that an activity is "carried on for a profit" if it makes a profit during at least three of the last five tax years, including the current year. However, determination of whether an activity is a hobby or a business is determined by a number of factors, including an analysis of the following:

- Does the effort put into the activity indicate an intention to make a profit?
- Does the taxpayer depend on income from the activity?
- If there are losses, are they due to circumstances beyond the taxpayer's control, or did they occur in the start-up phase of the business?
- Has the taxpayer changed methods of operation to improve profitability?
- Does the taxpayer or his advisors have the knowledge needed to carry on the activity as a successful business?
- Has the taxpayer made a profit in similar activities in the past?
- Does the activity make a profit in some years?
- Can the taxpayer expect to make a profit in the future from the appreciation of assets used in the activity?

Income from a hobby is taxable and reported on Form 1040 line 21. Hobby income is generally not subject to self-employment tax, and the use of losses from a hobby to offset income is limited. Expenses related to a hobby activity are deductible, but only up to the amount of hobby income. Hobby expenses must be itemized on Schedule A. If a taxpayer does not have enough expenses to itemize, then the hobby expenses are not deductible. Also, any expenses that exceed hobby income are not deductible.

> **Example:** Chester breeds aquarium fish as a hobby. Twice a year, he goes to an Exotic Fish convention and sells some of his fish. Although he makes money on occasion, he mainly does this activity for pleasure. Chester plans to continue attending the conventions whether he makes money or not. Therefore, the income is hobby income. The convention costs are hobby expenses and deductible only up to the amount of his hobby income.

Court Awards and Damages

Court awards for compensation for lost wages or profits are generally taxable as ordinary income, as are punitive damages.

Compensatory damages for personal physical injury or physical sickness are not taxable income, whether they are from a settlement or from an actual court award.

> **Example:** Felix was injured in a car accident in 2016. His legs were broken, and he suffered other serious physical injuries. He received an insurance settlement for his injuries totaling $950,000. This is nontaxable income because it is payment for a physical injury.

Damages received for emotional distress due to physical injury or sickness are treated the same way as damages for physical injury or sickness, so they are not included in income.

If emotional distress is not due to a physical injury (for example, an employment lawsuit in which a taxpayer suffers emotional distress for injury to reputation), the proceeds are taxable, except for any damages received for medical care due to that emotional distress. Emotional distress includes physical symptoms such as headaches, insomnia, and stomach disorders.

> **Example:** Kristina won a court award for emotional distress caused by unlawful discrimination. The emotional distress resulted in her hospitalization for a nervous breakdown. The court awarded Kristina damages of $100,000, including $20,000 to refund the cost of her medical care for the nervous breakdown. In this case, $80,000 ($100,000 - $20,000) would be considered a taxable court award. The $20,000 of damages for her medical care would not be taxable.

Civil damages, restitution or other monetary awards that the taxpayer received as compensation for a wrongful incarceration are not taxable.

> **Example:** Reuben was wrongfully convicted of murder and later released after spending almost 15 years in prison. Reuben was awarded $50,000 per year of wrongful imprisonment. None of the award is taxable income to Reuben.

Prizes and Awards

Prizes and awards are usually taxable and are reported on line 21. If the prize or award is in the form of property rather than cash, the fair market value of the property is treated as the taxable amount. The winner may avoid taxation of the award by rejecting the prize. The taxpayer may also avoid taxation by having the payer directly transfer the prize to a charity or other nonprofit organization.

> **Example:** A national education association chooses Jerry, a college instructor, as its teacher of the year. He is awarded $3,000, but he does not accept the prize. Instead, Jerry directs the association to transfer his winnings to a college scholarship fund. Jerry never receives a check or has control over the funds; therefore, the award is not taxable to him.

Employee awards for safety, length-of-service, or achievements are generally not taxable to the employee unless they exceed specified limits.[29]

Educational Assistance

Many types of educational assistance are tax-free if they meet certain requirements.

Scholarships and Fellowships: A scholarship is an amount paid to an undergraduate or graduate student to pursue studies. A fellowship is an amount paid to an individual to pursue research. A scholarship or fellowship is excluded from income only if:

- The taxpayer is a degree candidate at an eligible educational institution that has been nationally accredited.
- It does not exceed qualified educational expenses.

---

[29] Employee awards are covered in greater detail in Book 2, *Businesses*, because they are a common employee fringe benefit. Fringe benefits are generally tested on Part 2 of the EA exam.

- It is not designated for other purposes, such as room and board.
- It does not represent payment for teaching, research, or other services.

Qualified educational expenses include tuition, required fees, and course-related expenses such as books.

> **Example:** Aubrey is a graduate student who received a scholarship of $3,000. Under its terms, she must serve as a part-time teaching assistant. From the $3,000 scholarship, she receives $1,250 for teaching, which is listed as income on her Form W-2. She had expenses of more than $5,000 for tuition and course-related books. Aubrey may exclude $1,750 of the scholarship funds from income, but the $1,250 is taxable and must be included in her gross income.

An athletic scholarship is tax-free only if it meets the requirements described above.

Pell Grants: A Pell Grant is a need-based grant that is treated as a scholarship for tax purposes. It is tax-free to the extent it is used for qualified educational expenses during the specified grant period.

Payment to Service Academy Cadets or Midshipmen: An appointment to a United States military academy is not a scholarship or fellowship. Cadets and midshipmen receive free tuition and room and board, which is nontaxable. However, they also get government pay while at the military academy; these amounts are taxable income.

Veterans' Educational Benefits: Veterans' benefits for education are tax-free if administered by the Department of Veterans Affairs.

> **Example:** Moises served in Afghanistan and has since returned to college. He receives two education benefits under the GI bill: a $1,534 monthly basic housing allowance and $3,840 tuition paid directly to his college. Neither of these benefits is taxable to Moises, and he is not required to report them on his tax return.

Section 529 Plans

Qualified Tuition Programs: QTPs, also known as section 529 plans, are established and maintained by states or educational institutions. These plans allow a taxpayer to either prepay a student's qualified educational expenses at an eligible educational institution or contribute to an account that will be used to pay future expenses. The amounts contributed to a section 529 plan are not deductible for federal tax purposes.

Eligible institutions include virtually all accredited colleges, universities, vocational schools, and other postsecondary educational institutions. Qualified expenses include tuition, fees, books, computer equipment and software, and room and board for any time the beneficiary is enrolled in college. A beneficiary may be anyone the taxpayer designates: himself, a child, a grandchild, or an unrelated person.

Distributions from a 529 plan are reported to the taxpayer on Form 1099-Q. The part of a distribution representing the amount paid or contributed to the plan is not included in income.

The beneficiary also generally does not have to include in taxable income any earnings distributed from a 529 plan if the total distribution is less than or equal to a student's qualified education expenses (after reduction of the latter by other tax-free education assistance received during the year).

If the total distribution is greater than a student's adjusted qualified expenses, an allocable portion of the earnings is taxable. In this type of taxable distribution, an additional tax of 10% generally applies on the amount included in income.

Example: Seven years ago, Emma's parents opened an account for her with a Qualified Tuition Program maintained by the state of Virginia. Over the years, they contributed $22,000 to the account. The total balance in the account was $33,000 on the date the distribution was made. In September 2016, Emma enrolled in college and had $10,000 of qualified education expenses for the rest of the year. She paid her college expenses from the following sources:

- QTP distribution: $7,500
- Partial tuition scholarship (tax-free): $4,000
- Gift from her parents: $1,000

Emma must reduce her qualified educational expenses by the tax-free scholarship ($10,000 minus $4,000), so she has $6,000 of adjusted qualified educational expenses. Since that amount is less than the QTP distribution, part of the earnings shown on Form 1099-Q is taxable and would be reported on Line 21 of Form 1040.

Any amount distributed from a 529 plan is not taxable if it is rolled over to another 529 plan for the use of the same beneficiary or for a member of the beneficiary's family. The amount must be paid to another educational account within 60 days after the date of distribution.

Example: Yasir still had $3,000 left in his 529 plan after he graduated from college. He wanted to help his younger sister, who was still in high school. Within 60 days after distribution of the remaining portion of his 529 plan, he contributed the money to his sister's 529 plan, so the distribution was not taxable to him or his sister.

Starting in 2016, the definition of "qualified higher education expenses" for distributions from 529 accounts now includes the purchases of computer equipment and technology.

Coverdell Education Savings Accounts (ESAs)

A Coverdell ESA is a trust or custodial account set up to pay qualified elementary, secondary, or higher education expenses for a designated beneficiary. In order to contribute to an ESA, the contributor's MAGI must be below $110,000 in 2016 ($220,000 if married filing jointly). Contributions must be in cash (not property) and must be made by the due date of the contributor's tax return (not including extensions). There is no limit to the number of accounts that can be established for a beneficiary; however, the total contribution to all accounts on behalf of a beneficiary in any year cannot exceed $2,000, no matter how many accounts are established.

All contributions that exceed $2,000 for a single beneficiary in a taxable year will be treated as excess contributions. There will be a 6% excise tax if the excess contributions and earnings on them are not withdrawn from the child's accounts before June 1 of the following tax year. Any earnings withdrawn as part of a corrective distribution are taxable in the year of the excess contribution, even if the distribution occurs in the following year.

> **Note:** The penalty for excess contributions is imposed on the *beneficiary* of the account (usually a minor child), and not on the person who over-contributed to the account. The excise tax must be reported on the child's income tax return, using IRS Form 5329, *Additional Taxes on Qualified Plans (Including IRAs) and Other Tax-Favored Accounts.* This rule seems contrary to common sense, but the penalty is imposed on the child, not the child's parents, or the contributor of the excess funds.

Contributions must be made before the beneficiary reaches age 18 unless the beneficiary is special-needs. Contributions to a Coverdell are not deductible. The beneficiary needs to withdraw the balance from the account before age 30.

If there is a balance in the ESA when the beneficiary reaches age 30, it must be distributed within 30 days. The beneficiary can also choose to transfer the ESA to another beneficiary (such as a younger sibling or another family member) in order to avoid the tax. If the beneficiary is special-needs, the Coverdell account can continue in existence (without transfer to another beneficiary) after the beneficiary turns 30.

> **Example:** Three Coverdell ESAs were set up for Lindsay when she was born: one by her parents, one by her grandparents, and one by her great-uncle. In 2016, her grandparents contribute $1,500 to Lindsay's account. The most her parents and great-uncle can contribute is a combined $500, because the maximum contribution per year for a single beneficiary is $2,000.

> **Example:** Francis earned a full scholarship to Stanford University. He enrolled when he was 19, and had a Coverdell ESA with $52,000. Since his tuition was already paid by his scholarship, Francis only used the ESA for books and required lab fees. Francis graduated college four years later, and had only used a total of $9,000 from his Coverdell. Rather than withdrawing the money and paying the 10% tax, Francis transferred the Coverdell to his younger sister, who is 17 and still in high school. His sister can use the remaining amounts in the Coverdell for her own future college expenses.

The beneficiary of a Coverdell account can receive distributions to pay qualified education expenses that are tax-free if the amount of the distributions does not exceed the beneficiary's adjusted qualified education expenses. If a distribution does exceed the beneficiary's qualified education expenses, a portion of the earnings is taxable and is reported as "other income" on line 21 of Form 1040. An additional penalty tax of 10% applies to distributions that are not used for qualifying expenses.

If a beneficiary receives distributions from both a 529 plan and a Coverdell ESA in the same year and the total distributions exceed the beneficiary's adjusted qualified education expenses for that year, the expenses must be allocated between the distributions from each account. The total expenses must also be reduced by any amounts used in claiming an American Opportunity or Lifetime Learning Credit for that year.

Miscellaneous Line 21 Income Items

Other types of income that are taxable to the recipient and reported on line 21 include the following:

- Strike benefits
- Jury duty pay (when it is not turned over to the employee's employer and deducted as an adjustment to income)
- Fees paid by an estate to a personal representative/executor
- Gifts or gratuities received by a host or hostess of a party or event where sales are made

Example: Kathleen hosts a cooking party for 15 friends, which includes a live demonstration by a Pampered Chef consultant. At the end of the evening, the women order $1,000 worth of cookware and other products from the consultant. Kathleen receives a gift of $215 of products for hosting the party, which she must report as income at its fair market value.

Bartering Income

Bartering is an exchange of property or services, usually without an exchange of cash. Barter may take place on an informal, one-on-one basis between individuals and businesses, or it may occur on a third-party basis through a barter exchange company.

Taxpayers may barter for a variety of goods and services: computer services for auto repairs, or dental work for carpet cleaning, for example. The FMV of the goods or services exchanged must be reported as income by each party in the year of the exchange. If the parties have agreed ahead of time as to the value of services exchanged, the agreed-upon value will be accepted as the fair market value.

Example: Brayden builds custom kitchen cabinets. Annemarie is a veterinarian. Brayden builds new cabinets for Annemarie's kitchen, and Annemarie performs hip dysplasia surgery on Brayden's German shepherd. They agree in advance that the cost for the kitchen cabinets and the surgery is $2,500. They each must report $2,500 of income on their tax returns.

Bartering income from business services is reported on Schedule C or Schedule F if the taxpayers are self-employed.

A barter exchange is an organization that serves as a third party to coordinate barter transactions between members of the organization. Members contract with each other to exchange property or services. The barter exchange provides a record of the fair market value of all income a member receives from transactions on Form 1099-B, *Proceeds from Broker and Barter Exchange Transactions.*

Summary: Taxable vs. Nontaxable Income

TAXABLE INCOME	NONTAXABLE INCOME
Wages, salaries, tips, bonuses, vacation pay, severance pay, commissions	Most employer-provided fringe benefits
Interest on bank and money market accounts; CDs; dividends; Treasury bonds	Interest on most state and local bonds
Gains from sales of property, stocks and bonds, stock options, etc.	Life insurance proceeds
Fees paid to an estate's executor	Gifts and inheritances
Alimony	Child support
Social Security benefits (above the base amount and limited to 85% of benefits)	Welfare payments, food stamps, other forms of public assistance
Court awards for punitive damages and lost wages	Compensation or court awards for physical injury or illness, and awards for wrongful incarceration
Unemployment compensation; strike benefits	Worker's compensation
Barter and hobby income	Combat pay and certain veteran's benefits
Certain distributions from Coverdell savings accounts or qualified tuition programs	Scholarships, Pell grants, employer-provided educational assistance
Cancellation of debt income (unless excludable)	Canceled debt from a primary residence, bankruptcy, or insolvency
Gambling winnings; most prizes and awards	Certain employee awards for safety, achievement, or service

Unit 10: Study Questions

(Test yourself first, then check the correct answers at the end of this quiz.)

1. Penelope is under 18 and has two Coverdell accounts. One was set up by her grandparents, and the other was set up by her mother. Penelope received $3,200 in total contributions in her Coverdell accounts in 2016. Which of the following statements is true?

A. The contributions are tax deductible and can remain in the accounts until Penelope reaches 30 years of age.
B. Penelope has an excess contribution of $1,200. The excess contribution must be withdrawn, or it will be subject to an excise tax.
C. Penelope must invest the proceeds in a traditional IRA.
D. Penelope has an excess contribution of $200. She can transfer this excess contribution to another beneficiary.

2. In which of the following instances is canceled debt not excluded from income?

A. Mortgage debt of a rental property in foreclosure.
B. Insolvency.
C. Bankruptcy.
D. Debt as part of a farming business.

3. Under Cary's divorce decree, he must pay his ex-wife, Eugenia, $30,000 of alimony per year. The decree also requires that Cary pays child support of $12,000 per year. The payments will stop after 15 years. However, if Eugenia dies before the end of the 15-year period, Cary must still pay Eugenia's estate the difference between $450,000 ($30,000 annually × 15 years) and the total amount paid up to that time. Eugenia dies at the end of the tenth year, and Cary must pay her estate an additional $150,000 ($450,000 – $300,000). How are the payments that occurred after Eugenia's death characterized for tax purposes?

A. Child support.
B. Alimony.
C. Other income.
D. Taxable income.

4. Alexander, age 64, is single and retired. He earned the following income in 2016. To determine if any of his Social Security is taxable, Alexander should compare how much of his income to the $25,000 base amount?

Part-time job	$8,000
Bank interest	5,000
Social Security	11,000
Taxable pension	6,000
Total	**$30,000**

A. $11,000
B. $24,500
C. $25,000
D. $30,000

5. Karly is trying to get her finances in order. During the year, she negotiated a settlement with her credit card company, to which she owed a delinquent debt. She owed $10,000 on her credit card. As part of the negotiation, the credit card company agreed to accept a $2,500 settlement as payment in full. Karly was not insolvent and not in bankruptcy when the debt was canceled. What amount should be reported as "other income" on Karly's Form 1040, line 21?

A. $0
B. $10,000
C. $2,500
D. $7,500

6. Isabella had $9,000 of gambling winnings during the year. She also incurred $15,000 of gambling losses. How should these transactions be reported on her tax return?

A. The $9,000 of winnings are reported as income, and the $15,000 of losses are reported as an adjustment to income on Form 1040.
B. The $9,000 of winnings are reported as income, and the $15,000 of losses are reported as an itemized deduction subject to the 2% limit on Schedule A.
C. The $9,000 of winnings are reported as income, and $9,000 of losses are reported as an itemized deduction not subject to the 2% limit on Schedule A.
D. The $9,000 of winnings are reported as income, but the gambling losses are not deductible.

7. Ed received $32,000 of wages in 2016. He also won a prize from his homeowner's association for developing a new water conservation plan. The prize was free landscaping service for a year, valued at $600. Ed also received $7,000 in child support and $2,000 in alimony from his ex-wife. Ed has full custody of his children. What is Ed's taxable income (before deductions and adjustments) for 2016?

A. $32,000
B. $32,600
C. $34,600
D. $39,600

8. Expenses related to a hobby activity are deductible, but only up to the amount of:

A. Taxable income.
B. Ordinary income.
C. Passive income.
D. Hobby income.

9. In 2016, Mina was discharged from her liability to repay $10,000 of credit card debt. The lender reported the discharged debt on Form 1099-C. Immediately prior to the debt cancellation, Mina had liabilities of $15,000 and the fair market value of her assets was $2,000. What portion of the canceled debt must Mina include in income?

A. $10,000
B. $3,000
C. $5,000
D. $0

10. Beth and Clifton's divorce decree requires Clifton to pay Beth $250 per month of child support and $1,500 per month of alimony. Clifton makes all of his child support and alimony payments on time during 2016. How much of these payments is Beth required to report as taxable income on her 2016 return?

A. $0
B. $1,500
C. $18,000
D. $21,000

11. Archer is a former National Football League cornerback. In 2016, he is awarded a sizable settlement in a class action lawsuit for concussion injuries. The settlement will be paid in installments over a period of ten years. How should Archer report the damages he is awarded on his income tax return?

A. He must include the entire amount of his settlement in his gross income for 2016.
B. He must include in his gross income only the portion of the settlement paid to him each year when it is received.
C. He must report the settlement on his tax return, but it is not taxable income.
D. He may exclude the payments from his gross income.

12. Ginny had the following income in 2016:

Source	Amounts
Wages	$14,000
Interest	125
Gambling winnings	1,000
Gambling losses	2,000
Discrimination lawsuit settlement	10,000
Child support payments	1,000
Food stamp benefits	5,000

How much gross income must Ginny report on her tax return?

A. $14,125
B. $15,125
C. $25,125
D. $30,000

13. Which of the following is not taxable income to the recipient?

A. Long-term disability payments from a policy paid by the recipient's employer.

B. Bartering income.

C. Gains from the sale of stock.

D. $25,000 of group-term life insurance coverage provided by an employer.

14. Jean received the following income: wages, interest, child support, alimony, inheritance, worker's compensation, and lottery winnings. What amount of her income is taxable?

Source	Amounts
Wages	$13,000
Interest	15
Child support	6,000
Alimony	2,000
Inheritance	10,000
Worker's compensation	1,000
Lottery winnings	5,000

A. $13,015

B. $16,015

C. $20,015

D. $30,015

15. Paulo, 72, experiences age-related discrimination on his job and sues his company. After he files the lawsuit, he is physically attacked by the company owner, who breaks Paulo's arm. The court awards Paulo the following amounts:

- $4,000 for emotional distress attributable to the age discrimination and resulting lawsuit
- $10,000 for loss of wages
- $35,000 for physical injury related to the assault
- $16,000 reimbursement for medical expenses

How much of this award is taxable to Paulo?

A. $4,000

B. $10,000

C. $14,000

D. $49,000

16. During 2016, Anaya received payments of $20,000 for alimony and $15,000 for child support. Based upon the terms of her divorce settlement, her ex-spouse was also required to pay $14,000 of mortgage payments for the house they owned jointly. What portion of the amounts above must Anaya include in income?

A. $27,000
B. $34,000
C. $35,000
D. $49,000

17. Sven and Samantha filed jointly and received the following income in 2016. How much income should be reported on their joint return?

- W-2 income for Samantha for wages of $40,000.
- W-2 for Samantha for $2,000, the value of a trip she won to the Bahamas. She is planning to take the trip in the following year.
- Court settlement of $10,000 paid to Sven from a car accident for serious injuries he suffered.
- $4,000 child support for Samantha's son from a previous marriage.

A. $40,000
B. $42,000
C. $46,000
D. $52,000

18. Which of the following would be considered taxable income to the recipient?

A. Life insurance proceeds paid to a beneficiary.
B. Adoption expense reimbursements.
C. Unemployment compensation.
D. Worker's compensation benefits.

19. Bart had a $15,000 loan from his credit union but stopped making payments. The credit union determined that the legal fees to collect might be higher than the amount Bart owed, so it canceled the remaining amount of $5,000 due on the loan. Bart did not file for bankruptcy, nor is he insolvent. How much income must he include from the debt cancellation?

A. $0
B. $5,000
C. $10,000
D. $15,000

20. Alimony does not include:

A. Noncash property settlements.
B. Payments to a third-party on behalf of an ex-spouse.
C. Medical expenses paid on behalf of an ex-spouse.
D. Cash payments.

21. Hank received Social Security in 2016 totaling $11,724. Also in 2016, Hank sold all of his stock and moved into senior housing. He received $31,896 of taxable income from the stock sale. What is the maximum taxable amount of Hank's Social Security benefits?

A. $31,896
B. $20,172
C. $11,724
D. $9,965

22. Brent, a dermatologist, agreed to exchange services with a handyman, Tevin. Brent removed a mole for Tevin and Tevin fixed Brent's running toilet in his medical office. Brent generally charges $200 for mole removal, and Tevin generally charges $150 to fix a toilet. They agreed in advance that the fee would be $150. They did not exchange cash. How much income must Brent recognize for this barter transaction?

A. $50
B. $150
C. $200
D. $250

Unit 10: Answers

1. The answer is B. Penelope has an excess contribution of $1,200. The excess contribution must be withdrawn by June 1 of the next tax year, or it will be subject to an excise tax of 6%, plus 6% of any interest or profits derived from the excess contribution. The maximum contribution to a Coverdell is $2,000 per year per beneficiary, regardless of how many accounts the beneficiary has. Any *earnings* withdrawn as part of a corrective distribution are taxable in the year of the excess contribution, even if the corrective distribution occurs in the following year.

2. The answer is A. Foreclosure of a rental property does not qualify for exclusion of canceled debt income. A taxpayer may exclude income realized as a loan modification or foreclosure of a taxpayer's principal residence. Canceled debt related to rental property, other business property, second homes, and vacation homes does not qualify.

3. The answer is A. For tax purposes; alimony cannot continue after the death of the receiving spouse. Since the payments are required even after Eugenia's death, none of the annual payments are considered alimony for tax purposes. The payments are considered "disguised child support" and cannot be deducted by Cary as alimony.

4. The answer is B. In order to figure out the taxable portion of Social Security, the taxpayer's total income, including tax-exempt interest, must be compared to the base amount for his filing status, which is $25,000. The amount of income that should be compared to the $25,000 base amount is calculated as follows:

Part-time job	$8,000
Interest	5,000
½ of Social Security	5,500
Taxable pension	6,000
Total	**$24,500**

Alexander does not have to pay tax on his Social Security. His income plus one-half of Social Security is less than the applicable base amount ($25,000). However, he is still required to file a tax return, because his overall income exceeds the minimum filing requirement.

5. The answer is D. Karly would report $7,500 in cancelled debt income ($10,000 - $2,500) on line 21 of her Form 1040.

6. The answer is C. The $9,000 of winnings are reported as income, and $9,000 of the losses are reported on Schedule A as an itemized deduction not subject to the 2% floor. The amount of losses deducted may not exceed gambling winnings.

7. The answer is C. The wages and the prize are both taxable income. Child support is not taxable to the receiver, nor deductible by the payer. The alimony is taxable to Ed and deductible by his ex-wife. The answer is calculated as follows: ($32,000 + $600 + $2,000) = $34,600.

8. The answer is D. Expenses related to a hobby activity are deductible, but only up to the amount of hobby income. Hobby expenses are only deductible on Schedule A as an itemized deduction. If a taxpayer does not itemize, he cannot deduct hobby expenses.

9. The answer is D. The amount of Mina's assets immediately prior to the debt cancellation exceeded the amount of debt that was discharged. Therefore, the entire amount of the debt cancellation can be excluded from income.

Liabilities	$15,000
Fair market value of assets	(2,000)
Amount of insolvency	13,000
Amount of debt cancellation	**$10,000**

10. The answer is C. Alimony is taxable income to the recipient and deductible by the payer. Therefore, Clifton can deduct $18,000 ($1,500 × 12 months) as alimony paid, and Beth must report $18,000 as alimony received. The amount paid as child support, $3,000 ($250 × 12), is not deductible by Clifton and is not reported as income by Beth.

11. The answer is D. Gross income does not include the amount of damages received due to physical injuries or sickness, regardless of whether the damages are paid as lump sums or as periodic payments.

12. The answer is C. The wages, interest income, gambling income, and settlement from a discrimination lawsuit must all be reported ($14,000 + $125 + $1,000 + $10,000 = $25,125). The child support payments and the food stamp benefits are not taxable. The gambling losses do not affect the inclusion of the gambling income within gross income. However, if Ginny chooses to itemize deductions, her gambling losses may be deducted on Schedule A to the extent of her gambling income. If Ginny does not itemize, the gambling losses are not deductible.

13. The answer is D. An employer may provide up to $50,000 of life insurance coverage as a nontaxable benefit to an employee. The value of any insurance coverage that exceeds $50,000 is a taxable benefit. All of the other items are taxable.

14. The answer is C. The wages, interest, alimony, and lottery winnings are taxable income ($13,000 + $15 + $2,000 + $5,000 = $20,015). Child support, inheritances, and worker's compensation are nontaxable income.

15. The answer is C. The amounts for loss of wages and emotional distress are taxable as ordinary income ($4,000 + $10,000 = $14,000). Damages for emotional distress that is not due to physical injury or sickness are usually taxable (as in this case where the distress was attributed to the job discrimination and lawsuit). The damages awarded for physical injury are not taxable.

16. The answer is A. Anaya must report the cash alimony payments and one-half of the mortgage payments as taxable alimony ($20,000 + $7,000). The child support payments are not taxable.

17. The answer is B. The answer is $42,000 ($40,000 wages + $2,000 prize). Samantha must recognize the prize even though she has not taken the trip because she had constructive receipt of the winnings. The accident settlement and the child support payments are not taxable.

18. The answer is C. Unemployment compensation is taxable income.

19. The answer is B. Bart's inability to pay his debt is not a result of bankruptcy or insolvency, so he must include the full amount of the canceled debt ($5,000) in his gross income.

20. The answer is A. Noncash property settlements do not qualify as alimony. Alimony does not include child support, noncash property settlements, payments to keep up the payer's property, or use of the payer's property. Payments made to a third party or medical expenses paid on behalf of a former spouse may qualify as alimony.

21. The answer is D. The maximum amount that is ever taxable on net Social Security benefits is 85%, which in Hank's case is $9,965.

22. The answer is B. Brent must include $150 in income. He can also deduct the cost of the repair ($150) if it qualifies as a business expense. If a taxpayer exchanges services with another person and both have agreed ahead of time on the value of those services, that value will be accepted as fair market value unless the value can be shown to be otherwise.

Unit 11: Adjustments to Gross Income

> **For additional information read:**
> Publication 529, *Miscellaneous Deductions*
> Publication 535, *Business Expenses*
> Publication 521, *Moving Expenses*
> Publication 970, *Tax Benefits for Education*
> Publication 590-A, *Contributions to Individual Retirement Arrangements*

An "adjustment to income" reduces taxable income and thus the amount of tax owed. They are reported on page 1 of Form 1040.

Adjustments are subtracted from gross income in order to derive adjusted gross income (AGI), whereas itemized deductions and the standard deduction are subtracted from AGI. Because adjustments are taken before AGI is calculated, they are designated as "above-the-line" deductions.

Adjustments are beneficial because they not only reduce taxable income, but a lower AGI may increase a taxpayer's eligibility for certain credits and deductions and the amounts that he can claim. Unlike "below-the-line" deductions, adjustments are not added back when calculating the alternative minimum tax.

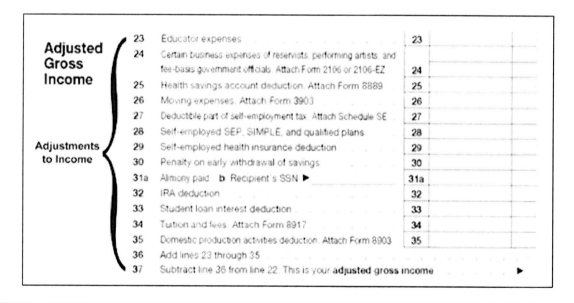

> **Note:** Form 1040 (the "long form") is needed for most tax deductions and adjustments; Form 1040-EZ cannot be used. Form 1040A can be used if a taxpayer is reporting only the following adjustments to income: educator expenses, traditional IRA deduction, student loan interest deduction, and tuition and fees deduction.

Common Adjustments to Gross Income

There are many types of adjustments to gross income, and we will cover the most common ones in this unit. These are the adjustments listed in the order they are reported on Form 1040:

- Educator expenses (Line 23)
- Certain business expenses of reservists, performing artists, and fee-basis government officials (Line 24)
- Health savings account deduction (Line 25)
- Moving expenses (Line 26)
- Deductible part of self-employment tax (Line 27)
- Self-employed SEP, SIMPLE, and qualified plans (Line 28)
- Self-employed health insurance deduction (Line 29)
- Penalty on early withdrawal of savings (Line 30)
- Alimony paid (Line 31a)
- IRA deduction (Line 32)
- Student loan interest deduction (Line 33)
- Tuition and fees (Line 34)
- Domestic production activities deduction (Line 35)
- Write-in adjustments (Line 36)
    - Archer MSA deduction
    - Jury duty pay remitted to an employer
    - Repayment of unemployment benefits
    - Other adjustments

Line 23: Educator Expense Deduction

An eligible educator is allowed to deduct up to $250 of unreimbursed expenses for books, supplies, computer equipment (including related software and services), other equipment, and supplementary materials used in the classroom.

Since this is an adjustment to income, teachers can deduct these expenses even if they do not itemize deductions. The PATH Act permanently extended the above-the-line deduction for eligible educators' classroom expenses. For courses in health and physical education, expenses are deductible only if they are related to athletics. Nonathletic supplies for physical education and expenses related to health courses do not qualify. Materials used for homeschooling cannot be deducted.

An eligible educator must work at least 900 hours a school year in a school that provides elementary or secondary education (K-12). College instructors do not qualify. For the purposes of this credit, an "educator" includes a:

- Teacher or instructor
- Counselor
- Principal
- Teacher's aide

222

Example: Devina is a third-grade teacher who worked 1,600 hours during the tax year. She spent $262 on supplies for her students. Of that amount, $212 was for educational software. The other $50 was for supplies for a unit she teaches on health. Only the $212 is a qualified expense that she can deduct.

On a joint tax return, if both taxpayers are eligible, they each may take the deduction, up to a maximum of $500. Any expenses that exceed the adjustment to income may be deducted as unreimbursed employee expenses on Schedule A, subject to the 2%-of-AGI limit.

Line 24: Certain Business Expenses of Reservists, Performing Artists, and Fee-Basis Government Officials

Certain employees are allowed to claim specified work-related expenses as an adjustment to income, rather than as a deduction on Schedule A. This adjustment applies only to reservists (members of the reserve component of the Armed Forces of the United States, National Guard, or the Reserve Corps of the Public Health Service); qualified performing artists; and state or local government officials who are compensated on a fee basis.

Line 25: Health Savings Account Deduction (HSAs)

A health savings account (HSA) allows a taxpayer to save funds intended to pay for health care expenses on a tax-preferred basis. The HSA contributions are deductible as an adjustment to income. The taxpayer can take tax-free withdrawals from the HSA to pay for his qualifying medical expenses.

An HSA must be established exclusively to pay medical expenses for the taxpayer, his spouse, and his dependents. HSA accounts are usually set up with a bank, an insurance company, or through an employer. To qualify, the taxpayer:

- Must not be enrolled in Medicare.
- Cannot be claimed as a dependent on anyone else's tax return.
- Must be covered under a high deductible health plan and have no other health coverage, other than for a specific disease or illness; a fixed amount for a certain time period of hospitalization; or liabilities incurred under worker's compensation laws or tort liabilities.

An employee and his employer are both allowed to contribute to the employee's HSA in the same year. If an employer makes an HSA contribution on behalf of an employee, it is excluded from the employee's income and is not subject to income or payroll taxes.

For 2016, taxpayers can contribute up to $3,350 for an individual and $6,750 for a family (in 2016, the limits for a family contribution were increased, but the single contribution limits stayed the same). HSA holders who are age 55 and older get to save an extra $1,000 as a catch-up contribution. Any excess contributions over these limits are subject to a 6% penalty.

2016 Health Savings Account (HSA) Contribution Limits

Taxpayer	Minimum Deductible	Maximum Out-of-Pocket	Contribution Limit	55 and Over
Single	$1,300	$6,550	$3,350	+$1,000
Family	$2,600	$13,100	$6,650	+$1,000

Allowable medical expenses are those that would generally qualify for purposes of the deduction for medical and dental expenses and which are not paid or reimbursed by the taxpayer's high deductible health plan.

Withdrawals from an HSA for purposes other than payment of allowable medical expenses are subject to income tax. They may also be subject to a 20% penalty, except in the following instances:

- When a taxpayer turns age 65 or older
- When a taxpayer becomes disabled
- When a taxpayer dies

Example: Teddy is 67, single, and has an HSA through his employer. In 2016, his car breaks down and he doesn't have the funds to repair it. Teddy withdraws $2,000 from his HSA to pay for the car repairs. Since he did not use the funds to pay for qualifying medical expenses, the entire withdrawal is subject to income tax. However, Teddy avoids the 20% additional penalty tax because he is over 65.

A taxpayer will receive Form 5498-SA from the HSA trustee showing the amount of contributions for the year. The deduction for an HSA is reported on Form 8889, *Health Savings Accounts*.

To claim the HSA deduction for a particular year, the HSA contributions must be made on or before that year's tax filing date (without extensions). For 2016, HSA contributions must be made on or before the 2016 tax year filing deadline (April 18, 2017).

Line 26: Moving Expenses

If a taxpayer moves due to a change of job or business location, he can deduct qualifying moving expenses that his employer does not reimburse. Moving expenses are reported on Form 3903, Moving Expenses. To qualify for the moving expense deduction, the taxpayer must satisfy these tests:

- The move must be related to work or business, and
- The taxpayer must meet the tests for time and distance.

Time Test: This test is different for employees than for those who are self-employed. For employees, moving costs are deductible only if the taxpayer works full-time at the new work location for at least 39 weeks in the first 12 months. For joint filers, only one spouse has to qualify for the time test in order to deduct moving expenses.

Self-employed taxpayers must work full-time for at least 39 weeks in the first 12 months at the new location, and at least 78 weeks within the first 24 months at the new location. For this test, any combination of full-time work as an employee or as a self-employed person qualifies.

Example: Randy quit his job and moved from Missouri to Georgia to begin a full-time job as a mechanic for Custom Motorcycles. He worked at the motorcycle shop 40 hours each week. Shortly after his move, Randy also opened a part-time motorcycle repair business from his home garage. Because Randy's principal place of business is Custom Motorcycles, he satisfies the time test by meeting the 39-week test as an employee. However, if Randy is unable to satisfy the requirements of the 39-week test during the 12-month period, he may instead be able to satisfy the 78-week test because he also works as a self-employed person.

If a taxpayer fails to meet the time test, he must report the moving expenses as "other income" in a later tax year or amend the tax return on which the moving expenses were claimed.

Exceptions to the Time Test: A taxpayer does not have to meet the time test and may still deduct moving expenses if any of the following applies:

- The taxpayer is in the armed forces and moved because of a change of station.
- The taxpayer's main job location was outside the United States, and he moved back to the United States because he retired from his position.
- A taxpayer is the surviving widow(er) of a person whose main job location at the time of death was outside the United States.
- The taxpayer's job at the new location ends because of death or disability.
- The taxpayer is transferred or laid off for a reason other than willful misconduct.

> **Example:** Darrell's company transfers him from New York to Tennessee, and he deducts his moving expenses. Darrell expects to continue his full-time employment in Tennessee and does not expect it to be a temporary move. A few months later, his employer goes bankrupt and closes the entire Tennessee division. Darrell is laid off. He does not have to satisfy the time test.

> **Example:** Shelby moves from Michigan to Ohio for a new job as a building manager. Six months after she starts the job, she dies. On Shelby's final tax return, her executor can deduct her moving expenses since the job ended due to her death.

Exceptions for Seasonal Work and Temporary Absences: For purposes of the moving expense deduction, if a taxpayer's trade or business is seasonal, the off-season weeks when no work is available may still be counted as weeks during which he worked full-time. In order to qualify, the off-season must be less than six months, and the taxpayer must work full-time before and after the off-season.

> **Example:** Chelsea moves from North Dakota to Jackson Hole, Wyoming for a job at a ski resort. She works full-time during the ski season and is off for five months during the summer. Chelsea may still count this time as full-time work since her employment is expected to be seasonal.

A taxpayer is still considered to be employed on a full-time basis during any week he is temporarily absent from work because of illness, labor strikes, natural disasters, or similar causes.

Distance Test: Under the distance test, the new job must be at least 50 miles farther from the taxpayer's old home than the old job location was from the taxpayer's old home. If the taxpayer had no previous workplace, the new job must be at least 50 miles from the old home (see diagram for clarification).

This means that if a taxpayer starts a job for the first time, the place of work must be at least 50 miles from his former home to meet the distance test. The location of the taxpayer's new home doesn't factor into the equation.

> **Example:** Gael graduated college in 2016 and was immediately offered a new job. Gael has always lived with his parents in Dallas, TX. His new job is located in Fort Worth, which is 33 miles away. Gael moves to Fort Worth in 2016 and starts his new job. He does not qualify for the moving expense deduction because he does not meet the distance test.

Example: Abe moved to a new city and took a job as an attorney in a different law firm. His old job was six miles from his former home. Therefore, in order to deduct his moving expenses, his new job location must be at least 56 miles from that former home. Abe calculates the distance between his new job and his old home and discovers that it is 58 miles. Abe's moving expenses are deductible.

A taxpayer who starts a first job or returns to full-time work after a long absence can also qualify for the deduction. Moving expenses incurred within one year of the date the taxpayer first reported to work at the new location can generally be deducted. There is no requirement that the job be in the same field. If a taxpayer does not move within one year of the date he begins the new job; the moving expenses are not deductible unless he can prove that circumstances prevented moving within that period. Failing to sell a former home, for example, would not be an adequate reason.

Members of the armed forces moving because of a permanent change of station or a military order are not required to meet the distance test or the time test.

Qualifying Moving Expenses: Expenses that qualify for the moving expense deduction include:

- The cost of packing and moving household effects and family members.
- Storage costs (only while in transit and for up to 30 days after the day of the move).
- The cost of connecting or disconnecting utilities required because a taxpayer is moving his household goods, appliances, or personal effects.
- The cost of shipping a car or a pet to a new home.
- Travel expenses (including lodging, but not meals) for one trip per person. Family members are not required to travel together.

Actual car expenses such as gas and oil are tax deductible if accurate records are kept, or a taxpayer can use the standard mileage rate instead (19 cents per mile driven for moving purposes in 2016). Parking fees and tolls are also tax deductible, but general car repairs, maintenance, insurance, and depreciation of a taxpayer's car are not deductible moving expenses.

> **Example:** Ethan and Jackie are married and file jointly. In February 2016, Ethan and Jackie moved from Rhode Island to Alabama where Ethan was starting a new job. He drove the family car to Alabama, a trip of 1,100 miles. His actual expenses were $281 for gas, plus $40 for tolls and $150 for lodging, for a total of $471. One week later, Jackie flew from Rhode Island to Alabama. Her only expense was a $400 plane ticket. The couple's moving expense deduction is $871 (Ethan's $471 + Jackie's $400).

Nondeductible Moving Expenses: Moving expenses that cannot be deducted include:
- Pre-move house-hunting expenses
- Temporary living expenses
- Meals while traveling
- Expenses of buying or selling a home, home improvements to help sell a home, or a loss on a home sale
- Real estate taxes
- Car tags and driver's license renewal fees
- Storage charges except those incurred in transit or for a foreign move

Employer-Reimbursed Moving Expenses: When an employer reimburses a taxpayer for deductible moving expenses, the reimbursement is excluded from taxable income. However, if an employer reimburses an employee for nondeductible expenses (such as the expense incurred from breaking a lease), the reimbursement is taxable as wages and must be included on the employee's Form W-2.

> **Example:** Gabriel was offered a job at XelCorp Engineering. He agreed to accept the offer if XelCorp paid all his moving expenses. The cost of his professional movers was $9,600, which the company paid. This amount is deductible by XelCorp as a business expense and not taxable to Gabriel since it is a deductible moving expense. XelCorp also reimbursed Gabriel for a $7,500 loss on the sale of his home. Because this is reimbursement of a nondeductible expense, it is taxable and must be included on Gabriel's Form W-2. The $7,500 is deductible to XelCorp, but it is categorized as a wage expense and therefore subject to payroll tax.

Line 27: Deductible Part of Self-Employment Tax

A self-employed taxpayer can subtract from income 50% of self-employment tax, equal to the amount of Social Security and Medicare taxes that an employer normally pays for an employee, which is excluded from an employee's income. The deduction is figured on Schedule SE. A self-employed taxpayer cannot deduct one-half of the additional Medicare tax on earned income.[30]

Line 28: Self-Employed Retirement Plans

Self-employed individuals can deduct contributions to the following types of retirement plans:
- Simplified Employee Pension (SEP) plans
- Savings Incentive Match Plan for Employees (SIMPLE) plans
- Qualified plans

---

[30] The additional Medicare tax and other provisions of the Affordable Care Act are covered later.

A taxpayer must have self-employment income in order to contribute to his own plan.[31] However, a self-employed taxpayer does not need to show a profit on Schedule C in order to contribute to an employee's retirement plan.

> **Example:** Tony is a self-employed kickboxing instructor. He has a full-time receptionist named Francine that works in his training gym. In 2016, Tony makes a large fitness equipment purchase for his training gym. The fitness equipment qualifies for accelerated section 179 expensing. As a result, Tony reduces his taxable income to zero for the year. He cannot contribute to a retirement plan because he has no taxable income on his Schedule C. However, Tony is still allowed to contribute to Francine's retirement plan.

Line 29: Self-Employed Health Insurance Deduction

A self-employed taxpayer may be able to deduct up to 100% of his health insurance premiums as an adjustment to income. Premiums paid by the taxpayer for his spouse and dependents under age 27 at the end of the year are also deductible. However, the deduction is limited to the net profit or other earned income from the business under which the health coverage is arranged, minus the deductions on Lines 27 and 28 of Form 1040. The taxpayer must either:

- Be self-employed and have a net profit for the year;
- Be a partner with net earnings from self-employment; or
- Have received wages from an S corporation in which he was a more-than-2% shareholder.

Long-term care insurance is also considered health insurance for purposes of this deduction. The policy can be in the name of the business or in the name of the business owner.

A self-employed taxpayer may not take the deduction if either he or his spouse (if MFJ) is eligible to participate in an employer-sponsored and subsidized health insurance plan, even if they decline coverage.

Line 30: Penalty on Early Withdrawal of Savings

If a taxpayer withdraws money from a certificate of deposit (CD) or other time-deposit savings account prior to maturity, he usually incurs a penalty for early withdrawal. This penalty is charged by the bank or other financial institution and withheld from a taxpayer's proceeds.

Taxpayers can take an adjustment to income for early withdrawal penalties. The penalties are reported on a taxpayer's Form 1099-INT, *Interest Income*, or on Form 1099-OID, *Original Issue Discount*, which lists interest income as well as the penalty amount.

> **Example:** Early in 2016, Gloria invested in a $15,000 one-year certificate of deposit. In November, she had an unexpected medical expense and had to liquidate the CD. She paid a penalty of three months' interest, which totaled $150. Gloria can claim the penalty ($150) as an adjustment to income.

---

[31] SEP, SIMPLE, and qualified retirement plans are primarily tested on the businesses section of the EA exam (Part 2), so they are covered primarily in Book 2 of the PassKey EA Review.

Note: Don't be confused by this concept! It is frequently tested. Only the penalty for early withdrawal from a timed deposit (a certificate of deposit) is tax deductible. The penalty for early withdrawal from an IRA or a retirement plan is never deductible.

Line 31a: Alimony Paid

As described in the preceding unit, alimony received is taxable income. Alimony paid is generally treated as the mirror image and is a deductible expense that is claimed on Page 1 of Form 1040.

By definition, Alimony is a payment to a former spouse under a divorce or separation instrument. The payments do not have to be made directly to the ex-spouse. For example, payments made on behalf of the ex-spouse for expenses such as medical bills, housing costs, and other expenses can also qualify as alimony. Voluntary payments not required by a divorce decree or separation instrument do not qualify as alimony.

Example: Yvette's divorce settlement requires that she pay her ex-husband $16,000 a year. Per the divorce agreement, she also must pay his ongoing medical expenses. In 2016, her ex-husband had $9,500 of medical expenses. She can deduct the full amount ($25,500) as an adjustment to income because it is required by her divorce agreement.

Example: Under the terms of Anthony's divorce decree, he must pay his ex-wife $12,600 in 2016. As a favor, he also makes $2,400 in payments to cover part of her vehicle lease so she can keep steady employment. Anthony can claim the $12,600 as an adjustment to income. He cannot count the lease payments because they were not required by the divorce agreement.

Line 32: IRA Deduction

An individual retirement arrangement (IRA) offers tax advantages for setting aside money for retirement. Some taxpayers can claim a deduction for the amounts contributed to a traditional IRA as an adjustment to gross income.

Amounts that do not qualify for deduction include:

- Contributions to a Roth IRA
- Contributions to a traditional IRA that are nondeductible because the taxpayer and/or spouse is covered by an employer-sponsored retirement plan and modified adjusted gross income (MAGI) exceeds certain limits
- Contributions that apply to the previous tax year
- Rollover contributions

Deductions are allowed in full for contributions to a traditional IRA by a taxpayer (and spouse, if married) who is not covered by a retirement plan at work. If the taxpayer (and/or spouse) is covered by a retirement plan at work, deductions are phased out at certain income levels.[32]

---

[32] The rules regarding IRA contributions, distributions (withdrawals), and rollovers are covered in detail later, in a dedicated unit for retirement plans.

Line 33: Student Loan Interest Deduction

Generally, personal interest (other than mortgage interest) is not deductible. However, interest on a qualified student loan is deductible. A qualified student loan is a loan used solely to pay qualified higher education expenses for the taxpayer, his spouse, or his dependents. A taxpayer can claim the deduction for 2016 if:

- He paid interest on a qualified student loan on which he was legally obligated.
- His filing status is not married filing separately.
- Neither he (nor his spouse, if filing jointly) can be claimed as a dependent on someone else's return.

The maximum deduction for student loan interest in 2016 is $2,500. A phaseout applies for taxpayers with modified adjusted gross income (MAGI) exceeding $65,000 ($130,000 MFJ). The deduction is completely phased out for taxpayers with modified adjusted gross income (MAGI) of $80,000 or more ($160,000 for MFJ). Taxpayers who file MFS are not allowed to take a deduction for student loan interest.

> **Example:** Veronica and her husband file jointly. Their modified adjusted gross income is $168,000. She completed her doctorate and paid $3,400 of student loan interest in 2016. Due to their high income, they cannot deduct any of their student loan interest as an adjustment to income.

In order for student loan interest to qualify, the student must have been enrolled at least half-time in a higher education program leading to a degree, certificate, or other recognized educational credential. A student who used the loan to take classes for other purposes does not qualify.

> **Example:** Peter graduated from a technical college where he had been enrolled full-time in a certificate program for automotive repair. Peter may take the student loan interest deduction.

A student loan is not eligible if it is from certain related persons (such as family members or certain corporations, partnerships, or trusts). Loans from an employer plan also do not qualify. The student loan interest deduction limit is per return, not per student. For example, if a taxpayer has three children and pays $2,000 in student loan interest for each of them, the maximum deduction is still only $2,500. Qualified higher education expenses are costs of attending an eligible educational institution, including graduate schools, such as:

- Tuition and fees
- Room and board
- Books, supplies, and equipment
- Other necessary school-related expenses, such as transportation

Qualified expenses must be reduced by the amounts of tax-free items used to pay them, such as the following:

- Employer-provided educational assistance benefits
- Tax-free withdrawals from a Coverdell Education Savings Account
- U.S. savings bond interest already excluded from income
- Tax-free scholarships and fellowships

- Veterans' educational assistance benefits
- Any other nontaxable payments (except gifts or inheritances) received for educational expenses

> **Example**: In 2016, Eva's college tuition expenses are $7,200. She also receives a gift of $1,000 from her aunt and $1,000 of her veterans' G.I. Bill. Therefore, Eva's qualified higher education expenses are $6,200 because veterans' assistance benefits must be subtracted. The gift from her aunt does not have to be subtracted.

Lenders are required to send the taxpayer Form 1098-E, *Student Loan Interest*, when the amount of interest paid is at least $600 or more.

Summary: Student Loan Interest Deduction

Rules	Description
Maximum deduction	$2,500 per tax return, per year.
Loan qualifications	The student loan: • Must have been taken out solely to pay qualified education expenses, and • Cannot be from a related person or made under a qualified employer plan.
Student qualifications	The student must be the taxpayer, a spouse, or a dependent, and must be enrolled at least half-time in a degree program when the loan was incurred.
Time limit	The taxpayer can deduct interest paid during the remaining period of the student loan.
MAGI phaseout ranges	Single: $65,000-$80,000; MFJ: $130,000-$160,000. MFS does not qualify to take this deduction, regardless of income threshold.

Line 34: Tuition and Fees

Taxpayers can deduct qualified tuition and related higher education expenses paid for academic periods beginning in 2016 and the first three months of 2017.[33] For example, if a taxpayer paid $1,500 in December 2016 for qualified tuition for the spring semester that begins in January 2017, the taxpayer would be able to deduct that $1,500 on their 2016 return.

The Tuition and Fees Deduction is up to $4,000 for qualifying tuition and fees paid for a qualified student (the taxpayer, a spouse, or a dependent). The deduction is reduced to $2,000 for taxpayers with income between the income phaseout thresholds. The phaseout begins at $65,000 ($130,000 for MFJ). A taxpayer whose modified adjusted gross income is greater than $80,000 ($160,000 for joint filers) cannot claim the tuition and fees deduction.

Qualified education expenses include: tuition, fees, and other required course materials. Qualified expenses do *not* include:

- Room and board, medical expenses (including student health fees), transportation, or other personal expenses

---

[33] At the time of this book's printing, the Tuition and Fees Deduction is set to expire on December 31, 2016, and has not been extended for 2017.

- Course-related books, supplies, equipment, and nonacademic activities and fees, unless they are *required* as a condition of enrollment
- Any course or other education involving sports, games, or hobbies, or any noncredit course

A taxpayer cannot claim the tuition and fees deduction based on expenses that have already been paid with a tax-free scholarship, fellowship, grant, or education savings account.

> **Note:** The expenses that qualify for the tuition and fees deduction are more limited than the expenses that qualify for the student loan interest deduction. Generally, for the tuition and fees deduction, qualified education expenses are only amounts paid for tuition expenses at an eligible college or vocational institution

Restrictions: A taxpayer filing MFS cannot take the tuition and fees deduction. If a taxpayer is claimed as a dependent on someone else's return, he cannot take the deduction for himself. Nonresident aliens also do not qualify for this deduction.

A taxpayer cannot claim the tuition and fees deduction and an education credit for the same student. A taxpayer who is eligible to claim the American Opportunity Credit or Lifetime Learning Credit is allowed to figure his return both ways and choose the deduction resulting in the lowest tax.

Line 35: Domestic Production Activities Deduction

The domestic production activities deduction is a tax deduction available to manufacturing businesses that have employees in the United States. The deduction is designed to stimulate domestic production. A sole proprietor could qualify for this deduction if his business has employees and pays wages,[34] although it is rare.

Line 36: Other Adjustments

Line 36 of Form 1040 is reserved for more obscure deductions. This line on the form allows the taxpayer to manually indicate what type of adjustment is being taken. Some of the miscellaneous adjustments that may be entered on line 36 include deductions to an Archer MSA; jury duty pay remitted to an employer; and repayment of unemployment benefits.

---

[34] The DPAD is covered more thoroughly in Part *2: Businesses.*

Unit 11: Study Questions

(Test yourself first, then check the correct answers at the end of this quiz.)

1. Kyle is 26 and has an HSA. He becomes permanently disabled in 2016 due to an auto accident. Which of the following statements is correct?

A. He may withdraw money from his HSA for nonmedical expenses, but the withdrawals will be subject to income tax and also an additional penalty of 20%.
B. He may withdraw money from his HSA for nonmedical expenses. The withdrawals will be subject to income tax, but will not be subject to a penalty.
C. He may not take nonmedical distributions from his account.
D. He must be at least 65 to take nonmedical distributions from an HSA.

2. Deborah was self-employed in 2016 and had self-employment tax of $4,896. Which of the following statements is correct?

A. She can deduct 100% of the self-employment tax she paid on Schedule C.
B. She can deduct 50% of the self-employment tax she paid on Schedule C.
C. She can deduct 50% of the self-employment tax she paid as an adjustment to income on Form 1040.
D. She cannot deduct self-employment tax.

3. Jermaine and Anna have MAGI of $45,000. They are married and file a joint return. Two years ago, they took out a loan so their daughter, Miranda, could earn her degree. Miranda is their dependent. In 2016, they paid $3,000 of student loan interest. How much student loan interest can Jermaine and Anna deduct on their tax return?

A. $0
B. $1,000
C. $2,500
D. $3,000

4. All of the following statements are correct about the educator expense deduction except:

A. A school counselor may qualify.
B. A part-time teacher may qualify.
C. A school principal may qualify.
D. A college instructor may qualify.

5. Under his divorce decree, Rick must pay the medical expenses of his former spouse, Linda. In January 2016, Rick sends a check totaling $4,000 directly to General Medical Hospital in order to pay for Linda's emergency surgery. Which of the following statements is correct?

A. This payment qualifies as alimony, and Linda must include the $4,000 as income on her return.

B. This payment does not qualify as alimony, but Rick can claim a deduction for the medical expenses on his return.

C. Linda must include the $4,000 as income on her return, but Rick cannot deduct the expense as alimony because it was paid to a third party.

D. None of the above.

6. Dave and Bea file jointly. In March 2016, they move from Arizona to Connecticut, where Dave is starting a new job. Dave drives his car to Hartford. His expenses are $400 for gas, $40 for bridge tolls, $150 for lodging, and $70 for meals. One week later, Bea quits her job and drives to Hartford to join her husband. Bea's expenses are $500 for gas, $40 for tolls, $35 for parking, $100 for lodging, and $25 for meals. A week later, they pay $600 to ship their pet, a miniature horse, to Connecticut. How much can they deduct for moving expenses?

A. $590
B. $1,265
C. $1,865
D. $1,960

7. Chuck and Mallory are married and file jointly. Chuck is self-employed, and his net profit was $50,000 in 2016. They pay $700 per month for health insurance coverage. Mallory was a homemaker until she started working for a construction company in early February. Mallory and Chuck became eligible to participate in her employer's health plan on March 1, 2016, but they did not want to switch insurance providers, so Mallory declined her employer's coverage. Which of the following statements is correct?

A. They can deduct $700 for both January and February, and $350 per month for each of the last ten months of the year, as self-employed health insurance premiums on Chuck's Schedule C.

B. They can deduct $1,400 in self-employed health insurance premiums, which is for January and February, the two months they were not eligible to participate in an employer plan.

C. They can deduct 100% of their health insurance premiums because they declined the employer coverage.

D. They can deduct 50% of their health insurance premiums on Chuck's Schedule C.

8. Years ago, Sammy took out a student loan for $90,000 to help pay his college tuition. He graduated and began making payments on his student loan in 2016. Sammy made 12 payments in 2016, which included $1,600 of interest and $2,000 of principal. How much is Sammy's student loan interest deduction?

A. $1,600
B. $2,000
C. $2,500
D. $2,600

9. Marshall lost his job last year and withdrew money from a number of accounts. He paid the following penalties:

Penalty for early withdrawal from a CD	$100
Penalty for early withdrawal from a traditional IRA	200
Late penalty for not paying his rent on time	50

What amount can Marshall deduct as an adjustment to income on his Form 1040?

A. $0
B. $100
C. $200
D. $250

10. Lynn was offered a position in another city. Her new employer reimburses her for the $9,500 loss on the sale of her home because of the move. How should this reimbursement be treated?

A. The employer can reimburse Lynn and make the payment nontaxable through an accountable plan if properly documented.
B. Because this is a reimbursement of a nondeductible expense, it is treated as wages and must be included on Lynn's Form W-2.
C. The reimbursement is tax-exempt because it is a qualified moving expense.
D. The expense is nontaxable as long as Lynn's employer makes the payment directly to her mortgage lender.

11. Bruce makes an excess contribution to his HSA by accidentally contributing over the maximum allowable amount. What is the penalty on excess contributions if Bruce does not correct the problem?

A. No penalty.
B. 6% penalty.
C. 10% penalty.
D. 20% penalty.

12. An adjustment to income is considered the most beneficial type of deduction because:

A. It favors taxpayers who choose to itemize their deductions.
B. It is simpler to figure out qualifying expenses for adjustments to income than it is other deductions.
C. It lowers a taxpayer's adjusted gross income, and thus can affect the amounts of certain credits and deductions he may be able to claim.
D. There is no significant difference between an adjustment to income and other tax deductions.

13. Emilio is a sophomore at his state university, working on his degree in anthropology. In 2016, he paid $3,000 of tuition and $10,000 to live in optional on-campus housing. In addition to tuition, he is required to pay a fee of $300 to the university for the rental of the equipment he uses in his anthropology program. What amount of qualifying expenses does he have for purposes of the tuition and fees deduction?

A. $3,000
B. $3,300
C. $13,000
D. $13,300

14. Drew borrowed $15,000 from his sister to pay for college. He signed a notarized loan statement and is making regular payments of $500 per month, including 10% interest. In 2016, he paid $1,400 of student loan interest. Which of the following statements is correct?

A. Drew can deduct all the interest as qualified student loan interest.
B. Drew can deduct $2,500 of the interest as qualified student loan interest.
C. Drew cannot deduct the interest.
D. Drew can deduct $6,000 ($500 × 12 months) as qualified student interest.

15. Jasmine is a part-time art teacher at an elementary school. She spends $185 on qualified expenses for her art students and $75 on materials for a health course that she also teaches. She worked 440 hours as an educator during the tax year. How much can she deduct in educator expenses as an adjustment to income?

A. $0
B. $185
C. $250
D. $260

16. George paid $14,000 of alimony to his ex-wife during the year. Which of the following statements is correct?

A. He can deduct alimony only if he itemizes deductions on his tax return.
B. The deduction for alimony is entered on Schedule A as an itemized deduction.
C. He can deduct alimony paid, even if he does not itemize deductions.
D. He can deduct alimony paid on Form 1040A.

17. Two full-time teachers who are married and file jointly can deduct a maximum of _____ in educator expenses:

A. $100
B. $250
C. $500
D. $750

18. Chase is moving for a new job. He has the following expenses:

Moving truck rental	$500
Moving family and pets	300
Storage unit while moving	200
Breaking his existing apartment lease	400
Pre-move house-hunting	500

Assuming that Chase passes all the required tests, what is his allowable moving expense deduction?

A. $500
B. $800
C. $1,000
D. $1,900

19. Which of the following qualifies as a deductible education expense for the tuition and fees deduction?

A. College club dues.
B. Student health fees.
C. Room and board.
D. Student activity fees required as a condition for enrollment.

20. Marina is a software specialist who works and lives in Boston. A company offers her a new job in Raleigh, North Carolina, more than 700 miles away. As part of the offer, she negotiates a deal to work part-time for the first six months. Marina's husband is a stay-at-home father to the couple's two young children. The family makes the move from Boston to Raleigh, and Marina begins work at her new job. Does she meet both the time and distance tests in order to deduct her moving expenses as an adjustment to income?

A. No, she does not meet the distance test.
B. No, she does not meet the time test or distance test.
C. She meets the distance test, but not the time test.
D. Marina meets both tests and is able to deduct her moving expenses.

21. Carlie had an HSA account set up with her employer that had $3,000 in the account at the end of the year. She then quit her job in late December and withdrew all the funds from her HSA. She did not use the $3,000 for qualifying medical expenses. What is the consequence of this action?

A. Nothing; taxpayers are allowed to withdraw from their HSA accounts at any time.
B. Nonmedical withdrawals from an HSA are prohibited and will result in a forfeiture of the funds.
C. Withdrawals from an HSA for non-eligible expenses are subject to income tax and a 20% penalty.
D. Withdrawals from an HSA for non-eligible expenses are subject to income tax and a 6% penalty.

Unit 11: Answers

1. The answer is B. Withdrawals for nonmedical expenses from an HSA are allowed, but are subject to income tax. Nonmedical distributions are also subject to an additional penalty tax of 20%, except when the taxpayer has turned 65, become disabled, or died. Kyle has become permanently disabled, in which case his HSA withdrawals are not subject to penalty.

2. The answer is C. Deborah can deduct 50% of the self-employment tax she paid as an adjustment to income on page 1 of her Form 1040.

3. The answer is C. The maximum deduction for student loan interest is $2,500. The deduction is limited to the lesser of $2,500 or the amount of interest actually paid. It doesn't matter how many qualifying student loans there are; the maximum is $2,500 per tax return (not per taxpayer).

4. The answer is D. College instructors do not qualify. An eligible educator must work 900 hours a year in a school that provides elementary or secondary education (K-12). Part-time teachers qualify, if they meet the yearly teachers requirement for hours worked. The term educator includes instructors, counselors, principals, and aides.

5. The answer is A. The payment may be treated as alimony for tax purposes because the medical payments are a condition of the divorce agreement. Payments to a third party on behalf of an ex-spouse under the terms of a divorce instrument can be alimony, if they qualify. These include payments for a spouse's medical expenses, housing costs (rent and utilities), taxes, and tuition. The payments are treated by the ex-spouse as if they were received directly, and included as income.

6. The answer is C. The cost of both trips is deductible. However, the cost of meals is not deductible. The costs of travel, transportation, and lodging are all deductible. The costs of moving personal items and pets are deductible. The answer is figured as follows:

Dave's deductible expenses: $400 + $40 + $150 = $590
Bea's deductible expenses: $500 + $40 + $35 + $100 = $675
Cost of shipping horse: $600
Total deductible expenses: $590 + $675 + $600 = $1,865

If a married couple files jointly, either spouse can qualify for the full-time work test. Family members are not required to travel together.

7. The answer is B. Chuck and Mallory can deduct only $1,400 ($700 X two months) of self-employed health insurance for the months that they were ineligible to participate in an employer plan. No deduction is allowed for self-employed health insurance for any month that the taxpayer has the *option* to participate in an employer-sponsored and subsidized plan. This is true even if the taxpayer declines the coverage. A self-employed taxpayer can deduct 100% of health insurance premiums as an adjustment to income, but only if neither he nor his spouse was eligible to participate in an employer health plan.

8. The answer is A. Only the interest is deductible. A payment toward the principal on the loan is not a deductible expense. Student loan interest is interest a taxpayer paid during the year on a qualified student loan. It includes both required and voluntary interest payments.

9. The answer is B. Early withdrawal penalties are deductible if made from a time deposit account, such as a certificate of deposit. The other types of penalties are not deductible.

10. The answer is B. Expenses of buying or selling a home (including closing costs, mortgage fees, and points) are never deductible as moving expenses. If an employer pays or reimburses expenses, the amounts are treated as taxable compensation and must be reported as wages on Lynn's Form W-2.

11. The answer is B. A 6% penalty applies to excess contributions to a health savings account. Excess contributions made by an employer must be included in an employee's gross income. Excess contributions to an HSA are not deductible.

12. The answer is C. Adjustments are deducted from gross income to derive adjusted gross income (AGI), and itemized and standard deductions are subtracted from AGI. The amount of a taxpayer's AGI is important, as it can affect his eligibility for certain deductions and the amounts that he can claim. For example, certain items are phased out at specified levels of AGI, and some itemized deductions must exceed specified percentages of AGI in order to be deductible. In addition, itemized deductions may be subject to the alternative minimum tax, or may total less than the taxpayer's applicable standard deduction.

13. The answer is B. The rental fee ($300) and the tuition costs ($3,000) qualify for the tuition and fees deduction, which Emilio can claim as an adjustment to income. Because the equipment rental fee must be paid to the university and is a requirement for enrollment and attendance, it is a qualified expense. Student-activity fees and expenses for course-related books, supplies, and equipment can be included in qualified educational expenses if the fees and expenses paid to the institution are required. The housing is not a qualified educational expense.

14. The answer is C. Interest paid to a family member is not qualified interest for purposes of the student loan interest deduction. Related persons include a spouse, brothers and sisters, half-brothers and half-sisters, ancestors (parents, grandparents, etc.), and lineal descendants (children, grandchildren, etc.).

15. The answer is A. Because Jasmine worked only 440 hours as an educator during the tax year, she cannot deduct her educator expenses as an adjustment to income. An educator must have at least 900 hours of qualified employment during the school year to take this deduction as an adjustment to income.

16. The answer is C. George can deduct alimony paid, even if he does not itemize deductions. He must file Form 1040 and enter the amount of alimony paid as an adjustment to income.

17. The answer is C. On a jointly filed tax return, if both taxpayers are teachers, they both may take the deduction, up to a maximum of $500 ($250 each).

18. The answer is C. The cost of breaking a lease is not a deductible moving expense. House-hunting before a move is also not deductible. Therefore, Chase can deduct $1,000 ($500 for a moving truck + $300 for moving his family and pets + $200 for a storage unit).

19. The answer is D. Only the student activity fees qualify for the tuition and fees deduction. Deductions are not allowed for room and board and other basic expenses of going to college, other than required tuition and fees. Student activity fees, course-related books, supplies, and equipment may be deductible only if they are required by the institution as a condition of enrollment.

20. The answer is C. Marina is not able to deduct her moving expenses. She meets the distance test because her old home in Boston is more than 50 miles from her new office in Raleigh. However, to meet the time test, she must work full-time for a period of at least 39 weeks in the first 12 months. Since she is only working part-time for six months, this does not fulfill the requirements of the time test. A spouse does not need to be employed for a MFJ couple to deduct moving expenses.

21. The answer is C. Withdrawals from an HSA for non-eligible expenses are allowed, but the withdrawal is subject to a 20% penalty, in addition to regular income tax.

Unit 12: Standard Deduction & Itemized Deductions

For additional information read:
Publication 502, *Medical and Dental Expenses*
Publication 600, *State and Local General Sales Taxes*
Publication 936, *Home Mortgage Interest Deduction*
Publication 526, *Charitable Contributions*
IRS Publication 1771, *Charitable Contributions–Substantiation and Disclosure Requirements*

A taxpayer generally may choose either to claim a standard deduction amount or to itemize deductions. The choice should be based on which option results in a lower tax liability.

The standard deduction is a specific dollar amount that reduces the amount of income on which a taxpayer is taxed. Using the standard deduction eliminates the need for a taxpayer to itemize his actual allowable deductions, such as medical expenses, charitable contributions, or state and local taxes. The standard deduction amounts are based on a taxpayer's filing status and are adjusted every year for inflation.

Filing Status	2016 Standard Deduction
Single	$6,300
Head of Household	$9,300
Married Filing Separately	$6,300
Married Filing Jointly	$12,600
Qualifying Widow(er)	$12,600
Dependent Standard Deduction	$1,050

Depending on the option selected, either the applicable standard deduction amount or the taxpayer's total itemized deductions is subtracted from his adjusted gross income.

An additional standard deduction is available to taxpayers who, at the end of the year, are:

- 65 or older, and/or
- Blind or partially blind.

The additional standard deduction amount in these cases is $1,250 per taxpayer for married filers and $1,550 for single or head of household filers. A taxpayer who is *both* blind and 65 or older may take the basic standard deduction and additional standard deduction amounts for both age and blindness.

Additional Standard Deduction Amounts-2016	
Taxpayers who are age 65 and/or blind	
Filing Status	Additional Amount Allowable
Single, HOH	$ 1,550
MFS, MFJ, QW	$ 1,250

Note: For filing purposes, a taxpayer is considered to be age 65 in tax year 2016 if they were 65 on December 31, 2016, or if they turned 65 on January 1, 2017.

The additional amount for blindness is allowed if the taxpayer is blind on the last day of the tax year, even if he was not blind the rest of the year. A taxpayer must obtain a statement from an eye doctor indicating that:

- The taxpayer cannot see better than 20/200 in the better eye, even when corrected with eyeglasses, or
- The taxpayer's field of vision is not more than 20 degrees (the taxpayer has disabled peripheral vision).

Example: Wade, 46, and Christine, 33, file jointly. Neither is blind. They decide not to itemize their deductions. Their standard deduction is $12,600 in 2016.

Example: Gilbert, age 52, and Lisa, age 51, are married and do not itemize deductions. Because they file jointly, their base standard deduction is $12,600 in 2016. Lisa is also blind, so she can claim an additional standard deduction amount of $1,250. Therefore, the total standard deduction of their joint return is $13,850 ($12,600 + $1,250) in 2016.

The standard deduction for a deceased taxpayer is the same as if the taxpayer had lived the entire year, with one exception: If the taxpayer died *before* his actual sixty-fifth birthday, the higher standard deduction for being 65 does not apply.

Example: Richard is single and died on November 1, 2016. He would have been 65 if he had reached his birthday on December 18, 2016. He does not qualify for a higher standard deduction because he died before his sixty-fifth birthday, even though it would have happened during the 2016 tax year. His standard deduction is $6,300 on his final income tax return, which must be filed by his executor before April 18, 2017.

Standard Deduction for Certain Dependents

The standard deduction for a dependent which can be claimed on another person's return is limited to the greater of:

- $1,050, or
- The dependent's earned income (such as wages) plus $350, but not more than the regular standard deduction amount. For a single person, this is generally $6,300 in 2016. However, the standard deduction amount can be higher if the dependent is 65 or older and/or blind.

Example: Amy is 19, single, and legally blind. She is claimed as a dependent on her parents' 2016 return. Amy has interest income of $1,300 and wages from a part-time job of $2,900. Because she is claimed as a dependent, Amy's base amount for the standard deduction is $3,250 ($2,900 wages + $350). Because she is also blind, she is also allowed an additional standard deduction amount of $1,550. Her standard deduction is $4,800 ($2,900 + $350 + $1,550).

> **Example:** Georgia is single, 22, and a college student with a part-time job. Her parents support her, so they claim her as a dependent on their 2016 tax return. Georgia files a return and takes the standard deduction, but she does not claim her own exemption (because her parents are claiming her as a dependent). She has wages of $780 from her part-time job, and taxes withheld from her wages totaling $35. Her standard deduction is $1,130 ($780 wages + $350).

Itemized Deductions

Itemized deductions may be taken instead of the standard deduction; they allow taxpayers to reduce their taxable income based on specific personal expenses.

If a taxpayer's total itemized deductions are greater than his applicable standard deduction amount, they will normally result in lower taxable income and a lower tax liability. In most cases, a taxpayer may choose whether to claim itemized deductions or the standard deduction, depending on which is more beneficial. However, taxpayers are *required* to itemize in the following cases:

- If married and filing separately and one spouse itemizes, the other spouse also must itemize.[35]
- If the taxpayer is a nonresident or dual-status alien (who is not married to a U.S. citizen or resident).
- If the taxpayer files a tax return for a period of less than 12 months due to a change in accounting methods.

If a taxpayer itemizes deductions, he must complete and file Schedule A along with his Form 1040. We will review the specific requirements for various itemized deductions in this and the next unit.

Limitation on Itemized Deductions (the Pease Limitation)

The "Pease Limitation" is named after Congressman Donald Pease, who originally introduced the legislation. This provision limits the amount of itemized deductions for taxpayers in higher income brackets.

The limitation reduces the total amount of a higher-income taxpayer's itemized deductions by the lesser of:

- 3% of the amount by which the taxpayer's AGI exceeds a specific threshold, or
- 80% of the total amount of the otherwise allowable itemized deductions.

Itemized Deduction AGI Threshold Amounts

2016 Pease Limitation	
Filing Status	AGI Phaseout Ranges
MFS	$155,650 to $216,900
Single	$259,400 to $381,900
HOH	$285,350 to $407,850
MFJ, QW	$311,300 to $433,800

---

[35] This rule only applies when *both* spouses are filing MFS. If one spouse is MFS, but the other spouse qualifies for HOH filing status (Head of Household), then the spouses are not forced to itemize, and they may choose the standard deduction if they wish.

The Pease Limitation only affects certain tax deductions. The limitation does not apply to the following itemized deductions:

- Medical expenses
- Investment interest expense
- Casualty or theft losses
- Gambling losses

The limitation applies to all other itemized deductions, including charitable contributions; mortgage interest; state, local, and property taxes; and miscellaneous itemized deductions. The Pease Limitation does not apply under the AMT.

Example: For tax year 2016 Andrew and Pauline are filing jointly. Their adjusted gross income is $325,500. Their itemized deductions on Schedule A are as follows:

Property taxes:	$17,900
Mortgage interest paid:	$45,000
Investment interest expense:	$41,000
Charitable gifts:	$21,000
Job search expenses:	$17,240
Total *before* applying Pease Limitation:	$142,140

Andrew and Pauline's investment interest expense deduction ($41,000) isn't subject to the overall limit on itemized deductions. They use the Itemized Deductions Worksheet in the Schedule A (Form 1040) instructions to figure their overall limit. Of their $142,140 total itemized deductions, they can deduct only $141,714 ($142,140 - $426). They enter $141,714 on Schedule A (Form 1040), line 29.[36]

Medical and Dental Expenses

Medical and dental expenses (other than self-employed health insurance premiums) are deductible only if a taxpayer itemizes deductions. Further, most taxpayers can deduct only the amount of unreimbursed medical expenses that exceeds 10% of adjusted gross income.[37]

Example: Tracy, age 53, had unreimbursed medical expenses totaling $2,500 in 2016. Her AGI was $40,000. Tracy cannot deduct any of her medical expenses on Schedule A because they are not more than 10% of her AGI ($40,000 × .10 = $4,000).

Example: Manuel, age 46, paid $12,000 in out-of-pocket expenses for knee surgery in 2016. His AGI was $100,000. The amount of medical expenses in excess of $10,000 (AGI of $100,000 × 10% limitation), or $2,000, is allowed as an itemized deduction on Schedule A.

---

[36] Example adapted from Publication 17, chapter 29.
[37] The change from the original 7.5% medical expenses threshold to 10% was introduced in 2014 as part of the Affordable Healthcare Act and applies until the end of 2016.

Special Rules for Taxpayers 65 and Over: Only through 2016, a taxpayer (and spouse, if married) age 65 or over can deduct the amount of unreimbursed medical expenses that exceeds 7.5% of AGI, rather than 10%. The 7.5% floor also would apply if *either* spouse reaches age 65 by the end of the tax year.[38]

A change in the applicable AGI percentage can occur because of marriage, divorce, or annulment.

Example: Meredith, age 59, and Rudy, age 66, had unreimbursed medical expenses of $8,000 in 2016. Their AGI was $70,000. Because Rudy is older than 65, they may use the 7.5%-of-AGI threshold and deduct $2,750 on their Schedule A, the amount in excess of the 7.5% floor ($70,000 × .75 = $5,250). The 7.5% limitation applies to all their medical expenses, regardless of which spouse incurred them.

Example: Neil, age 61, is married to Cora, age 66. Their unreimbursed medical expenses total 9% of their AGI. They can deduct the amount that exceeds the 7.5% floor because Cora is over age 65. However, on November 2, 2016, Neil and Cora divorce. Now they must both file as single for 2016. Neil, who is age 61, now can deduct only the amount of his unreimbursed medical expenses that exceeds 10% of his AGI, while Cora may continue to use the 7.5% floor.

Note: The special 7.5% threshold for taxpayers 65 and older is only temporary—starting in 2017, regardless of age, all taxpayers will be subject to a 10%-of-AGI limit for medical expenses.

Qualifying Medical Expenses

A taxpayer may only deduct medical expenses they paid during the year, regardless of when the services were provided. Qualified medical expenses include expenses paid for:

- The taxpayer or the taxpayer's spouse
- Dependents (the individual must have been a dependent at the time the medical services were provided or at the time the expenses were paid). However, there is an exception to this rule for children of divorced or separated parents.

A taxpayer can deduct medical expenses paid on behalf of an adopted child, even before the adoption is final. A taxpayer can also deduct medical expenses paid for a dependent parent. All the standard rules for a dependency exemption apply, so the dependent parent does not have to live with the taxpayer to qualify.

Note: If a child of divorced or separated parents is claimed as a dependent on either parent's return, each parent can deduct medical expenses they individually paid for the child. This is true even if the other parent claims the child's dependency exemption. Basically, it doesn't matter which parent claims the child—the medical expenses are deductible for the parent that pays them.

Example: Julie pays all the medical expenses for her father, age 62, who is her dependent, but does not live with her. The medical expenses are deductible on Julie's tax return as an itemized deduction to the extent they exceed the 10% threshold.

---

[38] The floor for medical expenses is 10% for all taxpayers, regardless of age, after December 31, 2016.

> **Example:** Raymond and Carmen are divorced. Their son, Colby, lives primarily with Carmen, who claims him as a dependent on her tax return. Carmen also deducts Colby's annual medical and dental bills, including orthodontia expenses for his braces. However, in April, Colby falls on the playground and fractures his arm. The out-of-pocket expenses for Colby's broken arm are $5,500. Colby's father, Raymond, pays for the emergency room visit and the expenses related to the injury, and Raymond can deduct the expenses on Schedule A, even though he does not claim his son as a dependent.

Qualifying medical expenses include the costs of diagnosis, cure, mitigation, treatment, or prevention of disease, and the costs of medical (but not cosmetic) treatments. They include the costs of:

- Medically necessary equipment, supplies, and diagnostic devices
- Dental and vision care
- Transportation to obtain medical care
- Qualified long-term care insurance

Deductible medical expenses include:

- Fees paid to doctors, dentists, surgeons, chiropractors, psychiatrists, psychologists, and nontraditional medical practitioners
- In-patient hospital care or nursing home services, including the cost of meals and lodging charged by the hospital or nursing home
- Acupuncture treatments
- Lactation supplies
- Treatment at centers for alcohol or drug addiction, participation in smoking-cessation programs, and prescription drugs to alleviate nicotine withdrawal
- Weight-loss programs prescribed by a physician (but not diet food items)
- Insulin and prescription drugs (but prescription drugs brought in or shipped from a different country are generally not deductible)
- Admission and transportation to a medical conference relating to a chronic disease (but the costs of meals and lodging while attending the conference are not deductible)
- Veterinary care when it relates to the care of animals trained to assist persons who are visually-impaired, hearing-impaired, or disabled.

> **Example:** Olaf is a Gulf War Veteran. Olaf is recovering from severe Post-Traumatic Stress Disorder. Olaf's physician recommends that he obtain a service dog to help aid him with his recovery. The doctor gives Olaf a written physician's statement explaining the recommendation. With the help of a Veteran's support group, Olaf obtains a trained service dog in 2016. The dog's veterinary costs are deductible medical expenses on Olaf's individual tax return.

> **Note:** Medical expenses must be primarily to alleviate or prevent a physical or mental defect or illness. Medical expenses do not include expenses that are merely beneficial to general health, such as vitamins, spa treatments, gym memberships, or vacations. In addition, the cost of over-the-counter medications cannot be deducted.

Medical Insurance: If a taxpayer receives insurance reimbursement for medical care expenses, those amounts are not deductible. Qualifying medical expenses include medical insurance and long-term care insurance premiums that the taxpayer paid with after-tax dollars. A taxpayer cannot deduct insurance premiums paid by an employer-sponsored plan unless the premiums are included in Box 1 of his Form W-2.

> **Note:** The value of a taxpayer's annual health care coverage is reported on Form W-2. The amount includes the portions paid by both the employer and the employee. Although this amount is reported on Form W-2, it does not mean the amount is taxable; it is for informational purposes only. This is a recent requirement of the Affordable Care Act.

Payments for medical expenses out of a health savings account (HSA) are not deductible, but contributions to HSAs may be deducted as an adjustment to gross income.

Long-Term Care Services: A taxpayer may include limited amounts paid for qualified long-term care services and insurance premiums in his medical expense deductions.

Long-term care services include necessary diagnostic, preventive, therapeutic, rehabilitative, maintenance, and personal care services that are required by a chronically-ill individual and provided under a plan of care by a licensed doctor.

The deductibility of costs of qualified long-term care premiums is limited by the age of the taxpayer. The expenses generally cannot include costs that would be reimbursed under Medicare.

2016 Long Term Care Premiums - Deductibility	
Age	Maximum deduction for the year
Age 40 or under	$390
Over 40 but not more than 50	$730
Over 50 but not more than 60	$1,460
Over 60 but not more than 70	$3,900
Over 70 years of age	$4,870

The limits on deductible long-term care premiums are per individual, not per tax return. For example, a married couple over age 70 could deduct up to **$9,740** ($4,870 X 2 persons) on a joint return in 2016.

Other Medical Expenses: If a taxpayer or a dependent is in a nursing home and the primary reason for being there is medically related, the entire cost, including meals and lodging, is a medical expense.

A taxpayer can deduct legal fees necessary to authorize treatment for a mental illness. However, legal fees for the management of a guardianship estate or for conducting the affairs of a person being treated are not deductible as medical expenses.

Medical Expenses of Deceased Taxpayers: In addition to expenses paid before a taxpayer's death, his survivor or personal representative can elect to treat medical expenses paid by the estate within one year after his death as if the taxpayer had paid when the medical services were provided.

Example: Anne had heart surgery in November 2016 and incurred $20,000 of medical bills. When she died on December 2, 2016, her 2016 medical bills had not yet been paid. The executor of Anne's estate is her son, Benny. Benny pays his late mother's outstanding medical bills on February 3, 2017. As the executor, Benny may elect to deduct Anne's final medical expenses on her 2016 tax return (her final tax return), even though the medical expenses were not paid by him until 2017. This special election only applies to deceased taxpayers.

Cosmetic Surgery: Cosmetic surgery is only deductible if it is used to correct a defect or disease. A cosmetic procedure simply for the enhancement of someone's physical appearance is not a deductible medical expense.

Example: Bethany undergoes a mastectomy to remove her breasts as part of treatment for cancer. A cosmetic surgeon later reconstructs her breasts to correct a deformity that is directly related to cancer. The cost of the cosmetic surgery is deductible as a medical expense because the surgery corrects an earlier defect or disease.

Medically-Related Transportation, Meals, and Lodging: Vehicle mileage may be deducted if transportation is for medical reasons, such as trips to and from doctors' appointments. If a taxpayer uses his own car for medical transportation, he can deduct actual out-of-pocket expenses for gas and other expenses, or he can deduct the standard mileage rate for medical expenses, which is 19 cents per mile in 2016. A taxpayer can also deduct the costs of taxis, buses, trains, planes, or ambulances, as well as tolls and parking fees.

A taxpayer can deduct the cost of meals and lodging at a hospital or similar institution if the principal reason for being there is to receive medical care. The care must be provided by a doctor, hospital, or medical care facility, and there must not be any significant element of personal pleasure or recreation.

Capital Improvements for Medical Reasons: Capital improvements such as home improvements are usually not deductible. However, a home improvement may qualify as a deductible expense if its main purpose is to provide medical care to the taxpayer or to dependent family members.

The deduction for capital improvements is limited to the excess of the actual cost of the improvements over the related increase in the fair market value of the home. Home improvements that qualify as deductible medical expenses may include:

- Wheelchair ramps
- Lowering of kitchen cabinets
- Railings and support bars
- Elevators
- Special lift equipment

Tenants can deduct the entire cost of disability-related improvements since they are not the owners of the property.

Example: Lonnie, age 61, has a heart condition. He cannot easily climb stairs or get into a bathtub. On his doctor's advice, he pays for the installation of a special sit-in bathtub and a stair lift in his rented house. The landlord did not pay any of the cost. Lonnie can deduct the entire amount as a medical expense, subject to the 10% threshold.

Deductible Taxes

Taxpayers can deduct certain taxes if they itemize deductions. To be deductible, a tax must have been imposed on the taxpayer and paid by the taxpayer during the tax year. Deductible taxes include:

- State, local, and foreign income taxes
- State and local sales taxes
- Real estate taxes
- Personal property taxes

State and Local Taxes: Taxpayers are allowed to deduct either *sales/use* taxes or state and local *income* taxes, depending on which provides the larger deduction, but not both. Income taxes paid include taxes withheld from salaries and wages, amounts paid for prior years, and estimated tax payments.

Real Estate Taxes: State, local, or foreign real estate taxes based on the assessed value of the taxpayer's real property (such as a house or land) are deductible. If the taxes are paid from a mortgage escrow account, the taxpayer can deduct only the amount actually paid out of the escrow account during the year to the taxing authority.

Note: Foreign real estate taxes are deductible on Schedule A. The property does not have to be located in the United States for the real estate tax to be deductible.

Some real estate taxes are not deductible, including taxes imposed to finance improvements to property, such as assessments for streets, sidewalks, and sewer lines. In addition, itemized charges for services and homeowner's association fees are not deductible.

Example: Genevieve makes the following payments: state income tax, $2,000; real estate taxes, $900; local benefit tax for improving the sewer system, $75; homeowner's association fee, $250. Her total deductible taxes are $2,900 ($2,000 + $900 = $2,900). The $75 local benefit tax and the $250 homeowner's association fee are not deductible.

If a property is sold, the real estate taxes are prorated between the buyer and the seller according to the number of days that each owned the property, and adjustments are charged or credited on the settlement statement depending upon which party is responsible for paying the taxing authority.

Escrow accounts: If a portion of the taxpayer's monthly mortgage payment goes into an escrow account, and periodically the lender pays the real estate taxes out of the account to the local government, the taxpayer is only allowed to deduct the amount that was actually paid out of the escrow account during the year to the taxing authority.

Foreign Income Taxes: Generally, a taxpayer can choose between claiming the Foreign Tax Credit or claiming an itemized deduction on Schedule A for income taxes paid to a foreign country, depending on which option results in the lowest tax. The rules regarding which foreign taxes qualify for either the credit or the deduction are covered later.

Personal Property Taxes (DMV Fees): Personal property taxes are deductible if they are:
- Charged on personal property, including cars, boats, or items used in a business, such as equipment and furniture;
- Based on the value of the property; and
- Charged on a yearly basis, even if collected more or less than once a year.

Example: Patty receives an annual registration notice for her car from the California Department of Motor Vehicles. The bill is broken down as follows:
- Registration: $25
- Vehicle license fee: $58
- Weight fee: $32
- County fee: $13
- Owner responsibility fee: $15

The notice states that the vehicle license fee is based on the car's value. Only the vehicle license fee is tax deductible on Schedule A.

Deductible Interest

Taxpayers are allowed to deduct certain types of interest. Qualified interest payments are deductible as itemized deductions on Form 1040, Schedule A. Deductible interest includes:
- Home mortgage interest
- Points on a mortgage loan
- Mortgage insurance premiums
- Investment interest expense

Home Mortgage Interest

Home mortgage interest is paid on a loan secured by a taxpayer's home. The loan may be a mortgage, a second mortgage, a home equity loan, or a line of credit. A taxpayer is allowed to deduct the interest related to a primary residence and a second home. Under current laws, taxpayers may deduct interest on the loan balance of up to $1 million of home acquisition debt secured by a qualified primary or secondary residence.

Example: Kenji has a $150,000 mortgage on his main home where he lives. He also has a $75,000 mortgage on a beach cottage in North Carolina and a $90,000 mortgage on a condo in Utah. Kenji can deduct the mortgage interest on his main home and on the condo, but he cannot deduct the mortgage interest on the cottage because the deduction is limited to two homes.

A second home can include any other residence a taxpayer owns and treats as a home, but the taxpayer does not have to actually use the second home during the year in order to deduct the mortgage interest paid on the related loan.

Note: Although a taxpayer can deduct real estate taxes on more than two properties, he cannot deduct mortgage interest on more than two homes.

An empty lot does not qualify for the mortgage interest deduction. If a taxpayer builds a house that becomes a qualified home when ready for occupancy, he can deduct mortgage interest for a period of up to 24 months from when construction begins. A taxpayer can deduct late charges on a mortgage loan as mortgage interest.

Example: Reese owns his home and pays his mortgage on a monthly basis. In 2016, he falls behind on his mortgage payments and sends in his payment late on two occasions. The mortgage company charges Reese a $35 fee for each late payment. The late fees are deductible as mortgage interest.

Mortgage Deduction Limits

If all of the taxpayer's mortgages fit into one or more of the following three categories, he can deduct all of the interest:

- Mortgages obtained on or before October 13, 1987 (grandfathered debt).
- Mortgages obtained after October 13, 1987, to buy, build, or improve a home (called home acquisition debt), but only if these mortgages plus any grandfathered debt total **$1 million** ($500,000 if MFS) or less.
- Mortgages obtained after October 13, 1987, for purposes other than to buy, build, or improve the home (called home equity debt, or home equity lines of credit), but only if these mortgages are $100,000 or less.

If one or more of the taxpayer's mortgages does not fit in at least one of these categories, his interest deductions will be limited.

Example: Shirley has a mortgage of $800,000 against her primary residence and another of $500,000 against a vacation home. Both loans were used solely to acquire the homes. The loan amounts add up to $1.3 million. Since the total loan amounts exceed the $1 million limit for home acquisition debt, Shirley's mortgage interest deduction is limited.

Home Equity Lines of Credit (Special Rules)

The interest paid on home equity debt related to a main home and a second home is deductible, in most cases. Taxpayers can generally deduct interest paid on the first $100,000 of a home equity loan. The home equity debt limit is reduced to $50,000 for taxpayers who are married filing separately.

A taxpayer can deduct the interest on home equity debt, subject to the limits described above, no matter how he uses the proceeds.

Example: Jeremy and Ashley obtained two home equity loans totaling $90,000. They used the loans to pay off gambling debts, credit card payments, and medical expenses. The couple can deduct the interest on their home equity loans because the total does not exceed $100,000.

If the home equity line is used to improve the home, then the interest is deductible up to the one million dollar limit. Remember, the amount of deductible mortgage interest on an equity loan depends primarily on what the loan is used for.

If a taxpayer borrows $250,000 in a home equity line of credit, and all of the loan proceeds are used to substantially improve the home, then the entire amount would be considered a qualifying loan for the mortgage interest deduction. In that case, the mortgage interest would be deductible up until the $1 million limit.

Example: Noah owns his own home. He decides to borrow a $150,000 home equity line in order to consolidate his credit card debt and buy a new car. Only the interest on the first $100,000 of the loan is deductible. The interest on the remaining $50,000 of the loan is not deductible as mortgage interest.

Example: Griselda owns her home. In 2016, she decides to add an extra bedroom, a new bathroom, and she installs a new pool. The bedroom addition cost $66,000, the new bathroom cost $22,000, and the new pool cost $29,000, for a total cost of $117,000. Griselda applies for a home equity line of credit to finance the improvements. Since the home equity loan was used entirely to improve the property, all of the interest is deductible as mortgage interest, even though the loan amount exceeds $100,000.

Example: Carla purchased her home ten years ago and paid cash. Its fair market value is now $80,000. She did not have a mortgage until last year, when she took out a $45,000 home equity loan, secured by her home, to pay for her daughter's college tuition. This loan is home equity debt. Since it is less than the $100,000 limit, the mortgage interest on the equity line is deductible.

Equity Loans Exceeding Fair Market Value

If the home equity line is used for something other than home improvements, and the amount of the home equity loan exceeds the fair market value of the home,[39] a portion of the interest will be disallowed, even if the equity line does not exceed $100,000.

The taxpayer must calculate the percentage of deductible interest based on a percentage.[40]

Example: Kody bought his home five years ago. Its FMV is now $110,000, and the current balance on his original mortgage is $95,000. His bank offers him a home equity loan with borrowings up to 125% of the FMV of the home. To consolidate some of his other debts, Kody takes out a new $42,500 home equity loan ([125% × $110,000] – $95,000). Kody's home equity loan exceeds the FMV of the home minus the balance of his home acquisition debt ($110,000 - $95,000 = $15,000). Therefore, his deductible mortgage interest relating to the home equity loan is limited to the interest on $15,000.

---

[39] Lenders traditionally refuse to lend more money than a home's fair market value. Although it is now uncommon for a bank to lend a borrower more than a home's value, it was common for lenders to offer 125% of a home's value as an equity line of credit, before the housing crisis of 2007-2008. This issue is still covered in IRS Publication 17, so you must understand it.
[40] Internal Revenue Code Section 163(h)(3) provides additional guidance for the limitations on the home mortgage interest deduction.

Points and Other Prepaid Mortgage Interest

Points are interest charges a borrower pays up-front to obtain a loan. Points generally represent prepaid interest a borrower pays at closing in order to obtain a lower interest rate. Points may also be called loan origination fees, including VA and FHA fees, maximum loan charges, premium charges, loan discount points, or prepaid interest.

Loan fees paid for specific services, such as home appraisal fees, document preparation fees, VA funding fees, or notary fees are not interest and are not deductible. In order to deduct points, the following requirements must be met:

- The mortgage must be secured by the taxpayer's main home, and the mortgage must have been used to buy, build, or improve the home.
- The points must not be an excessive or unusual amount for the local area.
- The points paid must not be more than the amount of unborrowed funds.
- The points must be computed as a percentage of the loan principal, and they must be listed on the settlement statement.

If all these requirements are met, the taxpayer can deduct points in connection with the acquisition or construction of the home either in the year paid or over the life of the loan. Tax law treats "purchase" mortgage points differently from "refinance" mortgage points. Points paid to refinance a mortgage are generally not fully deductible in the year paid and must be deducted over the life of the loan unless the proceeds are used to improve a main home. A second home or vacation home would not qualify for this exception.

> **Example:** Abby refinanced her home in January 2016. She did not use the proceeds of the loan to improve the home. Instead, she used the loan proceeds to pay off other bills. She paid $1,500 in points for a 15-year refinance of her existing mortgage. She is entitled to deduct only $100 per year on her Schedule A ($1,500 ÷ 15 years).

Mortgage Insurance Premiums

A taxpayer can deduct qualified mortgage insurance[41] premiums (also called PMI) for coverage related to home mortgages after 2006. The deduction for mortgage insurance premiums is phased out for higher-income taxpayers.

2016 Mortgage Insurance Phaseout Ranges	
Single, MFJ, QW	$100,000 - $109,000
MFS	$50,000 - $54,500

A taxpayer cannot deduct any mortgage insurance premiums if the AGI on their return exceeds $109,000 ($54,500 if married filing separately).

---

[41] A lender may require mortgage insurance to protect itself in case a borrower defaults. Mortgage insurance protects the lender, not the borrower, and it generally allows the homebuyer to make a smaller down payment than would otherwise be required.

Form 1098: If a taxpayer paid more than $600 during the year for mortgage interest (including points and mortgage insurance premiums) in connection with any single mortgage, the amounts should be reported to the taxpayer on Form 1098, *Mortgage Interest Statement,* by the financial institution that received the payments.

Investment Interest Expense

When a taxpayer borrows money to buy property held for investment, interest he pays on that borrowed money is investment interest expense and may be deductible. The amount of investment interest expense a taxpayer can deduct each year is limited to the amount of net investment income earned. However, he can carry forward any disallowed investment interest expense to the next year.

> **Example:** Mariko borrows money from a bank to buy $3,000 worth of short-term bonds. The bonds mature during the year, and Mariko makes $400 of investment interest income. She also has $210 in investment interest expense, which she paid on the loan originally taken out to buy the bonds. Mariko must report the full amount of $400 as investment interest income. She can deduct the $210 of investment interest expense on Schedule A.

> **Example:** Jackson borrows money from a bank in order to buy $10,000 worth of U.S. gold coins. During the year, the coins lose value, and he has no investment income. Jackson paid $326 of investment interest expense on the loan he used to buy the coins. He may not take a deduction for the investment interest expense because he has no investment income, but he may carry over to the next tax year the investment interest expense he could not deduct.

The deductible amount of investment interest expense and any disallowed amount that may be carried over to the following year are calculated on Form 4952, *Investment Interest Expense Deduction.*

A taxpayer cannot deduct interest related to passive activities or incurred to produce tax-exempt income (such as state and local bonds that generate tax-exempt interest income) as investment interest expense.

Nondeductible Interest and Investment Expenses: The following expenses cannot be deducted:

- Interest on personal loans, such as car loans
- Fees for credit cards and finance charges for nonbusiness credit card purchases
- Loan fees for services needed to get a loan
- Interest on a debt the taxpayer is not legally obligated to pay
- Service charges
- Interest to purchase or carry tax-exempt securities
- Late payment charges paid to a public utility
- Expenses relating to stockholders' meetings or investment-related seminars
- Interest expenses from single-premium life insurance and annuity contracts
- Interest incurred from borrowing against an insurance policy
- Short-sale expenses
- Fines and penalties paid to any government entity for violations of the law

254

Example: José and Blanca file a joint return. During the year, they paid:

1. $3,180 of home mortgage interest reported to them on Form 1098
2. $400 of credit card interest
3. $1,500 to the home mortgage lender for an appraisal fee
4. $2,000 of interest on a car loan

José and Blanca can deduct only their home mortgage interest ($3,180). None of the other charges are allowable as a tax deduction.

Charitable Contributions

Taxpayers who itemize deductions can deduct certain charitable contributions to qualified organizations. Taxpayers may contribute cash, property (such as clothing and furniture), securities, or other assets. A taxpayer can deduct a contribution only in the year it is actually made. A donation charged to a credit card before the end of 2016 counts for 2016, even if the credit card bill is not paid until the following year. A donation made by check counts for 2016 if the donor mails it in 2016, even if the charity cashes the check in the following year.

In order to claim deductions for noncash donations, the donated items must be in good condition. In most cases, the taxpayer will be able to claim a deduction for the fair market value of the contribution (generally what someone would be willing to pay at a garage sale or thrift store). No deduction is allowed for items that are in poor or unusable condition. Deductible contributions may include:

- Unreimbursed expenses that relate directly to the services the taxpayer provided for the organization.
- The amount of a contribution in excess of the fair market value of items received, such as merchandise and tickets to a charity ball or a sporting event.
- Transportation expenses, including bus fare, parking fees, tolls, and either the actual cost of gas and oil or a standard mileage deduction of 14 cents per mile in 2016.

Volunteer Expenses: A taxpayer cannot deduct a monetary value for the hours he spends volunteering. However, taxpayers are allowed to deduct out-of-pocket costs related to their volunteer work for qualifying organizations.

Example: Emily is an attorney who donates time to her local church for its legal needs. In 2016, she spent ten hours drafting legal documents for the church, which is a qualified religious organization. She also had $200 of out-of-pocket expenses because she purchased a new printer for the church. The printer was delivered directly to the church rectory for its use. Emily can take a charitable deduction for $200, the amount she spent on behalf of her church. She cannot deduct the value of her time.

A taxpayer can deduct expenses incurred while traveling to perform services for a charitable organization only if there is no significant element of personal pleasure in the travel. However, a deduction will not be denied simply because the taxpayer enjoys providing the services. The taxpayer can take a charitable contribution deduction for the expenses if he is on-duty in a genuine and substantial way throughout the trip.

> **Example:** Francine regularly volunteers at her local animal shelter, a qualified animal rescue organization. She uses her own car to travel to and from the shelter. She is not reimbursed for mileage. Francine also fosters kittens on behalf of the shelter. She pays for cat food for the foster kittens and other supplies out-of-pocket. She receives an annual statement from the animal shelter substantiating her donations. Francine can deduct her mileage and her unreimbursed expenses as a charitable contribution, but cannot deduct the value of her time.

Exchange Students: A taxpayer can deduct some expenses paid for a foreign or American student who is living with him. The student must be sponsored by a qualifying organization, not be related to the taxpayer, and be part of a program to provide educational opportunities.

> **Example:** The Jensen family hosts a high school student from Portugal in their home for nine months during 2016. The exchange student is sponsored by AFS; Intercultural Programs USA, a qualifying organization. The Jensens can deduct up to $50 a month in expenses while the student lives with them.

Nonqualifying Organizations: Not all nonprofit organizations qualify as charitable organizations for purposes of donors being able to claim tax deductions. An organization may qualify for nonprofit status so that its own activities are not subject to income tax, but this designation does not automatically provide qualification for purposes of deductible contributions. The following are examples of items that do not qualify as deductible charitable contributions:

- Gifts to civic leagues, social and sports clubs, and Chambers of Commerce
- Gifts to groups run for personal profit
- Gifts to political groups, candidates, or political organizations
- Gifts to homeowner's associations
- Donations made directly to individuals
- The cost of raffle, bingo, or lottery tickets, even if the raffle is part of a qualified organization's fundraiser
- Dues paid to country clubs or similar groups
- Gifts and dues to labor unions (although union dues may be deductible on Schedule A as a miscellaneous itemized deduction)
- Blood donated to a blood bank or to the Red Cross
- Any part of a contribution that benefits the taxpayer, such as the FMV of a meal eaten at a charity dinner

> **Example:** Renee paid the Chamber of Commerce a $30 entry fee to run in a 10K race it was sponsoring on behalf of a cancer-related charity. The Chamber is not a qualifying charitable organization, so none of Renee's entry fee is tax deductible as a charitable contribution. If the race had been organized by the charity itself, part of her entry fee might have been deductible.

Example: Bill goes to a church fundraiser that includes a bingo game. Bill spends $200 on bingo cards but does not win anything. Even though the $200 went directly to the church, the cost of the bingo game is not considered a charitable gift and is therefore not deductible.

Substantiation Requirements for Charitable Gifts

There are strict recordkeeping requirements for taxpayers who claim deductions for charitable contributions, depending upon the nature and amounts. The IRS imposes recordkeeping and substantiation rules on donors and disclosure requirements on the charities themselves. Here are the basic rules for ALL charitable gifts:

- At a minimum, the donor must have at least a bank record **or** a written receipt (or written acknowledgment) from a charity for **any** cash contribution before the donor can claim a charitable deduction.
- The *donor* is responsible for obtaining a written receipt from a charity for any single contribution of $250 or more before he can claim a charitable deduction.
- Charitable organizations are required to provide a written disclosure to a donor who receives goods or services in exchange for a single payment in excess of $75.[42]

Rules for Cash Donations

Cash Donations of LESS than $250: Cash contributions include those paid by cash, check, debit card, credit card, or payroll deduction. If the value of an individual donation is less than $250, the taxpayer must keep a reliable written record, such as the following:

- A bank, credit union, or credit card statement that shows the name of the qualified organization, the date of the contribution, and the amount of the contribution.
- A receipt (or a letter or other written communication) from the qualified organization showing its name, the date of the contribution, and the amount of the contribution.
- For payroll deductions, a pay stub or Form W-2, plus a pledge card or other document showing the name of the qualified organization.
- For text donations, a telephone bill, as long as it shows the name of the qualified organization, the date of the contribution, and the amount given.

A donor should not attach the acknowledgment or receipt to his tax return, but must retain it to substantiate the contribution.

Example: Gary donates $25 per month to the Humane Society. Gary always pays by check, and he keeps the canceled check as a record of his contribution. This is a valid method of recordkeeping for donations under $250. He does not need to have an additional receipt from the organization to substantiate his deduction.

Cash Donations of $250 or MORE: For cash donations of $250 or more, the taxpayer must have a receipt or written acknowledgment from the organization that includes:

---

[42] See Publication 1771, *Charitable Contributions Substantiation and Disclosure Requirements*

- The amount of cash the taxpayer contributed.
- The date of the contribution.
- Whether the qualified organization gave any goods or services as a result of the contribution (other than certain token items and membership benefits). The absence of this simple statement by a charity has led to court cases in which major cash contributions have been challenged, and in some cases, disallowed.
- If applicable, a description and a good faith estimate of the value of goods or services provided by the organization as a result of the contribution.

The taxpayer must obtain the receipt on or before:
- The date the taxpayer files his tax return for the year he makes the donation, or
- The due date, including extensions, for filing the return.

If the donation is via payroll deduction, any amount of $250 or more must be substantiated with a pay stub or W-2, and a statement about whether goods or services were given by the qualified organization.

> **Note:** A single annual statement from the charitable organization may be used to substantiate multiple contributions of $250 or more.

Rules for Noncash Donations (Gifts of Property)

Noncash Contributions of Less than $250: For each contribution of less than $250, the taxpayer must obtain a receipt from the receiving organization and keep a list of the items donated.

> **Example:** Gary donated ten dress shirts to Goodwill during the year. He made a list of the items he donated and received a receipt from the organization when he dropped off his donation. In Gary's town, Goodwill sells dress shirts in their thrift shops for about $5 each. Based on the thrift store's valuation of his donation, Gary has made a charitable donation of $50.

Noncash Donations between $250 and $500: For each contribution of at least $250, but not exceeding $500, the taxpayer must have the same documentation as described above for noncash contributions less than $250. In addition, the organization's written acknowledgment must state whether the taxpayer received any goods or services in return and included a description and a good faith estimate of the fair market value of any such items.

Noncash Donations Over $500: If a taxpayer's total deduction for all noncash contributions for the year is more than $500, he must also file Form 8283, *Noncash Charitable Contributions.*

Noncash Donations Over $5,000: If any single donation or a group of similar items is valued at more than $5,000, a qualified appraiser is required to make a written appraisal of the donated property. The taxpayer must also complete Form 8283, Section B, and attach it to his tax return. He generally does not have to attach the appraisal itself, but must retain a copy for his records. For donations of artwork valued at more than $20,000, or property valued at more than $500,000, the appraisal itself must be included with the tax return.

Special Rules for Donated Vehicles

Special rules apply to any donation of vehicles, including boats and airplanes. If the taxpayer claims a deduction of more than $500, he can only deduct the smaller of:

- The gross proceeds from the sale of the item by the charity, or
- The fair market value on the date of the contribution.

The charitable organization should provide Form 1098-C, *Contributions of Motor Vehicles, Boats, and Airplanes*, which shows the gross proceeds from the sale of the vehicle donated. If the taxpayer does not attach Form 1098-C, the maximum deduction that can be taken for the donation is $500. Vehicles not in working condition may have zero donation value.

> **Example:** Kevin donates his used motorcycle to his church fundraiser. The FMV of the motorcycle is $2,500. The church sells the motorcycle 60 days later for $1,700 and sends Kevin a Form 1098-C. He can deduct only $1,700 on his Schedule A (the smaller of the FMV or the gross proceeds from the sale) and must attach a copy of the Form 1098-C to his tax return.

Two exceptions apply to the rules regarding vehicle donations:

- If the charity keeps the vehicle for its own use, the taxpayer can generally deduct the vehicle's FMV.
- If the charity gives or sells the vehicle directly to a needy person, the taxpayer can generally deduct the vehicle's FMV.

Deductible Contribution Limits

A taxpayer cannot deduct aggregate charitable contributions that exceed 50% of his adjusted gross income. For example, if a taxpayer had $100,000 of adjusted gross income in 2016, the maximum charitable contributions he could deduct would be $50,000 (50% of AGI). Contributions must be paid in cash or other property before the close of the tax year in order to be deductible. There are three major AGI limits:

- **The 50% limit** (this applies to most donations)
- **The 30% limit** (this applies to certain organizations and certain types of gifts)
- **The 20% limit** (this applies specifically to gifts of capital gain property to certain nonprofits)

Any amounts disallowed as a result of this limit could be carried forward to future years. Be aware that the 50% limit applies to *most* charitable contributions. The **50%-of-AGI contribution limit** applies to contributions made to:

- Churches, synagogues, and similar religious organizations,
- Hospitals,
- Most schools,
- State or federal government units, and
- Nonprofits organized solely for charitable, religious, educational, scientific, or literary purposes or for the prevention of cruelty to children or animals.

Certain organizations that foster national or international amateur sports competition also qualify (examples include the Olympics, Special Olympics, and the Paralympic Games).

> **Example:** Pandora likes to volunteer and donate to her local animal shelter. In 2016, her AGI for the year was $30,000. She has money saved in her bank account, and she makes a large donation of $18,000 to the shelter. Her maximum charitable deduction for the year would be $15,000 (50% of her $30,000 AGI). Her disallowed contribution, $3,000 ($15,000 allowable deduction -$18,000 donation), would be carried over to the following year and can be used on a future return.

A taxpayer's deductible contributions to certain other types of nonprofit organizations are limited to either 30% or 20% of his AGI.

The **30% limit** applies to organizations that include the following:

- Veterans organizations
- Fraternal societies (such as the Knights of Columbus or Elks)
- Nonprofit cemeteries

In addition, a **separate 30% limit** applies in the following cases:

- Gifts for use by the charitable organization (such as the donation of a refrigerator the organization uses for itself)
- Gifts of appreciated property (also called capital gain property)

The **20% limit** applies to contributions of capital gain property to organizations subject to the 30% limit.

> **Example:** Howard's adjusted gross income is $50,000. During the year, he gave appreciated stocks with an FMV of $15,000 to his church, which is a 50% limit organization. Howard also gave $10,000 cash to a veteran's organization. The $10,000 gift is subject to the 30% limit based on the nature of the organization. The $15,000 gift of appreciated property is subject to the separate 30% limit. However, both gifts are fully deductible by Howard, because neither is more than the 30% limit that applies ($15,000 in each case), and together they are not more than the 50% limit of Howard's AGI ($50,000 × 50% = $25,000).

Charitable Contribution Carryovers: To the extent a taxpayer's deductions for contributions are limited, they may be carried over to subsequent years. However, the carryover period is generally limited to five years. Any carryover amounts that cannot be deducted within five years due to the AGI limits are lost.

Any contributions made by the taxpayer and carried over to future years retain their original character. For example, contributions made to a 30% organization continue to be subject to the 30%-of-AGI limit.

Special Rules for Conservation Easements

Many taxpayers choose to donate real estate to their favorite charities. Special rules apply to conservation easements. Conservation easements are gifts of real property (real estate) that are specifically for conservation purposes.

There are very unique rules that apply to charitable gifts of this type. Unlike other capital gain property, if the real property has appreciated in value, the charitable deduction is not limited to 30% of adjusted gross income.

In 2016, the charitable deduction allowed for conservation property is 50% of adjusted gross income, regardless of whether or not the property has appreciated. There is also a separate, higher allowance that applies specifically to farmers and ranchers.[43]

The carryforward period for a donor to take tax deductions for a conservation agreement is fifteen years, rather than the usual five years for other types of charitable gifts.

> **Example:** In 2016, Gerald decides to make a donation of property to The Nature Conservancy. Gerald donates 500 acres of land with the intent to preserve the area for fishing and wildlife. Gerald purchased the land twenty years ago for $1,000,000. The land has appreciated in value. Gerald obtains a qualified appraisal of the property, stating that the land has a current fair market value of $1,400,000. In 2016, Gerald's AGI is $400,000. Because of the special threshold that applies to conservation easements, Gerald will be able to take a charitable deduction of up to 50% of his $400,000 AGI. Therefore, his $1,400,000 gift permits a deduction of $200,000 ($400,000 AGI X 50% =$200,000) in 2016 and charitable carryforward of $1,200,000 that he can use in future years to offset his taxable income. If Gerald had been a qualified farmer or rancher, he would have been able to deduct up to 100% of his AGI for the year, for a full $400,000 deduction on Schedule A.

---

[43] The PATH Act created numerous incentives for charitable contributions of capital gain real property that is set aside for conservation purposes.

Unit 12: Study Questions

(Please test yourself first, and then check the correct answers at the end of this quiz.)

1. Vera and Jack are married and file jointly. They contributed $15,000 of cash to their synagogue during 2016. They also donated $3,000 to a private foundation that is a nonprofit cemetery organization to which a 30% contribution limit applies. Their adjusted gross income for 2016 was $30,000. Vera and Jack's deductible contributions for 2016 and carryover to the next year are:

A. An allowable charitable deduction of $18,000, with zero carryover to next year.
B. An allowable charitable deduction of $15,000, with a $2,100 carryover to next year.
C. An allowable charitable deduction of $7,500, with a $2,100 carryover to next year.
D. An allowable charitable deduction of $15,000, with a $3,000 carryover to next year.

2. Angie and Sheldon, both age 41, file a joint return and claim their two children as dependents. They have adjusted gross income of $68,400. In 2016, the family accumulated $6,620 of unreimbursed medical and dental expenses that included the following:

Prescription medications filled in the U.S.	$2,300
Prescription medications ordered and shipped from another country	320
Prescription contact lenses for Angie	400
Teeth whitening procedure by Angie's dentist and custom bleach trays	600
Smoking cessation program for Sheldon	3,000

What amount can they deduct for their medical expenses?

A. $6,020
B. $5,700
C. $3,020
D. $0

3. Which of the following taxes can taxpayers deduct on Schedule A?

A. Federal income tax.
B. Real estate tax.
C. Taxes on alcohol and tobacco.
D. Foreign sales taxes.

4. Christopher and Ariel file a joint return. During the year, they paid:

Home mortgage interest	$5,000
Credit card interest	600
Auto loan interest	4,000
Loan interest on an empty lot that was purchased to build a second home	3,000

What amount can they report as deductible mortgage interest?

A. $0
B. $5,000
C. $8,000
D. $8,600

5. Which of the following taxpayers must either itemize deductions or claim zero as their deduction?

A. Mindy, who files a joint return with her husband.
B. Leslie, who is single, claims two dependents, and files Form 1040.
C. Pearl, whose itemized deductions are more than the standard deduction.
D. Gabe, whose wife files a separate return and itemizes her deductions.

6. Amelia donates $430 in cash to her church. Which of the following is required on the receipt to substantiate the donation correctly for IRS recordkeeping requirements?

A. The reason for the contribution.
B. Amelia's home address.
C. The amount of the donation.
D. Amelia's method of payment.

7. Which of the following home improvements cannot be deducted as an itemized medical expense?

A. The cost of installing porch lifts and other forms of lifts.
B. The cost of lowering cabinets to accommodate a disability.
C. The cost of making doorways wider to accommodate a wheelchair.
D. An elevator that costs $4,000 and adds $5,000 to the FMV of the home.

8. Which of the following contains none of the deductions subject the reduction of total itemized deductions for certain higher income taxpayers (the Pease Limitation)?

A. Gambling losses, investment interest expense, and medical expenses.
B. Charitable contributions, employee business expenses, and medical expenses.
C. Charitable contributions, theft losses, and the mortgage interest deduction.
D. Miscellaneous itemized deductions, casualty losses, and real estate taxes.

9. Which of the following taxes can taxpayers deduct on Schedule A?

A. Local sales taxes.
B. Fines for speeding.
C. Social Security taxes.
D. Homeowner's association fees.

10. Justin, age 37, had the following medical expenses in 2016:

- Contributions to health savings account (HSA): $6,000
- Treatment of a broken leg: $9,000 (of which $8,000 was reimbursed by his insurance)
- Doctor-prescribed back brace: $1,900
- Child care while in the hospital: $200

What is his medical expense deduction before limitation based on the 10%-of-AGI threshold?

A. $1,900
B. $2,900
C. $7,900
D. $8,900

11. Which of the following taxpayers is required to itemize deductions and cannot take the standard deduction?

A. Sophie, who has one dependent child.
B. Andrea, who wants to deduct the alimony she paid to her ex-husband.
C. Gabrielle, whose itemized deductions are more than the standard deduction.
D. Samir, who is a nonresident alien.

12. For a tax to be deductible, all of the following must be correct except:

A. The tax must be imposed during the tax year.
B. The taxpayer must be legally liable for the tax.
C. The tax must be paid during the tax year.
D. The tax must be paid by the taxpayer.

13. All of the following factors determine the amount of a taxpayer's standard deduction except:

A. The taxpayer's filing status.
B. The taxpayer's adjusted gross income.
C. Whether the taxpayer is 65 or older, or blind.
D. Whether the taxpayer can be claimed as a dependent.

14. Iris is single and has the following income and expenses:

Wages	$70,000
Net investment interest income	3,000
Mortgage interest	24,000
Investment interest expense	5,000
Personal credit card interest	3,400
Car loan interest	1,200
Late fees on her mortgage	50

What is Iris's total allowable deduction for interest expense on her Schedule A?

A. $24,000
B. $27,000
C. $27,050
D. $32,400

15. Thomas donates to his church multiple times during the year. Which one of the donations listed below will require a qualified appraisal before the contribution can be deducted on his return?

A. A cash donation of $1,000.
B. A donation of antique furniture valued at $5,500.
C. A donation of appreciated stock with a fair market value of $12,500.
D. A donation of a motorcycle valued at $450.

16. Herschel and Angeline will file separate tax returns in 2016. Herschel plans to itemize his medical expenses, therefore, _____.

A. They will have to file jointly.
B. Angeline must take the standard deduction.
C. Angeline must either itemize her deductions or claim a zero standard deduction.
D. Angeline may choose to itemize or take the standard deduction.

17. Kiara donates her used car to a qualified charity. She bought it three years ago for $15,000. A used car guide shows the FMV for this type of car is $5,000. Kiara's friend, Buck, offered her $4,500 for the car a week ago. Kiara receives Form 1098-C from the organization showing the car was sold for $1,900. How much is Kiara's charitable deduction?

A. $15,000
B. $5,000
C. $4,500
D. $1,900

18. Harold, age 65, and his wife Marie, age 59, incurred the following medical expenses:

Physician and hospital fees	$10,000
Dental and orthodontic fees	5,000
Medical and dental insurance premiums	12,000
Prescription eyeglasses and contact lenses	1,000
Health club dues	1,000
Prescription medications	3,000
Nonprescription medicines	1,000
Pre-cancerous mole removal at doctor's office	805

The insurance premiums were paid through Harold's employer-sponsored health insurance plan and were not reported as income in box 1 of his Form W-2. Harold and Marie had adjusted gross income of $100,000 in 2016. What is the amount of their medical expense deduction?

A. $9,805
B. $12,305
C. $19,805
D. $33,805

19. Oscar donated a leather coat to a thrift store operated by his church. He paid $450 for the coat three years ago. Similar coats in the thrift store sell for $50. What is Oscar's charitable deduction?

A. $0
B. $50
C. $400
D. $450

20. Which of the following taxes is not deductible on Schedule A?

A. Property taxes paid on a vacation home.
B. Special assessments to improve the sidewalks.
C. Property taxes based on a vehicle's value.
D. Property taxes paid on a home in Mexico.

21. Don owns three homes and has an AGI of $128,000 in 2016. His primary residence is in Chicago. He also owns a mountain cabin in Lake Tahoe and a small condo in Las Vegas, which he uses several times a year. In 2016, Don did not use the cabin, and it sat empty all year. He pays property tax and mortgage interest on all three properties.

Home Location	Mortgage Interest	Property Tax
Main Home in Chicago	$18,500	$7,500
Cabin in Tahoe	$5,200	$2,800
Condo in Las Vegas	$4,500	$1,950

Based on the information above, which of the following statements is correct?

A. Only the mortgage interest and property tax on his main home in Chicago are deductible. Don has a mortgage interest deduction of $18,500 and a property tax deduction of $7,500.

B. The mortgage interest and property tax on both his main home and the cabin are deductible. The mortgage interest and the property tax on the third property, the condo in Las Vegas, are not deductible. Therefore, Don has a mortgage interest deduction of $23,700 and a property tax deduction of $10,300.

C. The mortgage interest and property tax on all three homes are deductible. Therefore, Don has a mortgage interest deduction of $28,200 and a property tax deduction of $12,250.

D. Only the mortgage interest on the first two properties is deductible. The property tax on all three homes is deductible. Therefore, Don has a mortgage interest deduction of $23,700 and a property tax deduction of $12,250.

22. In 2016, Martin donates $3,900 of cash and contributes a painting with a fair market value of $16,000 to his church. Martin has a basis of $5,000 in the painting. He also donates $4,000 of cash to his local chamber of commerce. His AGI for the year is $45,000. What is the maximum amount he can deduct for charitable contributions for the year?

A. $9,000
B. $17,400
C. $22,500
D. $25,000

23. Carroll, age 66, and his wife, Ellen, age 59, file jointly. Which of the following statements is correct regarding their qualified medical expenses, if they itemize deductions?

A. They can deduct 7.5% of their qualified medical expenses if they itemize their deductions.
B. They can deduct 10% of their qualified medical expenses if they itemize deductions.
C. They can deduct only the amount by which their total medical expenses for the year exceed 7.5% of adjusted gross income.
D. They can deduct only the amount by which their total medical expenses for the year exceed 10% of adjusted gross income.

24. Xavier, age 29, paid medical expenses of $6,200 during the year. His AGI is $46,000 in 2016. Taking into account the AGI limit, how much can Xavier deduct on his Schedule A?

A. $0
B. $620
C. $1,600
D. $6,200

25. Julio spent the entire day attending his human rights organization's regional meeting as a delegate. He spent $250 on a plane ticket to the meeting and $25 on materials for the meeting. In the evening, Julio went to the theater with two other meeting attendees. He spent $50 on movie tickets. The charity did not reimburse Julio for any of his costs. How much can he deduct as a charitable expense?

A. $0
B. $250
C. $275
D. $125

26. Bowen donated to all of the following nonprofit organizations in 2016. What is his allowable deduction for charitable gifts on Schedule A?

Organization	Amount
Methodist Church	$100
County animal shelter	120
Salvation Army	75
American Red Cross	25
Democratic party	50
Chamber of Commerce	300
Total contributions	**$670**

A. $320
B. $370
C. $220
D. $670

Unit 12: Answers

1. The answer is D. Vera and Jack cannot deduct more than $15,000, which is 50% of their income of $30,000. The remaining amount must be carried forward to a future tax year. The carryforward period is five years for most charitable deductions.

2. The answer is D. Angie and Sheldon cannot deduct any of their medical expenses. Only the portion of total medical expenses that exceeds 10% of the taxpayer's AGI is deductible. The total of Angie and Sheldon's medical expenses, $6,620, is less than $6,840 ($68,400 × 10%). Further, of the items listed, only the smoking cessation program, the contact lenses, and the prescription medications filled in the United States are qualified medical expenses. Prescription medications shipped from other countries are ineligible. The teeth whitening procedure would be considered a cosmetic enhancement and would not be a qualified medical expense, whether performed by a dentist or not.

3. The answer is B. Only the real estate taxes are deductible. Taxpayers can deduct real estate tax on Schedule A as an itemized deduction.

4. The answer is B. Only their home mortgage interest ($5,000) is deductible as interest on Schedule A. The other types of interest are all personal interest, which is not deductible. Interest paid on a plot of land is not deductible as mortgage interest, even if the taxpayer later decides to build a home on the property. Only the interest secured by an actual home (not land) is deductible as mortgage interest.

5. The answer is D. A married taxpayer who files separately and whose spouse itemizes deductions must either itemize his deductions or claim zero as his deduction. He is not permitted to utilize the standard deduction.

6. The answer is C. A taxpayer can claim a deduction for a contribution of $250 or more only if she has a receipt or acknowledgment from a qualified organization. The receipt must include:
- The amount of cash contributed
- Whether the qualified organization gave the taxpayer any goods or services in return
- If applicable, a description and good faith estimate of the value of any goods or services provided in return by the organization

A receipt must also show the date of the donation and the name of the organization that was paid.

7. The answer is D. The deduction for capital improvements is limited to the excess of the actual cost of the improvements over the increase in the fair market value of the home. Since the increase in fair market value of the home exceeds the cost of the improvements, none of the cost can be deducted as a medical expense.

8. The answer is A. The limitation on itemized deductions does not apply to deductions for medical expenses, investment interest expense, casualty or theft losses, and allowable gambling losses. The following itemized deductions are limited for higher-income taxpayers:
- Charitable contributions,
- Mortgage interest,
- State, local, and property taxes, and
- Miscellaneous itemized deductions (answer continued).

It reduces the total amount of otherwise allowable itemized deductions by 3% of the amount by which the taxpayer's AGI exceeds specific thresholds. The limitation cannot be more than 80% of the otherwise allowable itemized deductions.

9. The answer is A. A taxpayer has the option of claiming state and local sales taxes as an itemized deduction on Schedule A instead of claiming state and local income taxes. A taxpayer cannot claim both. The other expenses listed are not deductible on Schedule A.

10. The answer is B. His medical expense deduction before limitation is $2,900 ($1,900 + $1,000). The child care cost is not deductible, even though it was incurred while Justin was obtaining medical care. The amount reimbursed by insurance is not deductible. Contributions to an HSA may be claimed as an adjustment to gross income, but not as a medical expense deduction. Payments for medical expenses out of an HSA are not deductible.

11. The answer is D. A nonresident or dual-status alien (who is not married to a U.S. citizen or resident) must itemize deductions. He cannot use the standard deduction. The other taxpayers listed are not required to itemize their deductions, but may elect to do so if they wish.

12. The answer is A. Taxpayers can deduct tax imposed during a prior year, as long as the taxes were paid during the current tax year.

14. The answer is B. The standard deduction amount is based on the taxpayer's filing and dependent status, and whether the taxpayer is blind or at least 65 years old. It is not based on a taxpayer's income.

13. The answer is C. The answer is calculated as follows: $24,000 + $3,000 + $50 = $27,050. The deduction for investment interest expense is limited to net investment income ($5,000 - $3,000). The excess amount of interest expense must be carried over to the next tax year and may be used to offset net investment income in future tax years. Late fees paid on a qualifying mortgage are deductible as interest. The credit card interest and car loan interest are not deductible.

15. The answer is B. The IRS requires a taxpayer to obtain a written appraisal by a qualified appraiser for any noncash contribution of more than $5,000. The antique furniture would require a qualified written appraisal before the taxpayer could deduct the donation on his tax return. The taxpayer must complete Form 8283 and attach it to his tax return. Thomas must retain a copy of the appraisal for his own records, but in most cases, does not have to attach the appraisal with his tax return. Answer A is incorrect because a cash donation does not require an appraisal. Answer C is incorrect because the donation of stock or other securities does not require an appraisal. A donation of a vehicle valued at less than $500 does not require an appraisal or any other type of documentation beyond a written acknowledgment from the organization.

16. The answer is C. Since they are both filing MFS, Angeline is forced to either itemize her deductions or claim a zero standard deduction. A taxpayer whose spouse itemizes deductions must either itemize deductions or claim zero as the standard deduction. This only applies in situations when both taxpayers are filing MFS. If one spouse qualifies for Head of Household filing status, then neither spouse would be forced to itemize.

17. The answer is D. Kiara can deduct $1,900 for her donation. She is allowed to take the lesser of the car's FMV or the amount for which the charity was able to sell the car. Since the charity sold the car for only $1,900, that is the amount of the donation, regardless of any other estimates of its value.

18. The answer is B. The insurance premiums are not deductible because they were paid through an employer health insurance plan and were not reported in box 1 of Form W-2. Neither club dues nor nonprescription medicines (except insulin) are deductible. The deductible costs listed total $19,100. Deductibility of the resulting total of $19,820 is limited to the amount in excess of 7.5% of adjusted gross income (because Harold is 65 or over), which is $7,500, so their medical expense deduction calculated on Schedule A would be $12,305.

Calculation for Deductible Medical Expenses	
Physician and hospital fees	$10,000
Dental and orthodontic fees	5,000
Eyeglasses and contact lenses	1,000
Prescription medications	3,000
Pre-cancerous mole removal at doctor's office	805
Total deductible expenses	**$19,805**
Adjusted gross income $100,000	
7.5% deduction limit ($7,500)	
Applying the limitation ($19,805 - $7,500) =$12,305	
Allowable Medical expense deduction on Schedule A $12,305	

19. The answer is B. Oscar's donation is limited to $50. Generally, the FMV of used clothing and household goods is far less than original cost. For used clothing, a taxpayer should claim as the value the price that a buyer typically would pay in a thrift shop or at a garage sale.

20. The answer is B. The assessment to improve sidewalks is not deductible. Many local governments impose taxes that finance improvements to property, such as assessments for streets, sidewalks, and sewer lines. These taxes cannot be deducted, but rather must be added to the basis of the taxpayer's property.

21. The answer is D. The mortgage interest and property tax on both, his main home in Chicago and the cabin, are deductible. The property tax on all the homes is deductible. The mortgage interest on a second home is deductible, even if the taxpayer did not use the home during the year. A taxpayer may deduct mortgage interest on up to two homes. There is no limitation on the deduction for property tax, so a taxpayer may deduct property tax on more than two homes. The answer is calculated as follows:

Home Location	Mortgage Interest	Property Tax
Main Home in Chicago	$18,500	$7,500
Cabin in Tahoe	5,200	2,800
Condo in Las Vegas	Not Deductible	1,950
Totals	**$23,700**	**$12,250**

22. The answer is B. The contribution to the Chamber of Commerce is not deductible. The cash contribution to his church is fully deductible. However, charitable gifts of appreciated property, such as Martin's painting, are subject to a maximum deduction of 30% of the taxpayer's adjusted gross income. Martin calculates his charitable contribution as follows:

(AGI of $45,000 × 30%) =	$13,500
Cash contribution to the church	3,900
Total allowable deduction in 2016	**$17,400**
Carryover = $2,500 ($16,000 FMV- $13,500 30% AGI Limitation)	

Martin must carry over $2,500 to the following year. There is a five-year carryover period for any excess charitable contribution deductions.

23. The answer is C. Since one spouse (Carroll) is over 65, and they file jointly, both taxpayers may deduct the medical expenses that exceed 7.5% of their AGI. A different threshold applies to taxpayers who are under 65. A taxpayer who is under the age of 65 can only deduct medical expenses for the year that exceed 10% of their adjusted gross income.

24. The answer is C. Xavier can deduct only $1,600 of his medical expenses because that is the amount that exceeds 10% of his AGI ($46,000 AGI × 10% = $4,600), the applicable threshold. So his allowable medical expenses are figured as follows:

Total medical expenses for the year	$6,200
AGI of $46,000 × 10% limitation	(4,600)
Total allowable medical deduction in 2016	**$1,600**

25. The answer is C. Julio's charitable contribution is $275 ($250 plane ticket + $25 materials= $275). He can claim his travel and meeting expenses as charitable contributions because they are directly related to his charitable activities. However, he cannot claim the cost of the evening at the theater, as that is a personal entertainment expense.

26. The answer is A. The contributions to the political organization and the Chamber of Commerce are not deductible on Schedule A. Bowen's allowable deduction is calculated as follows: $100 + $120 + $75 + $25 = $320.

Unit 13: Other Itemized Deductions

> **For additional information read:**
> Publication 587, *Business Use of Your Home*
> Publication 547, *Casualties, Disasters, and Thefts*
> Publication 529, *Miscellaneous Deductions*

There are a number of less common itemized deductions that are lumped together as "miscellaneous itemized deductions". Although these deductions are less frequently used than the more common deductions on Schedule A, you can still expect to see questions about them on Part 1 of the EA Exam. In addition to the deductions described in the previous unit, taxpayers may claim the following:

- Personal casualty and/or theft losses
- Miscellaneous expenses subject to the 2%-of-AGI limit
- Miscellaneous expenses **not** subject to the 2%-of-AGI limit

Casualty and Theft Losses

In this unit, we will cover personal casualty and theft losses.[44] A "casualty loss" is the damage, destruction, or loss of property resulting from an identifiable event that is sudden, unexpected, or unusual.

Casualty losses can include the damage caused by natural disasters, as well as financial losses from theft and other crimes. Other examples include a car accident, house fire, earthquake, flood, theft, act of vandalism, or act of terrorism. Losses that do not meet this definition and are thus not deductible include:

- Damage done by pets
- Progressive deterioration, such as the following:
  - Termite or moth damage[45]
  - Damage or destruction of trees and plants by a fungus, disease, or pests
  - Loss of property caused by drought
  - Damage to a water heater that bursts
  - Steady weakening of a building due to wind and weather conditions
- A car accident if the taxpayer's willful act or negligence caused it
- Arson if committed by or on behalf of the taxpayer
- Accidental breakage of china, dishes, or other items during regular use
- Losses in real estate value from market fluctuations

---

[44] Casualty losses are treated differently depending on whether the loss occurred to business property, investment property, or personal-use property. In this unit, we cover primarily casualty losses from personal-use property and investment property. Casualty losses from business and investment property will be covered in Book 2, *Businesses*.

[45] Note: there are several court cases where the taxpayer has been allowed (in certain situations) to deduct termite damage as a qualifying casualty event, but the IRS continues to hold their position that termite damage and other insect damage is not an allowable casualty loss. For the EA exam, you must answer questions based on the IRS' current position on a tax issue, regardless of any pending or past litigation that may have occurred.

- Losses in the value of an IRA account
- Lost property, unless it is the result of a sudden, unexpected, and unusual event

Example: A car door accidentally slams on Julia's hand, breaking the setting of her diamond ring. The diamond falls from the ring and is never found. The loss is deductible as a casualty because it is the result of an identifiable event that is sudden, unexpected, or unusual.[46]

In order to deduct a casualty or theft loss, the taxpayer must be able to prove:
- The type of casualty loss (car accident, fire, storm, etc.) and the date of occurrence
- That the taxpayer was the legal owner of the property, or legally liable for the damage (such as leased property when the lessee is responsible for damage)
- Whether the loss was subject to any insurance reimbursement

Example: Gregory rents a car from Reliable Rentals. He declines the optional insurance coverage and signs a contract stating he will be responsible for any damage. The rental car is stolen, and Gregory must reimburse Reliable Rentals for the cost of the car. His car insurance does not have rental car coverage, so he is liable for the full amount. Gregory can deduct the loss as a casualty loss, subject to the applicable rules.

Casualty losses are deductible only for actual damage to a property. Payments for the cost of cleaning up or making repairs are not part of a casualty loss itself, but generally may be used as a measure in determining a decrease in the FMV of a property. When calculating a decrease in the FMV of a property, a taxpayer may not consider the following:
- The replacement cost of stolen or destroyed property
- An item's sentimental value
- Related expenses such as the cost of temporary housing or a rental car
- A decline in market value of property near a casualty area

Example: Don purchased an antique vase at a garage sale for $600. Later, he discovered the vase was a rare collectible and its FMV was $20,000. He told a bunch of his friends, and then the vase was stolen from his home two months later. His casualty loss is limited to the $600 he paid for it, which is his basis in the vase. Don cannot claim a casualty loss deduction for $20,000, the actual value of the item.

Example: Nicole purchased a condo for $200,000. Two months later, a hurricane destroyed five properties on her block. Although her property was undamaged by the hurricane, a later appraisal showed that properties within a five-mile radius had declined 15% in fair market value because people were afraid to purchase homes in "hurricane territory." The reduction in her home's FMV is not a deductible casualty loss.

Casualty losses are subject to the "single event rule." This means that events closely related in origin are considered a single event. For example, it is a single casualty when the damage comes from two or more closely related causes, such as wind and flood damage from the same storm. A single

---

[46] This example is taken from IRS Publication 547, *Casualties, Disasters, and Thefts.*

casualty may also damage two or more pieces of property, such as a hailstorm that damages both a taxpayer's home and his car parked in the driveway.

Reporting a Casualty Loss or Gain

A taxpayer must complete Form 4684, *Casualties and Thefts*, to report a gain or loss resulting from a casualty or theft. The net deductible amount can be claimed by an individual taxpayer only if he itemizes deductions. A loss on personal use (nonbusiness) property is subject to certain limits (described next). It is calculated on Form 4684 and reported on Schedule A.

If an insurance reimbursement for a casualty loss exceeds the taxpayer's basis in the property, he will have a gain that may need to be reported. However, reporting the gain on damaged, destroyed, or stolen property can be postponed if the insurance reimbursement is spent to restore the property or to purchase similar property within a specified period of time.

> **Example:** Forty years ago, Albert bought a vacation cottage for $18,000. A storm destroyed the cottage, now valued at $250,000. Albert received $146,000 from his insurance company. He had a gain of $128,000 ($146,000 – $18,000 basis). Albert spent the full amount of $146,000 to rebuild his cottage. Since he used the insurance proceeds to rebuild his cottage, he can postpone reporting or recognizing the gain until the cottage is sold.

The replacement period begins on the date the property was damaged, destroyed, or stolen, and ends two years after the close of the first tax year in which any part of the gain is realized.

For a main home or its contents located in a federally-declared disaster area, the replacement period is generally four years rather than two. For disaster area losses, taxpayers may choose to deduct the loss on the previous year's tax return, rather than in the year the disaster loss occurred. This may result in a lower tax for that year, often producing or increasing a cash refund.

Nonbusiness Casualty Loss Limits

A taxpayer can deduct casualty and theft losses related to personal-use property only to the extent they exceed two separate limits:

$100 Rule: First, each separate casualty or theft loss is deductible only to the extent that it exceeds $100. It does not matter how many pieces of property are damaged, destroyed, or stolen in a single event; the taxpayer has to reduce his total loss for each event by $100.

> **Example:** During the winter, a hurricane came through Colleen's town. The hurricane caused extensive damage to her car and her house. This event would be considered a single casualty, even though multiple pieces of property were damaged. Colleen must calculate all her losses from this event, and reduce the loss by $100.

> **Example:** Nahor has a $750 deductible on his car's collision insurance. Nahor gets into an auto accident and his car is damaged. His insurance company pays to repair all the damage minus the $750 deductible. Since the deductible is his only out-of-pocket expense, Nahor's casualty loss is based solely on his deductible. His casualty loss is $650 ($750 – $100) because the first $100 of a casualty loss on personal-use property isn't deductible.

Example: A fire damaged Rick's house in January, causing $3,000 in damage. In September, a storm damaged his house again, causing $5,000 in damage. These two disasters are considered separate events. Therefore, Rick must reduce each separate casualty loss by $100.

The 10% Rule

Second, a taxpayer can deduct the total of all casualty or theft losses during the year (after the reduction of each one by $100) only to the extent the total is more than 10% of his AGI. This rule does not apply to a net disaster loss within a federally-declared disaster area.

However, married couples filing jointly who have a loss from the same event are treated as if they were one person; the $100 limit is applied only once to each shared loss event and the 10% limit is applied to their joint AGI to determine deductibility of their aggregate losses. For losses on personal-use property, this is how the taxpayer determines his deduction:

1. Calculate the *lesser* of the FMV or adjusted basis of the item prior to the loss.
2. Subtract reimbursements from insurance (if any).
3. Subtract $100 for each event.
4. Subtract 10% of the taxpayer's AGI.

Example: Inga's house was burglarized on July 1, 2016. Her total theft losses were $20,000. Her homeowner's insurance reimbursed $18,000 of her loss. Therefore, Inga's remaining casualty loss after the insurance reimbursement was $2,000 ($20,000 loss - $18,000 insurance reimbursement). Inga's AGI for 2016 is $29,500. In order to figure her deductible loss, she must first apply the $100 rule and then the 10% of AGI rule. Inga's theft loss deduction is figured as follows:

Casualty Loss Calculation	
Loss after insurance	$2,000
Subtract $100	($100)
Loss after "$100 rule"	$1,900
Subtract 10% x $29,500 AGI	($2,950)
Allowable theft loss deduction	**$0**

Inga does not have a deductible theft loss deduction because her loss after applying the $100 rule ($1,900) is less than 10% of her AGI ($2,950). The loss is disallowed due to the 10% of AGI rule that applies to nonbusiness casualty losses.

Example: Raquel bought a new leather sofa four years ago for $3,000. In April, a fire destroyed the sofa. Raquel estimates that it would now cost $5,000 to replace it. However, if she had sold the sofa before the fire, she probably would have received only $1,900 because the sofa was already four years old. Raquel's casualty loss is $1,900 (the FMV of the sofa immediately before the fire), subject to the $100 and 10% rules. Her loss is not $3,000 (her basis), and it is not $5,000 (the replacement cost). Raquel's AGI for 2016 was $15,000. Her deductible loss is calculated as follows: $1,900 loss minus $100 = $1,800. 10% of her AGI is $1,500. Her deductible casualty loss is, therefore, $300, the amount by which $1,800 exceeds $1,500.

Insurance Reimbursements

Taxpayers can deduct qualified casualty and theft losses to their homes, household items, and vehicles. However, if the property is covered by insurance, a taxpayer cannot deduct a loss unless he files a claim for reimbursement. If the taxpayer decides not to file an insurance claim but has a deductible, he can claim the amount of the insurance deductible as his loss, since that amount would not have been covered by the policy anyway.

> **Example:** A small fire causes $8,000 in damage to Maria's home. She does not want her homeowner's insurance premium to go up, so she declines to file a claim and pays to repair the fire damage out-of-pocket. Maria cannot deduct the full amount of the loss because she did not file an insurance claim. However, she can deduct the amount of her insurance deductible, subject to the $100 and 10%-of-AGI limitations. This is because she would have had to pay the deductible whether she filed a claim or not.

A taxpayer does not have to reduce his casualty loss by insurance payments received to cover living expenses in the following situations:

- When a taxpayer loses use of his main home because of a casualty.
- When government authorities do not allow a taxpayer access to his main home because of a casualty or a threat of one.

If the insurance payments are more than the temporary increase in his living expenses, a taxpayer must generally include the excess in his income. However, if the casualty occurs in a federally-declared disaster area, the excess insurance payments are not taxable.

The taxable part of the insurance payment should be included in income for the year the taxpayer gains use of his main home, or in a later year when the taxable part of the insurance payment is received.

> **Example:** A tornado damages Olivia's main home in January 2016. After repairs were made, she moved back into her home in September 2016. She received insurance payments that were $1,500 more than the temporary increase in her living expenses. Olivia includes this amount in income on her 2016 Form 1040. In January 2017, she receives a final insurance payment of $500 to cover any remaining living expenses that she incurred in the previous year. She must include the final insurance payment on her 2017 tax return.

Theft Losses

A theft loss may be deducted in the year the theft is discovered, regardless of when it actually occurred. The taking of property must be illegal under the law of the state where it occurred, and it must have been done with criminal intent. Qualifying theft losses include those resulting from blackmail, burglary, embezzlement, extortion, kidnapping for ransom, larceny, robbery, and mail fraud. A taxpayer is not required to show that someone was convicted of theft.

If a taxpayer takes a deduction for stolen property and authorities later recover the property, he must report the recovery as income in the year the property is recovered, but only to the extent of the amount that actually reduced his tax in an earlier year.

Insurance Cost: The cost of insurance or other protection is not deductible as a casualty loss, but it is deductible as a business expense by business taxpayers.

> **Example:** Jordan pays for renter's insurance to cover the furniture and appliances in his main home from theft or other disaster losses. Jordan cannot deduct the cost of the renter's insurance as a casualty loss.

> **Example:** Danny is a self-employed mechanic and owns a small auto shop. He pays for business property insurance to protect his equipment from casualty and theft. Since the insurance covers his business property, the cost of the insurance is deductible as an expense on his Schedule C.

Miscellaneous Expenses Subject to the 2% Limit

Certain miscellaneous expenses, including unreimbursed employee expenses, are deductible on Schedule A to the extent they exceed 2% of a taxpayer's AGI. The taxpayer must figure their allowable deduction by subtracting 2% of their adjusted gross income from the total amount of these expenses.

Unreimbursed Employee Business Expenses

An employee can deduct certain work-related expenses as itemized deductions. These expenses are first reported on Form 2106, *Employee Business Expenses*, and the amount is transferred to Schedule A. The taxpayer can deduct only unreimbursed employee expenses that are:

- Paid or incurred during the tax year,
- For carrying on the business of being an employee, and
- "Ordinary and necessary."

An expense does not have to be required to be deductible. However, it must be a common expense that would be accepted in the taxpayer's trade or profession. The following are examples of unreimbursed employee expenses that may be deductible:

- Business bad debts of an employee
- Business liability insurance premiums
- Malpractice insurance
- Depreciation on an asset the employer requires for work
- Dues to professional societies or to a chamber of commerce
- Subscriptions to professional journals
- Expenses of looking for a new job in the taxpayer's present occupation
- Licenses and regulatory fees
- Union dues
- Work clothes and uniforms (if required and not suitable for everyday use)
- Tools and supplies used for work
- Passport for a business trip
- Work-related education
- Travel, transportation, meals, and lodging related to the taxpayer's work

Unreimbursed Meal and Entertainment Expenses

An employee can deduct unreimbursed business-related meals and entertainment expenses he incurred for entertaining a client, customer, or another employee. The deduction for business meals and entertainment is generally limited to 50% of the unreimbursed cost. The taxpayer must apply the 50% limit before including the expenses on Schedule A (and applying the 2%-of-AGI limit). The taxpayer can deduct meals and entertainment expenses only if they meet the following tests:

- The main purpose of the meal or entertainment was the active conduct of business,
- The taxpayer conducted business during the entertainment period, and
- The taxpayer had more than a general expectation of some other specific business benefit at a future time.

Employee Travel Expenses: A taxpayer cannot deduct commuting expenses, which are expenses incurred when an employee travels from his home to his main workplace. However, there are numerous instances where an employee can deduct mileage or other travel expenses relating to his employment. Deductible employee travel expenses may include those related to:

- Going from one work location to another in the course of business.
- Visiting clients or customers.
- Going to a business meeting away from the regular workplace.
- Traveling from a first job to a second job in the same day.
- Going from the taxpayer's home to a temporary workplace.

Any amounts reimbursed by an employer are not deductible by the employee.

> **Example:** Andy's AGI is $45,000. He works as a salesman for a radio station, selling advertising to local businesses. He frequently travels to the businesses in order to talk to the owners in person and encourage them to purchase more radio advertising. Andy's employer (the radio station) does not reimburse Andy for his mileage. In 2016, Andy has $1,100 in miscellaneous deductible work-related expenses. In order to figure his deductible expenses, he must first determine the 2%-of-AGI limit (2% × $45,000 = $900). He can therefore deduct only $200 of those expenses ($1,100 - $900 = $200).

Tax Home and Work Location

A taxpayer's tax home is his principal place of work, regardless of where he actually lives. A taxpayer's tax home is used to determine if travel expenses are deductible. Travel and meal expenses are considered deductible if the taxpayer is traveling away from his tax home, which is determined based on the following two factors:

- The travel is away from the general area or vicinity of the taxpayer's tax home.
- The trip is long enough or far enough away that a taxpayer cannot reasonably be expected to complete the roundtrip without sleep or rest.

Example: Seville is a truck driver who lives in Tucson, Arizona with his family. He is employed by a trucking firm that has its main terminal in Phoenix. At the end of his long trucking runs, Seville returns to the terminal in Phoenix and spends one night there before returning home. Seville cannot deduct any expenses he has for meals and lodging in Phoenix or the cost of traveling from Phoenix to Tucson. This is because Phoenix is Seville's tax home.

When a taxpayer is traveling away from his tax home, he can deduct ordinary and necessary expenses incurred while traveling on business, such as:

- The cost of getting to a business destination (air, rail, bus, car, ferry, etc.)
- Meals and lodging while away from home (the deduction for business meals is generally limited to 50% of the unreimbursed cost)
- Taxi fares
- Dry cleaning and laundry
- Use of a car while at the business location
- Computer rental fees
- Baggage charges, including shipping samples and display materials to the destination
- Tips on eligible expenses

Special Department of Transportation Rules: Certain taxpayers subject to the Department of Transportation's "hours of service" limits can deduct 80% of meal expenses while traveling away from their tax home. These workers include the following:

- Certain air transportation workers such as pilots, crew, and mechanics regulated by the Federal Aviation Administration
- Interstate truck operators and bus drivers regulated by the Department of Transportation
- Certain railroad employees such as engineers and conductors regulated by the Federal Railroad Administration
- Certain merchant mariners regulated by the Coast Guard

Temporary Work Assignments

There are special rules for temporary work assignments that are expected to last for one year or less. When a taxpayer is working away from his main place of business, and the job assignment is temporary, his tax home does not change. The taxpayer can deduct his travel expenses because the job assignment is of a temporary nature, and therefore, the travel is considered business-related.

However, travel expenses paid in connection with an indefinite work assignment are not deductible. Any work assignment longer than one year is considered indefinite. A taxpayer cannot deduct travel expenses at a work location if it is realistically expected that he will work there for more than one year.

Example: Terry is a construction worker who lives and works primarily in Los Angeles. Because of a shortage of jobs, he agrees to work at a construction site in Fresno for ten months. Since the job lasts less than one year, the Fresno job is considered temporary, and Terry's tax home is still in Los Angeles. Therefore, his travel expenses, including meals and lodging, are deductible while traveling between his temporary place of work and his tax home in Los Angeles.

Special Rule for Military Members

Members of the armed forces on a permanent duty assignment overseas are not considered to be traveling away from home. Therefore, they cannot deduct their travel expenses for meals and lodging while on permanent duty assignment.

Convention Travel

A taxpayer can deduct the cost of travel and attendance to conventions in the U.S. or the "North American area," including Canada and Mexico.[47] For conventions outside of the North American area, travel expenses are normally not deductible unless the convention is directly related to the business of the taxpayer (or the employer of the taxpayer) and it is as reasonable for the convention to be held outside of the "North American area" than inside the area.

For cruises, there is a $2,000 annual cap on deductions or $4,000 if both spouses went on qualifying cruise ship conventions and they file jointly. The IRS imposes strict substantiation requirements on taxpayers who claim this deduction. A deduction is not allowed for conventions focused exclusively on investments or financial planning.

Home Office Deduction

If a taxpayer uses a portion of his home regularly and exclusively for business purposes, he may be able to deduct a portion of the operating expenses and depreciation of the home. In order to qualify as a home office, the space must be used exclusively and regularly:

- As the taxpayer's principal place of business, or
- As a place to meet with patients or clients in the normal course of business, or
- In the case of a separate structure not attached to the home, in connection with the trade or business.

The regular and exclusive use must be for the convenience of the employer, and not just helpful to the employee's job. The home office deduction is calculated based on the percentage of the home that is used for business. A taxpayer can use any reasonable method to compute business percentage, but the most common methods are to:

- Divide the square footage of the home used for business by the total square footage of the home, or

---

[47] The IRS maintains a list of these countries, many of which are tourist destinations and not normally associated with the "North American area." Examples include Aruba, Jamaica, Costa Rica, Barbados, Bermuda, Panama, the Marshall Islands, and the Netherlands Antilles (Revenue Ruling 2016--16).

- Divide the number of rooms used for business by the total number of rooms in the home (if all rooms in the home are about the same size).

Taxpayers cannot deduct expenses for any portion of the year during which there was no business use of the home.

> **Example:** Lillian is a part-time medical transcriptionist with a qualified home office. The entire square footage of her home is 1,200 square feet. Her home office is 240 square feet, so her home office percentage is 20% (240 ÷ 1,200) of the total area of her home. Her business percentage is 20%.

Simplified Home Office Deduction

The IRS has recently developed a simplified option for taxpayers who claim the home office deduction. The criteria for who qualifies remain the same, but the calculation and recordkeeping requirements have been simplified. Highlights of this simplified deduction include:

- A deduction of $5 per square foot for the space in the home that is used for business, with a maximum allowable square footage of 300 square feet (for a maximum deduction of $1,500)
- No depreciation deduction or recapture of depreciation upon sale of the home
- Home-related itemized deductions, such as for mortgage interest and real estate taxes, may be claimed in full on Schedule A, without allocation of portions to the home office space

Each year, a taxpayer must choose whether to elect the simplified method or the regular method for calculating the home office deduction. If he chooses the regular method after having used the simplified method, depreciation is calculated using an optional depreciation table for the property.

Job Search Expenses

A taxpayer can deduct job search expenses if the expenses relate to the same occupation. Expenses can be deducted even if the taxpayer does not find a new job. If the job search qualifies, the taxpayer can deduct the costs of using an employment agency or career counselor, of traveling to interviews, and of printing and mailing resumes. The following expenses are not deductible:

- Job search expenses for a new occupation
- Living expenses incurred during a period of unemployment between the end of a job and the next period of employment
- Job search expenses incurred by a taxpayer looking for a job for the first time

Job-Related Education

The cost of courses designed to maintain or improve the skills needed for a taxpayer's present job (or required by his employer or the law) is deductible as an employee business expense. The education must meet at least one of the following tests:

- The education must maintain or improve skills required for the taxpayer's current line of work.
- The education must be required by law or by the taxpayer's employer as a condition of his employment.

If a taxpayer has a regular job and enrolls in work-related education courses on a temporary basis, he can also deduct the round-trip costs of transportation between his home and school. This is true regardless of the location of the school, the distance traveled, or whether the taxpayer attends school on non-work days.

In some cases, a taxpayer may be able to take an education credit for his education expenses and may choose between the credit and the miscellaneous itemized deduction, depending upon which produces a lower tax.

Note: A taxpayer cannot deduct the cost of travel that in itself constitutes a form of education. For example, an individual who works as a Chinese-English interpreter cannot deduct the costs of a personal vacation to China, simply because it might benefit his language skills.

Uniforms

The cost of uniforms and other special work clothes required by an employer can be deducted as a work-related expense. The uniforms must not be suitable for everyday use. The taxpayer can also deduct the cost of upkeep, including laundry and dry cleaning bills.

Examples of employees who can deduct the cost of their uniforms include delivery workers, firefighters, health care workers, law enforcement officers, letter carriers, professional athletes, and transportation workers.

Musicians and entertainers can deduct the cost of theatrical clothing and accessories that are not suitable for everyday wear. An employee can also deduct the cost of protective clothing, such as safety shoes or boots, safety glasses, hard hats, and work gloves.

Full-time active-duty military personnel cannot deduct the cost of their uniforms. However, they may be able to deduct the cost of insignia, shoulder boards, and related items.

Gifts to Clients

A taxpayer can deduct no more than $25 for business gifts he gives to a single client or customer during the tax year. A gift to a member of the customer's family is generally considered a gift to the customer himself. If both a taxpayer and his spouse give gifts, they are treated as one taxpayer, even if they have separate businesses. Incidental costs such as packaging and shipping expenses are generally not included in determining the cost of a gift for purposes of the $25 limit.

Example: Noelle tutors students to prepare them for their SAT exams. She gives eight students dictionaries in December to thank them for their business. Each gift is worth $29. Noelle can deduct $200 on her tax return ($25 × 8 = $200).

Investment Expenses

Investment expenses directly connected with the production of investment income are allowed as a deduction. Examples include investment counseling fees and the rental of a safe deposit box to keep investment documents.

Hobby Expenses

An activity is considered a hobby rather than a business when it is not carried on to make a profit. Expenses related to a hobby are deductible, but only up to the amount of hobby income.

> **Example:** In 2016, Sadie earned $2,000 from selling her quilts at craft shows and had $5,000 in expenses. For Sadie, the vast majority of the quilts that she made were for pleasure, and she never had any intent to make a profit selling them. She would be able to claim $2,000 of these expenses, the amount equal to her hobby income. However, her deduction is further limited to the amount by which this item and any other applicable miscellaneous deductions exceed 2% of her AGI. Sadie's AGI was $40,000 in 2016, and she had no other miscellaneous itemized deductions to report. Therefore, her deductible hobby expenses are limited to $1,200 ($2,000 - $800 [2% × $40,000 AGI]).

Deductible Legal Fees

Most legal expenses are not deductible by individual taxpayers because they are considered personal expenses. But some legal expenses are deductible if they are incurred when a taxpayer is attempting to produce or collect taxable income, such as legal advice related to collecting alimony or earning investments.

To be deductible, tax advice fees must be separately stated on an attorney's bill. A taxpayer can deduct fees for legal advice on federal, state, and local taxes of all types, including income, estate, gift, and property taxes, even if the advice is related to a divorce.

> **Example:** The lawyer handling Ben's divorce consults another law firm, which handles only tax matters, to obtain information on how Ben's divorce will affect his taxes in the future. Since Ben consulted with the second law firm specifically to discuss tax issues, he can deduct the part of the fee paid to the second firm and separately stated on his bill as an itemized deduction, subject to the 2% limit.

> **Example:** Jenna pays an attorney $4,500 for handling her divorce. This fee is not deductible. She pays an additional $1,500 fee for services to collect alimony that her former husband refuses to pay. Jenna can deduct the fee for collecting alimony ($1,500), subject to the 2% limit if it is separately stated on the attorney's bill.

Tax Preparation Fees

A taxpayer may generally deduct tax preparation fees in the year he pays them. Deductible fees include the cost of tax preparation software and tax publications and any fee the taxpayer paid for electronic filing of his return. A taxpayer can also deduct fees paid to appraisers, actuaries, and accountants for services in determining the correct tax.

Miscellaneous Deductions Not Subject to the 2% Limit

There are some miscellaneous expenses that a taxpayer can deduct on Schedule A, without regard to the 2% limit. These expenses include:

Gambling losses to the extent of gambling winnings: The full amount of a taxpayer's gambling winnings is reported on line 21 of his Form 1040. Gambling losses are deducted on Schedule A, up to the total amount of gambling winnings. Taxpayers must have kept a written record of their losses. Gambling losses in excess of winnings are not deductible.

> **Example:** Jason likes to gamble at the blackjack tables at his local casino. In 2016, he wins $6,200 playing blackjack but has $9,500 in gambling losses. He is required to report the full amount of the winnings on Form 1040. His deduction for gambling losses is limited to $6,200 on Schedule A. He cannot write off the remaining $3,300 in losses. He also cannot or carry the losses forward to future years. If Jason chooses not to itemize his deductions, then none of his gambling losses would be deductible.

Work-related expenses for individuals with a disability: These are expenses that enable a disabled person to work, such as special equipment or attendant care services at his workplace.

> **Example:** Erin has a visual disability. She requires a large screen magnifier in order to see well enough to perform her work. Erin purchased her screen magnifier for $550. She can deduct its cost as an itemized deduction not subject to the 2% floor.

Amortizable premium on taxable bonds: If the amount a taxpayer pays for a bond is greater than its stated principal amount, the excess is called a bond premium. Annual amortization of the premium is treated as a miscellaneous itemized deduction not subject to the 2% limit.

Casualty or theft losses from income-producing property: A taxpayer can deduct a casualty or theft loss as a miscellaneous itemized deduction, not subject to the 2% limit if the damaged or stolen property was income-producing property (meaning property held for investment, such as stocks, bonds, gold, silver, vacant lots, and works of art).

Estate tax on income in respect of a decedent: Income in respect of a decedent (IRD) is income owed to a decedent at the time he died. If a decedent's estate has paid federal estate taxes on IRD assets, a beneficiary may be able to claim an IRD tax deduction, not subject to the 2% floor.

Deductions for Nonresident Aliens

Specific limitations on deductions apply to nonresident aliens who are required to file Form 1040NR. They cannot claim the standard deduction. Further, except for personal exemptions and certain itemized deductions, they can claim deductions only to the extent they are connected with income related to their U.S. trade or business. The following itemized deductions are allowed:

- State and local income taxes
- Qualifying charitable contributions to U.S. nonprofit organizations
- Casualty and theft losses
- Miscellaneous itemized deductions

Itemized deductions related to mortgage interest are not allowed.

Bad Debt Deductions

There are two kinds of bad debts: **business bad debt** and **nonbusiness bad debt**. If a taxpayer cannot collect money owed to him, he may have a bad debt. To deduct a bad debt, the taxpayer must have a basis in it: The taxpayer must have already included the amount in income or must have already loaned out the cash.

Note: Unlike the other deductions discussed in this and the prior unit, bad debt deductions usually are not itemized on Schedule A. Deductible business bad debts are generally reported on an individual taxpayer's Schedule C (or other corresponding schedule such as Schedule E or F, depending on the type of business). Business bad debts incurred by an employee are a rare exception and may be deductible as miscellaneous itemized deductions, subject to the 2% limit. Deductible nonbusiness bad debts are reported on Schedule D.

Business Bad Debts

A business bad debt is a loss from the worthlessness of a debt that either was created or acquired in operating a trade or business or was closely related to the business when it became partly or totally worthless. Business bad debts are typically the result of credit sales to customers, but they can also be the result of loans to suppliers, clients, employees, or distributors. Goods and services customers have not paid for are shown in the business's books as either accounts receivable or notes receivable.

If the business is unable to collect any part of these accounts or notes receivable, the uncollectible part is a business bad debt. However, the business can take a bad debt deduction for these accounts and notes receivable only if the amount owed was included in gross income either for the year the deduction is claimed or for a prior year.

Thus, a business that uses the cash method of accounting would normally report income when payment is received and would not usually have a bad debt deduction for amounts owed that are not received because those amounts would not previously have been included in income.

Nonbusiness Bad Debts

All other bad debts are classified as "nonbusiness" bad debts. In order to be deductible, a nonbusiness bad debt must:

- **Be totally worthless:** A partly worthless nonbusiness debt cannot be deducted.
- **Be genuine:** A debt is genuine if it arises from a debtor-creditor relationship based on a valid and enforceable obligation to repay a fixed or determinable sum of money. There must be a profit motive in order for the loan to qualify as a true debtor-creditor relationship. If a taxpayer lends money to a relative or friend with the understanding that it will not be repaid, it is considered a gift and not a loan. Unless a taxpayer has documentation that proves otherwise, the IRS generally considers loans to relatives or friends to be gifts. For example, when minor children borrow from their parents, there is no genuine debt, and bad debt cannot be deducted.
- **Have basis to the taxpayer:** The taxpayer must have already included the amount in income or loaned out cash. Thus, a cash method taxpayer generally cannot take a bad debt deduction for unpaid salaries, wages, rents, fees, interest, dividends, and similar items.
- **Be claimed only in the year the debt becomes worthless:** The taxpayer does not have to wait until a debt is due to determine it is worthless, if there is proof that the debt is already

worthless (for example, if the debtor has all of his debts completely discharged through bankruptcy). A debt becomes worthless when there is no longer any chance that the amount owed will be paid.

It is not necessary to go to court if it can otherwise be demonstrated that a debt would be uncollectible. However, the taxpayer must document that he has taken reasonable steps to collect the debt. Bankruptcy of a debtor is generally good evidence of the worthlessness of a debt.

> **Example:** In January 2016, Stephanie loans her friend, Jed, $14,000 to buy a car. Jed signs a note and promises to pay the entire debt back with interest by December 31, 2016. Jed has a stroke in June 2016 and cannot pay his debts, so he files for bankruptcy. The bankruptcy court notifies all creditors that no amounts will be paid to Jed's creditors. Stephanie does not have to wait until the debt comes due. Jed's bankruptcy means the loan has become worthless since there is no longer any chance the amount owed will be paid. Stephanie can deduct the nonbusiness bad debt.

A legitimate nonbusiness bad debt is reported as a short-term capital loss on Form 8949, *Sales and Other Dispositions of Capital Assets,* and Schedule D. It is subject to the capital loss limit of $3,000 per year, or $1,500 if the taxpayer files MFS. The taxpayer must include a detailed bad debt statement with a description of the debt, the amount, and the date it became due; the name of the debtor; the efforts made to collect the debt; and the reason the debt is worthless.

Nondeductible Expenses

The IRS has a lengthy list of expenses that individual taxpayers cannot deduct.[48] These are just a sample of personal expenses the IRS lists as nondeductible:

- Lunch with coworkers or meals while working late
- Country club dues, athletic club fees, and gym memberships
- Residential telephone lines and home security systems
- Home repairs, insurance, and rent
- Losses from the sale of a home, furniture, or a personal car
- Brokers' commissions
- Burial or funeral expenses, including the cost of cemetery lots
- Fees and licenses, such as car license or registration costs (except certain portions that may be considered deductible property taxes), marriage licenses, and dog tags
- Fines and penalties for breaking the law, such as parking tickets
- Life and disability insurance premiums
- Investment-related seminars
- Lost or misplaced cash or property
- Political contributions
- Expenses of attending stockholders' meetings

---

[48] A basic rule is that most personal, living, or family expenses are not deductible.

- Voluntary unemployment benefit fund contributions
- Adoption expenses (although a taxpayer may be able to claim a credit for these expenses)
- Travel expenses for another individual
- Interest on a personal credit card
- Expenses of earning or collecting tax-exempt income

Example: Nirali received taxable interest income of $2,400 and tax-exempt interest of $600 during 2016. In connection with this income, she had total investment expenses of $250 for the year. She cannot specifically identify the amounts of individual expense items that relate to each type of interest income. Therefore, 80% ($2,400/$3,000) of the expense is allocated to the taxable interest income and 20% ($600/$3,000) is for the tax-exempt interest. Subject to the 2% limit, she can deduct expenses of $200 (80% of $250).

Unit 13: Study Questions

(Test yourself first, then check the correct answers at the end of this quiz.)

1. Brady's toolshed caught fire in 2016. The shed is not attached to his primary residence. The shed is completely destroyed and the equipment inside the shed is also badly damaged. Brady estimates the property damage at $6,000. He fixes the damage himself, so he does not file an insurance claim. Brady pays $3,000 for the cost of the materials and estimates the value of his labor to be $2,800. His insurance company has a $1,000 deductible for any casualty loss claim filed. What is Brady's deductible casualty loss before any deductions or income limitations?

A. $0
B. $1,000
C. $5,800
D. $6,000

2. Marissa works as a tax preparer. In 2016, her employer requires preparers to take several courses in order to keep their current positions. Marissa incurred the following expenses when she took these courses:

Required supplies	$100
Tuition	550
Required books	120
Credit card interest from paying tuition	50
Bus passes to and from school	65
Total business related educational expenses	**$885**

What is Marissa's deductible work-related educational expense on her Schedule A *before* applying the 2% limitation?

A. $550
B. $670
C. $835
D. $885

3. All of the following miscellaneous itemized deductions are subject to the 2% of AGI limit except:

A. Tax preparation fees.
B. Malpractice insurance.
C. Baggage fees during a business trip.
D. Gambling losses to the extent of gambling winnings.

4. Stanton is a salesman in Oregon who attends a four-day convention for his industry in Las Vegas. He has the following expenses that are not reimbursed by his employer:

Roundtrip airfare	$400
Airline baggage fee	25
Car rental	125
Hotel	650
Business meals	300
Entertaining prospective clients	120

What amount can Stanton deduct on his Schedule A, before applying the 2%-of-AGI floor?

A. $1,200
B. $1,410
C. $1,500
D. $1,620

5. Alfred lives in Baltimore where he has a seasonal job for eight months each year and earns $25,000. He works the other four months in Miami, also at a seasonal job, and earns $9,000. Where is Alfred's tax home?

A. Miami.
B. Baltimore.
C. Alfred is a transient for tax purposes.
D. Alfred has no tax home.

6. Kim uses her home office while she works as a translator for an online company. She meets the requirements for deducting expenses for the business use of her home. Her home office is 480 square feet, and her home is 2,400 square feet. She chooses not to use the simplified option for calculation. What is Kim's business use percentage in order to figure her allowable deduction?

A. 5%
B. 10%
C. 15%
D. 20%

7. Monique is an attorney who reports the income from her practice on the accrual basis. In 2016, she receives $2,000 from the settlement of a bankruptcy case of a former client who owed her $15,000. What amount of bad debt deduction can Monique claim?

A. $15,000
B. $13,000
C. $2,000
D. None, because she uses the accrual basis.

8. Connor is deaf. He purchased a special device to use at work so he can identify when his phone rings. He paid for the device out-of-pocket, and his employer did not reimburse him. How should Connor report this on his tax return?

A. Connor can deduct the purchase as an itemized deduction, not subject to the 2% floor.
B. Connor can deduct the purchase as an itemized deduction, subject to the 2% floor.
C. Connor cannot deduct the purchase because he is not totally disabled.
D. Connor cannot deduct the purchase because he is not self-employed.

9. Enrique and Crystal had adjusted gross income of $75,000 in 2016 and incurred the following miscellaneous expenses:

Homeowner's association dues	$1,000
Fine from homeowner's association for violation of bylaws	100
Loss from burglary of their home	9,000
Tax preparation fees	250

Based upon the information provided, what is the amount of expenses they can deduct for 2016?

A. $1,750
B. $10,250
C. $1,350
D. $1,400

10. Which of the following is deductible as an employee business expense?

A. Employer-reimbursed expenses under a tuition reimbursement (nontaxable) program.
B. Taking classes that maintain or improve skills needed in the taxpayer's present work.
C. Taking classes that are required by a taxpayer's employer or the law to keep his present salary or job.
D. Both B and C.

11. Eli purchased a used car for $11,000 in 2016. He did not purchase auto insurance, and three months later he totaled his car in an auto accident. The car's FMV on the date of the accident was $10,000. He was able to sell the damaged car to a salvage yard for $300. Eli's AGI for 2016 was $50,000. What is Eli's deductible casualty loss on Schedule A?

A. $0
B. $4,200
C. $4,600
D. $9,700

12. Joshua's adjusted gross income was $20,000 in 2016, and he had the following expenses:

Tax preparation fee	$100
Safe deposit box rental to store bonds	75
Life insurance premiums	600
Home security system	175
Loss on sale of personal vehicle	(1,800)
Investment journals and newsletters	250
Investment advisory fees	200
Attorney fees for preparation of a will	1,000

What is the amount of Joshua's total qualified miscellaneous itemized expenses (before the application of the AGI limitation)?

A. $2,400
B. $1,225
C. $800
D. $625

13. All of the following may be claimed as miscellaneous itemized deductions except:

A. Unreimbursed commuting expenses to and from work.
B. Union dues.
C. Expenses of looking for a new job in the same career field.
D. Work-related expenses for individuals with a disability.

14. Patrice's antique Persian rug was damaged by a new puppy. Patrice estimates the loss at $4,500. Her AGI for the year is $30,000. How much of the casualty loss can she deduct?

A. $0
B. $4,500
C. $4,400
D. $1,400

15. Isaac's home was damaged by a tornado. He had $90,000 worth of damage, but $80,000 was reimbursed by his insurance company. Isaac's employer had a disaster relief fund for its employees. Isaac received $4,000 from the fund and spent the entire amount on repairs to his home. What is Isaac's deductible casualty loss before applying the deduction limits?

A. $0
B. $4,000
C. $6,000
D. $10,000

16. Hosanna is working on a temporary work assignment in another city. She is not sure how long the assignment will last. She travels overnight every week. So far, the work assignment has lasted 11 months in 2016, and Hosanna has incurred $800 of travel expenses and $300 of meal expenses. What is her deductible expense for this activity in 2016?

A. $0
B. $800
C. $950
D. $1,100

17. Using the simplified option to calculate a home office deduction, the maximum area that can be taken is:

A. 100 square feet
B. 250 square feet
C. 300 square feet
D. 500 square feet

18. All of the following may be claimed as miscellaneous itemized deductions except:

A. Funeral expenses.
B. Union dues.
C. Laundry costs for work uniforms.
D. Investment expenses.

19. Simon's AGI is $75,000. Therefore, the first_____ of miscellaneous employee work-related expenses is not deductible.

A. $1,000
B. $1,500
C. $5,625
D. $7,500

20. Which of the following types of destruction could create a potentially deductible casualty loss?

A. Dry rot
B. Terrorist attack
C. Termite damage
D. Carpet beetles

21. If a taxpayer's main home is destroyed in a flood and the area is later declared a federally-declared disaster area, how long would he typically have to purchase replacement property?

A. Two years.
B. Three years.
C. Four years.
D. Ten years.

22. Roberto is a nonresident alien who files Form 1040NR. Which of the following is he not allowed to claim as an itemized deduction on his income tax return?

A. A loss on a stolen laptop and audiovisual equipment used in his business in the U.S.
B. A charitable deduction to the American Cancer Society.
C. Mortgage interest on his main home.
D. Amounts paid for his state income tax.

23. Sandy has the following income and losses in 2016:

Wages	$45,000
Gambling winnings	10,000
Gambling losses	(13,000)
Attorney fees for a divorce	1,500

How should these transactions be treated on her tax return?

A. She should report $55,000 of income and $10,000 of miscellaneous itemized deductions on Schedule A, not subject to the 2% floor.
B. She should report $53,000 of income and $13,000 of miscellaneous itemized deductions on Schedule A, subject to the 2% floor.
C. She should report $55,000 of income and $13,000 of miscellaneous itemized deductions on Schedule A, subject to the 2% floor.
D. She should report $45,000 of income and $14,500 of miscellaneous itemized deductions on Schedule A, not subject to the 2% floor.

24. Brooke had adjusted gross income of $20,000 in 2016. Her home sustained damage from a storm, and she incurred a loss of $3,000. Her home insurance policy had a deductible of $2,500 for this type of loss, so she elected not to file a claim. Based upon the information provided, what is the amount of casualty loss Brooke can deduct for the year, after the application of the $100 and 10% of AGI limitations?

A. $400
B. $900
C. $2,000
D. $3,000

25. Ali is a single taxpayer who has AGI of $100,000 in 2016. He loaned $8,000 to his friend Phoebe in 2011 and Phoebe has not yet repaid him. What amount of bad debt deduction can Ali claim?

A. $1,500
B. $3,000
C. $8,000
D. $0

26. During the year, Leon paid $350 to have his tax return prepared. He also paid union dues of $450 and paid an attorney $3,000 to draft his will. What are Leon's total miscellaneous itemized deductions on his Schedule A before the 2% limitation?

A. $350
B. $450
C. $800
D. $3,800

27. All of the following statements are correct except:

A. A taxpayer can deduct job-related expenses, subject to the 2%-of-AGI limit.
B. Job search costs, such as the use of an employment agency, are deductible expenses.
C. The job search does not have to result in a new job for the taxpayer in order for his expenses to be deductible.
D. A taxpayer can deduct expenses related to the search for a job in a new occupation.

28. Marilyn won the lottery and then made personal loans to several friends. Each loan was a true debtor-creditor relationship but not business related. She could not collect on many of these loans. How does Marilyn report these transactions?

A. The losses from the uncollectible loans are not deductible since they were personal loans.
B. The losses are deductible as nonbusiness bad debts on Schedule D.
C. The losses are deductible as a business expense on Schedule C.
D. The losses are deductible on Schedule A as casualty losses.

29. Which of the following is an allowable miscellaneous deduction, subject to the 2%-of-AGI limit?

A. Veterinarian expenses for a family pet that is not a service animal.
B. Casualty loss for $50 cash that a dependent daughter lost at a shopping mall.
C. Cost of takeout meals for a live-in girlfriend.
D. Expenses related to earning taxable interest.

30. Wes had a fire in his garage that destroyed his car and two antique desks. He had recently bought the car for $30,000. The FMV of the car just before the fire was $27,500. Its FMV after the fire was $500 (scrap value). He had purchased the desks for $2,500, and their FMV just before the fire was $5,000. Wes's insurance company reimbursed him a total of $24,000. Wes's AGI in 2016 was $70,000. What is his casualty loss deduction?

A. $0
B. $3,500
C. $1,000
D. $900

31. Addison is a real estate agent who sold seven homes to seven buyers in 2016. She likes giving each of her clients a gift after closing. Addison purchases an $80 gift basket for each customer. She can deduct a total of _____ for the gifts as a business expense.

A. $0
B. $25
C. $175
D. $560

32. Hector works as part of the crew on an Amtrak train. He regularly travels away from his tax home on long train trips. In 2016, he incurs $3,760 of unreimbursed meal expenses during his business travels. Before application of the 2% threshold, how much can Hector deduct on his Schedule A?

A. $1,880
B. $2,820
C. $3,008
D. $3,760

33. Which of the following expenses are all itemized deductions subject to the 2%-of-AGI limitation?

A. Home office expense, hobby expenses, educator expenses.
B. Donation to a qualified charity, gambling losses, business-related entertainment expenses.
C. Cost of safety goggles required for work, tax preparation fees, dues to a professional society.
D. Impairment-related work expenses of a disabled employee, legal fee to collect alimony, union dues.

34. Blair teaches high school Spanish classes. In order to improve her Spanish language skills, she spends two months during the summer of 2016 in Madrid. She incurs the following costs:

Airfare	$5,000
Apartment rental	4,000
Meals	3,000
Other miscellaneous costs	1,500

Before application of the 2% threshold, what amount can Blair claim as a miscellaneous deduction for work-related education expenses?

A. $13,500
B. $12,000
C. $9,000
D. $0

Unit 13: Answers

1. The answer is B. If a taxpayer's property is covered by insurance and the taxpayer declines to file an insurance claim, the eligible casualty losses are limited to the amount that is not normally covered by insurance, such as the amount of an insurance deductible.

2. The answer is C. Marissa can deduct all the costs as work-related educational expenses except the credit card interest, which is a personal expense and not deductible.

3. The answer is D. Gambling losses, to the extent of gambling winnings, are not subject to the 2%-of-AGI limit.

4. The answer is B. Stanton can deduct 100% of the air fare, baggage fee, car rental fee, and hotel costs as unreimbursed employee expenses, before applying the 2%-of-AGI floor. However, he can deduct only 50% of the business meals and entertainment expenses, for a total of $1,410 ($400 + $25 + $125 + $650 + $150 meals + $60 entertainment).

5. The answer is B. Baltimore is Alfred's main place of work because he spends most of his time and earns most of his income there. Therefore, Baltimore is Alfred's tax home for IRS purposes.

6. The answer is D. Kim uses 20% of her home for business, as her office is 20% (480 ÷ 2,400) of the total area of her home.

7. The answer is B. Monique can claim the difference between the $15,000 owed to her (and previously reported as accrual-basis income when earned) and the $2,000 received in the bankruptcy settlement as a business bad debt deduction. The former client's bankruptcy provides evidence to support the worthlessness of the remaining amount owed to Harriet.

8. The answer is A. Connor can deduct the expenses for the special device as an impairment-related work expense. If a taxpayer has a physical or mental disability that limits employment, he can deduct the expense as a miscellaneous itemized deduction, not subject to the 2%-of-AGI floor.

9. The answer is D. Neither the homeowner's association dues, nor the fine are deductible. The tax preparation fees did not exceed 2% of adjusted gross income, and therefore are not deductible. The amount of the burglary loss, minus $100, that exceeds 10% of adjusted gross income is deductible as a casualty loss.

Loss from theft	$9,000
Minus $100 threshold	(100)
Loss after $100 limit	8,900
Adjusted gross income	75,000
Multiply by 10% limit	7,500
Casualty loss deduction ($8,900 - $7,500)	**$1,400**

10. The answer is D. A taxpayer can deduct the costs of qualifying work-related education as employee business expenses. Amounts that are reimbursed by an employer cannot be deducted by the taxpayer.

11. The answer is C. Eli's deductible casualty loss on Schedule A is $4,600. This is a nonbusiness casualty loss, so Eli must first reduce his loss by $100 and then by 10% of his AGI. Although his basis in the car is $11,000, he must use the FMV to determine his loss because it is lower.

FMV	$10,000
Insurance	0
Salvage value	(300)
Statutory reduction	(100)
10% of AGI	(5,000)
Deductible loss	**$4,600**

12. The answer is D. The expenses deductible as miscellaneous itemized expenses are the income tax preparation fee ($100); the safe deposit box rental ($75); the investment journals and newsletters ($250); and the investment advisory fees ($200). His total deduction before application of the 2% floor is $625.

13. The answer is A. The expense of commuting to and from work is not deductible.

14. The answer is A. A casualty loss is not deductible if the damage is neither unexpected nor unusual, such as when it is caused by a family pet.

15. The answer is C. Isaac's casualty loss before applying the deduction limits is $6,000. Isaac must reduce his loss ($90,000) by the $80,000 insurance proceeds and the $4,000 he received from his employer.

16. The answer is A. Hosanna cannot deduct any of the expenses, because travel expenses paid in connection with an indefinite work assignment are not deductible.

17. The answer is C. If a taxpayer chooses the simplified option for calculating the home office deduction, the maximum allowable area is 300 square feet at $5 per foot, for a maximum deduction of $1,500.

18. The answer is A. Funeral expenses are not deductible as a miscellaneous itemized deduction. All of the other expenses listed are deductible as itemized deductions on Schedule A.

19. The answer is B. Simon's employee work-related expenses are subject to a limit, based upon 2% of adjusted gross income. Therefore, Simon must calculate his deduction on Schedule A by first subtracting 2% of his AGI ($75,000 × .02 = $1,500) from the total amount of these expenses.

20. The answer is B. A loss due to a terrorist attack would qualify as a casualty loss. A "casualty loss" is the damage, destruction, or loss of property resulting from an identifiable event that is sudden, unexpected, or unusual. Loss of property due to progressive deterioration isn't deductible as a casualty loss.

21. The answer is C. For most casualty losses; taxpayers have two years to purchase a replacement for damaged or destroyed property. However, in the case of most federally-declared disaster areas, the period is four years. In certain extreme cases, the replacement period is extended to five years.

22. The answer is C. Nonresident aliens are limited as to the types of itemized deductions they can claim. Among other restrictions, they are not allowed to claim the deduction for mortgage interest.

23. The answer is A. The full amount of income ($45,000 + $10,000 = $55,000) must be reported on Form 1040. The gambling losses are deductible on Schedule A, but only up to the amount of gambling winnings. Gambling losses are not subject to the 2% of income limitation. Attorney fees for a divorce are not deductible, but separate legal advice related to collecting alimony is deductible.

24. The answer is A. Because the property was covered by insurance and Brooke did not file a claim, the casualty loss deduction is limited to the amount of the insurance deductible, as this amount would have been her out-of-pocket cost if a claim had been filed. This amount is further subject to a reduction of $100 and limited to the net amount that exceeds 10% of adjusted gross income.

Loss from storm	$3,000
Limited to amount of deductible	2,500
Minus $100	(100)
Net loss	2,400
Adjusted gross income	20,000
Multiply by 10% limit	2,000
Casualty loss deduction ($2,400 - $2,000)	$400

25. The answer is D. Based on the information presented; it appears unlikely that Ali would be able to claim a nonbusiness bad debt deduction. In order to do so, he would need to be able to demonstrate that: 1) he had a debtor-creditor relationship with Phoebe that included a valid and enforceable obligation for her to repay the loan; 2) he had taken reasonable steps to collect the debt; and 3) the debt was totally worthless.

26. The answer is C. The attorney's fee for drafting the will is not deductible. The tax preparation fees and union dues are deductible, but are subject to the 2%-of-AGI floor.

27. The answer is D. For job search expenses to be deductible, they must relate to the taxpayer's current occupation. A taxpayer cannot deduct expenses if they are connected with the search for a job in a new field. A taxpayer who starts a first job or who returns to full-time work after a long absence can also qualify for the deduction.

28. The answer is B. Nonbusiness bad debts are reported as short-term capital losses on Schedule D. They are subject to the capital loss limit of $3,000 per year.

29. The answer is D. Expenses related to earning or collecting tax-exempt income are not deductible; however, the expenses of earning taxable interest are. The other items listed are personal or family expenses that are not deductible.

30. The answer is A. Wes does not have a deductible casualty loss. Since the fair market value of the car was lower than its cost, it is used as the starting point to determine his loss. Net of the salvage value, he had a loss of $27,000 on the car. His loss on the desks is limited to his original cost since it was lower than FMV. Thus he had total losses of $29,500 before the insurance reimbursement, and a net loss of $5,500. After subtracting the $100 deduction, he had potentially deductible losses of $5,400. However, his deduction is limited to the amount of the losses that exceeds 10% of his AGI, or $7,000 (see calculation, next).

Calculations	Car	Desks
Basis for the casualty loss	$27,000	$2,500
Insurance reimbursement		24,000
Net loss after insurance reimbursement ($29,500 - $24,000)		5,500
Subtract $100		5,400
AGI × 10% ($70,000 × 10%)		7,000
Allowable casualty loss		$0

31. The answer is C. Addison can deduct $25 for each of the presents because there is an annual limit of $25 per gift per customer. Her total deduction would be (7 × $25 = $175).

32. The answer is C. Hector is an employee who falls under the special Department of Transportation hours of service rules, meaning he can deduct 80% of his unreimbursed meal expenses ($3,760 × .80 = $3,008), rather than the normal 50%.

33. The answer is C. This is the only answer where all three items are subject to the 2%-of-AGI floor. In answer A, educator expenses are an adjustment to income. In answer B, charitable donations are not a miscellaneous deduction, and gambling losses are a miscellaneous deduction not subject to the 2% floor. In answer D, impairment-related work expenses of a disabled employee are a miscellaneous deduction not subject to the 2% floor.

34. The answer is D. Blair cannot claim a miscellaneous deduction for these costs. Although her travel to Spain may be somewhat educational, the related costs do not qualify as work-related education expenses.

Unit 14: Tax Credits

For additional information read:
Publication 972, *Child Tax Credit*
Publication 503, *Child and Dependent Care Expenses*
Publication 596, *Earned Income Credit*
Publication 970, *Tax Benefits for Education*

A tax credit directly reduces a taxpayer's liability on a dollar-for-dollar basis, which means it is usually more valuable than a tax deduction of the same dollar amount that only reduces the amount of taxable income. Various types of tax credits are either refundable or nonrefundable.

Note: New due diligence requirements apply to Tax Preparers who prepare returns claiming the Earned Income Tax Credit (EITC), the Child Tax Credit (CTC), and the American Opportunity Tax Credit (AOTC). Starting with the 2016 tax year, preparers must complete Form 8867, *Paid Preparer's Due Diligence Checklist,* for each EITC, CTC/ACTC or AOTC claim they prepare. This new requirement is covered in more detail in Book 3, *Representation.*

Nonrefundable Tax Credits

A nonrefundable tax credit reduces a taxpayer's liability for the year to zero but not beyond that, so any remaining credit is not refunded to the taxpayer. Among the most common nonrefundable tax credits are:

- Foreign Tax Credit (covered later)
- Credit for Child and Dependent Care Expenses
- Child Tax Credit
- Adoption Credit
- American Opportunity Credit (partially refundable)
- Lifetime Learning Credit
- Retirement Savings Contributions Credit
- Residential energy credits

Credits cannot be claimed if the taxpayer is filing Form 1040EZ.

Refundable Tax Credits

A refundable tax credit can reduce a taxpayer's liability to zero and also generate a refund to the taxpayer for the amount by which the credit exceeds the amount of tax he would otherwise owe. Refundable tax credits include the following:

- Additional Child Tax Credit
- Earned Income Tax Credit[49]

---

[49] Note: The Protecting Americans from Tax Hikes Act prevents retroactive claims of the Earned Income Tax Credit, the Child Tax Credit, and the American Opportunity Credit for any individual that did not have a valid ITIN or SSN for the taxable year. In the past, a taxpayer was allowed to amend their return in order to claim these credits retroactively after a valid taxpayer identification number was issued.

- Premium Tax Credit (related to the Affordable Care Act, covered later)
- American Opportunity Tax Credit (partially refundable)

Child and Dependent Care Credit

The Child and Dependent Care Credit allows a taxpayer a credit for a percentage of child care expenses for children under age 13 and for disabled dependents of any age. This is a nonrefundable credit for child care expenses that allow taxpayers to work or to seek work. The credit offsets regular tax and the alternative minimum tax.

The credit ranges from 20% to 35% of qualifying expenses, depending on a taxpayer's income. For 2016, the limit on qualifying expenses is $3,000 for one child and $6,000 for two or more children. If a taxpayer receives a reimbursement under a flexible spending account, the amount is treated as being pre-tax, and the taxpayer must deduct the reimbursed amount from his qualified expenses to determine the credit. A taxpayer must pass five eligibility tests to qualify for the Credit for Child and Dependent Care Expenses:

- Qualifying person test
- Earned income test
- Work-related expense test
- Joint return test
- Provider identification test

Test #1. Qualifying Person Test

For purposes of the Child and Dependent Care Credit, a "qualifying person" is:

- A dependent child under the age of 13 (at the time the care was provided)
- A spouse who is physically or mentally unable to care for himself
- Any other disabled person who is unable to care for himself and that the taxpayer either claims as a dependent or could claim if not for certain specified circumstances

> **Example:** Rocky paid someone to care for his disabled wife, Janet, so he could work. Janet requires an in-home care aide. Rocky also paid to have someone prepare meals and babysit his 12-year-old daughter, Tamara. Both Janet and Tamara are qualifying persons for the Dependent Care credit.

Test #2. Earned Income Test

Both the taxpayer and his spouse, if married, must have earned income during the year to qualify for this credit. This generally means both spouses must work. The credit is not available to MFS filers. In the event one spouse does not have earned income, for purposes of this test the taxpayer's spouse is treated as having earned income for any month he is:

- A full-time student, or
- Disabled.

For any month that a spouse has no actual earned income, but has deemed earned income because they were a full-time student or disabled, the amount of deemed earned income by that nonworking spouse is $250 per month if the couple has a pre-qualifying individual for this credit; or $500 per month if the taxpayer has two or more dependents.

> **Example:** Jessica and Quincy are married. Quincy worked as a custodian in 2016. Jessica attended school full-time from January 1 to June 30. She was unemployed during the summer and did not attend school the rest of the year. Jessica is treated as having earned income for the six months she attended school full-time.

The amount of work-related expenses to figure the credit cannot be more than:

- The taxpayer's earned income for the year, if he is single at the end of the year, or
- The smaller of his or his spouse's earned income for the year if he is married at the end of the year.

Test #3. Work-Related Expense Test

Child and dependent care expenses must be work-related to qualify for this credit, meaning a taxpayer must be working or searching for work. Expenses incurred so that a spouse may do volunteer work or take care of personal business, or so that a married couple can go on a "date night" do not qualify.

> **Example:** Patsy is a stay-at-home mom who volunteers several hours a week for a local autism information hotline. Her husband works full-time as a maintenance worker. They pay a babysitter to stay with their daughter during the hours Patsy volunteers. The couple does not qualify for the credit because the babysitting expense is not work-related. Since Patsy does not have a job, is not disabled, and is not a full-time student, the child care expenses are ineligible.

> **Example:** Darcy's four-year-old son attends a daycare center while she works three days a week. The daycare charges $150 for three days a week and $250 for five days a week. Sometimes Darcy pays the extra money so she can run errands on her days off. This extra charge is not a qualifying expense. Darcy's deductible expenses are limited to $150 a week, the amount of her work-related daycare expense.

The following kinds of expenses qualify for the credit:

- Education: Preschool or other programs below the level of kindergarten; before or after-school care for a child in kindergarten or above
- Care outside the home for a child under 13 or in a care center for a disabled dependent
- Transportation for a care provider to take a qualifying person to or from a place where care is provided
- Fees and deposits paid to an agency or preschool to acquire child care
- Household services, if they are at least partly for the well-being and protection of a qualifying person

> **Example:** Roger's 10-year-old child attends a private school. In addition to paying for tuition, Roger pays an extra fee for before and after-school care so he can be at work during his scheduled hours. Roger can count the cost of the before and after-school program when figuring the credit but cannot count the cost of tuition.

> **Example:** Maura is single and her elderly mother, Edna, is her dependent. Edna is completely disabled and must be in an adult daycare. Maura pays $8,000 per year for Edna to be in the adult daycare. Maura may take the credit because Edna is disabled and incapable of self-care.

Examples of child care expenses that do not qualify include:

- Tuition costs for children in kindergarten and above
- Summer school or tutoring programs
- The cost of sending a child to an overnight camp (but day camps generally do qualify)
- The cost of transportation not provided by a care provider
- A forfeited deposit to a daycare center (since it is not for care and therefore not a work-related expense)

> **Example:** Ellie is divorced and has custody of her 12-year-old daughter, Destiny, who takes care of herself after school. In August, Ellie spends $2,000 to send Destiny to an overnight camp for two weeks. She also sends Destiny to a Girl Scout day camp for a week in July while Ellie is working. The cost of the Girl Scout camp is $75. Ellie may only count the $75 toward the credit because the cost of sending a child to an overnight camp is not considered a work-related expense. Next summer, when Destiny turns 13, she will no longer be a qualifying child under the rules for this credit.

Care expenses do not include amounts paid for food, clothing, education, or entertainment. Small amounts paid for these items, however, can be included if they are incidental and cannot be separated from the cost of care.

> **Example:** Krista takes her three-year-old child to a nursery school that provides lunch and activities as part of its program. The meals are included in the overall cost of care, and they are not itemized on her bill. Krista can count the total cost when she figures the credit.

Payments for child care will not qualify for the credit if made to a family member who is either:

- The taxpayer's own child under age 19
- Any other dependent listed on the taxpayer's tax return

Taxpayers may combine costs for multiple dependents. For example, if a taxpayer pays daycare expenses for three qualifying children, the $6,000 limit on qualifying expenses does not need to be divided equally among them.

> **Example:** Alec has three children. His qualifying daycare expenses are $2,300 for his first child; $2,800 for his second child; and $900 for his third child. Alec can use the total amount, $6,000, when figuring his credit.

> **Example:** Diego and Valeria both work and have three children. They have $2,000 of daycare expenses for their first child; $3,000 for their second child; and $4,000 for their third child. Although their total child care expenses are $9,000, they may use only the first $6,000 as their basis for the credit.

> **Example:** Lori is a single mother with a five-year-old son. She takes him to daycare five days per week so she can work. Lori makes $46,000 of wages and spends $5,200 per year on daycare. The maximum amount of qualifying expenses she can claim for the credit is $3,000 since she only has one qualifying child, even though her actual expenses exceed that amount.

Test #4. Joint Return Test

The joint return test specifies that married couples who wish to take the credit must file jointly. However, a married taxpayer can be "considered unmarried" for tax purposes if he qualifies for head of household filing status. With divorced or separated taxpayers, only the custodial parent is allowed to claim the credit.

Test #5. Provider Identification Test

This test requires that taxpayers provide the name, address, and taxpayer identification number of the person or organization who provided the care for the child or dependent. If a daycare provider refuses to supply its taxpayer identification information, the taxpayer may still claim the credit.

He must report whatever information he has (such as the provider's name and address) and attach a statement to Form 2441, *Child and Dependent Care Expenses,* explaining the provider's refusal to supply the information.

Child Tax Credit

Taxpayers with income below certain threshold amounts can claim the Child Tax Credit for each qualifying child under the age of 17. This is a nonrefundable credit of up to $1,000 per qualifying child. A taxpayer whose tax liability is zero cannot take the Child Tax Credit because there is no tax to reduce. However, he may be able to take the Additional Child Tax Credit, which is refundable.

The Child Tax Credit is reduced if the taxpayer's modified adjusted gross income is above certain thresholds.

In 2016, the phaseout threshold is $55,000 for married couples filing separately; $75,000 for single, head of household, and qualifying widow(er). The phaseout is $110,000 for couples filing jointly. For each $1,000 (or fraction thereof) of income above the phaseout threshold, the child tax credit is reduced by $50. In addition, the Child Tax Credit is limited to the amounts of regular income tax and any alternative minimum tax owed.

> **Example**: Cordell and Roxana file jointly and have two children who qualify for the Child Tax Credit. Their MAGI is $86,000, and their tax liability is $954. Even though their MAGI is less than the threshold limit of $110,000, they can claim only $954, reducing their tax to zero. Since their tax liability is zero, Cordell and Roxana cannot claim the maximum Child Tax Credit of $1,000 per child, but they may be eligible for the Additional Child Tax Credit, which is a refundable credit.

> **Example:** Clint files as head of household and has three children who qualify for the Child Tax Credit. His MAGI is $54,000, and his tax liability is $4,680. Clint is eligible to take the full credit of $1,000 per child ($3,000) because his MAGI is less than $75,000 and his tax liability is greater than $3,000.

Definition of a Qualifying Child: To be eligible to claim the Child Tax Credit, the taxpayer must have at least one qualifying child. To qualify, the child must:

- Be claimed as the taxpayer's dependent.
- Meet the relationship test: be the son, daughter, adopted child, stepchild, foster child, brother, sister, stepbrother, stepsister, or descendant of any of them (for example, a grandchild, niece, or nephew).
- Meet the age criterion: be under age 17 at the end of the year.
- Not have provided over half of his own support.
- Have lived with the taxpayer for more than six months of the tax year.[50]
- Be a U.S. citizen, a U.S. national, or a resident of the U.S. However, foreign-born adopted children qualify if they lived with the taxpayer all year, even if the adoption is not yet final.[51]

Example: Edward's son, Jeff, turned 17 on December 31, 2016. He is a U.S. citizen and has a valid Social Security number. According to the Child Tax Credit rules, he is not a qualifying child for this credit because he was not *under* age 17 at the end of the year. Disability has no effect on the eligibility for this credit.

Example: Laura's adopted son, Nash, is 14. He is a U.S. citizen and lived with Laura for the entire tax year. Laura provided all of her son's support. Nash is a qualifying child for the Child Tax Credit because he was under age 17 at the end of the tax year; he meets the relationship requirement; he lived with Laura for more than six months of the year, and Laura provided his support.

Additional Child Tax Credit

The Additional Child Tax Credit is available for certain individuals who do not qualify for the full amount of the nonrefundable Child Tax Credit. In order to claim the Additional Child Tax Credit, a taxpayer must be able to claim the Child Tax Credit, even if he does not qualify for the full amount.

Since the Additional Child Tax Credit is refundable, it can produce a refund even if the taxpayer does not owe any tax. The Additional Child Tax Credit allows eligible taxpayers to claim up to $1,000 for each qualifying child after subtracting the allowable amount of Child Tax Credit. For taxpayers with earned income over $3,000, the credit is based on the lesser of:

- 15% of the taxpayer's taxable earned income that is more than $3,000, or
- The amount of unused Child Tax Credit (caused when tax liability is less than the allowed credit).

---

[50] There are special rules for children of divorced or separated parents, as well as children of parents who never married. In some cases the noncustodial parent may be entitled to claim the dependency exemption for a child and thus the Child Tax Credit and Additional Child Tax Credit. In addition, there is an exception for an infant who is born during the tax year and has not lived long enough to meet the six-month requirement.

[51] Remember, retroactive claims of the child tax credit are now prohibited. The PATH Act prohibits retroactively claiming the child tax credit by amending a return (or filing an original return if the taxpayer failed to file) for any prior year in which the individual or a qualifying child for whom the credit is claimed did not have a valid ITIN.

> **Example**: May and Dimitri have two dependent children, MAGI of $66,000, and owe tax of $850. Because their tax liability is less than the full amount of the Child Tax Credit, they may be able to take the Additional Child Tax Credit of up to $1,150 ($2,000 for two children- $850 their tax liability).

Schedule 8812, *Child Tax Credit*, is used to report both the Child Tax Credit and the refundable Additional Child Tax Credit.

A taxpayer can no longer claim the additional child tax credit if he files Form 2555, *Foreign Earned Income Exclusion*.

Adoption Credit

In 2016, a nonrefundable credit of up to $13,460 per child can be taken for qualified expenses paid to adopt a child. For a special needs child, the maximum credit amount is allowed even if the taxpayer does not have any adoption expenses.

If a taxpayer receives employer-provided adoption benefits that are excluded from income, he may still be able to take the Adoption Credit. However, the exclusion and the credit cannot be claimed for the same expenses, and any allowable exclusion must be claimed before any allowable credit.

The exclusion is limited to the same dollar amount as the credit. The phase-out ranges are the same for all taxpayers, regardless of filing status (in 2016, the phase-out range is $201,920-$241,920). Married taxpayers generally must file jointly to claim either the credit or the exclusion.

Although the Adoption Credit is nonrefundable, any unused credit may be carried forward for up to five years. Qualified adoption expenses are directly related to the adoption of a child. These include:

- Adoption fees and court costs
- Attorney fees
- Travel expenses related to the adoption, including meals and lodging
- Re-adoption expenses to adopt a foreign child

Qualified adoption expenses do not include:

- Illegal adoption expenses
- A surrogate parenting arrangement
- Adoption of a spouse's child[52]

An eligible child is:

- Under 18 years old, or
- Physically or mentally disabled, regardless of age.

Special Needs Child: A taxpayer can claim the full credit for a special needs child regardless of actual expenses paid or incurred. For the purposes of this rule, a special needs child must be a United States citizen or U.S. resident when the adoption begins.[53]

Further, one of the following must apply:

- The state has determined the child cannot or should not be returned to his parents' home, or

---

[52] Although a taxpayer cannot deduct adoption expenses to adopt a spouses' child, qualified adoption expenses *does* include expenses paid by a registered domestic partner to adopt his or her partner's child, as long as those expenses otherwise qualify for the credit.
[53] Foreign children aren't considered to have special needs for purposes of the adoption credit.

- The state has determined the child will not be adopted unless assistance is provided to the adoptive parents.

In making the determination about special needs, a state may take into account the following factors: a child's ethnic background and age; whether he is a member of a minority or sibling group; and whether he has a physical, mental, or emotional handicap.

> **Example:** Noel and Cassie adopt a special needs child, and the adoption is finalized in 2016. Their actual adoption expenses are $7,500. They are allowed to claim the full $13,460 credit in 2016 because they adopted a special needs child. Their actual tax liability is 8,000, so the adoption credit will reduce their tax liability in 2016 to zero. They can carryforward any unused adoption credit for up to five years.

Unsuccessful Adoptions: A taxpayer who has attempted to adopt a child in the U.S. and been unsuccessful is still eligible for the credit or exclusion from taxable income for employer-provided adoption assistance payments. Eligible expenses may include those related to unsuccessful attempts to adopt as well as an adoption attempt that is ultimately successful. However, if the eligible child is from a foreign country, the taxpayer cannot take the credit or exclusion unless the adoption becomes final. A foreign child is defined as a child who was not a citizen or resident of the United States at the time the adoption effort began.

Timing of Payment: For a domestic adoption, qualified expenses paid before the year in which the adoption becomes final may be claimed in the year after the expenses were paid. Once the adoption becomes final (or if it is unsuccessful), the taxpayer can claim the expenses in the year paid. For a foreign adoption, expenses paid before or during the year of finality are allowable in that year.

Education Credits

Two education credits are available based on qualified expenses a taxpayer pays for postsecondary education:

- American Opportunity Tax Credit (also called the AOC or AOTC)
- Lifetime Learning Credit[54]

Certain general rules apply to both of these credits, in addition to specific rules for each. A taxpayer may take education credits for himself, his spouse, and his dependents who attended an eligible educational institution during the tax year.

Eligible educational institutions include colleges, universities, vocational schools, and community colleges. Taxpayers can claim payments that are prepaid for an academic period that begins in the first three months of the next calendar year.

> **Example:** Tom paid $1,500 in December 2016 for college tuition for the spring semester that begins in January 2017. Tom can claim $1,500 of education credits on his 2016 return, even though he will not start college until 2017.

---

[54] If a taxpayer does not qualify for either of these education credits, he may still qualify for the Tuition and Fees Deduction (as an adjustment to income), which can reduce the amount of taxable income by up to $4,000. A taxpayer must choose to take either the tax credit(s) or the deduction, and should consider which provides the greatest tax benefit.

A taxpayer cannot claim education credits if he:

- Can be claimed as a dependent on someone else's tax return
- Files MFS
- Has adjusted gross income above the phaseout limit for his filing status
- Has a spouse who was a nonresident alien for any part of the tax year[55]

To claim the credit for a dependent's education expenses, the taxpayer must claim the dependent on his return, but he does not necessarily have to pay for all of the dependent's qualified education expenses. If a taxpayer does not claim an exemption for a dependent who is an eligible student, the student may be able to claim an education credit on his own return.

> **Example:** Cathy has a 19-year-old son named Trent who is a full-time college student. Trent's grandmother paid his tuition directly to the college. For purposes of claiming an education credit, either Cathy or Trent is treated as receiving the money as a gift and paying for the qualified tuition and related expenses. If Cathy claims Trent as a dependent, she can claim an education credit. Alternatively, if Trent claims an exemption for himself on his own return and his mother does not, he can claim the credit.

If a taxpayer has education expenses for more than one student, he may be eligible to take the American Opportunity Credit for one student and the Lifetime Learning Credit for another student on the same tax return.

> **Example:** Reed is 49 and pays college expenses for himself and his dependent daughter, Ivy, age 18. Reed is attending graduate school to earn a doctorate degree. Reed qualifies for the Lifetime Learning Credit. Ivy is an undergraduate and qualifies for the American Opportunity Credit. Reed can take both credits on his tax return for each eligible student, Ivy and himself.

> **Example:** Elias is a college senior studying to be a dentist. This year, in addition to tuition, he pays a fee to the university for the rental of the dental equipment he is required to use in the program. Elias's equipment rental fee is a qualified education expense.

Form 8863 is used to figure and claim both education credits. Qualified education expenses are tuition and related expenses, such as books and other course materials required as a condition of enrollment.

Any course of instruction or other education involving sports, games, or hobbies is not a qualifying expense unless the course is part of the student's degree program (or if taken to improve job skills, in the case of the Lifetime Learning Credit). Qualified education expenses must be reduced by the amount of any tax-free educational assistance received, such as Pell grants, tax-free portions of scholarships, and employer-provided educational assistance. Education expenses that do <u>not</u> qualify include:

- Room and board

---

[55] This rule does not apply if the nonresident spouse elects to be treated as a resident alien for tax purposes.

- Any medical expenses, including health insurance or student health fees, even if charged by the college
- Other insurance costs
- Transportation costs
- Personal, living, or family expenses

Tuition expenses are reported to the student on Form 1098-T, *Tuition Statement*, issued by the school.

> **Example:** Faith received Form 1098-T from the college she attends. It shows that her tuition was $9,500 and that she received a $1,500 tax-free scholarship. Her maximum qualifying expenses for the education credit are $8,000 ($9,500 - $1,500).

> **Example:** Jacqueline paid $3,000 for tuition and $5,000 for room and board at her university. She was also awarded a $2,000 tax-free scholarship and a $4,000 student loan. To qualify for an education credit, she must first subtract the tax-free scholarship from her tuition, her only qualified expense. A student loan is not considered tax-free educational assistance because it must be paid back. To calculate her education credit, Jacqueline has $1,000 of qualified expenses ($3,000 tuition - $2,000 scholarship).

American Opportunity Tax Credit (AOTC or AOC)

The American Opportunity Tax Credit (AOTC) allows taxpayers to claim a credit of up to $2,500 based on qualified tuition and related expenses paid for each eligible student. The credit covers 100% of the first $2,000 and 25% of the second $2,000 of eligible expenses per student. Qualified expenses include tuition and required fees, books, supplies, equipment, and other *required* course materials (but not room and board).

Unlike other education credits and deductions, the American Opportunity Credit is partially refundable. Up to 40% of the credit is refundable, which means the taxpayer can receive up to $1,000 even if no taxes are owed. The credit is not refundable if the student is subject to the "kiddie tax" rules. Requirements for the AOC are as follows:

- **Degree requirement:** The student must be enrolled in a program that leads to a degree, certificate, or other recognized educational credential.
- **Workload:** For at least one academic period of the year, the student must carry at least half of the normal full-time workload for his course of study.
- **No felony drug conviction:** The student must be free of any felony conviction for possessing or distributing a controlled substance.
- **Four years of postsecondary education:** The credit can be claimed only for expenses related to a student's postsecondary education and only for the first four years.

For 2016, the AOTC phases out for joint filers with modified adjusted gross income between $160,000-$180,000, and between $80,000-$90,000 for taxpayers filing as single, head of household, or qualifying widow(er).

If a student does not meet all of the conditions for the American Opportunity Credit, he may still be able to take the Lifetime Learning Credit.

Lifetime Learning Credit

The Lifetime Learning Credit is a nonrefundable tax credit of 20% of qualified tuition, fees and any amounts paid directly to the educational institution for required books, supplies and equipment, up to $10,000, paid during the tax year. The maximum credit is $2,000 per tax return, not per student. A family's maximum credit is the same regardless of the number of qualified students. The requirements for the Lifetime Learning Credit differ from those for the AOTC as follows:

- **No workload requirement:** A student is eligible no matter how many or how few courses he takes.
- **Non-degree courses eligible:** A student qualifies if he is simply taking a course to acquire or improve job skills.
- **All levels of postsecondary education:** A student may be an undergraduate, graduate, or professional degree candidate.
- **Unlimited number of years:** There is no limit on the number of years for which the credit can be claimed for each student.
- **Felony drug convictions permissible:** A student can be convicted for a felony drug conviction and still qualify.

Example: Roland attends Creek Community College after spending six months in prison for a felony cocaine conviction. He paid $4,400 for the course of study, which included tuition, equipment, and books required for the course. The school requires that students pay for books and equipment when registering for courses. The entire $4,400 is an eligible educational expense under the Lifetime Learning Credit. Although he meets all the other requirements for the American Opportunity Credit, Roland does not qualify for the AOC because he has a felony drug conviction. He may claim the Lifetime Learning Credit instead.

Example: Lai works full-time and takes one course a month at night school. Some of the courses are not for credit, but she is taking them to advance her career. She is not pursuing a degree. The education expenses qualify for the Lifetime Learning Credit, but not for the American Opportunity Credit.

For 2016, the Lifetime Learning Credit is phased out for single filers with modified adjusted gross income between $55,000 and $65,000. For joint filers, the phase-out is between $111,000 and $131,000 of MAGI. If the taxpayer's MAGI is over $65,000 ($131,000 for joint filers), they cannot claim the credit.

Earned Income Tax Credit

The Earned Income Tax Credit (EITC), also known as the Earned Income Credit (EIC)[56], is a fully refundable federal income tax credit for lower-income people who work and have earned income and adjusted gross income under certain thresholds. There are very strict rules and income guidelines for the EITC. To claim the EITC, a taxpayer must meet all of the following tests:

- Have a Social Security number that is valid for employment. Any qualifying child must also have a valid SSN.
- Have earned income from wages, combat pay, or self-employment.
- Not have investment income that exceeds $3,400 in 2016.
- Not file as MFS.
- Not be claimed as a dependent by another taxpayer.
- Be a U.S. citizen or legal resident all year (a nonresident alien married to a U.S. citizen or resident alien filing jointly can still qualify).

Qualifying Income for the EITC: Only earned income, such as wages, tips, union strike benefits, and net earnings from self-employment, qualifies for the EITC. For EITC purposes, "earned income" does not include the following income:

- Social Security benefits
- Workfare payments
- Alimony or child support
- Pensions or annuities
- Unemployment benefits
- Inmate wages, including amounts paid while in work release programs
- Income from investments, rental activities, or other passive sources.

Example: Malika earns $11,500 in wages during 2016. Her wages would qualify her for the Earned Income Tax Credit, but she also has $4,000 of investment income during the year, from a certificate of deposit that she inherited from her grandmother. A taxpayer with $3,400 or more of investment income in 2016 does not qualify for the EITC, regardless of her earnings. So Malika would not qualify for the EITC in 2016 due to her investment income.

Income that is excluded from tax is generally not considered earned income for the EITC. Nontaxable combat pay is an exception. A taxpayer can choose to include their nontaxable combat pay in their earned income if it gives them a better tax result.

Taxpayers without Qualifying Children

Low-income taxpayers without children may qualify for the EITC in certain cases, but the rules are stricter, and the amount of the credit is lower. A taxpayer with a qualifying child can claim the EITC without any age limitations, but a taxpayer *without* a child can only claim the EITC if all of the following tests are met:

---

[56] The IRS uses both terms. For consistency's sake, we refer to this credit as the Earned Income Tax Credit (EITC).

- Must be at least age 25 but under 65 at the end of the year (if married, either spouse can meet the age test)
- Must live in the United States for more than half the year
- Must not qualify as a dependent of another person
- Cannot file Form 2555 (related to foreign earned income exclusion[57])

Qualifying Children for EITC Purposes

The definition of a "qualifying child" for purposes of the EITC is stricter than it is for the dependency exemption. The taxpayer's qualifying child must meet <u>all</u> the following tests:

- **Relationship test**
- **Age test**
- **Joint return test**
- **Residency test**

Relationship Test: The child must be related to the taxpayer in one of the following ways:

- Son, daughter, stepchild, eligible foster child, adopted child, or descendant of any of them (for example, a grandchild), or
- Brother, sister, half-brother, half-sister, stepbrother, stepsister, or descendant of any of them (for example, a niece or nephew).

> **Example:** Rusty is 27 and supports his younger sister, Colleen, who is 16. He has taken care of her since their parents died five years ago. Colleen is Rusty's qualifying child for purposes of the Earned Income Tax Credit.

An adopted child is generally treated as the taxpayer's own child. However, special rules apply for foreign adoptions. Any qualifying child listed on Schedule EITC also must have a valid SSN. Since an ATIN is not sufficient, then a taxpayer with an ATIN is not a qualifying child for EITC purposes. A foster child must be placed in the taxpayer's home by an authorized placement agency or by court order in order to be eligible.

Age Test: To qualify for the EITC, the child must be:

- Age 18 or younger,
- A full-time student age 23 or younger, or
- Any age, if permanently disabled.

In addition, the qualifying child must be younger than the taxpayer claiming him, unless the child (dependent) is permanently disabled.

> **Example:** Garth, age 45, supports his older brother, Jeremiah, age 56. Jeremiah, who is mentally challenged and permanently disabled, lives with Garth. In this case, Jeremiah meets the criteria to be Garth's qualifying child for purposes of the EITC.

---

[57] A taxpayer who elects not to exclude foreign income from his gross income may still be eligible for the EITC.

Joint Return Test: The qualifying child (dependent) cannot file a joint return with a spouse, except to claim a refund.

> **Example:** Margaret's 18-year-old son and his 18-year-old wife had $800 of interest income and no other income. Neither is required to file a tax return. Taxes were taken out of their interest income due to backup withholding, so they file a joint return to get a refund of the taxes withheld. The exception to the joint return test applies, so Margaret's son may still be her qualifying child if all the other tests are met.

Residency Test: The child must have <u>lived with</u> the taxpayer in the United States for more than half the year. For purposes of the EITC, U.S. military personnel stationed outside the United States on extended active duty are considered to live in the U.S. during that duty period, so their children meet the residency test. This means that only a custodial parent can claim the EITC.

A child who was born or died during the year meets the residency test for the entire year if the child lived with the taxpayer the entire time he was alive in 2016.

> **Example:** Gwynne gave birth to a baby girl in March. The infant died one month later. The child is still a qualifying child for purposes of the EITC because she meets the other tests for age and relationship.

Earned Income and AGI Limits

Both the taxpayer's earned income and his adjusted gross income must be less than the following limits:

Filing Status	Qualifying Children Claimed			
	Zero	One	Two	Three or more
Single, HOH, or QW	$14,880	$39,296	$44,648	$47,955
MFJ*	$20,430	$44,846	$50,198	$53,505

*MFS filers do not qualify to take the EITC, so they are not listed on this table.

> **Example:** Graham is single and his AGI is $39,600. He has one qualifying child. Graham cannot claim the EITC because his AGI exceeds the income threshold for single filers with one child.

EITC Fraud and Penalties: If the IRS audits a taxpayer's return and disallows all or part of the EITC, the taxpayer:

- Must pay back the amount in error with interest;
- May need to file Form 8862, *Information to Claim Earned Income Credit after Disallowance*;
- Cannot claim the EITC for the next two years if the IRS determines the error is because of reckless or intentional disregard of the rules; or
- Cannot claim the EITC for the next ten years if the IRS determines the error is because of fraud.

Note: Paid tax preparers face significant due diligence requirements in preparing EITC claims for their clients. Preparers must use Form 8867, *Paid Preparer's Earned Income Credit Checklist,* to determine eligibility for every EITC claim, EVERY SINGLE YEAR. The four-page, five-part form is required for each client who is claiming the EITC each year. The preparer must attach the checklist to the tax return of any client who is claiming the EITC. A preparer who fails to meet his EITC due diligence requirements is subject to a preparer penalty per failure. Due diligence requirements for EITC claims are covered in more detail in Book 3, *Representation.*

Retirement Savings Contributions Credit

Qualified individuals are allowed a nonrefundable credit of up to $1,000 ($2,000 MFJ) for eligible contributions to an IRA or an employer-sponsored retirement plan. The amount of the credit is the eligible contribution multiplied by the applicable credit rate, which is based on filing status and AGI.

Note: On past exams, the IRS has also referred to this credit as the "Saver's Credit". Either term may be used on the EA exam, since both terms are currently used on the IRS website as well as IRS publications.

To be eligible for the Retirement Savings Contributions Credit, a taxpayer must be at least 18 years old and must not be a full-time student or be claimed as a dependent on another person's return. AGI for 2016 must not be more than:

- $61,500 for married filing jointly.
- $46,125 for head of household.
- $30,750 for single, married filing separately, or qualifying widow(er).

Example: Truman is 24 and earns $35,000 during the year. He is single and contributes $3,000 to his 401(k) plan at work. Truman is not eligible for the credit because his income exceeds the threshold limit for single filers.

Eligible contributions include those to both traditional IRAs and Roth IRAs, elective deferrals to 401(k) or other qualified employer-sponsored retirement plans, and voluntary employee contributions to other qualified retirement plans.

Most workers who contribute to traditional IRAs already deduct all or part of their contributions. The Saver's Credit is in addition to these deductions.

When figuring the credit, a taxpayer generally must subtract the amount of distributions received from his retirement plans, in the two years before the year the credit is claimed; the year the credit is claimed; and the period after the end of the credit year but before the due date, including extensions, for filing the return for the credit year.

The Saver's Credit amount can be as low as 10% or as high as 50% of a maximum annual contribution of $2,000 per person, depending on filing status and AGI.

Also note that foreign income cannot be included in the taxpayer's adjusted gross income for the purposes of calculating this credit.

Residential Energy Credits

A number of tax credits for residential energy efficiency expired at the end of 2016, but are still valid for the 2016 tax season. These tax credits apply to equipment purchases made in 2016.[58]

Residential Energy Efficiency Property Credit

This credit applies to solar, wind, geothermal and fuel-cell technology. A credit is available for property that is used in the taxpayer's principal residence and a second home. The credit for fuel-cell equipment only qualifies if it is installed in the taxpayer's main home. The credit is equal to 30% of the cost of the equipment, including installation. Rental properties do not qualify for this credit. The following property is included:

- Geothermal Heat Pumps
- Small Wind Turbines (Residential)
- Solar Energy Systems[59]
- Fuel Cells (Residential Fuel Cell and Micro-turbine Systems)

There is no maximum credit threshold for qualifying solar, wind, and geothermal equipment, but the maximum credit for fuel cells is $500 for each half-kilowatt of power capacity, or $1000 for each kilowatt.

Nonbusiness Energy Property Tax Credit

For this credit, only equipment and property that meets technical efficiency standards set by the Department of Energy qualifies. The credit is 10% of cost up to $500, or a specific amount from $50-$300. For this credit, the IRS distinguishes between two kinds of property. The first is "residential energy property costs." It includes:

- Stoves that use biomass fuel
- Air source heat pumps
- Air conditioning units
- Natural gas, propane or oil furnaces and fans
- Insulation
- Roofs
- Water heaters (non-solar)
- Windows, doors & skylights

The second type of property is referred to as "qualified energy efficiency improvements," and includes:

- Home insulation
- Exterior doors
- Exterior windows and skylights

---

[58] The tax credit for home solar Photovoltaics and water heating systems does not expire until 2021.
[59] The credit is not available for solar panels that are used exclusively to heat swimming pools or hot tubs.

- Certain roofing materials

This credit is extremely limited. It is a maximum of $500 for all years combined, from 2006 to the present. These credits to not apply to new construction or rental property. Of that $500 limit, a maximum of $200 can be allocated for energy-efficient windows. Energy credits are reported on Form 5695, *Residential Energy Credits*.

Unit 14: Study Questions

(Test yourself first, then check the correct answers at the end of this quiz.)

1. Gail's earned income from wages is $7,000 in 2016. She has interest income of $3,500. She is single and has a valid Social Security number. She does not have any dependents. Which of the following statements is correct?

A. Gail qualifies for the Earned Income Tax Credit.
B. Gail does not qualify for the Earned Income Tax Credit.
C. Gail qualifies for the Earned Income Tax Credit and the Child Tax Credit.
D. Gail qualifies for the Child Tax Credit.

2. Orlando is a university senior studying to be an optometrist. Which of the following expenses is a qualifying expense for the American Opportunity Tax Credit?

A. The rental of the vision equipment he is required to use to enroll in this program.
B. Student health fees.
C. Room and board.
D. A physical education course not related to his degree program.

3. Which of the following individuals could be a qualifying child for the Child Tax Credit?

A. An 18-year-old dependent who is a full-time student.
B. A six-year-old nephew who lived with the taxpayer for seven months.
C. A child actor who is 15 years old and provides over half of his own support.
D. A foster child who has lived with the taxpayer for four months.

4. Which of the following expenses is not a qualified expense for purposes of the Adoption Credit?

A. Court costs.
B. Re-adoption expenses to adopt a foreign child.
C. Attorney fees for a surrogate arrangement.
D. Travel expenses.

5. Beatrice has three dependent children, ages 10, 12, and 18, who live with her. Assuming she meets the other criteria, what is the maximum Child Tax Credit she can claim on her 2016 tax return?

A. $0
B. $1,000
C. $2,000
D. $3,000

6. Which of the following individuals is eligible for the American Opportunity Credit?

A. Garrett, who is enrolled full-time as a postgraduate student pursuing a master's degree in biology after having completed a four-year undergraduate degree.
B. Lucy, who is taking a ceramics class at a community college for fun.
C. Doug, who is a full-time undergraduate student and was convicted of a felony for distributing marijuana.
D. Beth, who is pursuing a degree in computer science degree and who attended classes the entire school year.

7. In 2016, John and Hannah adopt a special needs child who is completely disabled. Their adoption expenses are $7,000, and their travel expenses related to the adoption are $1,200. Their modified AGI for 2016 is $175,000. What is their maximum Adoption Credit in 2016?

A. $7,000
B. $8,200
C. $13,460
D. $0

8. Noah, 29, decides to go to college for the first time. Which of the following will disqualify him from taking the Lifetime Learning Credit?

A. Noah is not seeking a degree, and is only taking two courses to improve his job skills.
B. Noah is pursuing a graduate degree.
C. Noah is attending school less than half-time.
D. Noah is already claiming the tuition and fees deduction.

9. Rocco has three kids in college. They are all his dependents:

- Cosima, age 21, a college sophomore working on her first bachelor's degree
- Marico, age 19, a college freshman working on his first bachelor's degree
- Kasha, age 23, a graduate student, working on her first master's degree. Kasha had a four-year bachelor's degree from the same college

Based on the above scenario, what is the maximum amount in American Opportunity Credits (AOC) Rocco can claim on his tax return?

A. $2,500
B. $6,000
C. $5,000
D. $7,500

10. All of the listed expenses are deductible for the Lifetime Learning Credit except:

A. Required books.
B. On-campus childcare in order to attend class.
C. Tuition.
D. Required fees.

11. The American Opportunity Credit has a maximum credit of up to _____.

A. $2,500 credit per eligible student
B. $2,000 credit per eligible student
C. $2,500 credit per tax return
D. $4,000 credit per eligible student

12. Samira and Rishi are married and file jointly. Their daughter, Chetana, was enrolled full-time in college for all of 2016. Samira and Rishi obtained a loan in 2016 and used the proceeds to pay for Chetana's tuition and related fees for 2016. They repaid the loan in 2017. When will they be entitled to claim an education credit?

A. They cannot claim an education credit.
B. 2016.
C. 2017.
D. Either 2016 or 2017.

13. Edwin is a professional bookkeeper. He takes an accounting course at the local community college to improve his work-related skills. Edwin is not a degree candidate. Which educational credit does he qualify for?

A. The American Opportunity Credit.
B. The College Saver's Credit.
C. The Lifetime Learning Credit.
D. The General Education Credit.

14. To qualify for the Earned Income Tax Credit, which of the following statements is correct?

A. The taxpayer must have a dependent child.
B. The taxpayer must be a U.S. citizen or legal U.S. resident all year.
C. The taxpayer's filing status can be MFS or MFJ.
D. The taxpayer's only income can be from Social Security benefits.

15. Nina pays for daycare costs for the following individuals so she can work. Each is a qualifying individual for purposes of the Child and Dependent Care Credit except:

A. Nina's husband, who is totally disabled.
B. Nina's son, age 13, who is Nina's dependent.
C. Nina's nephew, age 12, who is also Nina's dependent.
D. Nina's niece, who is 35, lived with her all year and is completely disabled.

16. Zoe attends college full-time, pursuing an undergraduate degree in business. Because she changed majors in her junior year, she is now in her fifth year of college. She has a $4,000 Pell grant for 2016, and her parents have claimed the American Opportunity Credit for Zoe the past four years. What amount can they claim for the AOC in 2016 based upon the following expenses for Zoe?

Tuition	$15,000
Room and board	12,000
Required Student Health Fees	1,000

A. $0
B. $2,500
C. $2,000
D. $11,000

17. Vincent has two kids in graduate school. His wife, Olivia, also attends a doctorate program at a local university. Vincent and his wife file jointly. What is the maximum amount of the Lifetime Learning Credit that Vincent can claim on his 2016 return?

A. $2,000 per student (up to a maximum of $4,000 per tax return)
B. $2,500 per student.
C. $6,000 maximum ($2,000 per qualifying student).
D. $2,000 per tax return.

18. For purposes of the EITC, the following type of income is considered earned income:

A. Alimony.
B. Interest and dividends.
C. Capital gains
D. Household employee income reported on Form W-2.

19. Generally, which is most beneficial to taxpayers when it comes to reducing income tax liability: a nonrefundable credit, a refundable credit, or a deduction?

A. A nonrefundable credit.
B. A refundable credit.
C. A deduction.
D. All are equally beneficial in reducing income tax liability.

20. Which of the following education tax benefits listed below is refundable?

A. The Tuition and Fees Deduction
B. The American Opportunity Credit
C. The Lifetime Learning Credit
D. Student Loan Interest Deduction

21. Couples who file jointly may be eligible to claim up to _____ per year for contributions to an IRA under the Retirement Savings Contributions Credit?

A. $500
B. $1,000
C. $2,000
D. $5,000

22. Which of the following filing conditions would prevent an individual from qualifying for the Earned Income Tax Credit?

A. MFS filing status.
B. A taxpayer with nontaxable combat pay.
C. Investment income of $3,100.
D. A taxpayer who is 68 years old with one qualifying child.

23. All of the following are qualified expenses for purposes of the Child and Dependent Care Credit except:

A. A $500 payment to a grandparent for child care while the taxpayer is employed.
B. A $300 payment to a daycare center while the taxpayer is looking for employment.
C. A $500 child care expense while the taxpayer obtains medical care.
D. A $600 adult daycare expense for a disabled spouse while the taxpayer works.

24. Orrin was audited in 2016, and the IRS determined that he claimed the Earned Income Tax Credit erroneously due to reckless disregard of the EITC rules. For how many years is Orrin prohibited from claiming the EITC?

A. None.
B. Two years.
C. Five years.
D. Ten years.

25. Which of the following statements is correct regarding a paid preparer's EITC due diligence requirements?

A. He is subject to a $50 penalty for each failure to meet his due diligence requirements.
B. He is required to complete Form 8867, the EITC checklist, for every client who is claiming the Earned Income Tax Credit. The preparer must retain a copy for his records and make it available to the IRS upon request.
C. He is required to complete and attach Form 8867, the EITC checklist, to the tax return of every client who is claiming the Earned Income Tax Credit.
D. He is required to complete and attach Form 8867, the EITC checklist, to the tax return of every client, regardless of whether the taxpayer is claiming the Earned Income Tax Credit.

26. Which of the following credits are refundable for 2016?

A. Lifetime Learning Credit.
B. The Residential Energy Credit.
C. The Additional Child Tax Credit.
D. The Dependent Care Credit.

27. Scott is 43 and unmarried. Scott's half-brother, Alexander, turned 16 on December 30, 2016. Alexander lived with Scott all year, and he is a U.S. citizen. Scott claimed Alexander as a dependent on his return. Which of the following statements is correct?

A. Alexander is a qualifying child for the Child Tax Credit.
B. Alexander is not a qualifying child for the Child Tax Credit because he is too old to be eligible.
C. Alexander is not a qualifying child for the Child Tax Credit because siblings do not qualify.
D. Alexander only qualifies for the Child Tax Credit if he is a full-time student.

Unit 14: Answers

1. The answer is B. Gail does not qualify for the Earned Income Tax Credit because her investment income exceeds $3,400 in 2016. She does not qualify for the Child Tax Credit because she does not have a qualifying child.

2. The answer is A. Because Orlando's equipment rental fee must be paid to the university as a condition for enrollment, it is considered a qualified related expense. For AOTC purposes, "qualified education expenses" do not include insurance or medical expenses (such as student health fees), room and board, transportation, or similar personal, living, or family expenses, or any course of instruction or other education involving sports, games, or hobbies, unless the course is part of the student's degree program.

3. The answer is B. A nephew who lived with the taxpayer for seven months may qualify. In order to qualify for the Child Tax Credit, the taxpayer must have a qualifying child who lived with him for more than six months and who is under the age of 17. The child cannot have provided more than half of his own support.

4. The answer is C. Expenses related to a surrogate arrangement are not a qualified adoption expense. Qualified adoption expenses are expenses directly related to the legal adoption of an eligible child. These expenses include adoption fees, court costs, attorney fees, travel expenses (including amounts spent for meals and lodging) while away from home, and re-adoption expenses to adopt a foreign child.

5. The answer is C. Beatrice can claim $2,000 as a maximum credit, or $1,000 for each qualifying child. For purposes of this credit, she only has two qualifying children, because one of her dependents is already over 17 and therefore no longer eligible for the credit.

6. The answer is D. Beth is eligible for the American Opportunity Credit because she is pursuing a degree and is enrolled at least half-time for at least one academic period during 2016. Courses that do not lead to a degree, certificate or other recognized credential do not qualify for the AOC. Students with felony drug convictions are ineligible for this credit.

7. The answer is C. John and Hannah can take the full Adoption Credit of $13,460 in 2016 because they adopted a special needs child. Under a special rule for taxpayers who adopt special needs children, the maximum Adoption Credit is allowed, even if the taxpayer has a lesser amount of adoption expenses.

8. The answer is D. A taxpayer cannot take an education credit and the tuition and fees deduction for the same student.

9. The answer is C. The American Opportunity Tax Credit is worth up to $2,500 per student. Rocco can potentially claim $5,000 in AOC credits on his tax return ($2,500 each for Cosima and Marico). Cosima and Marico would be qualifying students for AOC purposes because they are working on their first undergraduate degree. Kasha would not qualify, because she is working on a graduate degree after having completed a four-year undergraduate degree. The American Opportunity Credit is only available for four years of postsecondary school.

10. The answer is B. Child care is not a qualifying education expense, even if the child care is offered on-campus. For purposes of the Lifetime Learning Credit, qualified education expenses are tuition and certain related expenses required for enrollment or attendance at an eligible educational institution.

11. The answer is A. The American Opportunity Tax Credit is worth up to $2,500 per eligible student. The maximum credit equals 100% of the first $2,000 and 25% of the next $2,000 of qualified expenses.

12. The answer is B. Samira and Rishi are eligible to claim an education credit for 2016. The credit should be claimed for the year in which the taxpayer paid the expenses, not the year in which the loan is repaid.

13. The answer is C. Edwin qualifies for the Lifetime Learning Credit. He does not qualify for the American Opportunity Credit because he is not a degree candidate and because his course does not meet the requirements. The "College Saver's Credit" and the "General Education Credit" do not exist.

14. The answer is B. The taxpayer must be a U.S. citizen or legal resident all year. A taxpayer cannot claim the EITC if his filing status is MFS. Taxpayers do not need to have a dependent child in order to qualify for the Earned Income Tax Credit. However, the amount of the credit is greatly increased if the taxpayer has a qualifying child. A taxpayer must have earned income to qualify for the EITC; Social Security benefits do not qualify.

15. The answer is B. Nina's son does not qualify because he is over the age limit for the credit. To qualify for the Child and Dependent Care Credit, the dependent must be *under* the age of 13 or completely disabled.

16. The answer is A. Zoe does not qualify for the AOC because she is in her fifth year of college and her parents have already claimed the credit the prior four years. If she had been eligible for the credit, she would have had $11,000 of qualifying expenses. Room and board and student health fees are not qualifying expenses for the AOC, and the qualifying tuition cost must be reduced by any tax-free scholarships, such as the Pell grant. The AOC is a maximum credit of $2,500 per student (100% of the first $2,000 of eligible expenses and 25% of the next $2,000). Zoe qualifies for the Lifetime Learning Credit.

17. The answer is D. The maximum credit is $2,000 per tax return. The credit is allowed for 20% of the first $10,000 of qualified tuition and fees paid during the year. The credit is per tax return, not per student, so only a maximum of $2,000 can be claimed each year, no matter how many qualifying students a taxpayer may have.

18. The answer is D. Household employee income is considered earned income because it is a type of wages. Alimony, workfare payments, and interest and dividends are not considered earned income for purposes of the EITC.

19. The answer is B. A refundable credit, such as the Earned Income Tax Credit, is not limited by an individual's tax liability. The taxpayer can receive a refund even if he has zero tax liability.

20. The answer is B. Up to 40% of the American Opportunity Credit (up to $1,000) is refundable, meaning that the taxpayer can receive a refund even if they have zero tax liability.

21. The answer is C. Married couples who file jointly are allowed a nonrefundable credit of up to $2,000 for eligible contributions to an IRA or an employer-sponsored retirement plan. The credit is $1,000 per year for single filers.

22. The answer is A. Taxpayers cannot claim the EITC if they file Married Filing Separately. All the other choices would not disqualify a taxpayer from claiming EITC. Combat pay is considered qualifying income for EITC purposes. The investment income threshold for EITC in 2016 is $3,400. A taxpayer who is 68 years old may be eligible for EITC if they have a qualifying child.

23. The answer is C. Child care costs to obtain medical care are not a deductible expense. Deductible costs must be work-related and for a child under 13, a disabled dependent, or a disabled spouse of any age. Child care costs incurred so that the taxpayer can volunteer, obtain medical care, run errands, or do other personal businesses do not qualify.

24. The answer is B. Orrin cannot claim the EITC for two tax years. There are restrictions on EITC claims by taxpayers for whom a previous claim was denied or reduced due to any reason other than a math or clerical error. If a taxpayer was determined to have claimed the EITC due to reckless or intentional disregard of the EITC rules, he cannot claim the EITC for two tax years. If the error was due to fraud, the taxpayer cannot claim the EITC for ten tax years.

25. The answer is C. As part of his due diligence requirements, a paid preparer must complete and attach Form 8867, *Paid Preparer's Earned Income Credit Checklist*, to the tax return of every client who is claiming the EITC. The checklist is a four-page form with questions the preparer must ask to determine client eligibility for the credit. A preparer faces a $500 fine for each failure to meet the EITC due diligence standards.

26. The answer is C. The Additional Child Tax Credit is refundable, meaning it can result in a refund even if a taxpayer does not owe tax.

27. The answer is A. Alexander is a qualifying child for the Child Tax Credit because he was under age 17 at the end of 2016. Siblings can be qualifying children for purposes of this credit, and half-siblings are treated the same as full siblings for tax purposes.

Unit 15: Affordable Care Act Tax Provisions for Individuals

> **For additional information read:**
> Publication 5187, *Health Care Law: What's New for Individuals & Families*
> Publication 974, *Premium Tax Credit*

The Affordable Care Act (ACA)[60] contains over 20 new taxes or tax increases that are, (or will be), administered by the IRS. The law requires most U.S. citizens and residents to have qualifying health insurance or to pay a penalty for not doing so. In recent years, a universal mandate, known as the *individual shared responsibility provision*, took effect.

> **Note:** In this unit, we provide an overview of the key ACA tax provisions you should understand for the EA exam. The ACA is extremely complex, and its provisions affect taxpayers in many different ways depending upon their individual situations. Parts of the ACA remain unsettled, with judicial and congressional challenges to some provisions and executive branch delays to others.[61]

Large employers also have annual reporting responsibilities concerning what health insurance they offered to their full-time employees. In this book, we will cover the ACA from the taxpayer's perspective. The ACA from the employer's perspective is covered in detail in Book 2, *Businesses*.

Important Forms for the ACA

In order to simplify reporting, the IRS has created a new group of forms to help handle some of the requirements of the ACA. If the taxpayer is covered by health insurance, he will most likely receive one of the forms listed below. The taxpayer must use the information from these statements when preparing his taxes. The forms are provided to different groups of people.

- **Form 1095-A**, *Health Insurance Marketplace Statement:* This form is for individuals who enroll in Marketplace[62] coverage. This form reports basic information about the insurance company that issued the taxpayer's policy, the exchange where he enrolled, and document coverage for each month.
- **Form 1095-B,** *Health Coverage:* This is for people whose insurance comes from a source other than the Marketplace.
- **Form 1095-C,** *Employer-Provided Health Insurance Offer and Coverage*: Individuals who work for applicable large employers will get this form (employees will also get this form if they enroll in self-insured coverage provided by an applicable large employer).

---

[60] Although commonly known as Obamacare, the actual name of the health care law is the "Patient Protection and Affordable Care Act," often shortened to the Affordable Care Act or ACA.

[61] In January, 2017, U.S. Senate approved a budget resolution that sets the stage for broad swaths of the Affordable Care Act to be repealed. At the time of this book's printing, no formal repeal of the ACA has yet taken place, although changes to the law are expected for 2017.

[62] The "Marketplace", also called the "Health Insurance Marketplace," is an online resource where taxpayers can learn about their health coverage options, compare health insurance plans based on costs, choose a plan, and enroll in coverage. In some states (such as California and New York), the Marketplace is run by the state government. In others, it is run by the federal government.

In December 2016, the IRS issued a notice delaying the reporting requirement for Forms 1095.[63] The due date for furnishing to individuals the 2016 Form 1095-B, *Health Coverage,* was extended from January 31, 2017, to March 2, 2017. [64]

The due date for furnishing to individuals the 2016 Form 1095-C, *Employer-Provided Health Insurance Offer and Coverage,* has changed from January 31, 2017, to March 2, 2017.

Some taxpayers will receive multiple forms in the same year. For example, if a taxpayer purchased health insurance through the Marketplace and then started a new job in the middle of the year that offered health coverage, depending on how the taxpayer's employer-sponsored insurance is set up, he may receive both Forms 1095-B and 1095-C on a single, combined form.

Minimum Essential Coverage

Under the Affordable Care Act, each individual must have qualifying health care coverage, known as *minimum essential coverage*, for each month of the year. This requirement applies to individuals of all ages. Coverage that qualifies includes:

- Employer-sponsored coverage, including self-insured plans, COBRA, and retiree coverage
- Coverage purchased in either federal or state health insurance Marketplaces (also known as exchanges)
- Medicare Part A and Medicare Advantage plans
- Most Medicaid coverage
- Certain types of veterans health coverage and most types of TRICARE coverage

Coverage that provides only limited benefits generally does not qualify as minimum essential coverage. For example, this includes stand-alone dental and vision insurance plans, accident or disability income insurance plans, worker's compensation insurance, and Medicaid family planning services.

An estimated three-quarters of taxpayers have qualifying health care coverage in 2016. They must self-report their coverage by checking the box on page 2 of Form 1040. Taxpayers are not required to send in proof of health care coverage to the IRS when filing their tax returns.

> **Example:** Rosalia, age 58, had health insurance through her employer for every month of 2016. Her husband, Benito, age 67, had Medicare coverage for all of 2016. On their joint return, they check the box attesting that they had full-year insurance coverage. They have fulfilled their "shared responsibility" of the Affordable Care Act, and will not owe a penalty to the IRS.

Health Coverage Exemptions

There are multiple coverage exemptions that will excuse an individual from the requirement to have minimum essential health insurance coverage. A taxpayer must apply to the Health Insurance Marketplace for certain types of exemptions. If an exemption is approved by the Health Insurance

---

[63] IRS Notice 2016-70

[64] The due date for filing with the IRS the 2016 Form 1094-B, *Transmittal of Health Coverage Information Returns,* and Form 1095-B, *Health Coverage,* remains unchanged. The due date is February 28, 2017; if filing electronically, the due date is March 31, 2017.

Marketplace, the taxpayer will receive an *exemption certificate number* (ECN), which must be entered into most software programs in order to e-file.

Form 8965, *Health Coverage Exemptions*, is the form used for reporting ACA Exemptions. Below are all health coverage exemptions for the 2016 tax year.

Income-Related Exemptions

- **Affordability exception:** Taxpayers who do not have access to coverage considered affordable based on their projected household income may be exempt from paying penalties. In this case, if the lowest-priced coverage available to the taxpayer, either through a Marketplace or job-based plan, would exceed 8.13% of household income in 2016, then the taxpayer is exempted from the penalty.
- **No filing requirement:** If the taxpayer doesn't have to file a tax return because his income is below the filing requirement, then he is exempted from the penalty.

Health Coverage-Related Exemptions

- **Short-Term Coverage Gap:** The taxpayer was uninsured for less than three consecutive months of the year. A taxpayer with a coverage gap of <u>3 months or more </u>is not exempt for any of those months.
- **State Did Not Expand Medicaid:** The taxpayer lived in a state that didn't expand its Medicaid program, but the taxpayer would have qualified if it had. In order to qualify for this exemption, the taxpayer would need to provide a copy of his Medicaid denial of eligibility notice.

> **Example:** Andres was covered by Medicaid until April 23, 2016. He started a new job, and his employer-sponsored health coverage started on June 1, 2016. Andres is eligible for the short coverage gap exemption because he was without coverage for less than three months.

Group Membership Exemptions

- **Recognized Tribe:** The taxpayer is a member of a federally-recognized tribe or eligible for services through an Indian Health Services provider.
- **Health Sharing Ministries:** The taxpayer is a member of a recognized health care sharing ministry.
- **Religious Objections:** The taxpayer is a member of a recognized religious sect with religious objections to insurance, including Social Security and Medicare.

Other Allowable Exemptions

- **Incarceration:** Taxpayers who are in jail, prison, or another correctional facility.
- **Citizens Living Abroad/Some Noncitizens:**
  - U.S. citizens or residents who spent at least 330 days outside of the U.S. during a 12-month period.
  - U.S. citizens who are bona fide residents of a foreign country

- Certain resident aliens who are citizens of a foreign country that has an income tax treaty with the U.S.
- Taxpayers who are not legally present in the U.S. (undocumented aliens)
- **Acceptable Hardships:** If the taxpayer experienced one of these listed hardships an exemption may potentially be granted:
  - The taxpayer was homeless.
  - The taxpayer was evicted or was facing eviction or foreclosure.
  - The taxpayer received a shut-off notice from a utility company.
  - The taxpayer experienced domestic violence.
  - The taxpayer experienced the death of a close family member.
  - The taxpayer experienced a fire, flood, or other natural or human-caused disaster that caused substantial damage to his property.
  - The taxpayer filed for bankruptcy.
  - The taxpayer had medical expenses that resulted in substantial debt.
  - The taxpayer experienced unexpected increases in necessary expenses due to caring for an ill, disabled, or aging family member.
  - The taxpayer expects to claim as a dependent a child who has been denied coverage for Medicaid, and another person is required by court order to give medical support to the child. In this case, the taxpayer doesn't have to pay the penalty for the child.
  - As a result of an eligibility appeals decision, a taxpayer is eligible for enrollment in a qualified health plan (QHP) through the Marketplace, lower costs on his monthly premiums, or cost-sharing reductions for a time period when he was not enrolled in health insurance through the Marketplace.
  - The taxpayer's individual insurance plan was cancelled during the year, and the taxpayer believes that other Marketplace plans are unaffordable.

Example: Jody is single. Her gross income for 2016 was $9,800. She did not purchase health insurance, but she is exempt from the individual shared responsibility provision because her income is below the filing threshold for filing a return. She does not file a tax return, and she is not required to file Form 8965 since she is automatically exempt from the penalty.

Example: Jonathan and his four children live in Wyoming, a state that did not expand Medicaid under ACA. Their household income is below 138% of the federal poverty line. They do not have qualified health coverage. When Jonathan files his tax return, he attaches Form 8965 and claims an exemption to the individual shared responsibility provision. Jonathan will not owe a penalty for failing to have minimum essential coverage.

Note: There's no "hardship" exemption based only on employment status. So if a taxpayer becomes unemployed during the year, that in itself is not considered a valid hardship. However, several exemptions apply to people with low income.

Penalties: The Shared Responsibility Payment

If a taxpayer (or any of his dependents) does not have minimum essential coverage for each month of the year and does not qualify for an exemption, he will face a penalty called the *shared responsibility payment* (SRP) when he files his tax return.[65]

> **Example:** Cory and Maryanne are married and have two dependent children under age 18. For half of the year, no member of their family had minimum essential coverage, and no one qualified for an exemption. Cory and Maryanne must calculate the shared responsibility payment for the six months of the year they did not have qualified health coverage.

For 2016, the annual Shared Responsibility Payment is the *greater* of:

- 2.5% of household income, or
- $695 per adult and $347.50 per child, up to a family maximum of $2,085.

The maximum penalty in 2016 is $2,085 per family. The Shared Responsibility Payment is capped at the national average premium for a bronze-level qualified health plan available through the Marketplace that would cover everyone in the tax household who does not have coverage or qualify for an exemption.

A taxpayer calculates the amount due for the shared responsibility payment by using the instructions to Form 8965. The payment is reported on page 2 of Form 1040 in the "other taxes" section.

> **Note:** The IRS is specifically prohibited from using enforcement actions such as liens and levies to collect an SRP that a taxpayer does not pay. However, if a taxpayer is due a refund, the IRS may offset the liability by subtracting the SRP amount from his current or future refund.

Premium Tax Credit

The Premium Tax Credit is a new refundable federal tax credit to help eligible taxpayers pay for health insurance premiums. The credit is based on a taxpayer's income and is only available for taxpayers who purchased their insurance through a federal or state exchange. The amount of the Premium Tax Credit is based on a sliding scale, so the higher the household income, the lower the amount of the credit. To be eligible for a Premium Tax Credit, a taxpayer must generally meet all of the following requirements:

- Purchase health insurance through the Marketplace.
- Be a U.S. citizen or legal U.S. resident.
- Be unable to get coverage from an employer or the government.

---

[65] On Jan. 20, 2017, an executive order signed by newly elected president Donald Trump directed federal agencies to exercise authority and discretion available to them to reduce potential burden of the ACA. On February 15, 2017, the IRS released the following statement regarding the Annual Shared Responsibility Payment: *"The IRS is currently reviewing the Jan. 20, 2017, executive order to determine the implications. Taxpayers should continue to file their tax returns as they normally would."* On February 3, 2017, the IRS disabled the e-file error related to the Annual Shared Responsibility Payment and will currently not reject an e-filed return that leaves the box unchecked or otherwise does not have either the appropriate penalty computed on Line 61 or have an exemption included with the return. At the time of this book's printing, the current legislative provisions of the ACA law are still in force, and taxpayers remain required to follow the law and pay what they may owe.

- Not be claimed as a dependent on anyone else's tax return.
- If married, the couple must generally file a joint tax return.[66] In general, taxpayers who file separate returns will not qualify for the credit.
- The taxpayer must meet certain household income requirements. Household income must be at least 100%, but not more than 400%, of the federal poverty line for the family size. For purposes of the Premium Tax Credit, a taxpayer's household income is the total of the taxpayer's modified adjusted gross income (MAGI), the taxpayer's spouse's MAGI (if filing jointly) and the MAGI of all dependents required to file a federal income tax return.

> **Example:** Don and Luna are married and file jointly. They have two dependent children. Luna works part-time and does not receive health insurance through her employer. Don was unemployed for several months during 2016 before starting a new job in April. His employer-sponsored health insurance started May 1, 2016. From January through April, the family purchased health insurance through the federal exchange. Assuming they meet the income guidelines, Don and Luna can claim the Premium Tax Credit for the four months that they had Marketplace coverage.

Advance Premium Tax Credit Payments

When a taxpayer first applies for a Marketplace plan, the amount of the credit is estimated using information the taxpayer provides about family size and projected household income. Since it can be difficult to know exactly how much income a taxpayer will earn in a given year and family circumstances can change during the year, the actual amount of the credit can vary from the estimated amount.

When enrolling in a plan, a taxpayer must choose whether to have some or all of the benefit of the expected credit paid in advance to his insurance company or wait to claim all of the benefits on his tax return. A taxpayer who chose advance credit payments must file a tax return, regardless of whether he meets any other filing requirements, in order to reconcile the advance credit payments with the actual Premium Tax Credit earned. This reconciliation is calculated on Form 8962. If the credit allowed is less than the advance credit payments received, normally the difference will be subtracted from the taxpayer's refund or added to his balance due.

> **Example:** Antoine is self-employed, and his income varies from year to year. When he enrolled in a health insurance plan through his state exchange, he estimated his 2016 earnings based on his prior year income. He learned he was eligible for the Premium Tax Credit, which he chose to take in full as advance credit payments. Antoine's business did well in 2016, and he made substantially more money than he expected, meaning his actual household income did not meet the guidelines for the Premium Tax Credit. He reconciles the advance credit payment amounts on Form 8962 and discovers he received a benefit of $1,000 in payments for which he is no longer eligible. Antoine is not owed a refund, so he must enter $1,000 on the excess advance premium tax credit repayment line of his Form 1040. That amount is added to his overall tax liability.

---

[66] In the case of married taxpayers who file separately, certain eligibility exceptions to the Premium Tax Credit apply, such as for domestic abuse or spousal abandonment.

Note: The Premium Tax Credit is refundable. If the amount of the credit is more than the amount of the tax liability of the return, a taxpayer may receive the difference as a refund. If no tax is owed, a taxpayer can receive the full amount of the credit as a refund.

Changes in family size due to marriage, divorce, birth, or adoption can affect the amount of the credit.

A taxpayer is supposed to report changes in circumstances to the Marketplace so the amount of the advance credit payments can be recalculated during the year. A taxpayer should also report changes in eligibility for government-sponsored or employee-sponsored health coverage, a move to a new address, an increase or decrease in the number of dependents, and other factors that may affect eligibility for the Premium Tax Credit.

Although the IRS is restricted in its ability to collect the shared responsibility payment, the agency may use full collection actions, including levies and liens, against a taxpayer who does not repay excess advance premium tax credits.

Net Investment Income Tax (NIIT)

The Affordable Care Act imposes a net investment income tax on higher-income taxpayers; it applies to individuals, estates, and trusts.[67] For individuals, a 3.8% tax is imposed on the lesser of:

- The individual's net investment income for the year, or
- Any excess of the individual's modified adjusted gross income for the tax year over the following thresholds:

Filing Status	Threshold Amount
MFJ or QW	$250,000
MFS	$125,000
Single or HOH	$200,000

These threshold amounts are not indexed for inflation. The NIIT is imposed only on U.S. citizens and resident aliens; nonresident aliens are not subject to the NIIT. Net investment income that is subject to the tax includes:

- Interest, unless it is otherwise tax-exempt
- Dividends
- Capital gains
- Rental and royalty income
- Non-qualified annuities
- Income from businesses involved in trading of financial instruments or commodities
- Income from businesses that are passive activities for the taxpayer

---

[67] The net investment income tax first went into effect in 2013.

Net investment income does not include wages, self-employment income, Social Security benefits, veterans' benefits, unemployment compensation, alimony payments, or distributions from IRAs or certain qualified retirement plans.

The NIIT does not apply to any gains excluded from gross income for regular income tax purposes. Additionally, net investment income does not include any gain on the sale of a personal residence excluded from gross income (Section 121 exclusion).

Example: Trey is single and earned a salary of $175,000 in 2016. He also had $15,000 of income from dividends and capital gains, for MAGI of $190,000. This amount is less than the $200,000 threshold for single filers, so Trey is not subject to the Net Investment Income Tax.

Example: Leanna is single and earned a salary of $175,000 in 2016. She also received $80,000 of dividend income, for a total MAGI of $255,000, which exceeds the threshold for single filers by $55,000. The Net Investment Income Tax is based on the lesser of $55,000 (the amount by which her MAGI exceeds the threshold for single filers) or $80,000 (her "net investment income"). Leanne owes NIIT of $2,090 ($55,000 × 3.8% = $2,090).

To the extent that gains are not otherwise offset by capital losses, the following are common examples of items included in computing net investment income:

- Gains from the sale of stocks, bonds, and mutual funds
- Capital gain distributions from mutual funds
- Gains from the sale of investment real estate
- Gains from the sale of interests in partnerships and S corporations, to the extent the partner or shareholder was a passive owner

---

Example: Reza and Zari are married and file jointly. They sell the main home that they have lived in for five years for $1.8 million and realize a gain of $850,000 on the sale. They may exclude $500,000 under section 121, so their gain subject to regular income tax is $350,000. They also have $75,000 of net investment income from other sources, for a total of $425,000. Their MAGI is $525,000, which exceeds the MFJ threshold amount of $250,000 by $275,000. They are subject to the NIIT on the lesser of $425,000 (NII) or $275,000 (the amount of excess MAGI). Reza and Zari owe NIIT of $10,450 ($275,000 × 3.8% = $10,450).

A gain from the sale of a second home that is not a primary residence would not be eligible for section 121 exclusion and therefore would be fully subject to the NIIT. Federal income tax credits generally may be used to offset net investment income.

Investment interest expense, investment advisory and brokerage fees, expenses related to rental and royalty income, and tax preparation fees can also be deducted to determine gross investment income, which is used to arrive at net investment income.

The NIIT is subject to estimated tax provisions, so taxpayers may need to adjust their withholding or estimated payments to avoid underpayment penalties. Employers are not required to withhold the tax from an employee's wages. The tax is computed on Form 8960, *Net Investment Tax: Individuals, Estates, and Trusts.*

ACA Due Diligence for Tax Return Preparers

A preparer is expected to resolve conflicting or contradictory statements from his clients during the return preparation process, as he does with other tax issues.

A preparer must ask if the client had minimum essential coverage for each month of the year. If a client had insurance through the Marketplace, he should have a Form 1095-A for the preparer to review in order to complete Form 8962.

In 2016, some clients may not have Form 1095-B or 1095-C for the preparer to verify minimum essential coverage. They may also receive these forms late in the tax year. If a client states that he had qualifying health coverage through an employer or through another qualifying plan, the preparer may ask to see an insurance card, insurance contract, or other documentation.

As part of his Affordable Care Act due diligence, a preparer should follow these general principles that apply to tax return preparation in general. A preparer:

- May rely in good faith without verification of information that a client provides.
- Should not ignore the implications of the information.
- Should make reasonable inquiries if the information appears to be incorrect, inconsistent, or incomplete.

To comply with the ACA tax requirements, some preparers may request that their clients fill out a worksheet or provide other written documentation regarding minimum essential coverage, eligibility for exemptions, and other provisions.

Additional Medicare Tax

The Affordable Care Act imposes an additional Medicare tax[68] of 0.9% that applies to a taxpayer's earned income. An employer is required to withhold the additional Medicare tax if an employee is paid more than $200,000, regardless of an employee's filing status or whether the employee has wages paid by another employer. There is no employer share of the additional Medicare tax. Self-employed taxpayers cannot deduct one-half of the 0.9% additional Medicare tax. The additional Medicare tax is computed on Form 8959, *Additional Medicare Tax.*

The tax is assessed on earned income in excess of the following thresholds:

Filing Status	Threshold Amount
MFJ	$250,000
MFS	$125,000
Single, HOH, or QW	$200,000

The thresholds are not adjusted for inflation. A taxpayer's earned income (including wages, taxable fringe benefits, bonuses, tips, commissions, and self-employment income) that is subject to regular Medicare tax is also subject to the additional Medicare tax to the extent it exceeds the applicable threshold amount for his filing status.

---

[68] The additional Medicare tax first went into effect in 2013.

Example: Norma is single. She earns $350,000 in wages during 2016. The additional 0.9% tax will be calculated on her earnings above $200,000. This means that $150,000 will be subject to additional Medicare tax ($350,000 wages - $200,000 threshold amount). She will pay $1,350 in additional Medicare tax on her 2016 tax return ($150,000 x 0.9% = $1,350). This additional tax is withheld from Norma's wages automatically by her employer.

A taxpayer may be subject to the additional Medicare tax even if amounts are not withheld from his wages.

Example: Steven is single and earned $145,000 of salary in 2016. Because his earnings are below the $200,000 threshold for single filers, his company did not withhold any amount for the additional Medicare tax. He also had $85,000 of self-employment income from selling custom watercolor paintings he created. Steven's total earned income is $230,000. He would be required to pay additional Medicare tax on the $30,000 of earned income that exceeds the $200,000 threshold. Steven would owe $270 in additional Medicare tax on his 2016 income tax return ($30,000 × 0.9% = $270). He must calculate the tax and attach Form 8959, *Additional Medicare Tax*, to his tax return.

Example: Steven gets married on December 31, 2016, to Elaine, who earned wages of $7,000 during the year. Because they are married as of the last day of the year and file jointly, their threshold for the additional Medicare tax is $250,000. Their combined earned income is $237,000, below the $250,000 threshold for MFJ. Steven and Elaine do not owe the additional Medicare Tax.

If an employer withholds amounts for an employee who earns more than $200,000, but the employee and his spouse's combined earnings are less than the $250,000 MFJ threshold, they can apply the overpayment against any other type of tax that may be owed on their income tax return.

Example: Quan and Kim are married and file jointly. Quan earned $120,000 of salary in 2016, and Kim earned $190,000. Their employers do not withhold amounts for the additional Medicare tax because neither has earnings above $200,000. However, their combined earned income is $310,000, which is above the $250,000 threshold for joint filers by $60,000. Quan and Kim will owe $540 of additional Medicare tax on their 2016 income tax return ($60,000 × 0.9% = $540). They must calculate the tax and attach Form 8959, *Additional Medicare Tax*, to their tax return.

Unit 15: Study Questions

(Test yourself first, then check the correct answers at the end of this quiz.)

1. Laverne had Minimum Essential Coverage (MEC) all year. On which form would she report her qualifying coverage?

A. Form 1040, Other Taxes.
B. Form 8965.
C. Form 1095-A.
D. Form 1095-B.

2. Terry and Lulu are married but choose to file separately because of Terry's past-due child support. Their household income for 2016 is at 200% of the federal poverty line. They enroll in the federal Marketplace for health coverage, which they had for 2016. Which of the following statements is correct?

A. They are not eligible for the Premium Tax Credit because their household income is too high.
B. They are not eligible for the Premium Tax Credit because of their filing status.
C. They are not eligible for the Premium Tax Credit and will owe a shared responsibility payment.
D. They are eligible for the Premium Tax Credit.

3. Which of the following taxpayers would be subject to the additional Medicare tax in 2016?

A. Randy, who files as HOH and earned $180,000 of wages and $50,000 of investment income.
B. Kerrie, who is single and earned $196,000 of compensation, fringe benefits, and bonuses.
C. Liz, who files separately from her husband and earned $140,000 of wages.
D. None of the above.

4. Which of the following taxpayers would not be subject to the net investment income tax (NIIT)?

A. An estate.
B. A nonresident alien.
C. A trust.
D. An individual with only rental income in 2016.

5. In 2016, Suzanne had health insurance through her employer for every month of the year. She does not receive Form 1095-B from her employer. All of the following statements are correct except:

A. Suzanne must attach proof of her insurance coverage when she files her income tax return.
B. Suzanne will not owe the individual shared responsibility payment.
C. Suzanne's employer is required to provide Form 1095-B to employees by March 31.
D. Suzanne is not eligible for the Premium Tax Credit.

6. Which of the following individuals would be eligible for the Premium Tax Credit, assuming he met applicable income guidelines?

A. A taxpayer who had minimum essential coverage through his employer.
B. A taxpayer who was enrolled for two months through the federal Marketplace.
C. A taxpayer who received Medicaid coverage for 12 months of the year.
D. All of the above are eligible for the PTC.

7. The additional Medicare tax is:

A. 0.9% on a taxpayer's earned income above a certain threshold.
B. 3.8% on a taxpayer's earned income above a certain threshold.
C. 0.9% on a taxpayer's investment income above a certain threshold.
D. 3.8% on a taxpayer's investment income above a certain threshold.

8. Which of the following does not qualify as minimum essential coverage under the Affordable Care Act?

A. COBRA.
B. Coverage purchased through a state Marketplace.
C. Medicare
D. Worker's compensation insurance.

9. Milka is single. She has the following income in 2016:

- $73,000 interest income
- $200,000 gain from selling her main home that she had lived in and owned for seven years
- $245,000 MAGI

Calculate Milka's net investment income tax, if any, for 2016:

A. $0
B. $1,710
C. $2,774
D. $10,374

10. The Premium Tax Credit is:

A. Nonrefundable.
B. Refundable.
C. Available to all taxpayers with essential minimum coverage.
D. Available to all taxpayers with essential minimum coverage who purchased insurance through the federal Marketplace (but not from a state exchange).

11. Which of the following is a correct statement about the net investment income tax?

A. The tax is 3.8% of the excess of MAGI over a threshold amount.
B. The tax is 3.8% of net investment income.
C. The tax is 3.8% of the greater of net investment income or the excess of MAGI over a threshold amount.
D. The tax is 3.8% of the lesser of net investment income or the excess of MAGI over a threshold amount.

12. The IRS may take the following actions to collect the shared responsibility payment from a taxpayer:

A. Offsetting his tax refund.
B. Offsetting his tax refund and putting a lien on his property.
C. Offsetting his tax refund, putting a lien on his property, and levying his property.
D. None of the above is allowed.

13. Kyong enrolled in the federal Marketplace for 2016 in order to obtain health insurance. She estimated her household income for the year, qualified for the Premium Tax Credit, and chose to have half of the expected credit paid in advance to her insurance company. What must Kyong do when she files her income tax return?

A. She must repay half of the credit that she received in advance.
B. She will not owe any additional amount but may be eligible for a larger amount of the credit.
C. She must reconcile the advance premium tax credit payments with the actual Premium Tax Credit that she calculates on Form 8962. Any excess amount will be counted as household income and used to project her credit for the next year.
D. She must reconcile the advance premium tax credit payments with the actual Premium Tax Credit she calculates on Form 8962. She may receive a refund, or she may have to repay any excess advance premium tax credit payments, depending on her individual situation.

14. Adrienne and Bill are married and file jointly. Adrienne has $133,000 of self-employment income. Bill earned $184,000 in wages. Compute the amount of their additional Medicare tax, if any.

A. $2,853
B. $1,053
C. $603
D. They do not owe the additional Medicare tax.

Unit 15: Answers

1. The answer is A. Taxpayers who have Minimum Essential Coverage all year will indicate this on Form 1040, page 2, by checking the box in the "Other Taxes" section. Answer B is incorrect because coverage exemptions are reported on Form 8965. Answers C and D are incorrect because these forms are used by the Marketplace and employers, not individual taxpayers.

2. The answer is B. Terry and Lulu have minimum essential coverage because they purchased health insurance through the federal exchange and had it for each month of the year. However, they are not eligible for the Premium Health Credit because they file separate returns. Unless one of a limited number of exceptions applies, a married couple cannot claim the credit unless they file jointly.

3. The answer is C. The additional Medicare tax is applied to MFS taxpayers whose earned income exceeds $125,000 in 2016. Liz will owe an additional .9% tax on the $15,000 of earned income that exceeds the $125,000 threshold ($15,000 × .009 = $135 additional Medicare tax).

4. The answer is B. A nonresident alien would not be subject to the net investment income tax. The net investment income tax applies to individuals, estates, and trusts. Only U.S. citizens and U.S. residents are subject to the tax.

5. The answer is A. Because Suzanne had employer-sponsored health coverage for all 12 months of 2016, she has fulfilled her obligations under the Affordable Care Act and does not owe the shared responsibility payment. She must check the box for "full-year coverage" on page 2 of Form 1040, but she is not required to send in proof to the IRS when she files her return. She must retain documentation of her coverage, as she would any other records needed to substantiate items on her tax return.

6. The answer is B. To be eligible for the Premium Tax Credit, a taxpayer, his spouse, or his dependents must have been enrolled in either the federal Marketplace or a state exchange at some point during the year. A taxpayer enrolled in an employer-sponsored plan, including retiree coverage, is not eligible for the Premium Tax Credit, even if the plan is unaffordable. A taxpayer who received coverage through Medicaid or other government health plans outside of the Marketplace is not eligible for the PTC.

7. The answer is A. The additional Medicare tax applies to 0.9% of a taxpayer's earned income above a threshold based on his filing status. For single, head of household, and qualifying widow(er) filers, the threshold is $200,000. For married couples filing jointly, the amount is $250,000. For married couples filing separately, the amount is $125,000.

8. The answer is D. Worker's compensation insurance, and other plans that offer only limited benefits, do not fulfill the minimum essential coverage requirements. Employer-sponsored plans, including self-insured, COBRA, and retiree plans, generally offer qualifying coverage. All plans purchased through a federal or state exchange also qualify as minimum essential coverage, so Medicare, Medi-Cal, and Medicaid would all qualify.

9. The answer is B. The NIIT applies to the lesser of Milka's investment income ($73,000) or her MAGI above the threshold for her filing status, which is $200,000 for a single filer ($245,000 MAGI - $200,000 threshold = $45,000). Thus, her NIIT is calculated as follows: $45,000 × 3.8% = $1,710. The $200,000 gain from selling her home is excluded from taxation under section 121 and is therefore not part of the calculation for the NIIT.

10. The answer is B. The Premium Tax Credit is refundable, meaning that a taxpayer may be able to receive the full amount of credit as a refund, assuming he has no other tax liability. The PTC is available only to a taxpayer, his spouse, or his dependents who had health coverage through a federal or state exchange for all or part of the year.

11. The answer is D. For individuals; the net investment income tax is 3.8% of the lesser of net investment income, or the excess of modified adjusted gross income over a threshold amount. For example, the threshold for spouses filing joint returns is $250,000; the threshold is $200,000 for single filers.

12. The answer is A. The IRS is not allowed to take any enforced collection measures to collect a taxpayer's liability related to the shared responsibility payment. However, if a taxpayer is owed a tax refund, it can be used to offset the unpaid SRP. In contrast, the IRS is not restricted in the collection methods it may use against a taxpayer who does not repay excess advance premium tax credits. Both liens and levies are allowed to collect excess advance premium tax credit payments.

13. The answer is D. Any taxpayer who claims the Premium Tax Credit (whether advance credit payments were made or not) must file a tax return and include Form 8962, *Premium Tax Credit* (PTC). Kyong must do a monthly calculation to determine the actual amount of her PTC, which must then be reconciled with the advance premium tax credits paid to her insurer to lower her premium payments. Kyong must enter the amount of any excess advance premium tax credit payments made on her behalf on her return and normally repay the excess. If there were no excess advance premium tax credit payments and the amount of the PTC is more than the amount of her tax liability, she may receive the difference as a refund.

14. The answer is C. Their combined compensation is $317,000, which is $67,000 above the applicable threshold of $250,000 for joint filers. Their additional Medicare tax is $603 ($67,000 × 0.9%).

Unit 16: Additional Taxes and Credits

More Reading:
Publication 54, *Tax Guide for U.S. Citizens and Resident Aliens Abroad*
Publication 519, *U.S. Tax Guide for Aliens*
Publication 514, *Foreign Tax Credit for Individuals*
Tax Topic 556, *Alternative Minimum Tax*
Publication 929, *Tax Rules for Children and Dependents*

In this unit, we cover a variety of other taxes and credits, including the taxation and reporting of foreign income, the "nanny tax," and the "kiddie tax." We start with a look at the alternative minimum tax (AMT).

Alternative Minimum Tax

As described in the preceding units, federal tax law provides special treatment for certain types of income and allows deductions and credits for certain types of expenses. These tax benefits can significantly reduce the regular income tax liabilities for some taxpayers. The AMT limits the extent to which these tax benefits can be used to reduce the total amount of income tax paid by higher-income taxpayers. Congress adopted the AMT in 1969 in an attempt to ensure that individuals and corporations pay at least a minimum amount of tax.[69]

When calculating the AMT, many common items considered in the computation of the regular income tax liability are either adjusted downward or eliminated entirely. These include personal exemptions; the standard deduction or certain itemized deductions, such as state, local, and foreign taxes; miscellaneous itemized deductions subject to the 2% floor; investment interest expense; and mortgage interest on home equity debt if the loan was not used to buy or improve the home. In addition, the benefits of the following tax preference items must be eliminated when calculating the AMT:

- Depletion
- Excess intangible drilling costs
- Interest on private activity bonds
- Accelerated depreciation on property placed in service before 1987
- Exclusion of gain on qualified small business stock

The AMT is a parallel tax system, with every taxpayer responsible for paying the higher of the regular tax or a calculated tentative minimum tax. The AMT is the excess of the tentative minimum tax over the regular income tax. Thus, the AMT is owed only if the tentative minimum tax is greater than the regular tax.

In general, the tentative minimum tax is computed by:

1. Starting with AGI minus itemized deductions, if any, for regular tax purposes,

---

[69] The American Taxpayer Relief Act of 2012 included provisions for the AMT to be permanently indexed for inflation, meaning the income threshold for an individual to be subject to the AMT will rise automatically each year.

2. Eliminating or reducing certain adjustments and preferences (the exclusions, deductions, and credits that are allowed in computing the regular tax, such as those mentioned above), to derive alternative minimum taxable income (AMTI),
3. Subtracting the AMT exemption amount,
4. Multiplying the amount computed in (3) by the applicable AMT rate, and
5. Subtracting the AMT Foreign Tax Credit.

The AMT exemption in step 3 is an amount that is deducted from alternative minimum taxable income before calculating the tentative minimum tax. The exemption phases out after a taxpayer's AMTI reaches a certain level, which is based on his filing status.

2016 AMT Phaseout Ranges			
Filing Status	AMT Exemption Amount	Excess Taxable Income (AMTI)	AMT Phaseout Income Level
MFJ, QW	$53,900	$186,300	$119,700
Single	$83,800	$186,300	$159,700
MFS	$41,900	$93,150	$79,850

Most tax preparation software will automatically compute whether a taxpayer owes the AMT. A taxpayer who prepares his own return without using software may need to complete Form 6251, *Alternative Minimum Tax-Individuals*, to determine whether he owes the AMT.

If a taxpayer received or claimed any of the following items in the tax year, he is required to complete, but may not necessarily need to file, Form 6251:

- Accelerated depreciation
- Stock received through incentive stock options that were not disposed in the same year
- Tax-exempt interest from private activity bonds
- Intangible drilling, circulation, research, experimental, or mining costs
- Amortization of pollution-control facilities or depletion
- Income (or loss) from tax-shelter farm activities or passive activities
- Interest from long-term contracts not figured using the percentage of completion-method
- Mortgage interest that is not used to buy, build, or substantially improve a home
- Investment interest expense reported on Form 4952
- Net operating loss deduction
- Alternative minimum tax adjustments from an estate, trust, electing large partnership, or cooperative
- Section 1202 exclusion (gains from qualifying Small Business Stock)
- Any general business credit in Part 1 on Form 3800
- Empowerment zone and renewal community employment credit
- Qualified electric vehicle credit

- Alternative fuel vehicle refueling property credit
- Credit for prior year minimum tax

Credit for Prior Year Minimum Tax

A nonrefundable credit may be available to individuals, estates, and trusts for alternative minimum tax paid in prior years to the extent that a taxpayer's regular tax in the current year is greater than his tentative minimum tax. If applicable, the credit is calculated on Form 8801, *Credit for Prior Year Minimum Tax – Individuals, Estates, and Trusts*.

The AMT is caused by two types of adjustments and preferences: exclusion items and deferral items. Exclusion items are those that affect only a single tax year and therefore cause a permanent difference between regular taxable income and alternative minimum taxable income (AMTI). AMT adjustments/preferences that are exclusion items and are not used to determine the minimum tax credit are as follows:

- Personal exemption
- Standard deduction
- Itemized deductions
- Percentage depletion
- Certain tax-exempt interest
- Exclusion of gain from qualified small business stock

For individual taxpayers, an example of an exclusion item is the deduction for state and local income taxes. These taxes are never deductible for AMT purposes, and they are added back into AGI in the calculation of AMTI in the year they are paid.

Deferral items are adjustment and preference items, such as depreciation, that affect more than one tax year. Because they affect the difference between regular taxable income and AMTI in multiple tax years, they generally do not cause a permanent difference in taxable income over time.

The minimum tax credit is allowed only for the portion of AMT caused by deferral items, which may generate credit for future years.

Example: Leland and Erika are married and file jointly. They had an AMT liability in the previous year after they exercised incentive stock options. They use Form 8801 to calculate how much of their AMT was related to that and other deferral items and discover they have a $1,500 credit carryforward. Their regular tax in 2016 is $4,000, and their tentative minimum tax is $3,000. They can use $1,000 of the minimum tax credit carryforward to reduce their regular tax, but they cannot reduce it below the tentative minimum tax amount. The balance of $500 can be carried forward.

Kiddie Tax on Investment Income

Years ago, wealthy families could transfer investments to their minor children and save tax dollars because the investment income would be taxed at the children's lower rates. Congress closed this tax loophole, and now investment income earned by dependent children may be taxed at the parent's rate. This law became known as the "kiddie tax".

The kiddie tax does not apply to earned income (such as wages); it applies only to investment income, such as interest, dividends, and capital gains distributions. Part of a child's investment income may be taxed at the parent's marginal tax rate if:

- The child's investment income is more than $2,100 (in 2016).
- The child is under age 18 or a full-time college student under age 24.
- The child is required to file a tax return for the tax year.
- At least one of the child's parents was alive at the end of the year.
- The child does not file a joint return for the tax year.

Parents can avoid paying the kiddie tax only if the child is age 18 or older and has enough earned income to provide greater than half of his own support. In that case, the tax would be based on the child's tax rate and not the parent's.

The kiddie tax only applies when a dependent child's investment income exceeds $2,100 in 2016. The first $1,050 in investment income is tax-free; the second $1,050 is taxed at the child's marginal rate. All of the child's investment income in excess of $2,100 is then taxed at the parent's tax rate. A taxpayer can report and pay the kiddie tax in either of two ways:

- The parents may include the child's investment income on their tax return (using Form 8814, *Parent's Election to Report Child's Interest and Dividends*), or
- The child may file a separate tax return (using Form 8615, *Tax for Certain Children Who Have Unearned Income*).

The tax on the child's income will be the same either way, unless an exception to the kiddie tax rules applies. A child's investment income is subject to the net investment income tax, which is calculated using only the child's income and not the parent's. However, the NIIT applies only if the child's net investment income exceeds the $200,000 threshold for single filers. This scenario would be very rare.

Example: Bill and Donna have a 15-year-old son named Jack. In 2016, Jack has $2,500 of interest income from a CD his grandfather gave him. He does not have any other taxable income. The first $1,050 of investment income is not taxable. The next $1,050 is taxed at the 10% income tax rate, which is Jack's marginal rate. The remainder, $400, is taxed at his parents' marginal rate.

Example: Kendra is 16 years old. She has a number of investments that she inherited when her parents died three years ago. Kendra lived with her grandmother, Edna, all year. Kendra has $5,600 in investment income during the year. Kendra is not subject to the kiddie tax rules because she does not have a living parent. In this case, Kendra would not be required to file Form 8615, and Kendra's grandmother would not have to file Form 8814, even if Edna claims her granddaughter as a dependent on her tax return.

Nanny Tax (Tax on Household Employees)

A taxpayer who has household employees may need to pay employment taxes. This obligation is commonly referred to as the "nanny tax," or the tax on Household Employees.

> **Example:** Daniel hires Candy to babysit his three children and do housework in his home. Daniel sets Candy's schedule and gives specific direction about household and child care duties. Daniel also provides all the equipment and supplies Candy needs to do her work. Candy is Daniel's household employee, and subject to the nanny tax rules.

If a taxpayer pays a household employee cash wages (including amounts paid by check, money order, etc.) of $2,000 or more in 2016, he must withhold the employee's share of Social Security and Medicare taxes, and remit them along with the employer's matching share, for a total of 15.3%, unless he chooses to pay both the employer's and employee's shares. If the amount of wages paid to an employee during the year is less than this threshold, no Social Security or Medicare taxes are owed.

> **Note:** An employer is not required to withhold income tax from a household employee's wages. However, income tax may be withheld at the employee's request. Even if the employer is not required to pay FICA (Social Security and Medicare) taxes, the employee's wages may be subject to income tax.

If a taxpayer pays wages of $1,000 or more[70] to a household employee in any quarter, he must also pay federal unemployment tax. The tax applies to the first $7,000 of wages per employee. The maximum FUTA tax rate is 6.0%, but credits reduce this rate to 0.6% in most cases.

A worker is the taxpayer's employee if the taxpayer can control not only what work is done, but how it is done, regardless of whether the work is full-time or part-time; the employee is paid on an hourly, daily, weekly, or per job basis; or the employee is hired through an agency. Examples of household employees include babysitters, housekeepers, private nurses, yard workers, and drivers.

A self-employed worker, such as a daycare provider who cares for several children from different families in her own home, is not considered a household employee.

> **Example:** Christopher hires Robby to do weekly yard maintenance and cut his grass. Robby runs a lawn care business and provides gardening services to many other clients. Robby also advertises his business in the local newspaper. Robby provides his own tools and supplies. Robby is self-employed and not considered Christopher's household employee.

> **Example:** Abner is a widowed single taxpayer with infant twin boys. Abner hires Tabitha to take care of his twin boys while he is at work. Tabitha usually works Monday through Friday, 9 AM to 6 PM. She is an experienced nanny, and she also cleans Abner's home during the day. Tabitha is a household employee. Abner is required to file payroll returns as well as Schedule H with his Form 1040.

A taxpayer who is required to pay Social Security and Medicare taxes or federal unemployment taxes for household employees, or who withholds income tax for them, must file Schedule H, *Household Employment Taxes,* with his Form 1040. The taxpayer will need an employer identification

---

[70] This FUTA tax threshold is different for other types of employees. In 2016, the FUTA tax reporting threshold is $1,000 in wages in any calendar quarter for household employees and farmworkers. The threshold is $1,500 or more (in any calendar quarter) for all other employees.

number (EIN) to file Schedule H. He also must file Form W-2, *Wage and Tax Statement,* and furnish a copy of the form to the employee.

A taxpayer who is an employer of household employees may need to increase the federal income tax withheld from his pay or pension or make estimated tax payments in order to avoid an estimated tax penalty resulting from his liability for employment taxes in connection with household employees, as shown on Schedule H. The taxpayer has several options. He can:

- Increase his federal income tax withheld by giving his employer a new Form W-4
- Increase his federal income tax withheld by giving the payor of his pension a new Form W4-P, *Withholding Certificate for Pension or Annuity Payments*
- Make estimated tax payments by filing Form 1040-ES, *Estimated Tax for Individuals*

Estimated taxes must be withheld or paid as the tax liability is incurred, so a taxpayer cannot wait until he files his tax return (and Schedule H) to pay household taxes owed.

Wages paid to a taxpayer's spouse, parent, or child under the age of 21 are exempt from the nanny tax rules.

> **Example:** Paula hires her mother, Rose, to take care of her children during the week. In this case, since Paula has hired her mother, the payments are exempt from the nanny tax rules. No Social Security and Medicare taxes will be owed by either Paula or her mother. No Federal Unemployment Tax (FUTA) would be owed. However, Rose would owe income tax on the amounts that she earned.

A taxpayer cannot claim a dependency exemption for a household employee such as a nanny, even if the employee lives with the taxpayer.

First-Time Homebuyer Credit Repayment

First-time homebuyers who claimed a special tax credit in 2008 are required to repay a portion of the funds received over a 15-year period. The First-Time Homebuyer Credit took the form of a loan in 2008. For example, a homebuyer who claimed the maximum credit of $7,500 must repay $500 per year as an additional tax. The amount is entered on line 60b on Form 1040.

A taxpayer who claimed the credit and sells a home purchased in 2008 must complete Form 5405, *First-Time Homebuyer Credit and Repayment of the Credit*. The repayment is limited to the amount of gain on the sale if the sale is to an unrelated taxpayer. The credit was also available in 2009 and 2010 but has since expired. A taxpayer who purchased his home and received the credit in either 2009 or 2010 does not have to repay the credit unless he sold the home within a three-year period following the purchase.

> **Example:** Alexa purchased her home in 2008 and claimed the full amount of the First-Time Homebuyer Credit. She still lives in the home and uses it as her main residence. She is required to pay back her credit in equal yearly installments of $500 over a period of 15 years. When she files her 2015 tax return, the repayment is listed on her Form 1040 as an additional tax.

Foreign Income and Taxes

Generally, all income of U.S. citizens and U.S. resident aliens is subject to tax by the United States, regardless of where the individual lives and even if the income is earned outside the United States. "Foreign earned income" is income received for services performed in a foreign country while the taxpayer's tax home is also in a foreign country. It does not matter whether the income is paid by a U.S. employer or a foreign employer.

> **Example:** Brenda and Sonny are married and file jointly. In 2016, they were both employed in Peru, with Brenda earning $80,000 and Sonny earning $26,000. Each qualifies for the foreign earned income exclusion. Brenda also has $6,000 of work-related expenses. She cannot deduct any of her expenses because she is already excluding all of her income from taxation by taking the foreign earned income exclusion.

Foreign Earned Income Exclusion: If a taxpayer is eligible for the foreign earned income exclusion, his income up to a certain threshold is not taxed. For 2016, the maximum foreign earned income exclusion is $101,300.

If married taxpayers file jointly and both individuals live and work abroad, each can claim the foreign earned income exclusion, for a total exclusion amount of $202,600.

Nonresident aliens do not qualify for the foreign earned income exclusion. A taxpayer must be either a U.S. citizen or a legal resident alien of the United States who lives and works abroad and must pass one of two tests in order to claim the exclusion:

- **Bona Fide Residence Test:** A U.S. citizen or U.S. resident alien who is a bona fide resident of a foreign country for an uninterrupted period that includes an entire tax year.
- **The Physical Presence Test:** A U.S. citizen or U.S. resident alien who is physically present in a foreign country or countries for at least 330 full days during 12 consecutive months. A taxpayer may qualify under the physical presence test, and the income may span a period of multiple tax years. If so, the taxpayer must prorate the foreign earned income exclusion based on the number of days spent in the foreign country.

> **Note:** The exclusion does not apply to the wages and salaries of members of the Armed Forces and civilian employees of the U.S. government.

The foreign earned income exclusion is calculated using Form 2555, *Foreign Earned Income,* which must be attached to Form 1040. If a choice is made to exclude foreign earned income, the choice remains in effect for subsequent years, unless revoked.

Foreign Housing Exclusion or Deduction: In addition to the foreign earned income exclusion, a taxpayer can claim an exclusion (or a deduction) for foreign housing costs. The maximum foreign housing exclusion for 2016 is $16,208, or $44.28 per day (16% of the maximum foreign earned income exclusion at $101,300).

The housing exclusion applies only to amounts paid by an employer, while the housing deduction applies only to amounts paid with self-employment earnings. Qualified housing expenses include reasonable expenses paid for housing in a foreign country. Only housing expenses for the part of the year that the taxpayer actually qualified for the foreign earned income exclusion are considered.

> **Example:** Sergio is a U.S. citizen who lived in Vietnam all of 2016 and was employed by a Vietnamese company as an advertising consultant. He lived rent-free in an apartment provided by his employer. Sergio received a salary of $95,000, and the fair rental value of his housing was $12,000, for a total of $107,000 of earned income. He qualifies for the foreign earned income exclusion and the foreign housing exclusion.

Foreign Income Taxes: Generally, income taxes paid to a foreign country can be deducted as an itemized deduction on Schedule A or as a credit against U.S. income tax. A taxpayer can choose between these options and use whichever one results in the lowest tax.

Foreign Tax Credit: U.S. citizens and resident aliens are eligible for the Foreign Tax Credit, which is designed to relieve taxpayers of the double taxation burden that occurs when their foreign source income is taxed by both the U.S. and a foreign country. Nonresident aliens are not eligible.

Four tests must be met to qualify for the credit:
- The tax must be imposed on the taxpayer.
- The taxpayer must have paid or accrued (if an accrual basis taxpayer) the tax.
- The tax must be a legal and actual foreign tax liability.
- The tax must be an income tax.

Although taxpayers can choose between taking the deduction or the credit for all foreign taxes paid, in most cases, it is to their advantage to take the Foreign Tax Credit, since a credit directly reduces tax liability. A taxpayer cannot claim both, the deduction and the tax credit on the same return, but may alternate years, taking a credit in one year and a deduction in the next year.

Taxpayers also cannot claim the Foreign Tax Credit for taxes paid on any income that has already been excluded using the foreign earned income exclusion or the foreign housing exclusion. Unlike the foreign earned income exclusion, which applies only to income that is earned while a taxpayer is living and working abroad, the Foreign Tax Credit applies to any type of foreign income, including investment income. Foreign tax paid may be reported to the taxpayer by a financial institution on Form 1099-INT or Form 1099-DIV.

Taxpayers can claim the credit on Form 1040 if, among other conditions, all foreign income is specified passive category income and total taxes paid do not exceed $300 ($600 MFJ). If the tax paid exceeds $300 ($600 MFJ), the taxpayer must file Form 1116, *Foreign Tax Credit*, to claim the credit.

> **Example:** Yusuf and Fatima are married and file jointly. They own a number of foreign stocks, and their Form 1099-DIV shows foreign tax paid of $590. The couple is not required to complete Form 1116 because their foreign taxes are less than $600.

> **Example:** Colette is a U.S. citizen who is also a shareholder of a French corporation. She receives $700 of income from the French corporation. The French government imposes a 10% tax ($70) on Colette's earnings. She must include the gross earnings ($700) in her income. The $70 of tax withheld is a qualified foreign tax for purposes of the Foreign Tax Credit.

Certain taxes do not qualify for the Foreign Tax Credit, including interest or penalties paid to a foreign country, taxes imposed by countries involved with international terrorism, and taxes on foreign oil or gas extraction income.

> **Note:** Currently, the foreign tax credit does not apply to any tax paid to Syria, Sudan, North Korea or Iran. These countries are sanctioned by the U.S.

The Foreign Tax Credit is nonrefundable, but the taxpayer is allowed a one-year carryback and a ten-year carryforward of any unused credit amount.

Fixed, Determinable, Annual, or Periodic (FDAP) Income

Fixed, Determinable, Annual, or Periodic (FDAP) income applies to foreign persons earning income in the U.S. FDAP income consists primarily of passive investment income, including interest, dividends, rents, royalties, pensions, and annuities. Deductions are not allowed against FDAP income, and it is taxed at a flat 30% rate or a lower rate if there is a tax treaty between the U.S. and the taxpayer's country of residency.

This 30% or lower rate only applies if the FDAP income or gains from U.S. sources are not "effectively connected" with a taxpayer's U.S. trade or business. A nonresident alien who receives income that is effectively connected with his trade or business in the United States is taxed at the rates that apply to U.S. citizens and residents. The IRS definition of FDAP includes all passive investment income except:

- Gains derived from the sale of real or personal property
- Items of income excluded from gross income, regardless of the U.S. or foreign status of the income's owner, such as tax-exempt municipal bond interest and qualified scholarship income

Compensation for personal services performed in the United States can also be FDAP income. If a nonresident alien receives income for personal services performed partly in the U.S. and partly outside the U.S., he must allocate the income based on the number of days where the services were performed.

> **Example:** Alain, a citizen, and resident of Canada, is employed as a professional hockey player by a U.S. hockey team. He received $200,000 in compensation for 120 days of play during 2016: 75 days in the U.S. and 45 days in Canada. The amount of U.S. source income is $125,000 ([75 days of play in the US ÷ 120 total days =.625] × $200,000).

Unit 16: Study Questions

(Test yourself first, then check the correct answers at the end of this quiz.)

1. Ahmed is a citizen and resident of Iran, a country that does not have a tax treaty with the United States. Ahmed is not a U.S. citizen or U.S. resident, but he owns several rental properties and other investments in the U.S. that produce passive investment income. His FDAP income is taxable at a flat _____ rate.

A. 25%
B. 28%
C. 30%
D. 35%

2. Colton is 22, a full-time college student, and is claimed as a dependent on his parents' tax return. He also has a part-time job at a local mall. Colton has $210 of dividend income in 2016. What is the maximum amount of wages Colton can earn in 2016 without triggering the kiddie tax?

A. $350
B. $2,100
C. $6,200
D. No maximum.

3. Ella hired a part-time nanny to work in her home. She paid the nanny $1,900 of wages in 2016. Which of the following statements is correct?

A. Ella is not required to issue a Form W-2 to the nanny and does not have to report or pay Social Security and Medicare taxes on the nanny's wages.
B. The income is not taxable to the nanny.
C. No reporting is required by either party if the wages are paid in cash.
D. Ella can deduct the nanny's wages as a business expense on Schedule C.

4. All of the following statements are correct about the alternative minimum tax except:

A. Congress passed the alternative minimum tax to ensure that individuals and corporations that benefit from certain exclusions, deductions, or credits pay at least a minimum amount of tax.
B. The tentative minimum tax is figured in addition to a taxpayer's regular tax.
C. The AMT is the excess of the tentative minimum tax over the regular tax.
D. The AMT is permanently indexed for inflation.

5. Natalie is a U.S. citizen who lives and works in Australia, which is her tax home. She does not maintain a residence in the U.S. In 2016, she received the following income:

- Annuity income from a U.S. investment: $12,500
- Taxable interest: $2,000
- Wages: $90,000

Natalie wants to take the foreign earned income exclusion on her individual tax return. What is the total amount of qualifying foreign earned income that Natalie can report on her Form 2555?

A. $101,300
B. $99,200
C. $92,000
D. $90,000

6. In 2016, when does an employer have to withhold and pay Social Security and Medicare taxes for a household employee?

A. When the taxpayer pays any employee for household services.
B. When the taxpayer pays a household employee $1,000 or more of wages a year.
C. When the taxpayer pays a household employee $2,000 or more of wages a year.
D. When the taxpayer pays his 20-year-old daughter to care for her younger siblings.

7. Which of the following taxpayers would not be eligible for the Credit for the Prior Year Minimum Tax by filing Form 8801?

A. An S corporation.
B. A trust.
C. An estate.
D. An individual.

8. Which of the following statements is correct regarding the Foreign Tax Credit?

A. The Foreign Tax Credit is a refundable credit.
B. The Foreign Tax Credit is available to U.S. citizens and nonresident aliens.
C. Taxpayers may choose to take a deduction for foreign taxes paid, rather claim than the Foreign Tax Credit.
D. Taxpayers can claim both a deduction and a tax credit for foreign taxes paid, provided the taxes were paid to different countries.

9. In determining a taxpayer's credit for prior year minimum tax, which of the following would not be considered?

A. Depreciation.
B. Mortgage interest.
C. Incentive stock options.
D. None of the above is considered in determining the credit for prior year minimum tax.

10. The Foreign Tax Credit applies to:

A. Taxpayers who have paid foreign taxes to a foreign country on foreign-sourced income and are subject to U.S. tax on the same income.
B. Taxpayers who have paid U.S. taxes while living and working abroad.
C. Taxpayers who have paid U.S. taxes while living and working abroad and who are subject to U.S. tax on their worldwide income.
D. Nonresident aliens who have paid foreign taxes to a foreign country on foreign-sourced income and are subject to U.S. tax on the same income.

11. The AMT was adopted by Congress in an attempt to ensure that individuals:

A. Pay a minimum amount of tax.
B. Pay zero tax.
C. Do not cheat on their taxes.
D. Pay tax at a lower rate than taxpayers in other countries.

Unit 16: Answers

1. The answer is C. Ahmed will be taxed at a flat 30% rate on his FDAP (Fixed, Determinable, Annual, or Periodical) income. A 30% (or lower treaty) tax rate applies to FDAP income or gains from U.S. sources, but only if they are not effectively connected with a taxpayer's U.S. trade or business. FDAP income consists primarily of passive investment income, including interest, dividends, rents, royalties, pensions, and annuities. FDAP income is all income except:

- Gains derived from the sale of real or personal property.
- Items of income excluded from gross income, without regard to the U.S. or foreign status of the owner of the income, such as tax-exempt municipal bond interest and qualified scholarship income.

2. The answer is D. The kiddie tax only applies to investment income, not to wages. Therefore, Colton's wage income will not be subject to the kiddie tax. Under the provisions of the kiddie tax, unearned income that is in excess of $2,100 will be taxed at the parent's marginal rate.

3. The answer is A. Ella is not required to issue a Form W-2 to the nanny, and does not have to report or pay Social Security and Medicare taxes on the nanny's wages. If an employer pays a household employee wages of less than $2,000 in 2016, the employer is not required to report or pay Social Security and Medicare taxes on that employee's wages. However, employers who withhold federal income taxes from their employee's wages must issue a Form W-2. Regardless of whether Form W-2 is issued, the nanny must report the income on Form 1040.

4. The answer is B. The tentative minimum tax is calculated separately from the regular tax. The AMT is owed only if the tentative minimum tax is greater than the regular tax.

5. The answer is D. U.S. citizens, and resident aliens who live abroad are taxed on their worldwide income. However, they may qualify to exclude a portion of their foreign earnings (up to $101,300 for 2016). A qualifying individual with qualifying income may elect to exclude foreign earned income, and this exclusion applies only if a tax return is filed and the income is reported. Natalie has $104,500 of gross income, but only her wages ($90,000) would qualify for the foreign earned income exclusion.

6. The answer is C. In 2016; the nanny tax applies when a taxpayer pays a household employee $2,000 or more of wages a year.

7. The answer is A. Only individuals, estates, and trusts are eligible to claim the Credit for the Prior Year Minimum Tax by filing Form 8801. The credit is calculated differently for corporations, which use a different form and set of instructions to determine whether they are eligible for the credit.

8. The answer is C. Taxpayers have the option to claim an itemized deduction for foreign taxes paid on Schedule A. They may choose either the deduction or the credit, whichever gives them the lowest tax. Taxpayers cannot claim both the deduction and a tax credit on the same return.

9. The answer is B. Itemized deductions, such as mortgage interest, are exclusion items not used to determine the minimum tax credit. Other exclusion items include personal exemptions and the standard deduction. Items such as depreciation are deferral items and are used to calculate the credit.

10. The answer is A. The Foreign Tax Credit applies to taxpayers who have paid foreign taxes to a foreign country on foreign-sourced income and are subject to U.S. tax on the same income.

11. The answer is A. The AMT was adopted by Congress in 1969 to ensure that individuals pay at least a minimum amount of tax. This means that individuals who reduce their taxable income using various methods (such as increasing their itemized deductions) may still be forced to pay tax.

Unit 17: Retirement Accounts

More Reading: Publication 590, *Individual Retirement Arrangements (IRAs)* Publication 575, *Pension and Annuity Income* Publication 560, *Retirement Plans for Small Business*

There are a variety of retirement accounts individuals can establish for themselves and retirement plans that can be established by employers and self-employed individuals.

In this unit, we primarily cover traditional individual retirement arrangements (traditional IRAs) and Roth IRAs, as they are tested heavily on Part 1 of the EA exam. We will also briefly address other types of retirement plans. Form 1099-R, *Distributions From Pensions, Annuities, Retirement or Profit-Sharing Plans, IRAs, Insurance Contracts, etc.,* is used to report distributions of $10 or more from a retirement plan or an IRA.

Traditional IRA: Amounts in a traditional IRA, including contributions and earnings, are generally not taxed until they are distributed. Typically, a taxpayer can deduct his traditional IRA contributions as an adjustment to gross income. However, the adjustment can be phased out at higher income levels.

Roth IRA: Contributions to a Roth IRA are paid with after-tax income and are not deductible. In contrast to a traditional IRA, withdrawals from a Roth IRA are generally not taxed. Income limits apply in determining who is eligible to participate in a Roth IRA.

A taxpayer cannot claim an adjustment for a deductible IRA contribution on Form 1040EZ; he must use Form 1040 or Form 1040A.

Note: The rules regarding IRAs and retirement plans apply to same-sex spouses who are legally married in any state.[71] A same-sex spouse is entitled to all spousal benefits and protections provided to heterosexual spouses from traditional IRAs, Roth IRAs, and qualified retirement plans. However, these rules do *not* apply to domestic partnerships and civil unions.

2016 IRA Contribution Limits

The limits for contributions to an IRA in 2016 are the lesser of qualifying taxable compensation (as described below) or the following amounts:

- **$5,500** per taxpayer (**$6,500** if age 50 or older)
- Taxpayers filing MFJ (even if only one had compensation): **$11,000** (or **$13,000** if both spouses are age 50 or older)

This yearly IRA contribution limit does not apply to:

- Rollover contributions (rolling over from one IRA account to another)
- Qualified reservist repayments[72]

---

[71] In June 2015, the landmark U.S. Supreme Court ruling *Obergefell v. Hodges* legalized same-sex marriage in every state.
[72] If a taxpayer was a reservist in the Armed Forces and was called to active duty, the taxpayer can contribute (repay) any IRA amounts equal to any qualified reservist distributions received. The taxpayer can make these repayment contributions even if the payments would cause the total yearly contributions to exceed the general limit on IRA contributions.

Traditional IRA Rules

To make contributions to a traditional IRA:

- The taxpayer must be under age 70½ at the end of the year.
- The taxpayer must have qualifying taxable compensation, such as wages, salaries, commissions, tips, bonuses, or self-employment income.

If either the taxpayer or his spouse is covered by an employer plan and his income is too high, his deductible IRA contribution will be phased out.

For purposes of making an IRA contribution, taxable alimony (but not child support payments) counts as qualifying compensation. This allows taxpayers to build retirement savings in IRAs even if they rely on alimony income for support. Nontaxable combat pay also qualifies as compensation for this purpose.

> **Example:** Stan is an Army medic serving in a combat zone for all of 2016. Although none of his combat pay is taxable, it is still considered qualifying compensation for purposes of an IRA contribution. He is allowed to contribute to a Roth or Traditional IRA if he wishes.

Compensation for purposes of contributing to an IRA does not include:

- Rental income
- Dividend and interest income
- Pension or annuity income
- Deferred compensation
- Prize winnings or gambling income
- Items (except for nontaxable combat pay) that are excluded from income, such as foreign earned income and excludable foreign housing costs

> **Example:** Larry is 54 and wants to contribute to his traditional IRA. He received $10,000 of rental income; $8,000 of interest income; and $3,000 of wages from a part-time job. The rental and interest income are not considered for purposes of determining his IRA contribution. Therefore, the maximum he can contribute to his traditional IRA is $3,000, the amount of his wages.

> **Note:** A taxpayer can never contribute more than he has earned for the year. Minors who want to start contributing to an IRA must abide by limits based on their own taxable income, *not* the income of their parents.

> **Example:** Penelope is 17 years old and has a part-time job. She is claimed as a dependent on her parent's return. She earns $4,300 in wages during 2016. She also has $3,500 in dividend income from stocks that she inherited from her grandmother. Penelope may contribute to an IRA in 2016 because she has earned income. Her IRA contribution would be limited to $4,300, the amount of her wages. The investment income is not qualifying compensation for IRA purposes.

IRAs cannot be owned jointly. Therefore, each spouse must have their own IRA account. However, a married couple filing jointly may contribute to each of their IRA accounts, even if only one taxpayer has qualifying compensation.

Example: Joaquin, 49, and Meg, 51, are married and file jointly. Joaquin works as a paramedic and makes $46,000 per year. Meg is a homemaker and has no taxable income. Even though Meg has no qualifying compensation, they may contribute to her IRA account. Their combined maximum contribution for 2016 is $12,000. Joaquin may contribute $5,500 to his IRA, and Meg may contribute $6,500 to her IRA because she is over 50 years old. This special rule only applies if the taxpayers file jointly.

If married taxpayers choose to file separately, they must consider only their own qualifying compensation for IRA contribution purposes.

Example: Greg is 35, works full-time, and earned $55,000 in wages during the year. His wife, Lila, is 34 and earned $3,600 in 2016. They choose to file MFS. Therefore, Lila is limited to a $3,600 IRA contribution, the amount of her qualifying compensation. Greg may contribute the full $5,500 to his own IRA account.

Contributions can be made to a traditional IRA at any time on or before the due date of the return (not including extensions). For the 2016 tax year, a taxpayer may make an IRA contribution up until April 18, 2017. This makes an IRA contribution a rare opportunity for late-stage tax planning because it can occur after the tax year has already ended.

A taxpayer can even file his return claiming a traditional IRA contribution before the contribution is actually made. However, if a contribution is reported on the taxpayer's return, but it is not made by the deadline, the taxpayer must file an amended return.

Example: Paul files his 2016 tax return on March 5, 2017, and claims a $4,000 deduction for an IRA contribution on the return. Paul may wait as late as April 18, 2017, the due date of the return, to make the IRA contribution.

If a person's only qualifying compensation for the year is from self-employment and the self-employment activity generates a loss for that year, he would not be able to contribute to an IRA.

However, if the taxpayer has wages in addition to self-employment income, a loss from self-employment would not be subtracted from the wages when figuring total "qualifying" compensation income for purposes of determining his IRA contribution.

Example: Marcy is 45 and earns $10,000 of wages working part-time for a library. She also works as a self-employed photographer, but her photography business has a net loss of $5,400 for the year. Even though Marcy's *net* income for 2016 is only $4,600 ($10,000 wages − $5,400 loss from self-employment), her qualifying compensation for purposes of an IRA contribution is still $10,000, the amount of her wages. This means that Marcy can make a full IRA contribution of $5,500 in 2016, assuming she has the funds to do so.

For married taxpayers filing a joint return, the combined IRA contributions cannot exceed their combined qualifying compensation.

> **Example:** Elliott and June are both age 49 and married. Elliott has $23,000 of passive rental income for the year. June has $13,000 of pension income and $7,000 of wages. Only June's wages count as qualifying compensation for purposes of an IRA contribution. If they file jointly, they can contribute a maximum of $7,000 to their IRAs. One of them can contribute up to the maximum annual amount ($5,500), and the other can contribute up to $1,500 (equal to the remaining amount of June's qualifying compensation), or they could split the $7,000 in another manner.

Splitting IRA Contributions Between Multiple Accounts

A person may have IRA accounts with multiple financial institutions and may split his annual contributions between accounts; his aggregate contributions for the year are subject to the limits described above.

Further, a taxpayer may choose to split his contributions between a traditional IRA and a Roth IRA; again, his combined contributions are subject to the maximum annual contribution limits outlined before.

> **Example:** In 2016, Leo has $3,200 in wages and $14,000 in rental income. He does not have any other earnings in 2016. His maximum IRA contribution is limited to $3,200 (the amount of his earned income). Leo decides to split his IRA contributions between a traditional IRA and a Roth IRA. He contributes $2,200 to a traditional IRA and $1,000 to a Roth IRA. The most Leo will be able to deduct as an adjustment to income is the $2,200 contribution to his traditional IRA. Roth IRA contributions are never deductible.

> **Example:** Alan is 32. He has a traditional IRA through his bank and a Roth IRA through his stockbroker. Alan wants to contribute to both accounts. Alan can contribute to both of his retirement accounts, but the combined contributions for 2016 cannot exceed $5,500, the annual maximum. Alan decides to contribute $3,000 to his Roth IRA and $2,500 to his traditional IRA.

> **Example:** Naomi, 25, has $3,000 of interest income and no other income in 2016. Naomi marries Carl during the year. Carl has taxable wages of $34,000, and he plans to contribute $5,500 to his traditional IRA. If he and Naomi file a joint return, each can contribute $5,500 to a traditional IRA. Naomi, who has no qualifying compensation, can use Carl's compensation, reduced by the amount of his IRA contribution ($34,000 − $5,500 = $28,500), to determine her maximum contribution to a traditional IRA.

Deductibility of Traditional IRA Contributions

A taxpayer may not be able to deduct all of his traditional IRA contributions. Deductibility is based on income, filing status, and whether the taxpayer or his spouse is covered by an employer retirement plan at work. A taxpayer is permitted to contribute to a traditional IRA regardless of whether he or his spouse is covered by an employer retirement plan; however, the deductible portion of the contribution may be limited.

If a taxpayer exceeds the income limits for making a fully deductible contribution to a traditional IRA, the excess portion can still be made as a nondeductible or after-tax contribution. Regardless of whether a portion of the contribution is nondeductible, the related earnings will grow on a tax-deferred basis.

Taxpayer (and Spouse) Not Covered by an Employer Plan: If neither the taxpayer nor his spouse is covered by an employer plan, there is no limitation on the deductibility of either of their traditional IRA contributions, other than as stated above. Thus, either can deduct the smaller of:

- $5,500 ($6,500 if 50 or older) or $11,000 ($13,000 if 50 or older) if filing MFJ, or
- 100% of qualifying compensation.

If a taxpayer makes nondeductible contributions to a traditional IRA, he must attach Form 8606, *Nondeductible IRAs*. Form 8606 reflects a taxpayer's cumulative nondeductible contributions, which is his tax basis in the IRA. If a taxpayer does not report nondeductible contributions properly, all future withdrawals from the IRA will be taxable unless the taxpayer can prove, with satisfactory evidence, that nondeductible contributions were made.

> **Example:** Tamara is single and earned $95,000 in 2016. She is covered by a retirement plan at work, but she still wants to contribute to a traditional IRA. She is phased out for the deduction because her MAGI exceeds the threshold for single filers covered by an employer plan. If she contributes to a traditional IRA in 2016, she must file Form 8606 to report her nondeductible contribution. She is still allowed to contribute to a traditional IRA, but the amounts would not be deductible on her Form 1040.

Taxpayer (or Spouse) Covered by an Employer Plan

If either a taxpayer or his spouse, or both, is covered by (participates in) an employer retirement plan,[73] the tax-deductible contribution to a traditional IRA is phased out at the following levels of modified adjusted gross income (MAGI):

Phase-outs when Taxpayer (or Spouse) is Covered by an Employer Plan		
Filing Status	**MAGI Range**	**Allowable Deduction**
Single, HOH, or MFS (did not live with spouse*)	$61,000 or less	A full deduction.
	more than $61,000 but less than $71,000	A partial deduction.
	$71,000 or more	No deduction.
MFJ (for the covered spouse*), QW	$98,000 or less	A full deduction.
	More than $98,000 but less than $118,000	A partial deduction.
	$118,000 or more	No deduction.
MFS (lived with spouse*)	less than $10,000	A partial deduction.
	$10,000 or more	No deduction.
If neither spouse is a participant in an employer retirement plan, their IRA contributions are fully deductible.		
*Note #1: If the taxpayer files MFS but <u>did not live</u> with their spouse during the year, the IRA deduction is determined under the "Single" filing status.		
*Note #2: If filing as MFJ and only one spouse is covered by a retirement plan, then for the non-covered spouse: a full deduction is allowed at MAGI of $184,000 or less; a partial deduction for more than $184,000 but less than $194,000; and no deduction at $194,000 or more.		

---

[73] This includes a qualified pension, 401(k), annuity, SEP, SIMPLE, etc.

If neither spouse is a participant in an employer-sponsored retirement plan, their IRA contributions are fully deductible.

Married taxpayers who file MFS generally have a much lower phaseout range than those with any other filing status. However, if a taxpayer files a separate return and *did not live* with his spouse at any time during the year, the taxpayer is treated as "single" for IRA contribution purposes.

> **Example:** Don, age 43, and his wife are not legally divorced, but they have lived in separate residences for the past three years. In 2016, Don earns $40,000 and files MFS. He is covered by an employer retirement plan, but is nevertheless allowed to deduct his full IRA contribution of $5,500. This is because he did not live with his spouse at any time during the year, and therefore is not subject to the lower IRA phaseout limits that normally apply to MFS filers.

Required Minimum Distributions (RMDs)

A person cannot keep funds in a traditional IRA account indefinitely. When the account owner reaches 70½ years of age, the funds must be distributed in annual required minimum distributions (RMDs).

The first RMD payment can be delayed until April 1 of the year following the year the taxpayer turns 70½. The distribution for each subsequent year must be made by December 31. The amount of each RMD is based on IRS tables.[74]

Failure to take an RMD can result in a penalty tax equal to 50% of the amount the taxpayer should have withdrawn, but did not. He must file Form 5329, *Additional Taxes on Qualified Plans*, to report the excise tax that applies as a result of the failure to take the RMD.

> **Example:** Dinah reaches age 70½ in 2016. Her first RMD must be distributed to her by April 1, 2017, in order to avoid the 50% excise tax. At the end of the year, her IRA account balance was $79,500. The applicable distribution period per the IRS tables for someone her age (71) on that date is 26.5 years. Her required minimum distribution for 2016 is $3,000 ($79,500 ÷ 26.5).

Required Minimum Distributions also apply to inherited IRAs. With an inherited IRA, the beneficiary generally needs to take annual distributions no matter what age he is. The same rule about taking a Required Minimum Distribution still applies. The beneficiary of the inherited IRA must begin withdrawing no later than December 31 of following year after the IRA owner died.

> **Example:** Judy dies May 1, 2016. Judy's only son, Russell, is the sole beneficiary of Judy's IRA account. Russell must begin withdrawing an RMD no later than December 31, 2017, the year after his mother's death. This rule applies no matter how old Russell is.

> **Note:** RMDs are not required if the beneficiary of an inherited IRA is a surviving spouse under 70½ years of age, and the spouse simply does a spousal rollover into his or her own IRA.

---

[74] An RMD is calculated by dividing the balance of the IRA account by a life expectancy factor that the IRS publishes in tables within Publication 590, *Individual Retirement Arrangements (IRAs)*.

> **Example:** Ulysses, age 72, and Layla, age 61, are married. Both spouses have traditional IRA accounts. Ulysses began taking required distributions from his traditional IRA in the previous year. However, in 2016, Ulysses dies, and his wife inherits his IRA account. Rather than take a distribution from her late husband's account, Layla decides to do a spousal rollover of the entire account balance into her own IRA. The rollover is not a taxable event. Layla is not required to take any minimum distributions from the account until she reaches age 70½.

Taxability of Distributions

Distributions from a traditional IRA are generally taxable in the year they are received, subject to the following exceptions:

- Rollovers to another retirement plan or account (other than conversions to a Roth IRA, as discussed below)
- Qualified charitable distributions
- Tax-free withdrawal of contributions
- Distributions of nondeductible contributions

Qualified Charitable Distributions (QCD)

A taxpayer who is 70½ or older may choose to make a qualified charitable distribution (QCD)[75] of up to $100,000 ($200,000 for MFJ) from his IRA to qualified charitable organizations. In order to qualify, the funds must come out of the taxpayer's IRA by the deadline for minimum distributions, (generally December 31).

The IRA trustee must make the distribution directly to the qualified charity (the taxpayer cannot request a distribution and then donate the money later). Likewise, any tax withholdings on behalf of the owner from an IRA distribution cannot qualify as QCDs.

> **Example:** Blanche regularly donates to the Red Cross. In 2017, Blanche turns 71. Instead of taking a minimum distribution from her IRA, she contacts her IRA trustee and requests to make a Qualified Charitable Contribution directly to the charity. The QCD counts towards her current year's RMD, as long as the funds are withdrawn from the IRA by December 31.

10% Penalty on Early Distributions

A taxpayer may withdraw funds at any time from a traditional IRA account. However, distributions before age 59½ will generally be subject to an extra 10% tax, in addition to normal income tax on the amount distributed. There are some exceptions to the general rule for early distributions. An individual may not have to pay the additional 10% tax in the following situations:

- To the extent the taxpayer has unreimbursed medical expenses that exceed 10% (or 7.5% if age 65 or older) of adjusted gross income.
- The distributions do not exceed the cost of the taxpayer's medical insurance while unemployed.

---

[75] The PATH Act made the QCD election permanent.

- The taxpayer becomes disabled.
- The distributions are not more than qualified higher education expenses.
- The distributions are used to buy, build, or rebuild a first home (up to $10,000).
- The distributions are used to pay the IRS due to a levy.
- Made as part of a series of substantially equal periodic payments for the life of the taxpayer.
- The distributions are made to a qualified reservist (an individual called up to active duty).

Even though distributions in these situations will not be subject to the additional 10% tax, they will be subject to income tax at the taxpayer's normal rates. Distributions that are properly rolled over into another retirement plan or account (other than conversions to a Roth IRA) are generally not subject to either income tax or the 10% additional penalty.

> **Example:** Lauren, age 39, takes a $5,000 distribution from her traditional IRA account. She does not meet any of the exceptions to the 10% additional penalty tax, so the $5,000 is an early distribution. Lauren must include the $5,000 in her gross income and pay income tax on it. In addition, she must pay a 10% penalty tax of $500 (10% × $5,000).

Roth IRA Vs Traditional IRA

Unlike a traditional IRA, none of the contributions to a Roth IRA are deductible, but the entire balance is generally tax-free at the time of withdrawal. However, distributions generally cannot be made until after a five-year holding period and after the taxpayer has reached age 59½. Further, income limits apply, which means high-income earners may be prohibited from contributing to Roth IRAs.

Whether or not a taxpayer can make a Roth IRA contribution depends on his filing status and modified adjusted gross income (MAGI). In 2016, the following income limits apply to Roth IRAs:

Filing Status	Roth IRA phaseout ranges
Single, HOH filers[76]	$117,000–$132,000
MFJ and QW filers	$184,000–$194,000
MFS (lived with spouse)	$0–$10,000

In general, a taxpayer cannot contribute to a Roth IRA if his income is above the phaseout thresholds. However, a "backdoor" Roth IRA is still possible in 2016. By this method, the taxpayer simply opens a traditional IRA, makes a contribution, and then converts the funds to a Roth in the same year. We will cover IRA conversions in more detail later.

The major differences between a Roth IRA and a traditional IRA are as follows:

- Contributions to a Roth IRA are not deductible by the taxpayer, and participation in an employer plan has no effect on the taxpayer's contribution limits.

---

[76] This phaseout range also applies to MFS taxpayers who did not live with their spouses at any time during the year.

- There are no required minimum distributions from a Roth IRA. No distributions are required until a Roth IRA owner dies.
- Unlike traditional IRAs, contributions to a Roth IRA can be made by individuals of any age, even those who are over the age of 70½.

IRA Rollovers

A rollover is a transfer from one retirement plan or account to another retirement plan or account. If executed properly, most rollovers are nontaxable events. However, taxpayers can also choose to convert a traditional IRA into a Roth IRA. In this case, the conversion will result in taxation of any previously untaxed amounts in the traditional IRA.

Beginning in 2016, a taxpayer can make only one rollover from an IRA to another IRA in any 12-month period, regardless of the number of IRAs the taxpayer owns.[77] There are two exceptions to this rule:

- Trustee-to-trustee transfers between IRAs are not limited
- Rollovers from traditional to Roth IRAs ("backdoor conversions") are not limited

Rollover Rules

If a taxpayer receives an IRA distribution and wishes to make a nontaxable rollover, he must complete the transaction by the 60th day following the day he receives the distribution.[78]

> **Example:** Adam quits his old job on September 1, 2016. On September 14, 2016, Adam begins a new job. He has an existing IRA account, and he decides to transfer the balance of his traditional IRA account to his new employer's retirement plan. Adam receives a distribution from his IRA of $50,000 in cash and $50,000 in stock. On October 9, 2016, he rolls over the entire amount of $100,000 into his new employer's plan. Because the transaction is completed within 60 days, it is completely nontaxable. The rollover must be reported on Form 1040.

If a taxpayer sells the distributed property (such as stocks distributed from an IRA) and rolls over all the proceeds into another traditional IRA or qualified retirement plan within the required time frame, no gain or loss is recognized. The sale proceeds (including any increase in value) are treated as part of the distribution and are not included in the taxpayer's gross income.

If a taxpayer receives both property and cash in a rollover distribution, he can roll over part or all of the property, part or all of the cash, or any combination of the two he chooses. He can also sell the property and roll over the proceeds into a traditional IRA.

But he cannot keep the property and substitute his own funds for property he receives.

---

[77] Internal Revenue Bulletin: 2014-16

[78] Starting in August, 2016, Rev. Proc. 2016-47 allows eligible taxpayers can now qualify for a waiver of the 60-day rollover limit and avoid possible early distribution taxes. Taxpayers will submit the self-certification to their plan administrator or an IRA trustee (NOT to the IRS). In the past, taxpayers who failed to meet the rollover time limit could only obtain a waiver by requesting a private letter ruling from the IRS.

> **Example:** Billy receives a distribution from his employer's plan of $20,000 cash and $30,000 worth of stock. He decides to keep the stock. He can roll over the $20,000 cash received, but he cannot substitute an additional $30,000 in cash in place of the stock and treat this amount as if it had also been rolled over.

A taxable distribution paid from an employer-sponsored retirement plan is subject to mandatory tax withholding of 20%, even if the taxpayer intends to roll it over. If the taxpayer does roll it over and wants to defer tax on the entire taxable portion, he will be forced to add funds from other sources equal to the amount of tax withheld.

In order to avoid this mandatory withholding, a taxpayer may request a "direct rollover". The distribution is then made directly from the custodian for the employer-sponsored plan to the custodian for the employee's IRA or his new employer's retirement plan. Under this option, the 20% mandatory withholding does not apply.

Rollover after the Death of an IRA Owner

Following the death of an IRA owner, the IRA usually passes to a beneficiary. There are very different rules if the beneficiary is a surviving spouse, versus any other type of beneficiary (such as a child or a sibling).

After the death of a traditional IRA's owner, a surviving spouse has two options: he or she can elect to treat the IRA as being his own by changing the ownership designation, or roll over the IRA balance to his own IRA account or certain other types of retirement plans.

> **Example:** Allison, 42, and Lorenzo, 53, are married. Allison dies suddenly in 2016, and at the time of her death, she has $83,000 in her traditional IRA account. Lorenzo chooses to roll over the entire $83,000 into his own IRA account, thereby avoiding taxation on the income until he retires and starts taking distributions.

For any beneficiary other than a surviving spouse, there are a number of factors that determine the period over which amounts remaining in an IRA upon the owner's death would be payable. These include whether the owner died on or before the date he was required to begin taking distributions, whether the beneficiary is an individual (or the owner's estate), and the life expectancies of the owner and the beneficiary in the year of death. If a Roth IRA owner dies and the sole beneficiary is the spouse, he can delay distributions until the owner would have reached 70½ or treat the IRA as his own.

For other beneficiaries, the account balance must generally be distributed by the end of the fifth calendar year after the owner's death, or be paid as an annuity over the beneficiary's life expectancy beginning the year following the year of death.

> **Example:** Delores, who was single and had no children, died in 2016. At the time of her death, Delores had a traditional IRA worth $42,000. The beneficiary of her IRA is her brother, Dean, age 42. Although he cannot roll over the IRA since he is not Delores's spouse, Dean can choose how he receives the IRA proceeds. Dean can choose a lump sum distribution, a five-year distribution, or a "stretch" IRA payout (an annuity paid over time). No matter what type of distribution Dean selects, the amounts will be subject to income tax. However, the 10% early withdrawal penalty is waived for a beneficiary of an IRA when the original IRA owner has died.

Traditional IRA vs. Roth IRA		
Issue	Traditional IRA	Roth IRA
Age limit	A person over 70½ cannot contribute.	No age limit for contributions.
2016 Contribution Limits	The lesser of $5,500 (or $6,500 if age 50 or older by the end of the year) and qualifying taxable compensation.	Same.
Deductibility of contributions	Generally deductible.	No. Contributions to a Roth IRA are never deductible.
Filing requirements	No filing requirement unless nondeductible contributions are made. Nondeductible contributions must be reported on Form 8606.	Filing requirement related to conversion of a traditional IRA to a Roth IRA. None related to contributions made directly to a Roth IRA.
Mandatory distributions	RMDs by April 1 of the year following the year a taxpayer reaches age 70½.	There are no required distributions unless the IRA owner dies.
How distributions are taxed	Distributions from a traditional IRA are taxed as ordinary income.	Distributions from a Roth IRA are generally not taxed.
Income limits	Phaseout of deductibility is based upon AGI if taxpayer and/or spouse are covered by an employer plan.	There are income limits for contributions, but conversions of a traditional IRA to a Roth IRA are still allowable.

Conversion of a Traditional IRA to a Roth IRA

In the past, taxpayers in higher income brackets were unable to contribute to a Roth IRA. They were also unable to convert from a traditional IRA to a Roth IRA. The IRS rules changed several years ago, and there is no longer an income threshold on IRA conversions. High-income taxpayers can convert to a Roth as long as they pay the appropriate tax on the conversion. This is frequently called a "backdoor conversion."

There is no 10% early withdrawal penalty if the funds from the traditional IRA are deposited into a Roth IRA within 60 days. If a taxpayer wishes to convert all or a portion of his traditional IRA to a Roth IRA, he is required to pay income taxes on the amount of pre-tax (deductible) contributions converted, as well as the growth in value resulting from earnings on those contributions. After the funds are converted to a Roth IRA, additional earnings are tax-free, and distributions are generally not subject to tax.

Example: Nancy converts her traditional IRA to a Roth IRA in 2016. The traditional IRA has a balance of $100,000. The entire balance represents deductible contributions and earnings that have not previously been taxed. She reports the amount of the balance that was converted to a Roth IRA as taxable income in 2016.

A Roth conversion is reported on Form 8606, *Nondeductible IRAs*. An inherited traditional IRA is generally not eligible to be converted to a Roth IRA unless it is inherited directly from a spouse. Non-spousal beneficiaries (for example, a child who inherits a traditional IRA from a deceased parent) are not allowed to convert a traditional IRA to a Roth IRA.

Recharacterization

A taxpayer may undo or reverse a rollover or conversion of one type of IRA to a different type of IRA through a *recharacterization.* Essentially, by recharacterizing an IRA, it is as if the conversion or rollover never occurred.

A recharacterization can only be done through a trustee, and it must be completed by October 15 of the year after the taxpayer made the initial conversion. The deadline applies even if the taxpayer did not request an extension to file his return, and filed his return on or before the filing deadline.

Example: On June 1, 2016, Andrew converts his traditional IRA to a Roth IRA. However, his investments perform poorly, and his account loses value after the conversion. Because he does not want to pay tax on the value of the converted funds, he decides to recharacterize the conversion and move the funds back to a traditional IRA. On January 10, 2017, Andrew opens a traditional IRA with the same trustee and instructs the trustee of the Roth IRA to make a trustee-to-trustee transfer of the Roth conversion contribution to the new traditional IRA. Due to the recharacterization, Andrew has no taxable income from the conversion to report for 2016.

If a taxpayer recharacterizes a contribution, he must do all three of the following:

- Include in the transfer any net income allocable to the contribution. If there was a loss, the net income might be a negative amount.
- Report the recharacterization on the tax return for the year during which the contribution was made.
- Treat the contribution as having been made to the second IRA on the date that it was actually made to the first IRA.

A taxpayer must report an IRA recharacterization on Form 8606, *Nondeductible IRAs.*

Excise Tax on Excess Contributions

If a taxpayer accidentally contributes more to his IRA than is allowed for the year, the excess contribution is subject to a 6% excise tax. Contributions made to a traditional IRA in the year a taxpayer reaches age 70½ are also considered excess contributions. However, the IRS will allow a taxpayer to correct an excess contribution if certain rules are followed.

If he makes a contribution that exceeds the annual maximum or his qualifying compensation, the excess contribution and all related earnings must be withdrawn from the IRA before the due date (*including* extensions) of the tax return for that year. If a taxpayer corrects the excess contribution within this period, the 6% penalty will apply only to the amounts earned on the excess contribution. The taxpayer must also report the earnings on the excess contribution as taxable income for the year in which the withdrawal is made. For each year that the excess amounts remain in the IRA, the taxpayer must pay the 6% tax. However, this tax can never exceed 6% of the value of the taxpayer's IRA at the end of the tax year.

> **Note:** A taxpayer cannot apply an excess contribution to an earlier year even if the taxpayer contributed less than the maximum amount allowable for an earlier year. However, the taxpayer is allowed to apply an excess contribution to a later year if the contributions for that later year are less than the maximum allowable for that year.

> **Example:** Betsy, age 62, is self-employed and owns several rental properties. She contributes $5,500 to her traditional IRA in December 2016. She files for an extension to prepare her tax return. When she finally gives her records to her accountant, he discovers that Betsy's taxable income from self-employment is only $4,500 and her rental income is $38,000. Only the self-employment income counts as compensation for purposes of contributing to her IRA, so Betsy has inadvertently made an excess contribution of $1,000. Betsy must withdraw the excess contribution and any earnings on it by the extended due date of her return or face an excise tax of 6% on both.

> **Example:** In 2016, Jonas is 49 years old and single. His wages for the year are $52,000. He has two IRA accounts, and he contributes $3,000 to each account in 2016. Jonas has accidentally made an excess contribution of $500 ($6,000 total IRA contributions - $5,500 2016 limit). The excess contributions earned $5 interest in 2016 and $6 interest in 2017. Jonas does not realize his mistake, and he does not withdraw the $500 in excess contribution or the interest it earned by the due date of his return. Since he doesn't discover the error until after his filing deadline, now Jonas is liable for an excise tax on his excess contributions. He figures the additional tax on Form 5329. To avoid the excise tax for 2017, he can correct the excess amount by allocating the $500 to the next year, or he can withdraw it from the account.

Prohibited Transactions

Generally, a prohibited transaction is the "improper use" of an IRA by the owner, a beneficiary, or a disqualified person (typically a fiduciary or family member). Prohibited transactions related to an IRA include:

- Borrowing money from it
- Using it as security for a loan
- Buying property for personal use with IRA funds
- Personally borrowing money from the IRA
- Selling, leasing, or exchanging property to the account
- Accepting unreasonable compensation for managing property or assets held by the IRA
- Granting account fiduciaries to obtain, use, or borrow against account assets for their own gain
- Transferring plan assets, lending money, or providing goods and services to "disqualified persons," usually a close family member, or a business that a close family member owns and controls.

For the purposes of the prohibited transaction rules, "family members" includes the taxpayer's spouse, parents, grandparents, children; and grandchildren and spouses of the taxpayer's children and grandchildren. Family members do not include in-laws, cousins, friends, aunts, uncles, siblings, and step-siblings.

> **Example:** Jada uses her traditional IRA as collateral for an auto loan. This is a prohibited transaction.

Although occurrences of prohibited transactions are rare, the consequences can be catastrophic. If a prohibited transaction occurs at any time during the year, normally the account ceases to be treated as an IRA and its assets are treated as if having been wholly distributed on the first day of the year. However, in situations where an IRA account, or a portion of an IRA account, is used as a security for a loan, only the amount used as security for the loan is treated as a distribution from the IRA as of the first day of the year that the loan was made, but the IRA continues to exist. If the total fair market value as of that date is more than the taxpayer's basis in the IRA, the excess amount is reportable as taxable income. It may also be subject to the additional 10% penalty on early distributions.

> **Example:** The fair market value of Noah's traditional IRA was $300,000 as of January 1, 2016. He had previously made $200,000 of nondeductible contributions to his IRA, so that was his basis in the account. On June 1, Noah, age 40, borrowed $150,000 from his IRA to purchase himself a vacation home. This is a prohibited transaction, and Noah's entire IRA account will no longer be treated as an IRA. Since the FMV of the IRA on the first day of the year, $300,000, is greater than Noah's basis, $200,000, the excess amount of $100,000 is reported as taxable income. Noah would also be subject to the additional 10% penalty for withdrawing funds before the age of 59½.

> **Note:** Prohibited transactions are rare occurrences, and they generally only occur when a taxpayer has a "self-directed" IRA. A self-directed IRA is a type of account that offers a taxpayer the ability to use his retirement funds to make almost any type of investment without requiring a financial institution or another custodian.

> **Example:** Paul is 52 and has $180,000 in his traditional IRA. His daughter, Lanie, wants to buy a home for $140,000 but does not have sufficient funds. As a result, Paul lends his daughter $140,000 from in his self-directed IRA to buy the home. This is a prohibited transaction. For Paul, the IRA is deemed immediately disqualified as of January 1, 2016 (the year in which the prohibited transaction occurred). The entire amount of the IRA is deemed distributed in 2016, and an early withdrawal penalty of 10% would also apply to the entire amount of the IRA ($180,000).

Prohibited IRA Investments

Almost any type of investment is permissible inside an IRA, including stocks, bonds, and real estate. However, there are some investments that are prohibited. For example, the law does not permit IRA funds to be invested in life insurance or collectibles. If the taxpayer invests in any of these using IRA funds, it is treated as a prohibited transaction. The following investments are prohibited:

- Collectibles such as artwork, rugs, and antiques
- Precious metals, coins, and gemstones (exceptions exist for U.S. coins and bullion)
- S corporation stock
- Insurance contracts

There is a narrow exception for investments in gold and silver coins minted by the U.S. Treasury Department. Investments in certain gold, silver, palladium, and platinum bullion are also allowable.

Retirement Plans for Businesses

Retirement plans for businesses include Simplified Employee Pension (SEP) plans, Savings Incentive Match Plan for Employees (SIMPLE) plans and qualified plans. The term "qualified" refers to certain IRS requirements that the plan and the employer must adhere to in order to obtain tax-favored status. SEP and SIMPLE plans must also meet certain requirements but are much less complex than those that apply to qualified plans.

> **Study Note:** Business retirement plans are covered in greater detail, and from the employer's perspective, in *PassKey EA Review Book 2: Businesses*, as much of the related information is tested on Part 2 of the EA exam. In Part 1 of the exam, you will need to understand the employee's perspective with regards to retirement plans. For Part 2, you must understand retirement plans from the employer's perspective.

If retirement plans are structured and administered properly, businesses can deduct contributions they make on behalf of their employees or, if self-employed, themselves. Both the contributions and the earnings are generally tax-free until distribution. Further, some plans also allow employees to make contributions, most commonly in pre-tax dollars (so that a portion of their salaries are not taxed until the amounts are later distributed to them by the plan).

SEP Plans: SEPs provide a simplified method for employers to make contributions to a retirement plan for themselves and their employees. Instead of setting up a profit-sharing plan with a trust, an employer can adopt a SEP agreement and make contributions directly to individual SEP-IRA accounts (similar to a traditional IRA as described previously) for himself and each eligible employee. A SEP plan is funded exclusively by employer contributions; employee contributions are not permitted.

SIMPLE Plans: An employer can generally set up a SIMPLE plan if the business has 100 or fewer employees who received at least $5,000 of compensation during the preceding year. Under a SIMPLE plan, employees can choose to make salary reduction contributions rather than receiving these amounts as part of their regular pay. An employer can contribute matching or nonelective contributions. A SIMPLE plan can be structured in one of two ways: using SIMPLE IRAs (again, similar to traditional IRAs as described previously) or as a SIMPLE 401(k) plan (similar to the qualified 401(k) plans described below).

Qualified Retirement Plans

There are two basic kinds of qualified retirement plans: defined contribution plans and defined benefit plans, and different rules apply to each. An employer is allowed to have more than one type of qualified plan, but contributions cannot exceed annual limits. Contributions for self-employed taxpayers are limited to 100% of compensation. If the business does not have any income for the year, no contribution can be made.

All qualified plans are subject to federal regulation under the Employee Retirement Income Security Act (ERISA). The federal government does not require an employer to establish a retirement plan, but it provides minimum federal standards for qualified plans.

Defined Benefit Plans

A defined benefit plan, often called a traditional pension plan, promises a specified benefit amount or annuity for each participant after retirement. Benefits are typically based on formulas that consider the participant's years of service with the employer and his earnings history.

The federal government and most state and local governments provide defined benefit plans for their employees. However, fewer businesses now offer defined benefit plans because they are costly to administer and inflexible.

The benefits promised by many defined benefit plans are protected by federal insurance. Contributions to a defined benefit plan are not optional. Contributions are typically based on actuarial calculations that estimate the amounts necessary to pay benefits in the future.

Defined Contribution Plans

A defined contribution plan provides an individual account for each participant in the plan depending upon how the plan is structured. It provides benefits to each participant based on the amounts contributed to the participant's account, along with subsequent investment income or losses, and, in some instances, allocations of forfeitures among participant accounts.

The participants, the employer, or both may contribute to the individual participant accounts. Examples of defined contribution plans include profit-sharing plans, 401(k) plans, 403(b) plans, and 457 plans.

Depending upon how a qualified plan is structured, salary reduction/elective deferral contributions are employee contributions based on a percentage of the employee's compensation and are generally made on a pre-tax basis.

This limitation applies to the aggregate amounts of contributions to any qualified plans, SEPs, and SIMPLE plans in which the individual participates during the year. However, the contribution cannot exceed the amount of the employee's compensation. Depending on the individual plan, the employer may provide matching contributions for employees who make elective deferrals.

> **Example:** Jon earns $80,000 per year as an insurance executive. He participates in his company's profit-sharing 401(k) plan. He contributes 3% of his pre-tax wages to the plan in 2016, or $2,400 ($80,000 × .03). Jon's company contributes a matching 3% to his individual 401(k) account.

Distributions: Distributions to participants may be made either on a periodic basis, such as annuity payments or as a lump sum. As is the case with distributions from traditional IRA accounts (as well as SEP and SIMPLE plans), distributions generally are not permitted prior to when the participant retires or otherwise terminates employment, dies, becomes disabled, or reaches age 59½.

Earlier distributions are generally subject to an additional 10% penalty tax.

Required minimum distributions from defined contribution plans must generally begin by April 1 of the year following the calendar year when the taxpayer retires, or the year in which the taxpayer reaches age 70½, whichever comes later.

Example: In 2016, Jon retires at age 63 after working 35 years at an insurance company. He would have been required to take distributions by April 1 of the year following the calendar year in which he reaches age 70½. However, he chooses to begin taking distributions from his 401(k) account in the same year he retires.

Note: For purposes of the net investment income tax, net investment income does not include distributions from a qualified retirement plan, such as a 401(k), or from traditional or Roth IRAs. However, these distributions are taken into account when determining the modified adjusted gross income threshold.

Restricted Loans from Qualified Plans

Unlike traditional IRAs and Roth IRAs, distributions from a qualified plan are generally restricted. This means that a taxpayer cannot withdraw from the account whenever he chooses. Generally, distributions of elective deferrals cannot be made until one of the following occurs:

- The taxpayer dies, becomes disabled, or has a severance from employment.
- The plan terminates, and no successor defined contribution plan is established or maintained by the employer.
- The taxpayer reaches age 59½ or incurs a financial hardship.

However, some borrowing is allowed. A qualified plan may allow its participants to borrow specified portions of their individual account balances, subject to certain restrictions. A loan can generally be no more than the lesser of $50,000, or the greater of $10,000 or 50% of the vested portion of the participant's account balance. If a loan is not repaid according to the specified payment terms, it may be considered a taxable distribution. This may apply if a participant terminates employment with the employer that sponsors the plan.

Hardship Distributions

A 401(k) plan may allow participants to receive hardship distributions because of an immediate and heavy financial need, such as sudden medical or funeral expenses.

Hardship distributions are limited to the amount of the employee's elective deferrals and generally do not include any income earned on the deferred amounts. The amount of the distribution may include amounts necessary to pay taxes or penalties anticipated to result from the distribution, including the 10% penalty levied on early distributions.

Example: Kendra's home is in foreclosure, and she is in immediate danger of being evicted. She requests a hardship distribution from her 401(k), which is granted. Since she is under age 59½, Kendra would likely have to pay the 10% early distribution penalty.

Unit 17: Study Questions

(Test yourself first, then check the correct answers at the end of this quiz.)

1. Frank, 72, and Sue, 61, are married and file jointly. In 2016, Frank earned wages of $30,000, and Sue earned $5,000. If Frank and Sue file jointly, how much can they contribute to their traditional IRAs?

A. $5,500
B. $6,500
C. $11,500
D. $13,000

2. An excess contribution to an IRA is subject to tax. Which of the following statements is correct?

A. The taxpayer will not have to pay the 6% tax on the excess contribution if he withdraws the excess contribution and any earnings on the excess contribution before the due date of the tax return for the applicable year, including extensions.
B. The 6% tax is due on both the excess contribution and any earnings on the excess contribution, even if the taxpayer withdraws the excess contribution from the account.
C. A taxpayer will not have to pay the 6% tax on the excess contribution if he withdraws the excess contribution and any earnings on the excess contribution before the due date of the tax return for the year, not including extensions.
D. A taxpayer will not have to pay the 6% on earnings on the excess contribution if he is disabled.

3. Contributions to a traditional IRA can be deducted for a given tax year if they are made:

A. Any time during the year or by the due date of the return, not including extensions.
B. Any time during the year or by the due date of the return, including extensions.
C. By December 31.
D. Any time during the year, but only while the taxpayer is employed.

4. Which of the following statements is correct regarding loans from a qualified plan?

A. Loans from a qualified plan are never permitted.
B. Loans are permitted up to the full amount of the employee's contributions to the qualified plan.
C. Loans are permitted, but generally cannot exceed $50,000, or the greater of $10,000 or 50% of the vested portion of the employee's account balance.
D. Loans are permitted, but only under specific and defined circumstances of hardship.

5. Elizabeth and Landon are age 62, married, and lived together all year. They both work and each has a traditional IRA. In 2016, Landon earned $4,000 of wages and received $11,000 of annuity income. Elizabeth earned $52,000. They prefer to file separately. If they file separate returns, what is the maximum that Landon can contribute to his IRA?

A. $1,000
B. $4,000
C. $5,500
D. $6,500

6. Lucas, an unmarried college student working part-time, earns $3,500 in 2016. He also receives $500 of interest income and $4,000 from his parents to help pay tuition. What is his maximum IRA contribution in 2016?

A. $0
B. $3,500
C. $5,500
D. $6,500

7. Kristin, 42, is a full-time graduate student with $1,200 of wages. She marries Adniel, 50, during the year. Omar has taxable compensation of $46,000 in 2016. What is the maximum they can contribute to their traditional IRA accounts in 2016 if they file jointly?

A. $1,200
B. $6,700
C. $11,000
D. $12,000

8. Penny, age 48, and William, age 49, are married and file jointly. Both are self-employed and report their business income on Schedule C. William's business has $9,900 in profits during the year. His wife, Penny, has an overall business loss of ($3,100) for 2016. Penny also earned $3,000 in wages from a seasonal job. What is their maximum allowable IRA contribution for 2016?

A. They are allowed to contribute $5,500 each.
B. William can contribute $5,500. Penny can only contribute $3,000.
C. William can contribute $5,500. Penny can only contribute $4,400.
D. William can contribute $5,500. Penny cannot contribute to her IRA, because she has an overall loss for the year.

9. Steve, age 36 and single, is in the Marines. He has the following income in 2016:

Nontaxable combat pay	$30,500
Regular wages	2,100
Interest income	4,600

What is the maximum amount that Steve can contribute to a traditional IRA?

A. $2,100
B. $4,600
C. $5,500
D. $6,500

10. Rafael, 40, earns $26,000 in wages during the year. Although he is allowed to contribute up to $5,500 to his IRA, he only has enough cash to contribute $2,500. On May 30, 2017, Rafael expects to receive a big commission bonus, and he wishes to make a catch-up contribution for 2016. Rafael filed a timely extension for his tax return, so his federal return isn't due until October 15, 2017. Which of the following statements is correct?

A. Rafael can contribute an additional $3,000 in May 2017 for the 2016 tax year as long as he files his tax return by the extended due date.
B. Rafael cannot contribute an additional $3,000 for the 2016 tax year after the normal filing deadline.
C. Rafael can contribute an additional $3,000 in May 2017 for the 2016 tax year only if he files his return by April 18, 2017.
D. Rafael cannot make a 2016 contribution to his IRA after December 31, 2016.

11. When does the IRS require the owner of a Roth IRA to start taking withdrawals?

A. After the death of the IRA owner.
B. At age 59½.
C. At age 70½.
D. Never.

12. Which of the following statements is correct?

A. A taxpayer can convert a traditional IRA to a Roth IRA. The transaction is tax-free.
B. A taxpayer can convert a traditional IRA to a Roth IRA. Any applicable tax must be paid on the conversion.
C. A taxpayer can rollover a traditional IRA to a Roth IRA only if his income is under $100,000.
D. A taxpayer cannot convert a traditional IRA to a Roth IRA.

13. Miguel is 37. In 2016, he contributed $1,500 to a Roth IRA. He also wants to contribute the allowable maximum to a traditional IRA account. What is the maximum he can contribute to a traditional IRA in 2016, assuming he had sufficient qualifying compensation?

A. $0
B. $3,000
C. $4,000
D. $5,000

14. Undoing or reversing an IRA is called a:

A. Conversion.
B. Rollover.
C. Recharacterization.
D. Distribution.

15. Jody is single, age 51, and has the following compensation in 2016:

Annuity income	$1,600
Wages	3,000
Alimony	2,300
Interest income	3,000
Rental income	6,000

What is the maximum amount that Jody can contribute to her traditional IRA in 2016?

A. $3,000
B. $5,500
C. $5,300
D. $6,500

16. Which of the following distributions from a traditional IRA is subject to an additional 10% penalty?

A. Distributions made prior to age 59½.
B. Distributions made after age 70½.
C. Distributions made to an unrelated beneficiary after the IRA owner's death.
D. Distributions made due to an IRS levy.

17. Shari received a distribution in 2016 from her IRA and wanted to roll it over to an IRA with another bank. How long does she have to complete the rollover in order to avoid income tax on the distribution?

A. 30 days.
B. 60 days.
C. Until the end of the year.
D. Until the due date of her return.

18. Which of the following is considered an excess contribution to an IRA?

A. A contribution to a traditional IRA by a taxpayer in the year he has reached age 70½.

B. A rollover to a Roth IRA.

C. A contribution to a Roth IRA by a taxpayer who is age 75.

D. A contribution made by a taxpayer who only has alimony income.

19. Doris is 58 years old and took a distribution of $8,000 from her traditional IRA in 2016. She had qualified higher education expenses of $6,000 during the year. What tax treatment would apply to the IRA distribution?

A. The entire distribution would be subject to regular tax plus the additional 10% applicable to early distributions.

B. Only $2,000 of the distribution would be taxable.

C. A portion of the distribution ($2,000) would be subject to regular tax, and the additional 10% applicable to early distributions would apply to the entire amount.

D. The entire distribution would be subject to regular tax, and the additional 10% tax would apply to $2,000.

20. Megan, age 36, is married and files jointly. She contributes $5,500 to a traditional IRA, and she is also a participant in her employer's retirement plan. She and her husband had modified adjusted gross income of $195,000 in 2016. Which of the following is correct regarding her IRA contribution?

A. It is fully deductible.

B. It is partially deductible.

C. It is not deductible.

D. She would be subject to a 6% excise penalty if she contributed to an IRA.

Unit 17: Answers

1. The answer is B. Only Sue can contribute to a traditional IRA. Frank cannot contribute because he is over 70½ years old. However, Sue is over 50 and can utilize Frank's qualifying compensation in order to contribute the maximum of $6,500 to her IRA.

2. The answer is A. The taxpayer will not have to pay the 6% tax on the excess contribution if the excess contribution and any earnings are withdrawn by the due date of his return, including extensions. If a taxpayer corrects the excess contribution in time, the 6% penalty will apply only to the earnings on the excess contribution.

3. The answer is A. A taxpayer cannot deduct a contribution to an IRA after the due date of his tax return, even if he files for an extension. IRA contributions for 2016 must be made by April 18, 2017.

4. The answer is C. Depending on its terms; a qualified plan may allow a participant to borrow funds from his account balance. A loan can be no more than the lesser of:
- $50,000, or
- The greater of $10,000 or 50% of the vested portion of the participant's account balance.

5. The answer is B. Since Landon is married and lived with his wife during the year but is filing separately, he can contribute no more than $4,000, the amount of his only qualifying compensation for IRA purposes.

6. The answer is B. His IRA contribution for 2016 is limited to $3,500, the total amount of his wages. The interest income and the gifted money from his parents are not qualifying compensation for IRA purposes.

7. The answer is D. They can contribute $12,000 if they file jointly. Kristin can contribute $5,500, and Adniel can contribute $6,500 because he is 50. Even though Kristin only has $1,200 of compensation, she can use her husband's compensation to determine her maximum contribution.

8. The answer is A. On a jointly filed return; they are both allowed to contribute and deduct the maximum allowable for their age bracket ($5,500 in 2016). William and Penny use their combined income to figure their maximum allowable IRA contribution in 2016. Even though Penny has an overall loss for the year, she does not have to offset her Schedule C losses from her wages when determining her allowable IRA contribution. The answer is figured as follows:

Qualifying Compensation: William: $9,900 + Penny: $3,000 = $12,800

If they file jointly, they can each contribute $5,500 ($5,500 X 2 = $11,000, which is less than the amount of their qualifying compensation).

9. The answer is C. Steve may contribute $5,500, the maximum contribution allowed for his age, because a taxpayer may elect to treat nontaxable combat pay as qualifying compensation for IRA purposes. The interest income is not considered compensation.

10. The answer is B. Rafael cannot contribute an additional $3,000 after April 18, 2017, the due date for filing 2016 tax returns, regardless of whether he files an extension. If contributions to a traditional IRA for the year were less than the limit, a taxpayer cannot contribute more after the original due date of the tax return to make up the difference. If Rafael wants to make an additional contribution for 2016, he must do it by the *normal* filing deadline, regardless of whether he files an extension or not.

11. The answer is A. Unlike traditional IRAs, Roth IRAs do not require withdrawals until after the death of the owner.

12. The answer is B. A taxpayer may convert his traditional IRA to a Roth IRA. If a taxpayer wishes to convert all or a portion of his traditional IRA to a Roth IRA, he is required to pay income taxes on the amount of pre-tax (deductible) contributions converted, as well as the growth in value resulting from earnings on those contributions. After the funds are converted to a Roth IRA, additional earnings are tax-free, and distributions are generally not subject to tax. However, penalties apply if the taxpayer withdraws from the Roth IRA within five years of the conversion. The conversion is reported on Form 8606, *Nondeductible IRAs*.

13. The answer is C. Assuming Miguel has sufficient qualifying compensation; he could contribute $4,000. The 2016 maximum for contributions to *all types* of IRAs is $5,500 per taxpayer (for taxpayers under 50). Taxpayers are allowed to have different types of IRA accounts, but the maximum contribution limits apply to their total contributions for the year.

14. The answer is C. When a taxpayer reverses a rollover or conversion of one type of IRA to a different type of IRA, it is called a recharacterization. A recharacterization can only be done through a trustee, and it must be completed by October 15 of the year after the year in which the taxpayer made the initial conversion. By recharacterizing an IRA, it is as if the conversion or rollover never occurred.

15. The answer is C. Her maximum contribution for 2016 is $5,300. Only Jody's wage income of $3,000 and the $2,300 of alimony qualify as compensation for purposes of an IRA contribution. The annuity income, rental income, and interest income do not qualify.

16. The answer is A. Distributions made prior to age 59½ are subject to a 10% early withdrawal penalty, if no exception applies. Some exceptions that allow early distributions from an IRA, as well as from qualified retirement plans, include the following:
- Distributions made to a beneficiary or estate after death
- Distributions made because of permanent disability
- Distributions to the extent of medical expenses (medical expenses that exceed 10%, or 7.5% for those age 65 and older, of adjusted gross income), whether or not the taxpayer itemizes deductions for the year
- Distributions made due to an IRS levy

The distributions listed above are not subject to the early distribution penalty, but they are subject to income tax at the taxpayer's normal tax rates.

17. The answer is B. Shari has 60 days to complete the rollover. If she does not complete the rollover within 60 days, the distribution is subject to income tax in 2016.

18. The answer is A. A taxpayer's contributions to a traditional IRA in the year he reaches age 70½ (and any later years) are considered excess contributions. An excess contribution and any earnings on it are subject to an additional 6% tax if the taxpayer does not withdraw the contribution and the earnings by the due date of the tax return, including extensions.

19. The answer is D. As Doris is not yet age 59½, early distributions from her traditional IRA would typically be subject to the additional 10% tax, in addition to regular tax at her marginal rate. However, the additional tax would apply only to the extent that her distributions exceeded her qualified higher education expenses for the year.

20. The answer is C. Contributions to a traditional IRA by an MFJ taxpayer who participates in an employer-sponsored retirement plan are allowed, but their deductibility is phased out at higher income thresholds. When MAGI reaches $194,000 (for joint filers) in 2016, the traditional IRA contribution is not deductible. If a taxpayer makes nondeductible contributions to a traditional IRA, she must attach Form 8606, *Nondeductible IRAs*, to her tax return.

Unit 18: FBARS and Foreign Financial Accounts

More Reading:
IRS FBAR Reference Guide
Reporting of Foreign Financial Accounts on the Electronic FBAR (IRS Webinar)
Instructions for FinCEN Form 114
Instructions for Form 3520

In this chapter, we will discuss foreign financial reporting requirements for U.S. taxpayers. The subject of foreign financial reporting is extremely complex, and the IRS continues to issue guidance on how taxpayers and tax professionals should approach this difficult topic. In past EA Exams, the issue of foreign financial reporting was not tested. However, it is possible that the IRS will begin to test on this important topic during the current testing cycle.

A person who holds a foreign financial account may have a reporting obligation even when the account produces no taxable income, and even if the person does not have an individual income tax filing requirement. For the purposes of foreign financial reporting requirements, a "United States person" includes U.S. citizens, U.S. residents, and U.S. entities. There are four major forms used for reporting foreign bank accounts, foreign assets, and foreign gifts. These are:

- The FBAR (Form 114, *Report of Foreign Bank and Financial Accounts*)
- Form 8938, *Statement of Specified Foreign Financial Assets*
- Schedule B, *Interest and Ordinary Dividends (Part III)*
- Form 3520, *Annual Return to Report Transactions with Foreign Trusts and Receipt of Certain Foreign Gifts*

Federal law requires that U.S. persons report all worldwide income, including income from foreign trusts and foreign bank accounts. In many cases, these taxpayers need to complete Schedule B and attach it to their tax return. Certain taxpayers may also have to fill out and attach Form 8938, *Statement of Foreign Financial Assets*. Form 3520 is used to report certain foreign gifts and bequests. Schedule B, Form 3520, and Form 8938 are filed together with a taxpayer's annual Form 1040.

The FBAR filing requirement, however, is considered a separate filing requirement than filing a regular tax return. FBARs are not filed with the IRS. These forms are filed directly with the Financial Crimes Enforcement Network (FinCEN), which is a division of the U.S. Treasury Department. The IRS is responsible for FBAR enforcement. Generally, records of accounts required to be reported on the FBAR should be kept for five years from the due date of the report, which is the year *following* the calendar year being reported.

FBARs in General

The term "FBAR" refers to Form 114, *Report of Foreign Bank and Financial Accounts*. In 2003, the Department of the U.S. Treasury delegated enforcement authority regarding the FBAR to the Internal Revenue Service (IRS). With regards to FBAR filings, the IRS is responsible for:

- Investigating possible civil violations,

- Assessing and collecting civil penalties, and
- Issuing administrative rulings.

The FBAR must be filed electronically and is only available online through the BSA E-Filing System.[79] Taxpayers cannot paper-file FBAR returns. A U.S. taxpayer is required to file an FBAR if:

- The person had a financial interest in, or signature authority over, at least one financial account located outside of the United States, and
- The *aggregate* value of all foreign financial accounts exceeded $10,000 (U.S. dollars) at any time during the calendar year reported.[80]

The IRS defines "signature authority" as the authority of an individual or individuals to control the disposition of assets held in a foreign financial account by direct communication with the bank or other financial institution.

Note: The recently enacted *Surface Transportation Act* changed the standard FBAR due date to April 15 beginning with the 2016 tax year.[81] Filers failing to meet the FBAR annual due date of April 15 are allowed an automatic extension to October 15. In prior years, no extensions were permitted.

The FBAR is due by April 15th of the year following the year in which the account holder meets the $10,000 threshold.

Example: Joel is a U.S. citizen. Joel's parents are citizens of Canada and live in Canada. Joel has signature authority on his elderly parents' accounts in Canada, but he has never written a check or made any withdrawals from his parents' bank account. The bank account balance reaches $10,000 for the first time in 2016. Joel is required to file an FBAR by April 18, 2017. Whether or not his signature authority is ever exercised is irrelevant to the FBAR filing requirement.

All FBAR forms are required to be filed electronically with the Treasury Department's Financial Crimes Enforcement Network (FinCEN); they are not filed as part of a tax return.

FBAR Penalties

The Treasury Department reports that FBAR filings have surged in recent years, with filings exceeding one million per year. The consequences of failure to timely file an FBAR can be severe. Both civil penalties and criminal sanctions can be imposed.

By law, civil penalties could be up to $10,000 per year for a "non-willful" failure to file. A "willful" failure could result in the greater of $100,000 or 50% of the balance in an unreported foreign account per year for up to six years. Criminal penalties may include a fine of up to $250,000 and five years in prison.

However, the IRS recently issued guidance[82] on penalties for failing to file an FBAR that caps the maximum percentage of the penalty. In most cases, the total penalty amount for all years under

---

[79] The BSA E-Filing System is a U.S. Treasury website, and is used for online filing of FBAR returns. The website also supports electronic filing of Bank Secrecy Act (BSA) forms through a secure network.

[80] Accounts are converted to U.S. currency based on the exchange rate as of the end of the calendar year, applied to the highest balance in the account during the year, even if the highest balance in the foreign account was sometime before the end of the year.

[81] The due date for FBAR filings for foreign financial accounts maintained during calendar year 2016 is April 18, 2017, consistent with the Federal income tax due date.

examination will be limited to 50% of the highest aggregate balance of all unreported foreign financial accounts during the years under examination.

The guidance also establishes procedures and documentation requirements for IRS examiners conducting examinations related to FBAR penalties.

Offshore Voluntary Disclosure Program (OVDP)

The IRS's Offshore Voluntary Disclosure Program (OVDP) offers taxpayers with undisclosed income from offshore accounts a way to disclose foreign accounts and possibly face reduced penalties and avoid criminal prosecution. Streamlined compliance procedures are also in effect. The IRS has FBAR submission procedures for taxpayers who do not need to use either OVDP or the streamlined procedures to report undisclosed income from offshore accounts. A taxpayer may avoid penalties for filing a delinquent FBAR if he:

- Has not filed a required FinCEN Form 114, *Report of Foreign Bank and Financial Accounts* (FBAR),
- Is not under a civil examination or criminal investigation by the IRS, and
- Has not already been contacted by the IRS about the delinquent FBARs.

The taxpayer should file the delinquent FBAR reports electronically, including a statement explaining why he is filing late. The IRS will not impose a penalty for failure to file the delinquent reports if the taxpayer properly reported and paid all tax on the income from the foreign financial accounts that are reported on the FBARs.

> **Example:** Ursula is a citizen of Spain and a legal U.S. resident. She travels frequently to her home country and maintains a bank account there with an average balance of $20,000. She is required to file an FBAR to report this foreign account. For tax year 2016, Ursula must file her FBAR by April 18, 2017.

Because foreign financial institutions may not be subject to the same reporting requirements as financial institutions located within the United States, the FBAR is designed to help the U.S. government identify persons or entities that use offshore accounts to hide income or illicit funds.

> **Example:** Alberto is a legal U.S. resident who has a bank account in Mexico. In prior years, the value of his foreign bank account totaled approximately $7,500. Therefore, Alberto did not have an FBAR requirement. However, in 2016, Alberto decides that he wants to build a vacation home in Mexico. He transfers $18,000 to his Mexican bank account on January 10, 2016, in order to begin construction on his new residence. Although he later withdraws all the funds, he is still required to file an FBAR. Alberto must file his FBAR by April 18, 2017, because the aggregate value of his foreign accounts reached $10,000 in 2016. However, he is not required to file Form 8938 (to be discussed later), because the value of his foreign assets is below the required thresholds.

> **Note:** A safe deposit box at a foreign financial institution is not considered a financial account for reporting purposes.

---

[82] May 13, 2015, *Interim Guidance for Report of Foreign Bank and Financial Accounts (FBAR) Penalties,* Department of the Treasury.

Form 3520: Reporting Foreign Gifts and Bequests

U.S. individuals who received large gifts or bequests from certain foreign persons may be required to file Form 3520, *Annual Return to Report Transactions with Foreign Trusts and Receipt of Certain Foreign Gifts*. A foreign person is defined as a nonresident alien individual or a foreign corporation, partnership, or estate. In 2016, a U.S. person must file Form 3520, *Annual Return to Report Transactions with Foreign Trusts and Receipt of Certain Foreign Gifts*, if he receives:

- Gifts or bequests valued at more than $100,000 from a nonresident alien individual or foreign estate, or
- Gifts valued at more than $15,671 in 2016 from foreign corporations or foreign partnerships.

Form 3520 is considered an "information return," not a tax return, because foreign gifts or bequests are not subject to income tax. However, failure to file a required Form 3520 can result in steep penalties. The penalty for reporting a foreign gift late is $10,000 or 35% of its value. However, no penalty applies if the failure to report was due to reasonable cause and not willful neglect.

The taxpayer is required to report a gift or bequest on Form 3520 when he constructively receives it. A taxpayer must aggregate gifts received from related parties.

> **Example:** Josephine is a US citizen that has many relatives living in Canada. In 2016, Josephine received $60,000 from her Canadian grandfather and $50,000 from her Canadian brother. Josephine must report the gifts because the total is more than $100,000. She is required to report them in Part IV of Form 3520. Gifts from foreign trusts must be treated as trust distributions and reported in Part III of Form 3520.

> **Example:** Ginny is a U.S. citizen who lives and works in the United States. Ginny's grandmother, Claudette, is a French citizen. In January 2016, Claudette dies and leaves Ginny a large inheritance of $250,000. After her grandmother's estate is settled by the executor, Ginny receives the inheritance via wire transfer on March 1, 2016. Since Ginny constructively received the funds in 2016, her Form 3520 is due on April 18, 2017.

Taxpayers file Form 3520 separately from their income tax return. The due date for filing Form 3520 is the same as the due date for filing an annual income tax return (generally April 15), including extensions.

> **Note:** A "foreign gift" to a U.S. person does not include amounts paid for qualified tuition or medical payments made on behalf of the U.S. person.

> **Example:** Jason is a U.S. citizen attending college in the United States. His aunt, Judith, is a citizen of Australia. Judith offers to pay her nephew's tuition. She makes a payment directly to Jason's college. There are no filing requirements for this foreign gift.

Form 8938: Statement of Specified Foreign Financial Assets

Generally, taxpayers who hold foreign financial assets with an aggregate value that exceeds $50,000 ($100,000 MFJ) on the last day of the tax year, or that exceeds $75,000 ($150,000 MFJ) at any time during the tax year, must also file Form 8938, *Statement of Specified Foreign Financial Assets*, with their tax returns. This is a separate filing requirement in addition to the FBAR filing requirements.

However, a taxpayer who is not required to file a return for the year does not need to file Form 8938, even if the value of his specified foreign assets is greater than one of the reporting thresholds.

> **Example:** Eloise is a U.S. citizen and resident with funds deposited in three different foreign banks. As of December 31, 2016, bank account #1 had $5,000; bank account #2 had $3,000; and bank account #3 had $2,500. Eloise is required to electronically file an FBAR by April 18, 2017, because the aggregate value of her accounts is more than $10,000. However, she is not required to file Form 8938, because the value of her offshore assets is below the required thresholds.

Schedule B, Reporting Foreign Accounts and Trusts

Schedule B is used to report interest and dividend income received during the tax year. However, the last part of Schedule B (Part III) is used by taxpayers who have financial accounts in foreign countries. This section of the form is where the taxpayer must disclose any foreign bank or investment accounts and whether or not the taxpayer received any distributions from a foreign trust.

The reporting requirements for these taxpayers have increased significantly in recent years as part of FATCA, which refers to the Foreign Account Tax Compliance Act. The law addresses tax noncompliance by U.S. taxpayers with foreign accounts by focusing on reporting by these taxpayers and by foreign financial institutions.

In general, federal law requires U.S. citizens and resident aliens to report any worldwide income, including income from foreign trusts and foreign bank and securities accounts. In most cases, affected taxpayers need to complete and attach Schedule B to their tax returns. Part III of Schedule B asks about the existence of foreign accounts, such as bank and securities accounts, and generally requires U.S. citizens to report the country in which each account is located.

On Part III, Schedule B, a taxpayer must check yes or no to the question of whether he had at any time during the year a financial interest in or signature authority over a financial account. A taxpayer who had a financial interest in a foreign account should check the "yes" box even if he is not required to file FinCEN Form 114, *Report of Foreign Bank and Financial Accounts* (FBAR).

A financial account includes securities, brokerage, savings, checking, deposit, time deposit, or other accounts that are maintained with a financial institution. A financial account also includes a commodity futures or options account, an insurance policy with a cash value (such as a whole life policy), an annuity policy with a cash value, and shares in a mutual fund.

> **Example:** Patty has an uncle who is a Greek citizen. In 2016, her uncle died, and Patty inherited $200,000 in foreign bearer bonds from her uncle. The bonds are held outside of a regular bank account. Patty is required to report the value of the bonds on Form 8938, even if she did not cash them out.

A financial account is considered to be located in a foreign country if the account is *physically located outside* of the United States. This includes accounts maintained with a branch of a U.S. bank if it is physically located outside the United States. However, a branch of a foreign bank is not a foreign account if it is physically located in the United States.

> **Note:** The potential penalties for willful failure to file an FBAR are huge. These penalties might include criminal prosecution as well as large civil penalties.

> **Example:** Ricky directly holds shares of a U.S.-based mutual fund. The mutual fund invests solely in foreign stocks. Since the foreign stocks are held in a mutual fund, Ricky does not need to report his ownership in the mutual fund or the holdings of the mutual fund.

Differences Between the FBAR vs. Form 8938		
Data	**FBAR**	**Form 8938**
Who must file?	U.S. persons, which includes U.S. citizens, resident aliens, trusts, estates, and domestic entities.	Specified individuals, which includes U.S. citizens, resident aliens, and certain nonresident aliens. This form does not apply to entities.
Reporting thresholds	$10,000 held in any foreign bank at any time during the calendar year.	$50,000 on the last day of the tax year or $75,000 at any time during the tax year.
When does the taxpayer have "an interest" in an account or asset?	Financial interest in an applicable foreign account, or signature authority on an applicable foreign account.	Any income, gains, losses, deductions, credits, gross proceeds, or distributions from holding or disposing of the account or asset that are (or would be required to be) reported, included, or otherwise reflected on the taxpayer's return.
What is Reported?	The maximum value of financial accounts.	The maximum value of specified foreign financial assets.
How are values determined and reported?	Converted to U.S. dollars using the end of the calendar year exchange rate and report in U.S. dollars.	Fair market value of the asset in U.S. dollars.
Due Date	Due by April 15 (extensions allowed).	The same due date as the taxpayer's individual return, including extensions.
Filing Procedures	File electronically through FinCEN's BSA E-Filing System. The FBAR is not filed with a federal tax return.	File with income tax return (Form 1040).
Penalties	Willful non-filing: up to the greater of $100,000 or 50% of account balances; Non-willful: up to $10,000; criminal penalties may also apply.	Up to $10,000 for failure to disclose, and an additional $10,000 for every 30 days of non-filing after IRS notice of a failure to disclose, up to a potential maximum penalty of $60,000; criminal penalties may also apply.

(Test yourself first, then check the correct answers at the end of this quiz.)

1. Which form are taxpayers required to submit with their individual tax return if they hold foreign financial assets with an aggregate value that exceeds $50,000 ($100,000 MFJ) on the last day of the tax year?

A. Form 8938.
B. Form 1040 G.
C. Schedule L.
D. FBAR.

2. Part _____ of the Schedule B is completed by taxpayers who have financial accounts in foreign countries.

A. Part I.
B. Part II.
C. Part III.
D. Schedule B is not used for this purpose.

3. Which of the following documents is completed to report foreign bank and financial accounts?

A. Schedule B.
B. Form 1116.
C. Form 2555.
D. FinCen 114.

4. Generally, U.S. citizens, resident aliens, and certain nonresident aliens must report specified foreign financial assets _____ if the aggregate value of those assets exceeds certain thresholds.

A. Form 1040.
B. FinCen 114.
C. Form 8938.
D. Form 9465.

5. Regarding the FBAR reporting requirement, the IRS issued guidance on penalties for failing to file the FBAR that caps the maximum percentage of the penalty. In most cases, the total penalty amount for all years under examination will be limited to _____ of the highest aggregate balance of all unreported foreign financial accounts during the years under investigation.

A. 50%
B. 75%
C. 25%
D. 10%

6. As a general rule, how long should taxpayers keep records related to an FBAR filing?

A. 3 years.
B. 5 years.
C. 7 years.
D. 10 years.

7. Louise is a U.S. citizen with funds deposited in three different Canadian banks. At the end of the tax year, bank account #1 had $5,500; account #2 had $3,250; and account #3 had $2,200. Is she required to file an FBAR, and if so, when is the due date?

A. No, each bank account has less than $10,000, so she is not required to file an FBAR.
B. Yes, Louise is required to file an FBAR by April 18, 2017.
C. Yes, Louise is required to file an FBAR by October 30, 2017.
D. Yes, Louise is required to file an FBAR as well as a Form 8938 by April 18, 2017.

8. Jim, a U.S. citizen who lives in Iowa, has a bank account located in Austria. He opened the account several years ago to send money to his mother, who is a citizen of Austria. He has signature authority on the account but does not withdraw money from it or collect any of the interest income on the account. On December 31, 2016, the account has a balance of $23,000. He otherwise does not have a U.S. filing requirement or any tax liability for the year. What is Jim's reporting requirement for this account?

A. He is not required to file returns since he does not have a filing requirement or owe U.S. tax.
B. He must file Form 8938, *Statement of Specified Foreign Financial Assets*, with the IRS when he files his tax return.
C. He must file an FBAR, *Report of Foreign Bank and Financial Accounts*, with the Treasury Department.
D. He must file an FBAR, *Report of Foreign Bank and Financial Accounts*, with the Treasury Department, and file Form 8938, *Statement of Specified Foreign Financial Assets*, with the IRS when he files his tax return.

9. A U.S. person who receives a gift or bequest valued at more than _____ from a nonresident alien or foreign estate must file an information return with the IRS.

A. $10,000
B. $25,000
C. $50,000
D. $100,000

10. Which of the following is a NOT considered United States person for the purposes of filing an FBAR?

A. A United States citizen who lives in Israel.
B. A U.S. Resident who lives in Russia.
C. A nonresident alien with U.S. investments.
D. A U.S. consular officer that lives and works overseas in a U.S. embassy.

Unit 18: Answers

1. The answer is A. Generally, taxpayers who hold foreign financial assets with an aggregate value that exceeds $50,000 ($100,000 MFJ) on the last day of the tax year, or that exceeds $75,000 ($150,000 MFJ) at any time during the tax year, must file Form 8938 with their returns. The FBAR is not included with the income tax return.

2. The answer is C. Part III of the Schedule B is completed by taxpayers who have financial accounts in foreign countries.

3. The answer is D. The FinCen 114 (FBAR) is the form used to report foreign bank accounts and foreign financial accounts.

4. The answer is C. U.S. citizens, resident aliens, and certain nonresident aliens must report specified foreign financial assets on the Form 8938 if the aggregate value of those assets exceeds certain thresholds.

5. The answer is A. In most cases, the total penalty amount for all years under examination will be limited to 50% of the highest aggregate balance of all unreported foreign financial accounts during the years under investigation.

6. The answer is B. Generally, records of accounts required to be reported on the FBAR should be kept for five years from the due date of the report, which is the year *following* the calendar year being reported.

7. The answer is B. The taxpayer is required to electronically file an FBAR by April 18, 2017, because the aggregate value of her accounts is more than $10,000. However, she is not required to file Form 8938, because the value of her offshore assets is below the required thresholds.

8. The answer is C. There are two separate reporting requirements for taxpayers who hold certain types of foreign assets or who have certain amounts of funds in foreign bank accounts. An FBAR generally must be filed with the Treasury Department if a taxpayer has more than $10,000 in offshore bank accounts. Taxpayers also must file a statement with the IRS if they hold foreign financial assets with an aggregate value that exceeds $50,000 ($100,000 MFJ) on the last day of the tax year, or that exceeds $75,000 ($150,000 MFJ) at any time during the tax year. In Jim's case, since the funds in his foreign account total $23,000, he is only required to file an FBAR. He is required to file the FBAR, even if he earns no money from the account and owes no U.S. tax.

9. The answer is D. Form 3520, *Annual Return to Report Transactions with Foreign Trusts and Receipt of Certain Foreign Gifts*, is an information return, not a tax return, because foreign gifts or bequests are not subject to income tax. In 2016, a U.S. person must file Form 3520 if he receives:
- Gifts or bequests valued at more than $100,000 from a nonresident alien individual or foreign estate, or
- Gifts valued at more than $15,671 from a foreign corporation or foreign partnership.

An individual who fails to file a required Form 3520 could be subject to steep penalties.

10. The answer is C. Nonresident aliens are not subject to the FBAR filing requirement. All of the following are subject to the FBAR filing requirement if they hold foreign bank accounts or applicable foreign assets.
- A citizen or resident of the United States
- A domestic entity
- A domestic corporation
- A domestic estate or trust

Unit 19: Estate and Gift Taxes

> **More Reading:**
> Publication 559, *Survivors, Executors, and Administrators*
> Publication 950, *Introduction to Estate and Gift Taxes*
> *Instructions for Form 1041*
> *Instructions for Form 706*
> *Instructions for Form 709*

Estates in General

An estate is a separate legal entity created when a taxpayer dies. The estate tax is a tax on the transfer of assets or property from an individual's estate to his beneficiaries after his death. The estate filing threshold for 2016 is $5,450,000.

Note: For Part 1 of the EA exam, you will be required to understand how estate and gift taxes affect individual taxpayers, especially the living beneficiaries of those estates. For Part 2 of the exam, you will be tested on the tax treatment of estates and trusts as legal entities. It is possible that questions will overlap, and therefore we cover the concept of estate taxation from various perspectives.

After a person dies, a personal representative, such as an executor, or an administrator appointed by a court, will typically manage the estate and settle the decedent's financial affairs. If there is no executor or administrator, another person with possession of the decedent's property may act as the personal representative. If a probate court proceeding is necessary, the judge will appoint an executor if one is not named in the decedent's will.

Note: The executor or "personal representative" must include fees paid to them from an estate in their gross income. If the executor is not in the trade or business of being an executor (for instance, the executor is a friend or family member of the deceased), these fees are reported on the executor's individual Form 1040, line 21. If the executor is in the "trade or business" of being an executor, they would report the fees received from the estate as self-employment income on Schedule C.

After a taxpayer dies, the following tax returns may need to be filed:

- **Form 1040:** Final income tax return for the decedent (for income received before death).
- **Form 1041**, *U.S. Income Tax Return for Estates and Trusts*: Fiduciary income tax returns for the estate for the period of its administration.
- **Form 706**, *United States Estate (and Generation-Skipping Transfer) Tax Return*: If the gross estate, based on the fair market value of its assets, exceeds the applicable threshold. This return is used to report tax on the taxable estate (the gross estate minus certain deductions).

Either the personal representative or a paid preparer must sign each required return. The personal representative is also responsible for determining any estate tax liability before the estate's assets are distributed to beneficiaries.

The tax liability for an estate attaches to the assets of the estate itself. If the assets are distributed to the beneficiaries before the taxes are paid, the beneficiaries may be held liable for the tax debt, up to the value of the assets distributed.

Final Income Tax Return (Form 1040)

The taxpayer's final income tax return is filed on the same form that would have been used if the taxpayer were still alive, but "deceased" is written after the taxpayer's name. The filing deadline is April 15 of the year following the taxpayer's death, the same deadline that applies for individual income tax returns.

The personal representative must file the final individual income tax return of the decedent for the year of death and any returns not filed for preceding years. If an individual died after the close of a tax year, but before the return for that year was filed, the return for that year will not be the final return. The return for that year will be a regular return, and the personal representative must file it.

Example: Milly dies on February 28, 2017. At the time of her death, she had not yet filed her prior year tax return. She earned $71,000 of wages in 2016. She also earned $16,000 of wages between January 1, 2017, and her death on February 28, 2017. Therefore, Milly's 2016 and 2017 tax returns must be filed by her representative or executor. The 2017 return will be her final individual tax return.

Example: James was unmarried when he died on April 20, 2016. His only daughter, Lillian, was named as the executor of his estate. James earned wages in 2016 before his death, so a final tax return is required for 2016. Lillian asks her accountant to help prepare her father's final Form 1040, which will include all the taxable income that James received before his death. The accountant also helps Lillian with the valuation of her father's estate. After determining the fair market value of all her father's assets, her accountant concludes that James' gross estate is valued at approximately $7 million on the date of his death. As this exceeds the filing threshold for 2016, an estate tax return (Form 706) is also required to be filed, and Lillian is responsible for filing both returns.

On a decedent's final tax return, the rules for personal exemptions and deductions are the same as those that apply for any individual taxpayer. The full amount of the applicable personal exemption may be claimed on the final tax return, regardless of how long the taxpayer was alive during the year.

Income in Respect of a Decedent (IRD)

Income in respect of a decedent (IRD) is any taxable income that was earned but not received by the decedent by the time of death. IRD is not taxed on the final return of the deceased taxpayer. IRD is reported on the tax return of the person (or entity) that receives the income. This could be the estate, in which case it would be reported on Form 1041, as described below. Otherwise, it could be the surviving spouse or another beneficiary, such as a child.

IRD retains the same tax nature that would have applied if the deceased taxpayer were still alive. For example, if the income would have been short-term capital gain, it is taxed the same way to the beneficiary. IRD can come from various sources, including:

- Unpaid salary, wages, or bonuses

- Distributions from traditional IRAs and employer-provided retirement plans
- Deferred compensation benefits
- Accrued but unpaid interest, dividends, and rent
- Accounts receivable of a sole proprietor

Example: Carlos was owed $15,000 of wages when he died. The check for these wages was not remitted by his employer until three weeks later and was received by his daughter and sole beneficiary, Rosalie. The wages are considered IRD, and Rosalie must recognize the $15,000 as ordinary income, the same tax treatment that would have applied for Carlos.

Example: Beverly died on April 30. At the time of her death, she was owed (but had not yet received) $1,500 of interest on bonds and $2,000 of rental income. Beverly's beneficiary will include $3,500 of IRD in gross income when the interest and rent are received. The income retains its character as interest income and passive activity rental income.

IRD is included in the decedent's estate and may be subject to estate tax. If it is received by a beneficiary and subject to income tax on the beneficiary's return, the beneficiary may take a deduction for estate tax paid on the IRD.

This deduction is taken as a miscellaneous itemized deduction on Schedule A and is not subject to the 2% floor.

Form 1041, Tax Return for Estates and Trusts

An estate is a taxable legal entity that exists from the time of an individual's death until all assets have been distributed to the decedent's beneficiaries. As investment assets will usually continue to earn income after a taxpayer has died, this income, such as rents, dividends and interest, must be reported. Form 1041 is a fiduciary return used to report the following items for a domestic decedent's estate, trust, or bankruptcy estate:

- Current income and deductions, including gains and losses from disposition of the entity's property, and excluding certain items such as tax-exempt interest (collectively, *distributable net income* or DNI);
- A deduction for income either held for future distribution or distributed currently to the beneficiaries (income distribution deduction) that are limited to DNI; and
- Any income tax liability.

Current income would include IRD if it was received by the estate rather than by specific beneficiaries. Expenses of administering the estate can be deducted either from the estate's income on Form 1041 in determining its income tax, or from the gross estate on Form 706 in determining the estate tax liability, but cannot be claimed for both purposes.

Schedule K-1 is used to report any income that is distributed or distributable to each beneficiary and is filed with Form 1041, with a copy also given to the beneficiary.

Estates are allowed some of the same tax credits that are allowed to individuals. The credits are generally allocated between the estate and the beneficiaries. However, estates are not allowed the Credit for the Elderly or the Disabled, the Child Tax Credit, or the Earned Income Tax Credit.

Note: Just like individual taxpayers, estates and certain trusts are subject to the Net Investment Income Tax (an additional tax of 3.8% on net investment income). The provisions for this tax are generally similar to those for individuals, and it must be reported on Form 8960, *Net Investment Tax: Individuals, Estates, and Trusts.*

The due date for Form 1041 is the fifteenth day of the fourth month following the end of the entity's tax year, but is subject to an automatic extension of five-and-one-half months if Form 7004 is filed. The tax year may be either a calendar or a fiscal year for an estate, subject to the election made at the time the first return is filed. Trusts must generally use a fiscal year. An election will be made on the first return as to the accounting method (cash, accrual, or other) of reporting the estate's income.

Form 1041 must be filed for any domestic estate that has gross income for the tax year of $600 or more or a beneficiary who is a nonresident alien (with any amount of income).

The Estate Tax

Estate tax may apply to the decedent's taxable estate, which is the gross estate minus any allowable deductions. In 2016, an estate valued at less than $5,450,000 would generally not be taxable or have a filing requirement.

Gross Estate: The gross estate is based upon the fair market value of the decedent's property, which is not necessarily equal to his cost, and includes:

- The FMV of all tangible and intangible property owned partially or outright by the decedent at the time of death
- Life insurance proceeds payable to the estate or, for policies owned by the decedent, payable to the heirs
- The value of certain annuities or survivor benefits payable to the heirs
- The value of certain property that was transferred within three years before the decedent's death

The gross estate does not include property owned solely by the decedent's spouse or other individuals. Lifetime gifts that are complete (so that no control over the gifts was retained) are not included in the gross estate.

Deductions from the Gross Estate: Once the gross estate has been calculated, certain deductions (and in special circumstances, reductions to value) are allowed to determine the taxable estate. Deductions may include:

- Funeral expenses paid out of the estate
- Estate administrative expenses, if not deducted on Form 1041
- Debts owed at the time of death
- The marital deduction (generally, the value of property that passes from the estate to a surviving spouse)
- The charitable deduction (generally, the value of property that passes from the estate to qualifying charities)
- The state death tax deduction (generally, any inheritance or estate taxes paid to any state)

The following items are not deductible from the gross estate:

- Federal estate taxes paid
- Alimony paid after the taxpayer's death; these payments are treated as distributions to a beneficiary

Property taxes are deductible only if they accrue under state law prior to the decedent's death.

Special Rule for Medical Expenses

Debts not paid before death, including medical expenses subsequently paid on behalf of the decedent, are liabilities that can be deducted from the gross estate on the estate tax return. However, if medical expenses for the decedent are paid out of the estate during the one-year period beginning with the day after death, the personal representative can alternatively elect to treat all or part of the expenses as paid by the decedent at the time they were incurred, and deduct them on the decedent's final tax return (1040).

Example: Frances, age 76, died on June 1, 2016, after a long battle with cancer. She incurred $42,000 of medical expenses, half during 2015 (the prior year) and half during 2016. The estate's executor paid the entire outstanding $42,000 bill in August 2016. He elects to file an amended return for Frances for 2015, claiming $21,000 as a medical expense deduction. The remaining $21,000 will be deducted on Frances' final income tax return, subject to the same limit. The medical expenses cannot also be claimed on the federal estate tax return.

The Marital Deduction

Transfers from one spouse to the other are typically tax-free. The marital deduction allows spouses to transfer an unlimited amount of property to one another during their lifetimes or at death without being subject to estate or gift taxes.

To receive an unlimited deduction, the spouse receiving the assets must be a U.S. citizen and a legal spouse, and must have outright ownership of the assets. The unlimited marital deduction is generally not allowed if the transferee spouse is not a U.S. citizen (even if the spouse is a legal resident of the United States).

Example: Walt and Martha are married, and both are U.S. citizens. Walt dies and leaves his wife, Martha, all his assets, which total $15 million on the date of his death. The transfer is tax-free to Martha because of the unlimited marital deduction. Martha's estate may or may not owe tax when she dies, but the transfer of assets to a surviving spouse is generally a nontaxable event, provided that the surviving spouse is a U.S. citizen.

Note: If the receiving spouse is not a U.S. citizen, assets transferred tax-free are limited to an annual exclusion amount. Non-citizen spouses can only receive $148,000 in 2016. This is true even if the spouse is a legal U.S. resident (a green card holder); it is one of the rare instances where U.S. citizens are taxed differently than legal U.S. residents.

The Estate Tax Return (Form 706)

An estate tax return is filed using Form 706, *United States Estate (and Generation-Skipping Transfer) Tax Return*. This return is due nine months after the death of the decedent. A six-month extension is allowed.

After the taxable estate is computed, it is added to the value of lifetime taxable gifts. The applicable estate tax rate is applied to derive a tentative tax, from which any gift taxes paid or payable are subtracted to determine the gross estate tax. The maximum estate tax rate is 40% in 2016.

However, all or a portion of the gross estate tax may be eliminated after applying the Basic Exclusion Amount.

This Basic Exclusion Amount is adjusted for inflation each year and may be used to reduce or eliminate gift and/or estate taxes. The exclusion is $5,450,000 in 2016. Most taxpayers never use the lifetime exclusion amount, and less than 1% of taxpayers are affected by the estate tax.

There is a special rule that applies to widows and widowers. A surviving spouse can add any unused exclusion of his deceased spouse who died most recently to his own estate tax return. This enables them together to transfer up to $10.9 million tax-free. This is also known as "portability."

Deceased Spousal Unused Exclusion (DSUE) and Portability

This is the unused portion of the decedent's predeceased spouse's basic exclusion (the amount that was not used to offset gift or estate tax liabilities). A portability election must be made to claim the DSUE on behalf of the surviving spouse's estate. This election can be made automatically by timely completion and filing of Form 706 for the estate of the predeceased spouse.

Portability is not automatic. This means that the executor, usually a surviving spouse, will need to transfer the unused exclusion to the surviving spouse. This is done by filing an estate tax return. The estate tax return is required when the first spouse dies, even if no tax is owed.

This return is due nine months after the death of the first spouse. A six-month extension is allowed.

Example: Marlene died in 2016 and left an estate valued at $3 million. She had not previously used any of her basic exclusion amount to avoid paying gift taxes, so the entire exclusion amount of $5.45 million is available to her estate. As this amount exceeds the estate's value, no estate tax is owed, and an estate tax return does not need to be filed.

Example: Matt died in early 2016 and left a gross estate valued at $9 million. His assets transferred to his wife, Leslie (who is a U.S. citizen), and none were taxed because of the unlimited marital deduction. Thus, none of the $5.45 million basic exclusion amount available to Matt's estate was used (and none had been used to offset gift tax liabilities during his lifetime). Leslie then died later the same year. Assuming Form 706 was timely filed for Matt's estate and Leslie had not used any of her basic exclusion amount, Matt's unused basic exclusion is added to Leslie's basic exclusion, for a total exclusion amount of $10.9 million. If Leslie's estate is valued at less than $10.9 million, the full amount can be excluded, and no estate tax will be owed.

Inheritances

For federal income tax purposes, cash inheritances are generally not taxable to the beneficiary, although the beneficiary may be responsible for if there is a related estate tax liability that has not been satisfied.

> **Example:** Hamid's aunt died and left him $100,000 cash in her will. Hamid does not owe any federal tax on the inheritance.

Distributions of retirement plan benefits or distributions from taxable IRA accounts to the decedent's beneficiaries are generally subject to income tax when received.

The decedent's surviving spouse may be able to defer taxation by rolling over the assets of a taxable IRA to another IRA or to a qualified plan.

Qualified distributions from a Roth IRA or of previously nondeductible contributions to a traditional IRA are generally not taxable.

> **Example:** Josepha dies and leaves her entire estate to her son, Lucas. At the time of her death, she had a significant cash balance in her bank account as well as several rental properties. The estate has a filing requirement, but Lucas ignores his accountant's advice and simply withdraws all the money from his late mother's bank account. He also sells all the rental properties and takes the money in order to take several lavish trips. Although inheritances are generally not taxable to the beneficiary, the fact that Lucas took possession of his mother's assets without filing her required estate tax return or satisfying the estate tax liability would make him directly responsible for the tax. The IRS can come after Lucas in order to satisfy the estate's debts.

Basis of Estate Property

Although cash inheritances are not subject to federal income tax, money received from the sale of inherited property may be taxable. The basis of property inherited from a decedent is generally one of the following:

- The FMV of the property on the date of death
- The FMV on an alternate valuation date, if elected by the personal representative
- The value under a special-use valuation method for real property used in farming or another closely-held business, if elected by the personal representative
- The decedent's adjusted basis in land to the extent of the value excluded from the taxable estate as a qualified conservation easement

> **Example:** Jared is the executor of his father's estate. His father's will directs that the estate be split equally between Jared and his four siblings. Their father dies on June 1, 2016, and Jared does not elect the alternate valuation date. The fair market value of his father's residence on the date of death is $500,000. In December 2016, the siblings agree to sell their late father's home for $550,000. Collectively, they must report a gain of $50,000 ($550,000 sale price minus $500,000 adjusted basis).

Alternate Valuation Date: If elected, the alternate valuation date is six months after the date of death. The estate value and related estate tax must be less than they would have been on the date of the taxpayer's death. However, for any assets distributed to a beneficiary after death, but prior to six months after death, the basis for these assets is the fair market value as of the date of distribution.

Jointly Owned Property: Property that is jointly owned by a decedent and another person will be included in full in the decedent's gross estate unless it can be shown that the other person originally owned or otherwise contributed to the purchase price. The surviving owner's new basis of property that was jointly owned must be calculated.

To do so, the surviving owner's original basis in the property is added to the value of the part of the property included in the decedent's estate. Any deductions for depreciation allowed to the surviving owner for his portion of the property are subtracted from the sum.

If property is jointly held between a husband and wife as tenants by the entirety, or as joint tenants with the right of survivorship (if they were the only joint tenants), one-half of the property's value is included in the gross estate, and there is a step-up in basis for that one-half. The other half is stated at the surviving spouse's cost basis, net of any deductions for depreciation allowed to the surviving spouse on that half. If the decedent holds property in a community property state, half of the value of the community property will be included in the gross estate of the decedent, but the entire value of the community property will receive a step-up in basis.

Example: Chen and Xia, brother and sister, owned rental property they purchased for $60,000 as joint tenants with right of survivorship. Chen paid $30,000 of the purchase price (for 50% ownership of the property), and Xia also paid $30,000 (for 50% ownership of the property). Under local law, each had a half interest in the income from the property and shared expenses equally. When Chen died, the FMV of the property was $100,000. Depreciation deductions allowed before his death were $20,000. Xia's original basis was $30,000. Upon Chen's death, she acquired his one-half share of the property and her basis in this portion of the property is stepped up to $50,000 (.50 × $100,000), resulting in a basis of $80,000 ($50,000 + $30,000 = $80,000). After subtracting her half of the depreciation deductions taken, Xia's adjusted basis in the property after Chen's death is $70,000 ($80,000 - $10,000).

Generation-Skipping Transfer Tax (GST)

In the past, wealthy families used various strategies to transfer wealth and assets to their grandchildren and other descendants. In response to this, Congress created the generation-skipping transfer tax, also known the GST, to close this tax loophole.

The generation-skipping transfer tax (GST) may apply to gifts during a taxpayer's lifetime or transfers occurring after his death, called bequests, made to "skip persons". A skip person is usually a grandchild, but it also applies to those who are more than 37½ years younger than the person making the gift or bequest. The most common scenario is when a taxpayer makes a gift to a grandchild.

The GST is assessed when the property transfer is made, including instances in which property is transferred from a trust. The GST is based on the amounts transferred to skip persons, after subtracting the allocated portions of the donor's available GST exemption. In 2016, the GST exemption is the same as the estate tax basic exclusion amount, and the GST tax rate is set at the maximum estate tax rate of 40%.

The GST is imposed separately and in addition to the estate and gift taxes.

> **Example:** Patrick sets up a trust that names his adult daughter, Helene, as the sole beneficiary of the trust. In January 2016, Patrick dies, and the trust passes to Helene. However, later in the year, Helene also dies, and the trust passes to her children (Patrick's grandchildren). Patrick's grandchildren are skip persons for purposes of the GST, and the trust's property may now be subject to the GST.

Any payments for tuition or medical expenses on behalf of a skip person that are made directly to an educational or medical institution are exempt from gift tax and GST.

> **Example:** Gordon wants to help support his grandchildren, but he tries to make sure that his gifts are not subject to gift tax, GST, or estate tax. In 2016, he pays his grandchild's college tuition in full and writes a check directly to the college for $25,000. Since the amounts were paid directly to the college, there is no tax consequence for this gift, and no additional reporting is required.

The Gift Tax

The gift tax may apply to the transfer of property by one individual to another, whether the donor intends the transfer to be a gift or not. Gift tax is imposed on the donor, not the receiver, of the property. However, under special arrangements, the donee may agree to pay the tax instead of the donor.

As discussed previously, an individual taxpayer's liability for estate tax and gift tax is subject to a combined basic exclusion amount ($5.45 million in 2016), and the use of any portion of this exclusion amount to reduce payment of gift taxes during the taxpayer's lifetime will reduce the amount available upon death to reduce applicable estate taxes. The following gifts are not taxable:

- Gifts to an individual that do not exceed the annual exclusion amount. In 2016, the gift exclusion amount is $14,000 per donee.
- Tuition or medical expenses paid directly to the educational or medical institution for someone else.
- Unlimited gifts to a spouse, as long as the spouse is a U.S. citizen.
- Gifts to a political organization for its use.
- Gifts to a qualifying charity.
- A parent's support for a minor child. This may include support required as part of a legal obligation, such as by a divorce decree.

Gift taxes are reported on Form 709, *United States Gift (and Generation-Skipping Transfer) Tax Return*. Form 709 must be filed if:

- A taxpayer gives more than the annual exclusion amount to at least one individual (except to a U. S. citizen spouse).[83]
- A taxpayer "splits gifts" with a spouse.

---

[83] For 2016, the exclusion from tax on a gift to a spouse who is <u>not</u> a U.S. citizen is $148,000.

- A taxpayer gives a future interest to anyone other than a U.S. citizen spouse.

If a gift tax return is required to be filed, Form 709 is generally due by April 15 of the following year. However, if the donor dies during the year, the filing deadline may be the due date for his estate tax return. Taxpayers who extend the filing of Form 1040 for six months using Form 4868 are deemed to have extended their gift tax returns, if no gift tax is due with the extension.

If the taxpayer does not extend their individual return, the gift tax return can be extended separately by using Form 8892, *Application for Automatic Extension of Time to File Form 709 and/or Payment of Gift/Generation-Skipping Transfer Tax*.

Definitions: A gift is considered a **present interest** if the donee has all immediate rights to the use, possession, and enjoyment of the property or income from the property. A gift is considered a **future interest** if the donee's rights to the use, possession, and enjoyment of the property or income from the property will not begin until some future date. Future interests include reversions, remainders, and other similar interests or estates. A gift of a future interest cannot be excluded under the annual exclusion ($14,000 per donee in 2016).

Example: Dion is 26, and Earlene is his mother. Earlene gives her son, Dion, a gift of $14,000 of cash during the year. She also pays his college tuition, totaling $21,000, and writes the check directly to the college. Earlene also pays for Dion's medical bills by issuing the check directly to his doctor's office. None of these gifts are taxable, and no gift tax return is required.

Example: Dave is single. In 2016, Dave gives his best friend Gary $18,000 to help start his first business. The money is not a loan, so Dave is required to file a gift tax return since the amount exceeds the $14,000 annual exclusion amount.

Applying the Applicable Credit to Gift Tax: After a taxpayer determines which of his gifts are taxable, he must calculate the amount of gift tax on the total taxable gifts and apply the applicable credit for the year.

Gift Splitting by Married Couples

Both the basic exclusion amount and the annual exclusion amount apply separately to each spouse, and each spouse must separately file a gift tax return if he or she made reportable gifts during the year. However, if a married couple or either spouse makes a gift to another person, the gift can be considered as being one-half from one spouse and one-half from the other spouse. This concept is known as *gift splitting*.

Gift splitting allows a married couple to give up to $28,000 (in 2016) to a single individual without making a taxable gift. Both spouses must consent to split the gift.

Example: Ronnie and his wife, Margie, agree to split gifts of cash. Ronnie gives a friend $21,000, and Margie gives her niece $18,000. Although each gift is more than the annual exclusion amount of $14,000, they can use gift splitting to avoid making a taxable gift to each donee. In each case, because one-half of the split gift is not more than the annual exclusion amount, it is not taxable. A gift tax return is required.

> **Example:** Felicia gives her cousin, Jessie, $24,000. Felicia elects to split the gift with her husband, Ralph, and Ralph is treated as if he gave Jessie half the amount, or $12,000. Assuming they make no other gifts to Jessie during the year, the entire $24,000 gift is tax-free. However, a gift tax return is required.

If a married couple splits a gift, each spouse must generally file his or her own individual gift tax return. However, certain exceptions may apply that allow for only one spouse to file a return if the other spouse signifies consent on the donor spouse's Form 709.

Basis of Property Received as a Gift

For purposes of determining gain or loss on a subsequent disposition of property received as a gift, a taxpayer must consider:

- The gift's adjusted basis to the donor just before it was given to the taxpayer,
- The gift's FMV at the time it was given to the taxpayer, and
- Any gift tax actually paid on appreciation of the property's value while held by the donor (as opposed to gift tax offset by the donor's applicable credit amount).

If the FMV of the gift was equal to or greater than the donor's adjusted basis in the gift right before the transfer, the donee's basis will be the donor's basis (transferred basis), adjusted for any gift tax paid on the donor's appreciation. If the FMV of the gift was less than the donor's adjusted basis in the gift right before the transfer:

- When the donee sells the property received as a gift, he calculates gain based upon the donor's adjusted basis.
- If the donee sells property at a loss, the taxpayer's basis would be the FMV at the time of the gift.
- If the donee sells the property at a price higher than the FMV at the time of the gift, but lower than the donor's adjusted basis at the time of the gift, the basis at the time of the sale will be the sales price, resulting in no gain or loss on the sale.

> **Example:** Edward's father gives him 20 shares of stock that are currently worth $900. Edward's father has an adjusted basis in the stock of $500. Edward's basis in the stock is also $500.

> **Example:** In 2016, Peggy received a gift of property from her uncle with an FMV of $50,000. Her uncle's adjusted basis was $20,000. For gift tax purposes, the amount of the gift was $36,000 ($50,000 minus the $14,000 annual exclusion). Peggy's uncle paid gift tax of $7,000. However, that amount is adjusted to $5,833 ($30,000 ÷ $36,000 = .83 × $7,000) to account for the gift tax paid on appreciation of the property's value. Peggy's basis is $25,833 (the donor's adjusted basis plus gift tax paid on the donor's appreciation).

> **Example:** Belinda receives an acre of land as a gift from her brother. Her brother's adjusted basis in the land is $50,000, and its FMV on the date of the gift is $40,000. A couple of years later, Belinda sells the gifted land for $35,000. Since she sold the property at a loss, her basis in the land is $40,000, because it is the lower of her brother's adjusted basis and the FMV at the date of the gift.

Generally, the value of a gift is its fair market value on the date of the gift. However, the value of the gift may be less than its fair market value to the extent that the donee gives the donor something in return.

> **Example:** Daniel sells his son, Nicolas, a house well below market value. Nicolas only pays $10,000 for the house. In 2016, the fair market value of the house is $90,000. Therefore, Daniel has made a gift to his son of $80,000 ($90,000 - $10,000 = $80,000). Daniel is required to file a gift tax return because the gift exceeds the $14,000 threshold for 2016.

The Unified Credit

The gross estate tax is reduced by the *applicable credit*, also referred to as the *unified credit*. For the 2016 tax year, the unified credit exclusion is $5.45 million per taxpayer. The annual gift tax exclusion is $14,000. The unified credit is the combination of the lifetime gift tax exclusion and estate tax exclusion.

Just as with the basic exclusion amount, any portion of the applicable credit amount used to avoid payment of gift taxes reduces the amount of credit available in later years that can be used to offset gift or estate taxes.

For example, if a taxpayer exceeds the annual gift tax exclusion amount in any year, the taxpayer can choose to either pay the tax on the excess or take advantage of the unified credit to avoid paying the tax.

> **Note:** For taxable gifts, each taxpayer has an aggregate lifetime exemption before any out-of-pocket gift tax is due. For example, a taxpayer can give away up to $5.45 million during their lifetime above the annual $14,000 exclusion and still avoid paying any gift tax.

> **Example:** Faye, who was single, died in 2016 and left an estate valued at $20 million. During her lifetime, she had used $1 million of her basic exclusion to offset payments of gift tax. That reduces the amount her estate may exclude to $4.45 million, which is then subtracted from her $20 million taxable estate. That leaves a total of $15.55 million to be taxed at the estate tax rate.

The due date for Form 706 is nine months after the decedent's date of death. An automatic six-month extension may be requested. However, the tax is due by the due date and interest is accrued on any amounts owed that are not paid at that time.

The assessment period for estate tax is three years after the due date for a timely filed estate tax return. The assessment period is four years for transfers from an estate.

Unit 19: Study Questions

(Test yourself first, then check the correct answers at the end of this quiz.)

1. Carl was divorced. He died in 2016, with a gross estate valued at $10,300,000. The estate also had the following activity:

Funeral and burial expenses	$42,000
Outstanding debt to a friend	200,000
Alimony paid to his ex-wife	75,000
State estate tax paid	25,000
Federal estate tax paid	125,000
FMV of land designated for donation to the American Humane Society	500,000

What is the total amount of the items listed that can be deducted from Carl's gross estate to determine the taxable estate?

A. $767,000
B. $892,000
C. $925,000
D. $967,000

2. In 2016, Jeffrey gives $25,000 to his girlfriend, Rachel. Which of the following statements is correct?

A. The first $14,000 of the gift is not subject to the gift tax, but the remainder is subject to gift tax, and Rachel is responsible for paying it.
B. Rachel is required to file a gift tax return and pay tax on the entire gift.
C. Jeffrey is required to file a gift tax return, Form 709.
D. Jeffrey may choose to report the gift tax on Form 1040, Schedule A.

3. Eileen's aunt gives her a gift of a remainder interest on her estate. Eileen will have full use of the estate after her aunt dies. Which is the correct statement about this gift?

A. Eileen can use the annual gift tax exclusion for this gift in 2016.
B. The gift is considered a present interest.
C. Eileen must pay estate tax on the gift in 2016.
D. Eileen cannot use the annual gift tax exclusion for this gift.

4. Max dies on May 1, 2016, and leaves his entire estate to his wife, Jeanne, a U.S. citizen. The estate is valued at $50 million. What amount of tax must Jeanne pay on her husband's estate in 2016?

A. $0
B. $5.45 million
C. $20 million
D. Unable to calculate because it depends on the amount of applicable credit.

5. Shawn, a single taxpayer, has never been required to file a gift tax return. In 2016, Shawn gave the following gifts:

- Tuition paid directly to a state university for an unrelated person: $18,000
- Payment to General Hospital for his brother's medical bills: $14,500
- Cash donations paid to his city's homeless shelter, a qualified 501(c)(3) organization: $50,000
- Political gift paid to the Libertarian Party (not a qualified 501(c)(3) charity): $15,000

Is Shawn required to file a gift tax return for 2016?

A. No.
B. Yes, because the donation to the political party is not an excludable gift.
C. Yes, because each of the gifts exceeded $14,000.
D. Yes, because the political gift is a reportable transaction.

6. Which of the following is not income in respect of a decedent?

A. Wages earned before death but still unpaid at the time of death.
B. Vacation time paid after death.
C. Taxable IRAs and retirement plans.
D. A royalty check that was received before death but not cashed.

7. When is an estate tax return due?

A. Four months after the close of the taxable year.
B. Six months after the close of the calendar year.
C. Nine months after the date of death.
D. Twelve months after the date of death.

8. Phil is unmarried and died in 2016. At the time of his death, he had assets of $4 million and owed debts of $500,000. He also had life insurance policies in place that paid $1 million to his only child. He had not used any of his basic exclusion amount during his lifetime. Based upon the information provided, what is the taxable amount of Phil's estate that must be reported on Form 706?

A. $0
B. $4 million
C. $4.5 million
D. $5 million

9. In general, who is responsible for paying gift tax?

A. The estate.
B. The donor.
C. The receiver of the gift.
D. The executor.

10. Delia's estate has funeral expenses for the cost of her burial. How should the executor deduct these costs?

A. Funeral expenses are an itemized deduction on Form 1040.
B. Funeral expenses are deducted on Form 1041.
C. Funeral expenses are deducted on Form 706.
D. Funeral expenses cannot be deducted as an expense.

11. Duncan died in 2015. Following his death, the executor of his estate paid the following bills. Which of these is not an allowable deduction in determining Duncan's taxable estate?

A. Administration expenses.
B. State inheritance taxes.
C. Charitable contributions.
D. Alimony paid after the taxpayer's death.

12. Alana had gifts totaling $28,000 in 2016 that were subject to gift tax. When is her gift tax return due?

A. March 15, 2017
B. April 18, 2017
C. October 15, 2017
D. September 15, 2017

13. Mandy was single. She died in 2016, and her executor did not elect the alternate valuation date. Given the following information, determine the value of Mandy's gross estate (all amounts listed are FMV at the date of her death):

- Household goods and personal effects: $25,000
- Antiques and collectibles: $300,000
- Certificates of deposit: $30,000
- Mortgage receivable on sale of property: $500,000
- Income tax refund due from Mandy's individual tax return: $6,000

A. $355,000
B. $361,000
C. $855,000
D. $861,000

14. Which of the following statements concerning the deceased spousal unused exclusion (DSUE) is correct?

A. The DSUE allows an unlimited estate tax deduction for a surviving spouse and his or her children.
B. The predeceased spouse must have died from natural causes.
C. The maximum DSUE available for a spouse who dies in 2016 is $14,000.
D. A portability election must be made by filing Form 706.

15. Emma's father dies during the year. Emma is the sole beneficiary of her father's traditional IRA. Emma is 46 years old when she takes possession of her father's IRA. Which of the following statements is correct about the distributions from the inherited IRA account?

A. Emma can avoid taxation by rolling over the assets of the IRA to another IRA or to a qualified plan.
B. The distributions are taxable to Emma, but not subject to an early withdrawal penalty.
C. Any tax on the distributions must be paid from her father's estate.
D. The distributions are taxable to Emma, and also subject to an early withdrawal penalty because Emma is younger than 59½.

16. Sandy and Matthew are married and have combined assets of $10 million. On May 10, 2016, Sandy dies. The FMV of Sandy's estate is $3.5 million on the date of her death. Matthew is the executor of his wife's estate and her sole heir. Since the value of Sandy's estate was below $5.45 million threshold, Matthew decides not to file an estate tax return, and he declines to take the portability election. What future impact does this have on Matthew, the surviving spouse?

A. There is no taxable effect on Matthew in this scenario.
B. Since Matthew declined to file an estate tax return, he did not elect portability. There will be estate tax due upon Matthew's death, assuming that the value of his assets does not decline, and there will be no deductions for estate tax purposes.
C. Matthew will owe tax in 2016 on his individual return from his inheritance.
D. Sandy's estate will owe estate tax in 2016. Her estate tax return must be filed by the executor.

17. The executor of Ophelia's estate is her sister, Elise. Elise decides to make a distribution of 100% of the estate's assets before paying the estate's income tax liability. Which of the following statements is correct?

A. The beneficiaries of the estate can be held liable for the payment of the liability, even if the liability exceeds the value of the estate assets.
B. No one can be held liable for the tax if the assets have been distributed.
C. The beneficiaries can be held liable for the tax debt, up to the value of the assets distributed.
D. None of the above.

18. Dustin pays $15,000 of college tuition for his niece, Delia, directly to her college. Which of the following statements is correct?

A. The gift is taxable, and Delia must report the gift tax on her individual tax return.
B. The gift is not taxable, but Dustin must file a gift tax return.
C. The gift is taxable, and Dustin must file a gift tax return.
D. The gift is not taxable, and no gift tax return is required.

19. Which of the following items is not an allowable deduction from the gross estate?

A. Debts owed at the time of death.
B. Medical expenses.
C. Funeral expenses.
D. Federal estate tax.

20. Bert and Sybil owned business property that they purchased for $100,000. They were joint tenants with right of survivorship. Each paid one-half of the purchase price. They took depreciation deductions prior to Sybil's death of $40,000. Under local law, each had a one-half interest in the income from the property. At the time of Sybil's death, the fair market value of the property was $200,000, one-half of which is includible in Sybil's estate. What is Bert's basis in the property after Sybil's death?

A. $80,000
B. $100,000
C. $130,000
D. $200,000

21. In which case must a gift tax return be filed?

A. A married couple gives a gift of $14,000 to an unrelated person.
B. A married couple gives a gift of $15,000 to a related person.
C. A single individual gives a gift of $4,000 to an unrelated person.
D. A wife gives a gift of $20,000 to her husband who is a U.S. citizen

22. All of the following gifts are excluded from the determination of the gift tax except:

A. A gift made to a political organization for its own use.
B. A cash gift given to a nonresident alien spouse of a U.S. citizen.
C. A medical bill paid directly to a hospital on behalf of a relative.
D. A gift made to a qualifying charity.

23. Janna is the executor for her father's estate. He died on November 5, 2016. Which of the following dates may she elect to use as an alternate valuation date for his estate?

A. January 1, 2017
B. April 15, 2018
C. May 5, 2017
D. October 15, 2017

24. Which of the following statements is incorrect regarding a married couple that uses gift splitting?

A. They must file a joint gift tax return along with their annual return (Form 1040).
B. They can give a gift of up to $28,000 to a single individual without using any of their basic exclusion amounts to avoid paying gift tax.
C. They must file gift tax returns even if no gift tax is owed.
D. Each must consent to split gifts.

25. Ida died in 2016. Which of the following assets would not be included in the calculation of her gross estate?

A. Life insurance proceeds payable to Ida's children.
B. The value of property transferred to Ida's son five years before her death.
C. The value of property owned jointly by Ida and her spouse.
D. The value of Ida's traditional IRA.

26. Cash inheritances are generally:

A. Taxable to the beneficiary.
B. Taxable for federal tax purposes, but not for state tax purposes.
C. Taxable in amounts over $2.5 million.
D. Not taxable to the beneficiary.

27. A taxpayer dies on May 4, 2016. Assuming that Form 706 needs to be filed for his estate, when is his estate tax due?

A. November 4, 2017
B. January 1, 2017
C. February 4, 2017
D. April 15, 2017

28. During 2016, prior to his death in December, Herman gave $30,000 to each of his two granddaughters. He also paid $80,000 directly to Birchland College for their college tuition costs. When Herman died, how much of his basic exclusion amount would he have used up as a result of these gifts?

A. $60,000
B. $140,000
C. $32,000
D. $112,000

29. Leighton received 100 shares of stock as an inheritance from her brother, who died on January 6, 2016. Her brother's adjusted basis in the stock was $14,750. The stock's fair market value on the date of her brother's death was $22,200. The executor of the estate elects the alternate valuation date for valuing the gross estate. Six months later, on July 6, 2016, the stock's fair market value was $23,100. Leighton finally received the stock on August 26, 2016, when its fair market value was $23,500. She sold the stock a week later for $23,450. What is Leighton's basis in the inherited stock?

A. $23,100
B. $23,500
C. $22,200
D. $14,750

Unit 19: Answers

1. The answer is A. Once the gross estate has been calculated, certain deductions (and in special circumstances, reductions to value) are allowed to determine the taxable estate. Federal estate taxes and alimony paid after the taxpayer's death are not deductible from the gross estate. Alimony payments are treated as distributions to a beneficiary and are therefore not included in the calculation of the taxable estate. The answer is calculated as follows: $42,000 funeral expenses + $200,000 outstanding debt + $25,000 state estate tax paid + $500,000 charitable gift of land = $767,000 allowable deductions.

2. The answer is C. Jeffrey is required to file a gift tax return. Gift tax is paid by the donor, not the recipient, of the gift. The first $14,000 of the gift is not subject to gift tax because of the annual exclusion. The remaining $11,000 is a taxable gift and must be reported on Form 709.

3. The answer is D. A gift of a future interest cannot be excluded under the annual exclusion ($14,000 per person in 2016). A gift is considered a present interest if the donee has all immediate rights to the use, possession, and enjoyment of the property or income from the property. A gift is considered a future interest if the donee's rights to the use, possession, and enjoyment of the property or income from the property will not begin until some future date. Future interests include reversions, remainders, and other similar interests or estates.

4. The answer is A. Jeanne will owe no estate taxes related to the value of Max's estate. The marital deduction allows for the transfer of an unlimited value of property from one spouse to another during his lifetime or from his estate after death without being subject to gift or estate taxes. To qualify for this unlimited deduction, the spouse receiving the assets must be a U.S. citizen and a legal spouse, and must have outright ownership of the assets.

5. The answer is A. None of the gifts are taxable, and no reporting is required. Tuition or medical expenses paid for someone directly to an educational or medical institution are not counted as taxable gifts. Nor are gifts to a political organization for its own use or gifts to a qualified charity.

6. The answer is D. Since the royalty check was received before the taxpayer died, it is not considered IRD income. Income in respect of a decedent is taxable income earned but not received by the decedent by the time of death. The fact that the royalty check was not cashed has no bearing on the nature of the income, and it should be reported as taxable income on the decedent's final income tax return (Form 1040).

7. The answer is C. Estate tax returns are due nine months from the date of death, although the executor may request an extension of time to file.

8. The answer is A. After calculating allowable deductions from the gross estate, Phil's net estate is valued at $4.5 million. This amount is less than the basic exclusion amount of $5.45 million for 2016, so no estate tax is applicable in this case. Also, because the gross value of the estate was less than $5.45 million an estate tax return is not required to be filed.

Assets	$4,000,000
Minus liabilities	(500,000)
Life insurance proceeds	1,000,000
Net Estate	**$4,500,000**

9. The answer is B. The donor is generally responsible for paying gift tax.

10. The answer is C. No deduction for funeral expenses can be taken on Form 1041 or Form 1040. Funeral expenses may be claimed only as a deduction from the gross estate on Form 706.

11. The answer is D. Alimony paid after a taxpayer's death is not deductible from the gross estate. It is considered a distribution to a beneficiary. Deductions from the gross estate are allowed for:
- Funeral expenses paid out of the estate and administration expenses for the estate
- Debts owed at the time of death
- The marital deduction, charitable deduction, and state death tax deduction

12. The answer is B. Alana would be required to file her gift tax return by April 18, 2017, the filing deadline for individual returns. Gift tax returns are typically due on April 15 of the following calendar year (the filing deadline), and payment of the tax is also due then, although the filing may be subject to a six-month extension. If the donor died during the year, the filing deadline is the due date for his estate tax return.

13. The answer is D. All of the property listed is included in determination of the gross estate. The gross estate is based upon the fair market value of the decedent's property, which is not necessarily equal to her cost, and includes:
- The FMV of all tangible and intangible property owned partially or outright by the decedent at the time of death
- Life insurance proceeds payable to the estate or, for policies owned by the decedent, payable to the heirs
- The value of certain annuities or survivor benefits payable to the heirs
- The value of certain property that was transferred within three years before the decedent's death

The gross estate does not include property owned solely by the decedent's spouse or other individuals. Lifetime gifts that are complete (so that no control over the gifts was retained) are not included in the gross estate.

14. The answer is D. The portability election allows a surviving spouse's estate the right to use a deceased spousal unused exclusion (DSUE), which is the remaining unused portion of the previously deceased spouse's basic exclusion amount. In 2016, an individual can leave $5.45 million estate tax-free at death. The portability election must be made by filing an estate tax return for the deceased spouse, even if no estate tax is owed.

15. The answer is B. The IRA distributions are taxable to Emma, but not subject to a penalty. Distributions of retirement plan benefits or distributions from taxable IRA accounts to a decedent's beneficiaries are generally subject to income tax when received. The decedent's surviving spouse may be able to defer taxation by rolling over the assets of a taxable IRA to another IRA or to a qualified plan. However, a child or other beneficiary is not allowed this same treatment. Qualified distributions from a Roth IRA or of previously nondeductible contributions to a traditional IRA are generally not taxable.

16. The answer is B. Since Matthew declined to file an estate tax return, he did not elect portability. No estate tax is due after Sandy's death because the value of her estate is below the exclusion amount. However, all her assets passed to her surviving spouse. Matthew's estate is now in excess of the annual exclusion amount.

Assuming there is no change in the value of Matthew's assets and no applicable deductions upon his passing, there will be estate tax due upon his death. He could have avoided this scenario if he had filed an estate tax return and elected portability.

17. The answer is C. The tax liability for an estate attaches to the assets of the estate itself. If the assets are distributed to the beneficiaries before the taxes are paid, the beneficiaries can be held liable for the tax debt, up to the value of the assets distributed.

18. The answer is D. Tuition or medical expenses paid directly to a medical or educational institution for someone else are not included in the calculation of taxable gifts, and there is no reporting requirement.

19. The answer is D. Federal estate tax is not deductible from the gross estate. The other items listed are allowable deductions from the gross estate. The decedent's unpaid medical expenses represent liabilities that can be deducted from the gross estate. Alternatively, if the expenses are paid by the estate during the one-year period beginning with the day after death, the personal representative can elect to treat all or part of the expenses as paid by the decedent at the time they were incurred, and deduct them on the decedent's final tax return (1040).

20. The answer is B. When they purchased the property, Bert's basis was $50,000 ($100,000 × .50. He was allowed half of the depreciation ($40,000 ÷ 2 = $20,000), which decreased his basis to $30,000. When Bert acquired the property in its entirety after Sybil's death, the fair market value of the portion owned by Sybil was included, based on the stepped-up basis of $200,000. The one-half portion representing Sybil's interest ($200,000 × .50 = $100,000) is added to Bert's basis for a final basis of $130,000.

21. The answer is B. In order to make a gift to one individual in excess of the annual exclusion of $14,000 and avoid using any of their basic exclusion amounts; a married couple can use gift splitting. Gift splitting allows married couples to give up to $28,000 to a person without making a taxable gift ($14,000 from each spouse), but they each must consent to the gift, and each may be required to file a gift tax return. Alternatively, the gift of $15,000 could be considered to have been from only one spouse (without using gift splitting); that spouse would need to file a gift tax return because the gift exceeds the annual exclusion of $14,000. Gifts to a spouse generally do not require a return to be filed, unless the spouse is not a U.S. citizen.

22. The answer is B. Although a full marital deduction is allowed for a spouse who is a U.S. citizen, a transfer of property to a noncitizen spouse is limited to $148,000 in 2016, and the excess amount would be subject to gift tax.

23. The answer is C. An estate is normally valued on the date of the decedent's death. However, an executor may elect an alternate valuation date for an estate, which would be six months after the date of death. The estate value and related estate tax must be less than they would have been on the date of the taxpayer's death.

24. The answer is A. If a married couple splits a gift, each spouse must generally file his or her own individual gift tax return. Couples cannot file a joint gift return. However, certain exceptions allow for only one spouse to file a return if the other spouse signifies consent on the donor spouse's Form 709.

25. The answer is B. The value of property transferred to Ida's son five years before her death would not be included in her gross estate. A taxpayer's gross estate includes the following:

- The FMV of all tangible and intangible property owned partially or outright by the decedent at the time of death
- Life insurance proceeds payable to the estate or, for policies owned by the decedent, payable to the heirs or beneficiaries
- The value of certain annuities or survivor benefits payable to the heirs or beneficiaries
- The value of certain property transferred within three years before the taxpayer's death (not five years, as stated in answer B)

26. The answer is D. For federal income tax purposes, cash inheritances are generally not taxable to the beneficiary, although the beneficiary may be responsible for a related estate tax liability that has not been satisfied.

27. The answer is C. If required to be filed, Form 706, *United States Estate (and Generation-Skipping Transfer) Tax Return,* must be filed nine months after the date of a decedent's death. The estate tax would be owed at this time. An executor may request a six-month extension to file Form 706, but the tax would still be owed on the earlier date.

28. The answer is C. Each granddaughter's cash gift of $30,000 would have been reduced by the annual exclusion amount of $14,000, and a portion of Herman's basic exclusion amount would have been used to avoid payment of gift tax on the excess amount of $16,000. Thus, he used a total of $16,000 for each granddaughter, or $32,000. Since the $80,000 was paid directly to Birchland College on behalf of the granddaughters, it was not subject to gift tax, and none of his basic exclusion amount would have been used as a result of these additional gifts. It should be noted that his cash gifts to the granddaughters would also be subject to generation-skipping tax.

29. The answer is A. The basis of property received from a decedent is generally the fair market value of the property on the date of the decedent's death. However, an executor has the option of choosing an alternate valuation date, which is six months after the date of death for valuing the gross estate. Since the alternate valuation date was elected by the executor, the Leighton's basis is the fair market value on the alternate valuation date, or $23,100.

INDEX

About the Authors

Richard Gramkow, EA, MST

Richard Gramkow is an Enrolled Agent with more than eighteen years of experience in various areas of taxation. He holds a master's degree in taxation from Rutgers University and is currently a tax manager for a publicly held Fortune 500 company in the New York metropolitan area.

Christy Pinheiro, EA, ABA®

Christy Pinheiro is an Enrolled Agent and an Accredited Business Accountant. Christy was an accountant for two private CPA firms and for the State of California before going into private practice.

Kolleen Wells, EA

Kolleen Wells is an Enrolled Agent and a Certified Bookkeeper who specializes in tax preparation for individuals and small businesses. She has worked in the accounting field for many years, including positions at a CPA office and at the county assessor's office.

Joel Busch, CPA, JD

Joel Busch is a professor of tax law at San Jose State University, where he teaches courses at both the graduate and undergraduate levels. Previously, he was in charge of tax audits, research and planning for one of the largest civil construction and mining companies in the United States.

CPSIA information can be obtained
at www.ICGtesting.com
Printed in the USA
LVOW09s0718301017
554271LV00006B/515/P